SEEMED LIKE A GOOD IDEA AT THE TIME

SEEMED LIKE

A GOOD IDEA

AT THE TIME

David Goodwillie

ALGONQUIN BOOKS OF CHAPEL HILL   2006

Published by
Algonquin Books of Chapel Hill
Post Office Box 2225
Chapel Hill, North Carolina 27515-2225

a division of
Workman Publishing
708 Broadway
New York, New York 10003

Lines on pages 123 and 337 from Adam Gopnik's *Paris to the Moon,* New York: Random House, 2000, reprinted by permission of the author.

This is a work of literary nonfiction, and as such, portrays real people and depicts true events. In some cases, names have been changed and descriptions of events slightly altered for obvious reasons. I have also done my best to protect the privacy of the places where I've worked. In the chapter on Kroll Associates, for instance, I created a composite case—the oil case—so as not to disclose confidential information. The Chinatown Mafia case is in the public domain and therefore happened as described.

Life has its slow moments but a book cannot, so on occasion I have also taken small liberties with the timing of events. But flipping through the pages again, I'm heartened by how much all of this occurred exactly as I wrote it.

DG

New York City, July 2005

Library of Congress Cataloging-in-Publication Data
Goodwillie, David, 1972–
    Seemed like a good idea at the time / David Goodwillie.—1st ed.
    p. cm.
    ISBN-13: 978-1-56512-465-3; ISBN-10: 1-56512-465-0
    1. Goodwillie, David, 1972. 2. Authors, American—21st century—Biography. 3. Private investigators—New York (State)—New York—Biography. 4. Baseball—United States. 5. Sports—Collectibles. 6. Auctions—New York (State)—New York. 7. Internet industry—United States. 8. New York (N.Y.)—Biography. I. Title.
CT275.G568A3 2006
974.7'044'092—dc22
[B]
    2005053074

10 9 8 7 6 5 4 3 2 1
First Edition

For my mother and father, of course.

CALVERA: What I don't understand is why a man like you took this job in the first place. Why, huh?
CHRIS: I wonder myself.
CALVERA: Oh, come on, come on. Tell me why.
VIN: It's like a fella I once knew in El Paso, one day he just took all his clothes off and jumped in a mess of cactus. I asked him the same question. "Why?"
CALVERA: And?
VIN: He said, "It seemed to be a good idea at the time."

—Eli Wallach, Yul Brynner, and Steve McQueen,
The Magnificent Seven

SEEMED LIKE A GOOD IDEA AT THE TIME

HERE HE IS AGAIN, *the man from across the hall. He doesn't care that my door was closed, that I was working, or trying to. He comes in, takes a seat in the corner, and produces a cigar from the depths of his crumpled jacket. It's one of those skinny hybrid cigars, the type smoked by street kids and men who no longer fit in the world. He rolls the thing around in his fingers, then lights it and sighs.*

"I'm here to save you," he says.

He says the same thing every time, he talks without breathing, streams of words rushing past thoughts. Today it's Edie Sedgwick and the fire. It was candles, he tells me, candles and coke and too much confusion. He says he was here in the hotel that night and I believe him. The names are what get me, so many famous names that I wonder if he ever knew anyone ordinary. Back when he knew people.

Arnold at the front desk laughed when I asked about him. Said he's some kind of writer, been here almost forty years, one of their permanent transients. He'd been a talent once, a voice of his generation and all that. There were a few published stories in the sixties, heady comparisons, soft fame, but then a book deal went wrong, addictions emerged, and the spotlight moved on. The requisite poetry came next, bitter and unreadable, and then nothing. Two decades of silence. For a while, in the mideighties, he'd started work on a new book, a history of everything left unsaid. But then his wife left him for a banker and he withdrew again, became the Joe Gould of Twenty-third Street—a sad loner spinning tales that never were. Arnold said I shouldn't listen.

But I can't help it. The man looks past me out the window and speaks of ghosts. Heroes of that New York. Leonard Cohen and Bob Dylan, William Burroughs and Gregory Corso. He was here the night Sid shot Nancy, the night Mapplethorpe met Patti Smith. Leaning forward, he describes Edie's skin, how the pills made it pale, how all that speed had her running in circles. He talks with his hands, conducts a symphony with every sentence, and when he's done, when the only story left to tell is his own, he gets up, looks solemnly at the pages piled on my desk, and walks out.

I've been toying with the idea of turning him into a character. But the thing is, I can't remember what the hell he looks like when he's gone. He vanishes into these thick, silent walls and I'm left with a vague impression of a Vonnegut gone to seed, a beard framing cracked yellow teeth. Anyway, this is no novel. He'd have to play himself. And I don't want the story to end like that.

My room was once a servant's quarters. There's just enough space for a desk, two chairs, and a bookcase full of dusty essays on the nature of things. On sunny days like this I open the window and let the city in. A half mile north the silver towers of Midtown push against the sky. Beckoning, even now. My father, my brother, my friends, they're all up there somewhere, surrounded by infra-structure. There is safety in numbers, wealth in billable segments. But I've learned I can't live like that. The hours fall too lightly.

Mine is a crowded city of loners and opportunists. Street-level music, played out of tune. I'm chasing the clunky promise of a life with a purpose. But it's risky. Live too fast and you end up running in circles, too. You tell unending stories to strangers, mumbling names from liner notes. Forgotten people from some other New York.

So I keep my head down, focus on the page. This is a haunted hotel. It's a beautiful place. I've been trying to get here for a long time.

PART ONE

Baseball as Metaphor for Life

"Some day — a day now postponed by my recent luck — I am going to retire from baseball and not knowing anything else, I plan to become a writer. So I start this account of my latest travels . . . and I am trying to remember the advice a friend gave me when I told him I had 'literary aspirations.' He advised me to read a lot and learn the new clichés. I like the old ones best myself. They are almost like a song."

—HOKE NORRIS, "Voo and Doo"

One

WE'RE ON A SUPERHIGHWAY in Ohio, racing past strip malls and industrial parks and billboards the size of city blocks. There were some fields before, miles back, clusters of discolored grass, but now just this gray steel and concrete. It's a warm Monday in May, and Kyle is driving, veering in and out of rush-hour traffic as if we're between heists. We're in a 1965 Mustang convertible—big, red, and loud. It's a fast car built for slower times, and it attracts attention. Kids wave from station wagons. Commuters glance suspiciously—longingly—from Toyotas, from Hondas, and I imagine them thinking back to when they were like we are now, two young men a week out of college, entering that first great summer of unknowing. Sometimes I catch a flicker of regret in their eyes at the moment they turn away. There's nothing worse than unscheduled nostalgia. It's almost like passion.

". . . if this doesn't work out?" Kyle is shouting through the stiff breeze.

"What?"

"If you don't make it?"

"What kind of question is that?"

"I'm just saying."

I know what he's saying. And he's right. Professional baseball . . . it just doesn't seem possible, even now. We speed past a sign for Singing Hills, another for a town called Maud. For a short time the factories give way to farmland again, spotted here and there with trailer homes and tract houses. Kyle lights a cigarette, looks around for an ashtray.

"We're in a convertible."

"What?"

"You can ash in the air," I shout. He turns the radio down.

"If you're asking what I'm going to do, I'm thinking about sales."

"Sales of what?"

"I don't know. It doesn't matter. I just think I'd be good at it."

"Probably," I say, feeling slightly depressed. Talk of the future makes me uneasy. At school, people were always going on about singing or painting or poetry. I have a friend who wants to bottle air and call it art, another who sings Canadian sea ballads at empty folk clubs. One of my closest friends writes postmodern short stories so vividly that the sentences stand up and live, completely on their own, without support or context. And yet she can't find a job, so she's going to grad school. Creative people have no place in the real world. So it's only logical that Kyle would embrace that world without pause. He's never been pestered by imagination. He's lucky that way.

I had cheery notions of becoming some kind of writer myself . . . until all *this* happened.

We pass the ring road on the outskirts of Cincinnati, and I bite my lip and lean forward, looking for signs of the city but seeing only rows of storage units stretching away toward the dull silver distance. I want to find the ballpark, maybe get out and walk around so we'll know what we're doing in the morning. But Kyle tells me not to worry. He's from Dayton and has been coming to Reds games all his life. Besides, he says, we'll see Riverfront Stadium from the highway, and a turn or two later we do, a massive concrete structure rising out of the Ohio River. It looks cold and unfriendly in the diminishing light, like an old photograph of Three Mile Island. We drive past in silence.

THE SCOUTS CALL ME a prospect. I like the word; it sounds unlimited. But it's misleading. Real prospects spend their college careers in weight rooms and field houses, swallowing supplement pills and studying slow-motion swing analyzers under buzzing halogen lights.

I went to Kenyon, a small New England college that got lost in the cornfields of central Ohio. The guidebooks rank it right up there with its elite East Coast cousins, but they're talking academics, not sports—certainly not baseball. The Kenyon College baseball team—we were the "Lords" and the women were the "Ladies"; that's the best they could do—was a curious mix of longhaired boarding-school benchwarmers and frat boys who needed a noncontact filler between parties. We wore purple uniforms and were cheered on by overzealous professors who kept careful score. Even our stadium wasn't quite right. It had an all-grass infield until eight of us were caught smoking pot during spring training in Florida. A week later they put dirt in to stop the jokes.

I wasn't much of a player until halfway through my sophomore year when, during a 6:00 A.M. indoor practice in the dead of winter, I turned around for no particular reason and started hitting left-handed. Suddenly I couldn't miss. That spring I transformed myself from a weak-hitting second baseman into a power-hitting center fielder. And we went from winning three games to beating some of the best Division III schools in the country. We developed a fan base. Girls came to our games with vodka-filled Evian bottles and short skirts, and the history teachers switched seats to get a good look at them. Fraternities had barbecues behind the left-field fence. The local paper started coverage. We became a cause célèbre. Still, baseball was a hobby for me, a diversion. I kept hitting line drives, kept diving for fly balls, and for a while I led the league in stolen bases. But this was Kenyon, not Florida State, and I wasn't fooling myself.

As graduation approached, I did what seniors do: drank bourbon and made vague plans to move to New York. My friends were all moving home— to New Canaan, Chevy Chase, Lake Forest—where decisions regarding futures could be made carefully and deliberately, from rooms still filled with prom dresses and Little League trophies; or they were breathlessly running off to Prague or Florence or Paris for museum internships or a summer with distant relatives; or they were driving to Austin or Boulder, in rusting Volvos with shoeboxes full of Jane's Addiction bootlegs and adopted dogs named Max. For four years we had heard how bad the economy was, and now we all believed it. Why look for a job when you could take the summer off? But my plan was New York. Move to the City and become a writer.

It was why I'd gone to Kenyon: the lure of a literary existence. Kenyon has a well-earned reputation for sending young wordsmiths into the world, but I'd gotten lost along the way, taken an easier route, majored in history. A high school interest in books became a college concentration in bars. I left the real writing to the real writers, the earnest students who carried Proust around in paperback and interned at *The Kenyon Review*. I couldn't compete with them. Call it a lack of confidence, call it laziness, call it *college*. I spent four years in the cornfields of Ohio without writing one creative word, until the very end, when I suddenly had no choice.

I was taking one of my *special* courses, The History of Baseball in American Culture, a seminar that met once a week for three hours. It sounded perfect. I'd spent my teenage years reading baseball books; I knew the sordid back story of our pastime, the names and dates, their small and wide significance. I knew the Red Sox really *were* cursed; I knew the old Brooklyn Dodgers made grown men cry. And I knew that baseball was bigger than a game. It was and is America, a stage where we can view the best and worst of ourselves—the heroics, the glory, the eternal optimism, and so, too, the cheating, the racism, the greed. I knew all the answers. Hell, I knew all the questions. That, and I *played* the damn sport, was captain of the team, doing my best to lead Kenyon to its first play-off appearance in years. It was an easy A, I thought, but the two wire-rimmed intellectuals who taught the class didn't see it that way. It was a problem of attitude, they said, but more so of attendance. As the Kenyon Lords went on their late season run, I was forced to miss two, three, four seminars in a row, including the final class, a bizarre exhibition contest against a group of middle-aged men who toured the Midwest re-creating 1860s baseball games.

My professors made the class practice for weeks. They laid out a small ballpark on the main lawn, read up on century-old rules, equipment, uniforms. They became completely obsessed, and so the news that I, the only athlete in the class, wouldn't be playing was greeted with minimal enthusiasm. That I needed to play a very real baseball game, a *play-off* game against nationally ranked Wittenberg University, was lost on them. There were pleas and then threats, awkward calls made from athletic offices to academic buildings. Deans got involved, but my professors held firm. I would play 1860s baseball or fail the course, and failing meant not graduating. Then a compromise was suggested, a last-minute deal negotiated by the dean of academics: I could write a research paper that expounded on some topic we'd covered in class. Determined to play center field in Wittenberg the following week, I agreed. I had no other choice.

But when I sat down to pound the thing out, I couldn't think of an appropriate subject. All our classroom heroes had proved hollow. I could write about Jackie Robinson, the paradigm of integration, or Joe Jackson, that tragic figure who played his heart out while his teammates threw the 1919 World Series, but Robinson inconveniently became a Republican, and Shoeless Joe still took the money even if he didn't *earn* it. Nothing is ever so sweet, so simple, as in the later telling. No, I'd write a different kind of American story, a fictional tale of a boy playing baseball in the bush leagues, my own fantasy future. I holed up in a corner of the library and wrote for two days, straight through, and finally came up for air seventeen pages later. The story was serviceable, would get me a diploma, but it was the process itself that stayed with me in the days that followed. For the first time in four years, I had gotten lost in something. And the result—the entire exercise— struck me as worthy, almost genuine.

I handed it in and got my C. We lost to Wittenberg, the class lost to the traveling sideshow act, and then, as the various seasons wound down and I turned toward the longer season of my life, it occurred to me that writing might be some kind of answer. I'd move to New York, where artists go, then find a job in a restaurant and figure it out from there. It was a *plan*.

But then my imagined life, my short-story existence, caught up with reality. It showed up in my mailbox wedged between credit card bills: an invitation to try out for the Cincinnati Reds.

It had been a chance encounter: a double-header against a school three times our size. A group of professional scouts, charts and radar guns in hand, were wedged into seats behind home plate, watching the other team's pitcher, a left-handed star in the making with a fastball in the upper eighties and an overhand curve he could throw for strikes. In a cold drizzle, the Kenyon nine, with their violet flannel jerseys and detached bohemian style, got shut out 9–0. In the second game I hit two doubles and a home run, but it didn't matter; we still lost 14–1. They were a national powerhouse and we were just filling out their schedule. But as we trudged back to the vans, one of the scouts approached me. He liked my swing, he said, and as I stood there shivering he produced a business card embossed with a raised Reds logo and asked about my plans for the future. I wiped the rain from my face, told him they were flexible.

He was only the first. By graduation I'd been invited to professional tryouts across the Midwest. It's a strange feeling when your dreams start coming true: you move more briskly through time and forget how much you cared before. No one from Kenyon had been drafted since the 1950s, but here I was, hugging my parents at graduation, then running down to the batting cages to practice while my friends packed up their young lives. They slapped me on the back, wished me luck, and said they'd check the box scores. Then they drove off in happy bunches, leaving me alone.

THE LOW RUNGS on the ladder of professional baseball are muddy with the famous footsteps of those climbing higher. Each major-league organization owns several minor-league teams, spread out like Wal-Marts across America. The journeymen, young and mostly going nowhere, ply their trade in near-anonymity, in seasonless suburbs and crumbling county seats. The truly talented pass through these places like rumors, glimpses of better selves, on their way to Louisville, Tucson, Pawtucket. Still, I couldn't think of anything more thrilling than playing in one of those small-town bandbox ballparks for people paying to watch, for coaches holding keys to stardom.

There were two routes I could take: get drafted by a major league organization (then report to one of its farm clubs) or get drafted by a small-town independent team and play well enough to sign on with a big-league club later on. The former was preferable, of course, and the Reds were my chance, but the road to Cincinnati was paved with the latter. If nothing else, the independent tryouts would be good practice.

The first stop was Chillicothe, Ohio, an hour and a half from campus. A week after graduation I drove south in a beat-up Pontiac station wagon, through rolling valleys scarred with barren fields. The towns had greeting signs with population figures, but the original numbers had been painted over — four figures changed to three, three to two. People were disappearing. Downtown Chillicothe was empty. A deserted gas station, its pumps uprooted, stood slowly decaying. I waited at a lonely traffic light, the only person on the road. There had been a time, I'm sure, when this corner was crowded, when there was too much traffic for stop signs alone. Now it was so quiet I rolled down the window and heard the click as the color changed, red to green.

I didn't make the lunchtime cut. I ran fast, threw as well as I could, but the hitting: You only got ten swings and mine were sluggish, the bat dragging itself lazily through the strike zone like the walk to class on so many mornings. It was an adjustment problem—metal bats to wooden, half-hearted throwing to real pitching. And I'd underestimated the talent level. These players were the real thing: Latin shortstops turned smooth double plays like they'd been born with baseball gloves on their hands; outfielders leaped over fences to steal home runs; rangy pitchers wound up like Juan Marichal and delivered effortless ninety-mile-per-hour fastballs. And the hitters: They all looked too big, as if on loan from some other more brutal sport. They lunged at every pitch with furious intensity, and the ball made such a perfect sound when it came off their bats that I kept flinching, like a rookie cop at a firing range.

But each tryout went better than the one before. I played well in Parkersburg, West Virginia, then drove to Zanesville, Ohio, where I made the most of my ten swings, hitting three home runs. I started making it past lunchtime. I was never the best player, but some days I was among them. After a strong showing in Newark, Ohio, the manager pulled me aside and asked where I'd come from.

"Kenyon College."

"Never heard of it."

"It's a half hour down the road."

"What's your plan after this?"

"I have a tryout with the Reds in a few days."

"If they're not interested come back and see us. We might have a spot for you."

I slept in roadside motels and ate in boxcar diners. I read old paperbacks and thought about grand New York, about exposed-brick lofts and pensive girls with choppy hair. And for the first time in my life, I felt alone. My father had given me $10,000 for graduation and told me not to spend it, so I stopped at a car auction in Lancaster and bought the Mustang for $6,000 (I threw in the station wagon to seal the deal). I felt it important to travel in style, and the vintage Ford looked and sounded flawless. Sure, I only had $4,000 left, but I'd be signing a contract soon.

The Reds tryout was on a Monday, two days away, so I pointed the car toward Dayton, where Kyle lived. Kyle had been my roommate and best

friend in college, and when he found out about the Reds tryout, he had in-
sisted on coming along. The Mustang sputtered and backfired its way west,
then died at the side of a road near a town called Washington Court House.
I didn't understand; when I'd test driven it, the engine had hummed with
expectation and the farmer who owned it said he hadn't had an engine
problem in years. He told me how he loved the car like a child but needed
money to feed his real kids. It was a good story, poignant and all, and when
it came time to negotiate, he named his price and I said fine. Now, $600
worth of repairs later, it was raining and the canvas roof was leaking, one of
the doors wouldn't close, and the stereo was making strange humming
sounds that increased and decreased along with the accelerator. I didn't
care. It was all just thrilling, this early chance to make it on my own. I
turned off the Interstate and drove through the winding heartland of the
country, the back roads, the blue highways, where people watered lawns
and sauntered down sidewalks. They waved as I passed, unknowing wit-
nesses to the origins of another American success story. Seeing so many
families, I realized I hadn't spoken to my own since graduation. But I'd
planned it that way. I'd vanish for a few weeks, then emerge phoenixlike
from the ashes of my education with a classic car, a signing bonus, and my
future all figured out. I'd fly my parents out to opening night, wherever it
was, and there they'd sit under the lights in a cozy ballpark with green trim,
together for the first time in years. They'd share peanuts and sip beer while
they watched their eldest son as he started his journey to the big leagues,
and how could they not take pride in that? Here, they'd say softly, we did
something right after all.

And my friends, wandering through the pockmarked landscape of post-
graduation, college products on the bargain shelves of the working world.
I pictured them in cubicles and crowded subways, in grad-school class-
rooms and messy painting studios, and it was fun for a while, building
other people's lives, but then I stopped. The back roads were confusing, and
besides, who could predict anything anyway? So much would happen, was
already happening, fates and coincidences forming, millions of them, the
tiny twists that lead lives one way or the other.

Two

THE OMNI IN DOWNTOWN Cincinnati is one of those grand, marble- and brass-filled hotels that still pepper the hollow insides of midwestern cities. The lobby is impressive but forlorn, and there's an air of slow submission, as if the building, the city, the whole state, has seen much better times and we've shown up for part of the long, relentless decline. We walk up to the counter, and Kyle starts leafing through the brochure rack while I check in. I ask for a room and the pale-faced clerk looks me up and down, then leans over the counter and looks at Kyle.

"We'd prefer you take two rooms," he says, "but if you insist on one, we ask that it have two beds."

"Well, that's what we want."

"Good, then," he says, looking relieved. He punches my credit card number into the computer, then produces two keys.

"Hold on. Did you think we were . . ."

"What?"

"Gay?"

"Excuse me, sir?"

"Gay. Is that what you were saying?"

His face turns red and he clears his throat. "It's not my business what people do behind closed doors."

"As long as they do it in separate beds."

"I didn't make the policy," he says.

"It's a *policy*?"

"Sir, there's no need to raise your . . ."

I walk away, letting his words die in the stagnant air. Kyle's reading a flyer about caves in Kentucky. I tell him what just happened, and at first he laughs, but then he sees how annoyed I am. We walk toward the elevators, and as we pass the front desk, he blows the feckless clerk a kiss. The guy freezes for a moment, then glances quickly around the lobby. He doesn't have to worry. We're the only ones there.

ACTUALLY, KYLE HAS SLEPT with more girls than anyone I know. He showed up at school freshman year with a reputation clattering along behind him like cans on a wedding car. The girls didn't care, though. Drawn by his All-American looks, his athletic prowess, his love of a good party, they appeared at our dorm-room door in late-night waves, lubed up with shots, with drugs, with *designs*. Kyle was recruited to play tennis, and he did, for a year, until the parties ran into practice time and something had to give. Classes had become obstacles, scheduling mishaps, and we worked hard to get around them. Sometimes we avoided daylight altogether. But enough of the same thing—even gluttony—becomes monotonous. The drinking was getting to me. Time became a meaningless sequence of events; I began to forget what had happened the day before. The weather, the assignments, the next girl's name—these became the only signifiers of change. Then spring came, and with it baseball. I took it seriously and it saved me. Kyle plowed forward without tennis, without me, and the trail he left behind became more and more destructive.

By sophomore year he needed rescuing, and it came in the form of a rich girl from a horse-breeding family. She took him home to Maryland for a weekend and he came back converted. He stopped drinking, stopped going out, and soon they were living together in her freshman dorm room. For the next year, on the few occasions I saw Kyle alone, we'd stop and try to catch up, but there was nothing to say. It was as if he'd had electroshock therapy—his eyes were glazed, his mind elsewhere. Among a certain jaded segment, Kyle became a punch line, a living testament to what relationships could do to a young man.

The girl broke up with him the summer before our senior year, then dropped out of school to marry a Thoroughbred trainer. And sure enough, the following fall, Kyle reappeared. He picked up his old habits as if he'd just left them on a shelf, and apart from a new fondness for the horse track, it was like he'd never left. He rejoined the tennis team and drank until dawn. He joked about having spent his junior year abroad, and we all laughed and opened the next beer, but somewhere underneath, it wasn't so funny. He had just dropped his life for a girl, and then, when it didn't work out, he pretended it hadn't happened. I'd never seen love up close. I think it scared me.

UP IN OUR HOTEL ROOM, Kyle's leafing through the newspaper.

"There's a good band playing in Over-the-Rhine," he says.

"Sounds like a German disco palace."

"It's not a club, you idiot, it's a neighborhood. It's the . . . the *seedy backwater* of Cincinnati. In high school we used to go there to score drugs. They keep talking about gentrification and all that shit, but it's still pretty sketchy."

"Sounds good," I tell him. And it does. The *seedy backwater*. Addicts and artists, desperation and desire, the day-to-day existence, where people and ideas come and go in unexpected bursts of living. I think of New York that way, as some grand experiment in finding oneself, and it scares and thrills me in equal measure. Why do I keep thinking of one life while I'm living another? The most important day of my life is tomorrow and I'm thinking of street scenes in Tompkins Square, of hipsters dripping in self-awareness. I pull the Reds invite from my pocket and read it one more time. "Just remember, we need to be at the stadium by nine tomorrow."

"Don't worry," Kyle says, "it's like two minutes away."

"Because it says here the workout starts at nine-thirty."

"We'll hit the hotel bar, then check out the band. We'll be back by midnight."

"You've never been back from anywhere by midnight."

LIKE SO MANY HOTELS of a certain age, the Omni has an exotic, heyday feel. The rooms are large, the ceilings high, the hallways oddly spacious. We head down to the bar off the lobby, Kyle off on some monologue about the history of the Reds, trying to get me focused on the significance of the event. But he's just making me nervous. Then the elevator opens and before I can stop him he's walking back up to the check-in counter. The same clerk is there. Kyle says something and the man physically recoils.

I wait until we're safely seated at the bar before asking what just happened.

"I asked him if he had any condoms."

"You're an asshole."

"Did you see him, though? You'd have thought I just killed someone."

"Try not to get us kicked out of here."

We order two drafts and make our way to the pool table. I was expecting a tranquil, old-world scene—well-dressed travelers with martinis and foreign magazines, married men making promises in shadows—but it's more like a sports bar. The Allman Brothers are playing on the jukebox. Reds and Bengals photos hang crookedly on water-stained walls. Kyle scans the room, then gets back to his history of baseball: "You know, the Reds started back in 1869 or something. And now *we're* here. Think of what that means. I remember when my dad took me to my first game when I was three or four. I think my parents got divorced because my dad was addicted to baseball."

"I'm sure that was it."

"He wanted to come watch you tomorrow, but I told him . . ."

Kyle's voice trails off. He's looking toward the door, where two girls are walking in. They're wearing eighties outfits—blousy shirts pulled off one shoulder, tight jeans, necklaces, bracelets, rings. Their hair is what one of my more snobbish prep-school friends calls "Midwestern blond," which is actually dark, teased, full of clips and curls.

"Cleveland Browns," Kyle says.

"What's that?"

"Good uniforms, bad helmets."

But not bad enough. Kyle downs his beer, orders a Jack and Coke, and wanders over to introduce himself. I watch him go to work. When he's on, there's no one better. He picked up the "hard listen" by studying President Clinton on TV, and he's doing it now as the girls start talking. He's leaning over with a look of grave earnestness, as if the words they're speaking may be the most important he's ever heard. Then he's talking again. He points at me and I give a meek wave. He could be saying anything. I order a third round, four drinks, and soon we're all crowding around, speaking over one another, while Kyle grins, like a modern-day Eddie Haskell. We play pool. We play the jukebox. We switch back to beer and play a sloppy game of quarters. They go to school across the river in Kentucky, some community

college near Lexington. They've come to Cincinnati to find summer jobs.
Instead they've found Kyle, who's going on about baseball again. Between
the talk and the music—Little Feat now, the same crap I've been hearing
for four years—and the pitchers of beer that arrive one after another like
planes in a landing pattern, the girls are confused and I realize after a while
that they think we're *both* ballplayers. One of them keeps asking what it's
like to play for the Reds, whether we have groupies in every city.

Kyle refines his efforts, as every good player must, and starts zeroing in
on the taller, prettier girl. He keeps touching her hand and she resists for a
while but gives in after a round of margaritas, and soon the two of them are
slow dancing in a corner to an Elvis song. I sit at the bar with Donna—I got
her name from her license; I told her I didn't believe she was twenty-one—
and watch them grope each other.

"I have a question," Donna says. "Aren't the Reds on the road this week?"

"Do you want another margarita?"

"We'll all be really hungover tomorrow if we keep mixing drinks."

She has a point; I'm getting drunk. And Kyle, bless him, is dancing with
his head buried in his partner's shoulder—for stability. I should slow
down. I order two Buds, then tell her the truth—that I'm only trying out
and the guy over there licking her friend's ear is just along for the ride. But
Donna doesn't seem to care. She leans in close and tells me she wants to be
an actress. There's a Greyhound bus that comes through her hometown
once a week, and for years she's watched it drive away without her. But all
that's about to end, she says, firmly. She reminds me of the unlucky kid in
an after-school special. I doubt she could even make it in dinner theater, or
porn. Still, the idea of a person's dreams boiled down to a seat on a bus, a
fresh chance at freedom every week . . . And so we talk like that, in broad
strokes, until the lights come on and our two lovebirds emerge from a corner, like bats at sunrise. The girls gather their purses. Kyle mumbles something about everyone coming upstairs for a nightcap, but he can barely
stand. Donna thanks us and we all kiss good night and Kyle follows them
out to the street because he's thorough like that. I raise my glass to a 1990
Reds World Series pennant hanging on the wall, then down the rest of my
beer. It's two thirty in the morning.

There's noise coming from the lobby—shouting, drunken slurs. I run out and sure enough, Kyle is at the front desk again, staggering back and forth as he reaches his arms over the counter. The clerk is speaking loudly into the phone, something about security. I run over and drag Kyle toward the elevator, but both of us are weaving like tangled puppets and it takes a little while. We must look ridiculous.

"What the fuck are you doing?" I ask, when we're finally in the elevator.

"I don't know," he says, helpfully pushing all the buttons so we stop on every floor. "All I did was ask for a wake-up call. Then the guy freaked out."

"What else did you say?"

"Nothing. Hey, let's go to that club."

"Tell me."

"Well, . . . I said we needed some lotion to make things go more smoothly."

"Oh, Jesus. There's no way that phone's ringing in the morning."

"It's okay," Kyle says, slumping into a corner. "I'll wake us up."

When we've finished our tour of four, five, and six, I drag my friend down the seventh-floor hallway and into our room, where he promptly passes out on the floor. Too drunk to lift him onto his bed, that's where I leave him.

In the darkness, Kyle snoring, I think of races and drills and coaches with clipboards. My head is spinning. What happened to a few beers and bed by midnight? I want to call someone and just talk a while, but I can't think of anyone who'd want to hear from me at this hour. I start playing that game where you try to think about nothing. You empty out your mind, but it never works, because even when you've blocked everything else out, you're still thinking about whiteness or space or an ex-girlfriend who seems perfect in hindsight. So it's back to baseball and that nervous sensation of succumbing to fate, my future whittled down to a few quick swings in a big-league ballpark. On the road the last few weeks, the sweeping sense of life moving from abstraction to reality has grown stronger with every tryout. What if I wake up in a few hours and run faster and hit it farther than everyone else? What then? Is it like that, life, where it just works out sometimes, where the choices are made for you?

I toss and turn, falling in and out of dreams. At one point I wake up with a start and realize I was just on a childhood beach on Long Island, catching pop flies hit with an old Donnay tennis racquet. My father was hitting them, higher and higher into the sun, until the wind picked up, capricious gusts blowing in off the ocean, and the tennis balls blew around in the high sky like lottery balls in a sorting machine. I kept running and diving in the hot sand, making every catch, until the entire beach was watching in stunned admiration. . . .

I open an eye and it's still dark. Kyle is talking to himself about horses. I put a pillow over my head and close my eyes again, and soon we're walking to the Quogue Beach Club, my father and I, and I'm tugging on his long arms, asking the same question over and over: What are the chances I'll make the major leagues? He laughs because I'm always asking stuff like this, always living in some more exciting future. But today I need an answer. I pick up a piece of beach glass and sidearm it into the water, watching it skip across the surface. I promise I'll never ask again if he'll just tell me. So then he does: if I work hard and still love playing, he says, the chances are one in ten. And that's all I need. Now there's a purpose to my young life, a timeline of goals and events, an arc of years falling neatly into place. The Beach Club that always seemed so far away materializes out of the horizon and the sky is full of falling tennis balls and I could catch them all if I only had the time. . . .

It's light outside. There's snoring coming from the floor beyond the bed. I roll over and read the blurry digits of the digital clock: 8:55. I look up at the ceiling, realize slowly where I am, then turn back to the clock and watch it flip tauntingly to 8:56.

And then confusion, panic. *We're so fucking late!* I jump on Kyle, then race around the room searching frantically for baseball belts and stirrups. Kyle saunters into the bathroom, complaining of a stiff back and asking what happened to the wake-up call. He doesn't remember his last conversation with the desk clerk. I yell through the bathroom door, try to get him moving faster, then start looking for the invite. Did it say the tryout started at 9:00 or 9:30? Miraculously, Kyle emerges mostly dressed, in a bright red T-shirt and jeans, and heads down to get the car while I gather the rest of my equipment like a disheveled little-leaguer who's late for his first practice. There's no time to pack or check out, so I leave the room a mess and am in the elevator when I remember that Riverfront Stadium has Astroturf. I've never played on a carpet and I don't know if I should wear sneakers or spikes. Sneakers, I decide, which are back up in the room, so I turn the creaking elevator around and head back upstairs to grab the shoes and the valet ticket that Kyle must have forgotten. This time I take the stairs down, jumping entire flights like they do in movies, and that's when it hits me, a sidesplitting headache that thumps like an amplified backbeat with every landing.

There's a different clerk in the lobby this morning, a short woman who watches me run past like a madman, my arms filled with gloves and caps and jerseys. I yell something about the wake-up call, but she stares back blankly. Out front there's no car and no Kyle. People are standing around with valet tickets. It must be almost 9:20. Then I hear that familiar stuttering rumble and suddenly the Mustang is roaring up from the depths. The top is already down and the sun is sparkling off Kyle's blond hair as he slows down. I try a Bo Duke jump over the door but catch my foot and land headfirst in the foot well, and that's how we strike off, all turned around, in a cloud of exhaust.

"There was only one guy on duty," Kyle says, "and I didn't have our ticket so I grabbed our keys from the little house of hanging keys then ran down the ramp and—"

"Do you remember if this starts at nine or nine thirty?"

"It says in your letter."

"I couldn't find it."

We merge onto the busy highway, Kyle sliding unevenly through the morning traffic. People start honking; a woman flips us off, but Kyle, veering across lanes, doesn't notice. I watch him casually light a cigarette; it's wonderfully out of context, a simple act in a moment of chaos, and I'm not sure why but it settles me down. Up ahead, I can make out the river and the stadium, smaller now in the daylight. I slip my sneakers on without untying the laces.

We're there but we're not there, and it's another tense ten minutes of missed exits and wrong-way ramps that we should have figured out last night before we finally descend on a cluster of cars parked near the players' entrance. I jump out with my gear and start sprinting into the depths of the concrete mass. Up ahead the sounds of baseball come echoing down the tunnel, and I run even faster until I reach the daylight and a scene that stops me short. It's the field I notice first, a green spectacle a shade shy of real grass, absorbing the morning heat like a giant sponge. Forty or fifty overgrown kids are split up in small groups, running and throwing and stretching, while coaches stand around barking instructions. The upper deck wraps around the entire stadium, and at any other time the sheer size of the place would have me questioning the exaggerated importance of sports in American society, but a man with a mustache and a Reds windbreaker is brusquely asking my name. He hands me a number and a safety pin, then tells me to get out to right field to do sprints. I drop my stuff in a pile and do what he says. Despite the headache and the lateness and the dozen other things that have gone awry, all I can think of at this moment is the future, firmly in my hands, just a few sun-filled hours away.

The sprints are my best—perhaps my only—chance to get noticed. In 1921 my grandfather, running in a Chicago high school track meet, set a world record in the 220-yard dash. The headline in the next day's *Tribune* proclaimed, "Goodwillie World's Fastest Human." He missed qualifying for the 1924 Paris Olympics, the *Chariots of Fire* Olympics, because he pulled a tendon in the trials. I didn't know him well—he died when I was three—but I think about that headline every time I run.

When I reach right field, a coach is already explaining the rules: we're to line up on the foul line ten at a time, and race sixty yards to another coach standing in center; the top six will run again, then the top four, then one final race with the winners from each group. I try my best to stretch but there's no time. My number is called and a moment later I'm crouching low behind the wide white stripe, watching heat rise off the turf in waves. I can see contours, the gentle arc of the field, and the size of everything—the outfield wall, the red-clay warning track, the seats that climb toward the sky—

"GO!" I catch it perfectly and in a few quick steps I'm out front, running full speed. But I can feel people right behind me, pumping, breathing . . . *gaining*. I almost hold them all off, but someone slips by at the very end. It's good enough to advance, but as I walk back, trying to catch my breath, I know I would have finished in the middle if I hadn't gotten such a good jump. I was running as hard as I could and they were catching up. Someone yells my name. It's Kyle, waving from a seat twenty rows up. He's by himself, a section away from the parents and young girlfriends sitting closer to home plate. His red shirt is tied around his head like a bandanna, his feet are spread over the seats in front, and it looks, if I'm not seeing things, like he's drinking a beer. I give him a little thumbs-up, and he raises his arm in response and it *is* a bottle he's holding. How did he . . . ? Another group sprints past in a blur so fast I can't focus.

I survive another round. With Kyle cheering loudly, I finish third this time, and now I'm in the semifinals. I'm the only white guy left in my group, a fact I hope might get me noticed in some kind of reverse affirmative-action way. We line up again. The heat is coming up through my sneakers and my eyes are watering. The last race was close and I think I can stay with these guys if I get another good start. At "GO" I come out of my crouch flat-out flying, my mind picturing glorious sprints on barren North Sea beaches. I shut my eyes and run faster than I've ever run before. We're closing in on the end when it happens—a twinge in my right hamstring, a little pop of disconnecting muscle, and though I haven't snapped it, it slows me by a half-step. I stagger through the finish a yard behind the others, and watch the final race from foul territory, with everyone else.

Still, I think I did well enough to get my name highlighted or starred or whatever it is they do when they see someone they like. I hope so, because throwing is next. I've never had a strong arm, a fact I try to make up for by hitting cutoff men and being as accurate as possible. They start marching us out to dead center field. We're halfway there, walking slowly to conserve energy, when there's a commotion in the stands. We all turn around to see three security guards surrounding someone with a red shirt on his head. Kyle's still holding a beer, and that's what the guards are pointing at. But he isn't handing the bottle over. The drills stop abruptly as all eyes shift to the impending altercation. For almost a minute it looks like the guards might make a move, but then Kyle chugs the rest of the beer, drops it loudly on the ground, and moves slowly toward the exit. A mock cheer goes up from the players. But just as everyone is turning back around, there's another eruption. Kyle tries to run, but they grab his arm, and to my horror I see him point at me with the other. He's cursing loudly and the guards are practically lifting him up the stairs. The last thing I see before he vanishes into the tunnel is his red shirt, whipping through the air like a flag of defiance. And then he's gone.

"What a fucking asshole," someone says.

I try to forget what I just saw, try not to wonder if he's being carted off to jail. A coach announces we'll each get three fly balls to throw all the way to home plate—without a cutoff man. With all the tryouts in the last few weeks, my already average arm has been throbbing every day. I've tried to ice it as much as I can, and I should have last night, but there's a lot I should or shouldn't have done last night. All I can do now is hope I have one or two good throws left. Through the heat waves on the horizon I can just make out the padded mirage of a catcher standing and waiting at home plate. My hamstring is tightening up. My head is still hurting. And my arm isn't loose because I didn't warm up.

The five players ahead of me are wearing crew cuts and practice jerseys from Division I schools. They're weight-room regulars, all progress charts and protein diets and, from the look of it, those naughty little needles with their hormone-enhancing concoctions. Still, there's no arguing with the results, and I watch in wonder as they throw baseballs on a line from the warning track to the catcher, each throw bouncing once, efficiently, between the mound and the plate. The throws are as taut as tightropes and just as straight, and as I move up the line I can hear the sound of the ball, the low hum of a hovering insect. It's a sound the baseball has never made for me. And I notice, too, how the best players get a running start as the balls fall from the sky. They catch them moving forward, momentum already driving them toward the plate, and crow-hop as they make the shift from glove to bare hand; then the arms come around, the legs push off, and the balls launch into the air.

When it's my turn, the coach hits a shallow fly ball, and I run in hard, catch it in stride, and try to get rid of it quickly. But the transfer isn't quite right and I never get a good grip on it. When my arm comes around, the ball isn't in my fingers but back in my palm. It's the way pitchers throw changeups, and that's exactly what I throw now. The ball sails out of my hand and heads skyward, tracing a flawless rainbow through the humid air. When it bounces, eventually, it is not with a sexy skid in front of the plate but with a wounded thud on the uphill part of the mound. It bounces straight up and straight back down, then slowly, ignominiously, trickles off the dirt and onto the turf, where it reaches its final resting place—sixty feet short of its target. Back in deepest center field, there is silence, the kind that speaks volumes. I have two more throws, but after that first effort they're more perfunctory than anything, and although they both eventually reach the catcher, they do so delicately.

We take a short break as the grounds crew wheels the batting cage onto the field. A lot of the players seem to know each other, because they're sitting and talking on the top step of the dugout. There's no sign of Kyle. I walk over, grab two bats from the rack, and start swinging them slowly, trying finally to loosen up. Then, with my first free minute of the day, I wander over to home plate and just stand there looking at the field spread out in front of me. It could be good, this baseball life.

Batting practice starts with what we call a "shot." A kid the size of Kansas hits the first pitch 450 feet to dead center. When bat and ball make contact, every player on the field turns instinctively as the ball shoots up and up and out. It lands in the Gods. Someone claps. The players, all of us, put our heads back down and go to work.

My number isn't called until an hour later, an hour filled with searing line drives and majestic home runs. When it was first wheeled out, the bat rack was filled with dark-stained Louisville Sluggers of all shapes and sizes, but now, as I jog in from the outfield for my star turn, all the good bats are broken. The few remaining specimens are far too heavy, but I have no choice. I pick up the lightest bat I can find, and it feels like a sledgehammer. It's like swinging through a clothesline hung with damp sheets. The batter in the cage hits one last bullet back through the middle, then adjusts his helmet and struts past me. My number is called again and I step in. I wonder what it would be like to describe all this on paper, years from now, from a desk with a view overlooking the Hudson River. It would be a small scene in my second or third book, the Americana novel, and still, a decade removed, I'd sketch the moment perfectly, the sounds, the heat, the overwrought emotions of the very second a life changes forever—

Come on: Focus. Breathe. The pitcher winds up and delivers a fastball right over the plate, but I don't swing. I'm gauging the speed. The difference between a good hitter and a bad one is his ability to *see* the pitch. Bad hitters guess; they guess curveball or fastball, inside or outside, and when they're wrong—and they usually are—they swing and miss by a foot. The good hitters *adjust*; they see what's coming when it's in the air, then react. They recognize a fastball on the outside corner, then drive it to the opposite field; they pick up a breaking ball and wait that extra split second before pulling it down the line. Ted Williams said he could see the seams on the ball as it left the pitcher's hand, and knew from the spin what pitch was coming. Doubtful, but he had quick hands, strong arms, and he never had to guess. My problem, I quickly realize, is that I will. The tree trunk I'm holding leaves me no choice but to start swinging as the ball is coming out of the pitcher's hand, and committing before I know where the pitch is going. Sure enough, the next one comes in high and hard, just below my shoulders. I swing early, unable to stop myself, and foul it back into the netting. The bat stings my hands and I step out to collect myself. From the corner of my eye I can see the Cincinnati coaches watching intently from the side of the cage. They're writing things down. I take another breath, try to block them out.

What I think of is the sound of solid contact, a sound rooted in hundreds of games, thousands of practices, tens of thousands of swings. Muscle memory: a culmination of moving parts coming together in one perfect moment. I can do this. This is my future: it found me naturally, the way all great talent is discovered, and so I'll let it lead me where it will, and other naively worthy aspirations will become footnotes, background romances. The third pitch is the same speed as the first two, only lower and over the inside corner. It's the kind of pitch I can turn on and drive to right center. I swing with a clear mind, and for an instant I can feel the contact, ball meeting bat, then violently reversing directions. Then there it is, *the sting*, moving up my arms like high voltage, followed by a feeling of weightlessness. I've hit it on the handle again. The bat is too long, and instead of getting it out in front of the strike zone, I've jammed myself. The ball is rolling slowly up the first base line, a perfect sacrifice bunt on another day, but it's something else that catches my eye, a flash against the sun, the barrel of the bat, spinning through the air like a rotor. I look down at my hands, and they're holding the jagged remains of the handle. A second passes, then the bat comes down with a quiet thud in front of the second baseman. It's traveled farther than the ball.

"Next hitter," someone shouts.

"But what about the rest of my—"

"*Next!*"

Ten swings. Ten chances to change my life. I've taken two and now I'm done. I look over at the coaches and they look back dispassionately, like postal workers. I'm still holding the thin, tapered bat handle in my right hand, the physical evidence in the mounting case against me. In a daze, I walk out of the cage and over to the dugout, where I pick up my glove, and try to disappear into the anonymous outfield. For twenty minutes I stand there, wondering how it could all be going so wrong. What was I thinking, going out last night, carrying on with Kyle like all this was some forgone conclusion? I don't deserve this, haven't *worked* for it. I watch the farm boy phenoms and inner-city superstars going through their drills with determined confidence. They all came ready to play. But I think I can still make it. The sprints must have caught someone's eye, and my college season . . . they have the scouting report, must know what I can do. Even if I'm not so sure myself.

Fifteen minutes later the cage is wheeled away and the coach in charge calls us all together near home plate. Spitting tobacco, he starts reading the names of those who will come back tomorrow. I watch the black juice sizzle as it hits the turf near his feet. All around, players pump their fists when they're called and head toward the dugout where—wouldn't you know it—someone has wheeled out a rack of new bats. The names keep coming, first, then last, one rolling into another. I look dead-on straight, listening for syllables, early sounds. Half the players are gone and the coach is coming to the end. He winds through the last few names, each a celebration for someone, and then the last one, strung out by the asshole for suspense . . . *and it's not mine.* He says something about keeping our heads up, other days and other tryouts, twenty-six teams looking for talent, keep working, keep in touch, thanks for your time and leave the way you came in.

The walk to the dugout is long. They're wheeling the batting cage back in place, a massive cave of netting that suddenly looks like a barrier, a wall protecting the prospects from the outsiders. I pick up my glove and take one more look around. The pitchers are pitching, the hitters are hitting, and the coaches are writing it all down. It's tough to watch. I start down the tunnel that leads from this world to the real one, and at the end I see Kyle's silhouette just outside the gate. I'm walking toward him, halfway down the tunnel, when I hear the sound from the field behind me. *The crack of the bat.* It echoes all around, and I can just imagine the ball soaring up and out and away. Oh, that sound; it's what I've been searching for. But it's coming from somebody else.

PART TWO

The Spy They Left Out in the Cold

"Wisdom is dead. Long live information."

—MASON COOLEY, *City Aphorisms*

Three

THE BULLETPROOF GLASS DOORS open onto a sinister reception area—gray walls, gray carpeting, and miniature gray cameras tucked into the corners above my head. The place looks like an underground bunker, and the receptionist could be a marine. He's a tall, barrel-chested man who at the moment is speaking into a headset and watching a bank of monitors built into his desk. I wonder if he's armed.

I'm in the seventh-floor lobby of Kroll Associates, the world's largest private investigative firm. The exotic office locales listed on the back wall—São Paulo, Moscow, Miami, Hong Kong, Paris, New Delhi, Los Angeles—hint at a corporate empire of espionage extending from this nondescript building in midtown Manhattan to every corner of the globe. I wander back behind the receptionist for a closer look at this great wall of cities, and when I turn around I glance at his embedded bank of monitors and in the middle—the one he's watching—I see myself, looking startled in a colorless version of some Big Brother future.

"Mr. Jeffries will see you now," he says, abruptly, though I haven't spoken yet.

"How do you know who I am?"

"If you would follow me, please. I can take your coat."

I'm led down a dim hall and into a windowless office. Jeffries is sitting behind a desk reading a folder. He's small and wiry and has a protruding mole on his cheek. There's a chair but he doesn't offer it, so I stand there in my ill-fitting suit and tie and wait for him to speak.

A WEEK AGO I stopped by my father's law office to tell him I'd sold the Mustang. I'd been in New York for two months, scraping by as a food runner at a Greenwich Village theme restaurant. When I walked in he was meeting with Jim Hawthorne, an old friend of his from London. My family had lived in London for most of the 1970s, and the memories of my childhood still come back like scenes from old movies: languid, unhurried frames of sophistication. My parents and their friends seemed so worldly. The men wore dashing suits and spoke in guarded voices; the women wore slim dresses, smoked long cigarettes, and spoke best with their eyes. I came up to their waistlines, my younger brother leveled off much lower, and during smoke-filled dinner parties in high-ceilinged rooms, we sat on laps and tugged on coattails and grew up to the talk of politics, oil, and England under Thatcher. Sometimes, when the women were in the kitchen, the men would turn grave and earnest. Even the football scores became serious business, the news of Arsenal beating Liverpool delivered like some solemn state secret.

One night, after a cocktail party of murmurs, I said, "Daddy, I think your friends are all spies."

"You do?" he said, arching an eyebrow, suppressing a smile.

"I think I want to be a spy."

Now, fifteen years later, I listened from the corner of my father's office on Sixth Avenue as Jim Hawthorne pitched security services—risk assessments, terrorism warnings, and international executive protection. My father nodded absently and said he'd think about it. Hawthorne turned to me. He said he hadn't seen me since I was *this* tall. Then he asked what I was up to. I told him I'd just moved to the city after being unceremoniously released from a professional baseball team. I left out the food running and told him I was thinking of writing. My father rolled his eyes. Hawthorne gave me a sympathetic smile, the kind people give babies.

"You should come talk to us at Kroll Associates," he said. "We're always looking for promising young investigators who can write. It's an interesting place, and if nothing else, you might find good material for your literary or journalistic . . . *endeavors*." Then he said his good-byes and walked out.

I looked at my father: "So you *did* hang out with spies."

"It was a different time. Ex-pats did things when they were asked."

"Did you *do* things?"

He smiled. "Your mother and I went to a party at Hawthorne's flat in

Kensington once. Four or five couples, all American. This must have been seventy-five, when we had just moved there. I remember, as the night went on, the conversation took a turn. I thought it was the wine, but finally your mother leaned over and asked why people were speaking in code. By dessert, they were all drunk and talking openly about safe houses and double agents, and I looked around and half-jokingly asked if everyone at the table was a spook. The room went silent. Then someone said, 'Jesus, you're not?' and they all burst out laughing. But I noticed they stopped talking shop."

"Maybe I should take Hawthorne up on his offer."

"A lot better than *writing*. When'd you get on that kick?"

"It's not a *kick*. And anyway, I sold the Mustang for ten grand. Doesn't that cut me any slack?"

"I hope whoever bought it paid you in cash."

I'VE SPENT THE LAST few days researching Kroll Associates at the public library on Fifth Avenue, and now, as I stand there waiting for Jeffries to stop ignoring me, I go over what I've learned one more time.

Investigating the investigators was easier than I thought: they're practically media darlings. I read about how a former prosecutor named Jules Kroll started the company in the early 1970s as a tiny agency specializing in employee theft. He scraped along, then found a niche as the economy picked up a decade later. Wall Street firms began hiring Kroll Associates for everything from employee screenings to major business fraud, and the more Jules Kroll dug up, the more important he became. Soon he had hired a full team of investigators and opened almost a dozen offices. When the market crashed in 1988, Kroll kept rolling ahead, moving past the boundaries of domestic finance to cases of a more global nature. His investigators became international bounty hunters, following money and people around the cities of the world. By the early 1990s Kroll Associates had become the largest investigative company in America. The *Times* called it a "CIA for hire" and dubbed its founder "the world's most famous gumshoe." Today the company has expanded into every conceivable area of information gathering and surveillance, and its executives include ex-FBI and CIA operatives, terrorism and computer experts, high-ranking ex-military personnel, investigative journalists, even the former commissioner of the New York police department.

But I don't remember any mention of a Mr. Jeffries.

"I've perused your résumé," he says, finally. "There's not much on it."

"I just graduated from college last spring."

"And you've been . . . what . . . recuperating since then?"

"I was playing baseball."

"Professionally?"

"Yes, sir. It's on the résumé."

"What does that have to do with being a private investigator?"

"I don't think anything." He still hasn't looked up at me. "I'm sorry, have I done something wrong?"

"Are you being smart?"

"Probably not. It's just that you—"

"Definitely not. What team did you play for?"

"The Newark Buffaloes. They're an independent single-A team in Ohio. I tried out for the Cincinnati Reds and a few others, but . . ."

"What?"

"I guess I wasn't good enough."

Jeffries perks up for the first time. "What was it like, playing professionally?"

"You really want to know?"

"Yes."

"It was really competitive, everyone out for themselves, their personal stats. And the towns we played in: Parkersburg, West Virginia; Erie, Pennsylvania; Zanesville, Ohio. . . . It was all so . . . *local*, you know, PR photos in the town square, signings at the mall, high school girls in—Anyway, I didn't last too long. With my Division Three background, I was pretty lucky to get drafted at all. I spent most of my time on the bench—pinch-running at the end of games, appearing as a late-inning defensive replacement. I don't know. I kept wondering what I was missing."

"Where?"

"Here. In New York."

"Let me ask you this," Jeffries says, frowning. "What sort of work would you like to do?"

"I'd like to be a private investigator."

"Your friend Mr. Hawthorne says you want to be a writer."

"Oh, no. Private investigator. It's been a lifelong dream." I'm not sure what else to say. I glance at his mole right as he looks up at me for the first time. I think he caught me because he turns his head so that I can't see it, and I get the sinking feeling that I've sealed my own fate just as I was warming to the idea of being an investigator or a corporate spy or whatever it is people do here. I'm sick of filling ketchup bottles.

"Well, we have a company softball team that plays in Central Park," Jeffries says, at last, his head turned completely now so that I have to move forward to hear him. "And I suppose we could use a good hitter."

FROM THE FIRE ESCAPE outside my bedroom window, I watch my friend Gustavo Chavez inch uptown in his little city-owned Ford. He's stuck in a rush-hour parking lot of yellow cabs and livery cars stretching down past Radio City. I know what he's thinking: another five minutes of this and he'll stick that *Starsky & Hutch* light on the roof, turn on the siren, and move this snarled mess himself.

I share my apartment on the corner of Fifty-eighth and Sixth with James Knight, a straitlaced Ivy League associate at my father's law firm. He sips scotch at the Yale Club and doesn't own a T-shirt, but he travels a lot and pays more than half the rent, so it's not too bad. Besides, I have this make-shift balcony to escape to when he starts playing Mozart. Out here, far above midtown Manhattan, the horns and jackhammers echo their way up the buildings and the people look like ants scurrying every which way. It's early winter and the air is raw and clean, almost soothing.

Gus is an hour late. He's coming straight from City Hall, where he works as an assistant press secretary for Mayor Giuliani—hence the car and its related benefits. He doesn't have a driver's license (he's never bothered to get one). He doesn't have glasses, either, and that's the bigger problem, because the world he inhabits is a blurry one. We went to college together, and like Kyle, Gus didn't exactly have a smooth four-year ride. The social probations could be excused as youthful excess, but when he skipped a week of classes because of "an adverse reaction to the liberal academic establishment," said establishment sent him on his way. We were sad. He had been the funniest guy in school, the centerpiece of our parties. But we were also worried; he was a financial-aid student, and though he never talked of his family situation, the little we gleaned wasn't rosy. Gus was a second-generation American. His Cuban father had deserted the family years ago, and his mother had raised him and his sister on a schoolteacher's salary. Gus was his family's big chance, and he'd blown it. Now, though, a year later, most of *us* are jobless and he's working for the mayor. No one knows how he did it, but that's part of his charm: he's always wavering between brilliance and impending disaster.

A block away, his arm comes out the window and the red light starts flashing. He flicks the siren on and off a few times and the cars in front part just enough to let him slide through. He double-parks in front of my building, puts a parking pass in the front window, and nods to my doorman, who thinks he's a fraud.

Gus strides in looking like a short, plump, Latin version of Robert Downey Jr. circa *Less Than Zero.* He's wearing a Brooks Brothers shirt and tie and faded Nantucket Reds. He always dresses like this, like he's headed for a cocktail party at the Racquet Club. It's part of his Republican veneer. I chalk it up to some deep-seated Castro resentment, because really, how can someone be so conservative with a background like that? It's as if he's playing a part, except he's never out of character.

"Important goings-on downtown," he says. "We're tackling the big issues, moving past partisan bickering and changing the city from the inside out."

"Kicking artists off the street again?"

"Don't believe everything you read in the *Times.*"

"Hey, I think I got a job offer."

"Do we have any gin?"

"In the kitchen."

"Where?"

"Next to the refrigerator."

"No, the job."

"Kroll Associates. It's a private—"

"I know what it is. What are they doing hiring you?"

"I'd be a PI."

"That's preposterous," Gus says, locating the bottle of Tanqueray. "Where are the limes? Don't tell me you don't have limes."

"Why is that preposterous? *You* work for the mayor."

"But I have a talent for communicating with *the people*. I can explain the complex machinations of government in sound bites tailored for the common man. You can't even find your shoes in the morning. And you're not a friend of law enforcement."

"And you are?"

"The mayor and police department work twenty-four hours a day to make New York the safest large city in the nation," Gus says, carefully adding a splash of tonic to his drink. He mixes it with his finger and walks over to the couch. "What's the latest with O. J.?"

"That he did it."

"I think he'll get off," Gus says, flipping on CNN, where Greta Van Susteren is arguing with a panel of attorneys.

"Aren't you sick of watching this shit?"

"You're missing the point. What we're watching here isn't 'shit,' as you so elegantly put it; rather it's the endgame of a remarkable cultural shift that began with the advent of television and has blossomed unabated into our current celebrity-strewn, substance-challenged, Clinton-pandering wasteland."

"And being a City Hall spin doctor is such a dignified profession?"

"It's called sacrificing for the greater good," Gus says, settling deep into the cushions, his feet resting on the Ikea coffee table. "So, what's Kroll paying you?"

"I'm not sure. It was kind of a strange interview."

"What about the great American novel you keep talking about?"

"Aren't you double-parked?"

ON THE FIRST BUSINESS day of 1995, I walk into Kroll Associates in a hand-me-down suit from the old Barneys Boys Town. The receptionist hands me a stack of papers to sign, and by lunchtime I'm a licensed private investigator in New York, New Jersey, and Connecticut. It's that easy: they give me a laminated photo ID stating that I'm "vested with all authorities allowed by law." I have no idea what that means. My office is a small cubicle lost in a maze of other cubicles. I spend ten minutes looking for my computer's On switch. I'm on my hands and knees tracing a cord to an out-let when I hear a voice behind me:

"The point of this job is to find things, not lose them."

"Oh, sorry. I was just—"

"I'm Eric. You'll be working for me, which is lucky because I get the best cases, the big ones, the ones you see in the news."

"Okay." He's a short, muscular guy, well dressed, maybe thirty. He screams Napoleon complex.

"I don't know how you got this job, or what you did before, but now you're on your own. We work like a law firm, on a billing system—at least eight hours a day. If you go to the bathroom, spend your time on the can thinking of a client you can bill. You need to memorize the American court system, learn all the databases we use, and be ready to work weekends or travel at a moment's notice. And your salary: it's twenty-five thousand a year, plus bonus. If you're lucky."

I sit quietly through the law-and-order speech, guessing it's partly a scare tactic. He discusses confidentiality rules while I try to figure out if $25,000 is a good starting salary. I guess it could be worse: I have a friend in retail who makes $18,500. She spent her first paycheck on dry-cleaning. Before Eric waves me away, he gives me a list of names and tells me to perform a background check on them. "No problem," I say.

I go back to my desk and sit there arranging pens. I still can't get the computer to work. I call Gus at City Hall but he's traveling with the mayor. At seven thirty, when I hear the last voices trail off toward the elevator, I wait five minutes and then slip out quietly. The lights in Eric's office are still on.

AND HE'S THERE in the morning, too.

"Find anything good?" he asks, as I walk past his door with an empty briefcase.

"I'm working on it."

"You have no idea how to perform a background check, do you?"

"No idea at all."

"Then why didn't you say something yesterday?"

"Because I figured you knew that."

He shakes his head. I can see he's trying not to smile. "Then ask one of the other investigators to show you. It's not that hard. And meet me back here at noon. Got a little murder mystery for you."

"Seriously?" I ask, as he closes his door in my face.

The investigator in the cubicle next to mine started yesterday, as well, but he already has a stack of confidential documents on his desk, along with a time sheet littered with case numbers. His name is Simon. He's tall, gaunt, and as pale as a mortician's son. Some kind of military uniform is hanging on his cubicle wall. "Civil Air Patrol," he says, following my eyes. I nod like I know what that is. Then Simon asks if I'm a fencer.

"With a sword?"

"An épée."

"I'm not, no."

He turns my computer on for me (the switch *was* under the desk) and starts punching in passwords. He shows me the basics: how to look up civil and criminal records, bank information, unlisted phone numbers, addresses, family members, bankruptcies, divorce proceedings, asset and property listings, DMV and voting records, press clippings . . .

"People's entire lives are available if you know where to look," he says. "It's like one of those Choose Your Own Adventure books we read when we were kids. Every name leads in fifty different directions, and the more money the client has, the farther we can travel. And then there's the Internet. We may get access from our desk computers soon, but for now we go up to the library."

I nod absently, like my father. Though people are starting to talk about it, the Internet is an abstract thought, something pending.

Simon goes through the names on Eric's list, carefully plugging them into databases. He finds a few interesting morsels—a ten-year-old felony conviction, an SEC investigation—but nothing earth-shattering. He writes it all up, prints it out, and after lunch I take the report to Eric.

"I see you've met Simon," he says, skimming the first page. "As a general rule, do what he does."

"He fences."

"You think you're really clever," Eric says, standing up and putting his jacket on. "Well, we're going to meet an important new client for the first time right now, and your job is to take notes and keep your mouth shut. Anything you think is interesting, for whatever reason, write it down. Do you think you can do that?"

I follow him down the hall and into a conference room, where two men in tan suits are waiting for us. The older one is wearing cowboy boots and a large silver belt buckle that cuts into his gut. He has a strong handshake and a Southern drawl. His younger associate barely speaks at all. He just sits there with a notebook, like me.

"Heard you boys can find people," the cowboy says, rubbing his hands together.

"Heard you're missing someone," Eric counters.

"Damndest thing."

Then Eric turns serious. "I know we've spoken on the phone, but I want to hear the whole story again. Everything you can think of that might be useful."

"I don't want to bore you with all the details—"

"The details are never boring."

"All right then, I'll take it from the beginning," he says, placing his palms face down on the table like a card shark trying to prove he's on the level. "We represent a large oil company that operates in Alaska, mostly in the North Slope and Prudhoe Bay, south of the Beaufort Sea. The North Slope produces over ninety percent of all oil drilled in Alaska, we're talkin' thirteen billion barrels by the end of the century. The Pipeline runs from Prudhoe to Valdez, bisects the state north to south with eight hundred miles of fourteen-inch insulated pipe. I swear you gotta see the thing, one of the great works of mankind. Snakes through mountains and rivers, above and below ground, oil takes five or six days to flow the whole way down. But those fields are drying up, which would be okay if we could tap new ones, but we can't—the liberals have been tying our hands since the Carter administration. The last two years, we've managed to get some North Slope satellite developments on line—Point McIntyre, West Beach, and that damn Indian one, Niakuk Pool. They're producing pretty good, but I ain't lyin' when I say every project is a battleground. Gore and his boys, the EPA . . . it's just the worst kind of bureaucracy, all half-baked studies and blanket policies. 'Let's just throw our lot in with the Saudis because of a few fuckin' penguins.' Understand, these are *remote* places with no one living within hundreds of miles. No tourism, no roads, nothing except ice and a whole lot of *oil*."

He's pretty worked up, and he pauses to wipe a handkerchief across his brow. Eric asks if he'd like some water, but he waves the question away. His young associate stares at us blankly, like a Southern Baptist at an abortion clinic.

"Anyway, what we've done as an industry is band together, form a *consortium* of sorts that's managed to sue the government to reopen parts of the arctic refuge to testing. Which is where you boys come in. There's a woman over at the EPA named Glenda Torrez. She's a national spokesman, or spokes*person* or whatever, for the Alaskan environmental cause—a real ballbuster if you don't mind my saying. But then, two years ago, out of nowhere she releases this study *attacking* the EPA's Alaska policies as too stringent. Of course, the fuckin' EPA tries to gag her, get her the hell out of the spotlight, but they couldn't. So last month we deposed her and I'm tellin' you, we had a star on our hands. She said everything we been sayin' all along. We could really use her. So everyone starts gearing up for a major courtroom showdown and then . . . then she *disappears*. Flat-out vanishes. It's been over a week now. Poor thing left for work last Monday and never got there. She lives in a split-level house in—what's that hippie place?—*Adams Morgan*. Our people knocked on her door, but there was no sign of her anywhere. Now, understand, we need to *find* this woman. I'm not exaggerating when I tell you the future of the American oil industry *depends* on it. We got a pretty good idea about foul play being involved. It's no secret bad things are going down in Washington. Vince Foster was just the tip of the iceberg. I've got a list of names I been authorized to share with you, but I need to stress this is extremely confidential. This is a war, gentlemen, a war that's turning very ugly."

Eric starts in with questions, but I'm too bewildered to pay much attention. I can't believe what I've just heard. A missing person, a life snatched up in broad daylight. All for the chance of finding oil in some icy corner of the country. I look down at my notes, a scribbled mess of names, dates, and statistics; they look like the beginnings of a dysfunctional movie treatment, some thriller no one would ever believe.

"Well?" Eric says, when they've gone.

"I don't trust him," I say, thinking it's the logical response, the next line of dialogue in the evolving screenplay.

"Me either. But he's paying the bills—remember that."

"What to you think happened to Glenda Torrez?"

"Doubt we'll ever find out. People at that level don't make mistakes too often."

"So you think she was kidnapped?"

"Maybe."

"Killed?"

"I don't know, but it's kind of funny, a big oil company paying all this money to look for a missing EPA employee. Why don't you do a preliminary background check on Torrez and her family, and I'll start making phone calls. Let's see if we can't track our girl down before they find her faceup in the Potomac."

I practically sprint back to my desk. It's only my first week, but I'm already getting a glimpse of that tangled underworld where the real buttons get pushed. And I'd like to think we're the good guys, sorting through this mess of immorality and keeping the playing field level. For the first time, I can almost imagine a *career*, a life lived at the white-hot center of things, where politics, business, and society intersect. I'll be a fixer, a hired gun, moving among the bold names who drink at private clubs, who slap your back and invite you to dinner at Rao's. They'll come to me for corporate intelligence, fraud investigations . . . or higher-stakes games like kidnappings and international espionage. I'll work in the shadows, but I'll have all the information. What more could a person want?

Four

On a cold night in February, Gus picks me up and we head downtown. He's been at Elaine's, the society saloon on the Upper East Side, and judging from the way he's driving, he's been there awhile. Elaine's is a striver's heaven, and Gus, with his City Hall credentials, has slipped in the side door. He sits with crime reporters, police brass, occasionally even Commissioner Bratton. When Gus took me there a few weeks ago, Al Goldstein was eating with Robin Byrd, George Steinbrenner was huddled in the corner with his Yankee lieutenants, and George Plimpton, his hair a shock of Warhol white, was holding court at a table in the back. I watched Plimpton walk up and introduce himself to some young writer of the moment. He stuffed accolades down the kid's throat until he was practically choking. My stomach dropped. I told Gus I had to go. It was such a great scene; it just wasn't mine. I hadn't earned it. On my way out I walked past Elaine herself watching over her brood of famous regulars with proprietary eyes.

Tonight we navigate our way down Second Avenue toward the Lower East Side. I light a skinny joint as Gus squints through the windshield, prattling on about *The New Yorker* and its controversial editor, Tina Brown. Gus isn't particularly well read—the two books he owns are biographies of Reagan and Kennedy, the former for politics, the latter for style—but he is something of a contemporary media scholar, a "Page Six" intellectual, and I listen intently as he rails against the coming cultural Armageddon.

". . . because what you don't understand is that *The New Yorker* used to be this staid mountain of literary integrity and now Tina's filling its pages with entertainment news and celebrity profiles and Richard Avedon photography. If she wanted to keep doing that she should have stayed at *Vanity Fair*."

"But you don't even read *The New Yorker*. Why do you care?"

"You're missing the point," Gus says, running a red light on Houston. "Don't you see what's happening? We're taking another step in the direction of backyard wrestling and Court TV, toward model-singer-actresses and best-selling eighteen-year-olds. We're embracing hype, buying air."

"I love it when you forget you work in PR," I say, but he's not listening.

"The great writers are still there, but they'll pack up soon. They're interested in content, not ad pages, and Tina thinks words are a distraction when it comes to chasing the zeitgeist." We turn right onto Ludlow and park in front of a hydrant.

"Where do you get all this shit about zeitgeists?"

"You need to open your eyes to the flow of the city, my friend. It has a rhythm to it. Sometimes, if you pick it up, you can tell what will happen next."

These days the Lower East Side is surging again. The energy on the streets is palpable. This is still the province of immigrants—Puerto Ricans and Chinese and Jews from a generation ago—but in a trend as old as the city itself, high rents are driving young creative types across rivers and seedy boulevard boundaries, and their necessary infrastructure, the dark bars and sultry lounges, has followed. I wish Kyle weren't in St. Louis, selling diagnostic machines to car dealerships, because he'd love it down here. This is our version of Over-the-Rhine, a place where lives rub up against each other, a place that could still go either way.

We make our way past the signs of change—boutiques opening beside bodegas, enotecas next to community theaters—and down a few icy steps into the Ludlow Street Café, a live-music bar with a pool table and cheap beer. Two young couples are playing eight ball, a few men are smoking at the bar, and a blond girl with crooked teeth is tuning a guitar at the edge of the small stage. Mostly, though, the place is dark and empty. We order drinks and are about to claim bar stools when the girl with the guitar starts yodeling into the microphone as part of her sound check. The place goes silent as she stands up and looks around the room. She's got an athletic build, a healthy robustness that's rare in this Kate Moss city. When she smiles, her teeth jut out at angles. Still, she's almost breathtakingly beautiful. Gus and I take a table in front of the stage, and she gives us a little wave. She's wearing jeans and a tight white T-shirt with "55" stretching across the front. When she starts strumming, uncertainly, she looks at her left hand as she changes chords the way students in typing class sneak peeks at their keyboards. "Okay, here goes," she says to the ten of us in the room. G, then C, then D, then . . . "Wait, that's not right, let me start over." The second time, she moves to an E-minor and now she's off and running.

Her first few songs are simple tunes about lovers and longings and mornings alone. But her *voice*: She opens her imperfect mouth and out comes this sweet, soaring sound that's so powerful it doesn't need amplification. She's singing from someplace else. The songs fly through us and out into the New York night, and I wonder if they can hear her on the frozen street, in the dominos clubs and hipster beer dives, this new voice in Gus's grand urban rhythm.

She tells a sanguine story about growing up in Alaska, then rushing off to chase her future. She ends up living in a VW van, singing in coffeehouses in California, and it would be so sappy coming from anyone else, but this girl makes you want to believe. She has this naked urgency for experience. She sings until she's out of songs, then answers our echoing applause by playing one more, a catchy little tune about soul saving amid the unstoppable roll of American culture. And then she's done. Gus gives her a standing ovation that's too long, and before I can even tell my friend I've fallen in love, the girl has pulled up a chair, ordered a beer, and thanked us for coming. And it's painful, the two of us sitting there, tossing out the same superlatives and asking the same questions she must get every night, at dozens of bars like this, from hundreds of guys like us. Even as I'm talking I wish I could stand out against all those other faces she sees, but I can't even stand out at this table because Gus is flashing his badge and feeding her some nonsense about New York being friendly to artists and all that Sinatra shit about making it here and making it anywhere. He sounds like a carnival barker, but he's got her smiling and she flips her hair back, crosses her legs, and starts to relax. She begs us to come back in two weeks, says she's on this never-ending tour of New York, Philadelphia, Boston, and D.C., trying to build a fan base and promote her first album, which isn't even out yet. Bring friends down, spread the word, maybe we can all go out for drinks afterward. She says it's so lonely on the road.

Then she hugs us good-bye and heads off to pack her equipment.

A FEW MORNINGS LATER I'm sipping coffee at my desk wondering why so many missing people are never found when I open the *Post* and Jewel Kilcher is staring seductively back at me, wearing that same little "55" shirt. Dan Aquilante, the paper's music critic, must have been down on Ludlow Street, as well. His review heralds Jewel as a breath of fresh air in our age of overproduced frat-boy bands. "She is absolutely reckless in avoiding showbiz slick," Aquilante writes.

I call Gus, who reads newspapers for a living.

"I know, I know, I saw her," he says, before I've even said her name. "I think we witnessed the humble birth of a career the other night. But the 'showbiz slick' part is bullshit. Just you watch; they'll get her, too."

"You're very cynical."

"Did you see the other story, about George Trow resigning from *The New Yorker*?"

"Who's George Trow?"

"He's, like, their best writer. He wrote that book I've been reading, *Within the Context of No Context*, which outlines the impending demise of everything. He predicted the coming of our TV-addicted, image-obsessed nation, and this was way back in 1980. Now look what's happened. That future has not only arrived, it's seeped into his austere little corner of the world and cost him his job."

"So Tina fired him?"

"I wonder if he sees the irony." I can hear Gus flipping pages of a book. "Here this poor guy was, reduced to working for the queen bee of gossip, of—what does he call it—'synthetic talk.' Do you know what he called Tina Brown? 'A great girl in the wrong dress.' That's so brilliantly condescending. And her response? 'I am distraught by your defection, but since you never actually write anything I should say I am notionally distraught.' I'm telling you, someday literate people will point to this as a seminal moment in our history, when our worst predictions of a country without a soul finally came true."

"You're spending too much time at Elaine's."

"All of which doesn't bode well for your little heart-on-her-sleeve friend Jewel. They'll get her—Tina Brown, MTV, the great swirl of mindless chatter. . . . Anyway, I can't keep giving you these free life lessons. I got to go. The mayor's starting his morning press conference."

I hang up, wondering how Gus is so culturally *aware*. I'm supposed to be the literary one, the one dropping names at Elaine's, and yet I'm completely unassociated with that New York. It's a different city, a hidden city, and I don't even know where to start searching. I look back down at Jewel. Will she make a dent in our cultural mind-set or glide quickly by, a near miss, a marginal note?

Eric appears around the corner as I'm eating a bagel and leafing through the rest of the *Post*. "I'm sorry," he says, "I didn't realize you were busy."

"I'm not. I mean I am, but not, you know, this second."

"Listen. Jeffries wants to see how you write a client report. Take the missing persons case you've been working on, round up the research and interviews performed to date, then summarize everything in five pages."

"But from what I've heard, we've done hundreds of hours of work and we're no closer to finding Glenda Torrez than we were in the beginning."

"You need to learn that endings aren't always happy."

ENDINGS AREN'T ALWAYS HAPPY. It takes another two weeks to get nowhere. None of the senior investigators connected to the oil case will share information, which makes writing a report nearly impossible. I have one more caseworker to interview, an operations guy in charge of the more *clandestine* parts of the case. I walk downstairs to the company nerve center, where the Missing Persons, Extortion, and Kidnapping & Ransom people do their sinister work. I'm shown into the operations office, which is packed floor to ceiling with blinking surveillance equipment, giant humming computers, and a half dozen TV monitors flickering from one office scene to the next in blurry black and white. This room must double as the security center for the whole company. The investigator starts in on today's version of the runaround, how he's still piecing together what little he knows, et cetera. He's halfway through when one of the monitors behind him catches my eye. It's a familiar office, *too* familiar: there's my coffee, my coat, my Laetitia Casta calendar . . . Fuck! Have they singled me out?

Back upstairs I take down the calendar, locate the small camera in question (it's in a vent in the ceiling), and try to work until Gus picks me up just after eight.

We're going back to Ludlow Street. This time there's a line outside, along with a guest list that we're not on. Gus fumbles for his badge, which can get us anywhere from VIP treatment to arrested. Tonight it gets us in, and soon we're squeezing our way to the bar, three deep with Ethan Hawke look-alikes. We order beers, then wade toward the back just as the lights dim and a man with slick hair and a dark suit steps up to the microphone and introduces "Atlantic Recording Artist *Jewel*." Tonight there are no forgotten lyrics, no wrong chords, no starting over. The songs and stories are the same, but something about them already sounds packaged and artificial, like Nutrasweet or Mariah Carey. When she sings "Who Will Save Your Soul," a group of teenage girls squeals loudly. The edge is gone but the soaring voice is the same, and when she finishes almost two hours later, she leaves the crowd cheering for more. As people clear out, Gus and I make our way up to the stage, where, surrounded by her bodyguard and label man, Jewel signs autographs and lends her crooked smile to snapshots. We wait in a greeting line, like royal subjects, until it's our turn.

"We came back," I say. "You sounded great."

"Thanks a lot," she replies, trying to place us, as the man in the suit whispers something in her ear. He has a cell phone clipped to his belt. Jewel nods, smiles, and withdraws. The label man holds his arms up to what's left of the line: "No more, no more, thank you for coming." A moment later Jewel is whisked outside; through the dirty window, we watch her climb into the only limo on Ludlow Street.

Gus shakes his head. "Guess she's not coming out for drinks."

CASES COME MY WAY fractionally, wrapped in tasty morsels of intrigue that prove unfulfilling. I do the research, then hand off the results to more senior investigators, never getting the whole story. It's like leaving a movie halfway through. I give Eric my client report on the missing woman and don't hear anything until late May, when he stops me in the hall with one of his increasingly frequent you-fucked-up looks.

"Jeffries called about the oil case."

"Did he like my report?"

"Did he *like* it? He thinks I should fire you. He said it was a dreadfully written document full of wild assumptions."

"Wild assumptions? The only *assumption* I made is that after, what, almost four months and God knows how many hours billed to the client, no one who works in this building has any idea if Glenda Torrcz is alive or dead. I spoke with every investigator who worked on that case, and no one would tell me anything. They said they couldn't have information like that flying around the office, which is ridiculous considering—"

"You *do* have a big mouth," Eric says.

"Whatever. They were all just covering their own asses."

"Well, Jeffries has it in for you, so try to stay out of his way. Maybe things will smooth over when the softball season starts. He's really into that company crap."

"So what *did* happen to Glenda Torrez?"

"I don't know. Murdered, probably. We're not the FBI. When the client stops paying, we stop looking."

That would have bothered me a few months ago, back before billing hours became the meaning of life, but it's something else that has me agitated—the description of the writing.

"I'm curious," I say. "Did he really use the word 'dreadful'?"

"No, but he did say the writing was long-winded."

"But every other client report I've seen is so dry and tedious that I tried to spruce this one up, you know, make it more interesting, add some color."

"Color?" Eric says. "Look at the walls in this place. They're all gray."

I WAKE UP HUNGOVER on a sunny Sunday morning in early summer, and blade up through the park to my cousin Deliah's apartment, looking for a cure. Deliah moved here from Chicago six months ago and in that way that certain girls have, already knows everyone worth knowing. She's a party girl who buys her drugs in price-club quantities, always searching for the perfect chemical balances, hard and soft, soaring and soothing. Last night was one of those temperate evenings when all of New York is out, eating on sidewalks and drinking on rooftops. Now everyone is inside, collectively recovering, and for a few hours the streets are the domain of dog walkers and starter families. When I get to Deliah's she's sprawled on her couch in a miniskirt, talking to a girl named Shelton, who is standing in the kitchen in a T-shirt and thong, eating potato chips. They both look fetchingly fucked up. Deliah says they haven't been to bed yet; they were at this dance club on the West Side until 3:00 or 4:00 A.M., then an after-hours bash in an abandoned Hell's Kitchen theater, where they acted out scenes from musicals on a crumbling stage until the sun shone through the sky-lights and the ecstasy ran out.

Whatever was happening, I definitely missed it, because now morale is low. The drugs have turned. It's like a bad eighties film in here, except this Shelton girl is striking. She's six feet tall and model thin, with choppy blond hair and barely any hips at all. I think she has the longest legs I've ever seen.

"They're forty-four inches, if you're wondering," she says, in a husky Southern accent.

"Busted," Deliah says, from the couch.

Shelton sneezes and rubs her nose. "Well, it's been real but I need to crash." She puts on sweatpants, kisses my cousin, and walks out the door. I look at Deliah.

"Don't worry," she says. "The weed is in the kitchen drawer and her number is on the counter."

A FEW NIGHTS LATER Shelton and I meet for drinks on Central Park South. There's a *Pocahontas* movie premiere going on in the park, and from our sidewalk table we watch kids dressed as Indians stream past with their parents in tow. Shelton's wearing jeans and a tank top under a tailored coat. She waits until the kids have passed to take it off.

"I almost worked at Disney World in high school," she says. "I tried out for Goofy but didn't get it."

"You would have walked around in that suit all summer?"

"Sure, it looked kind of fun but then me and my friends went back after we'd dropped acid which in the Magic Kingdom isn't a good idea and I went up to Mickey Mouse when I was really zooming and said, 'Hey Mickey I'm tripping so hard,' and then from behind his furry head Mickey said, '*So am I*,' and I ran out of that place so fast . . ."

Shelton has lots of stories like this, an outlandish trail of episodes that lead her from Florida's Redneck Riviera to her present incarnation in Manhattan. It's a rambling, unpunctuated narrative with gaps that make it tough to follow. For a while she's at the University of Florida, where she's dating the kicker on the football team. But he becomes a God-squadder who gets angry when she won't go to prayer group. Meanwhile, a childhood friend named Carolyn Murphy is making it big as a fashion model in New York, which sounds to Shelton a hell of a lot more exciting than football games and revival meetings. So she quits school and takes a bus up to New York, and now she interviews for fashion jobs all day, waits tables at night, and lives in a one-bedroom above Dorrian's, the bar where the Preppy Murderer seduced his victim. It's a loud apartment, directly above the jukebox, and the floor shakes until four o'clock every night from the sounds of Ace of Base and Hootie & The Blowfish played over and over and over, while two roommates, two cats, and a dog named Buster fight for space enough to sleep. "Whatever," she says, "it's cheap."

We order our fourth round of drinks, and Shelton shows no signs of slowing down. I realized, when I was waiting for her earlier, that this was my first real New York date. There have been a few token one-night stands, but nothing like this. No one who makes time stop and move too fast at the same time. I'm just trying to hang on.

Fireworks start going off in the park, and we watch them explode over the treetops. I look across at Shelton. In the glow of the streetlights she looks striking. I want her to talk all night. As if on cue, she sips her drink, leans forward across the table, and looks me in the eye.

"Well," she says. "What happens next?

Five

"This report doesn't exist," Eric says, tossing me a folder labeled Confidential. Yesterday I was transferred to the Monitoring Division. It sounds lackluster, but according to Eric, it's Kroll's most exciting new area. "And if you're thinking this is a promotion, it's not," he says. "We just hope you'll do better in the field than in the office. You certainly can't do any worse."

I'm not listening. I'm staring at the report in my hands, a binder filled with names and photographs straight out of *Goodfellas*. Most are mug shots and fuzzy long-distance surveillance photos. Some of the names sound familiar.

"You're holding one of the most important reports in American law enforcement. It's the culmination of years of work by the FBI, and I don't want you discussing it with anyone—not even people at Kroll."

"What is it, exactly?"

"A detailed blueprint of the five major crime families, a kind of genealogy of made men. Some of these guys are in jail, some are under federal protection, others have disappeared on their own." And from the look of it, a lot are dead, immortalized by a "deceased" banner stretching diagonally across their images, the mob version of a pageant ribbon.

"This is your new bible; study it carefully—names, ranks, families. You need to know who these people are because we're putting you on the Gambino case."

"Seriously?"

"Unless you want to stay in your cubicle."

"Is it dangerous?"

"You'll have an armed partner."

"What about *me*? I'm a good shot."

"You're a good target. Now, do you know anything about the Gambinos?"

"I know who John Gotti is."

Eric shakes his head and sighs. "All right, listen carefully. In the seventies and eighties, the Gambinos emerged as the strongest of the five families in New York. They had a piece of almost every major industry—finance, construction, garbage, trucking, real estate, fashion, nightlife, an enormous cash empire built on intimidation and violence. But the success bred infighting. You've probably heard of Paul Castellano."

"Former godfather. Gotti had him murdered outside Sparks's in 1985, then took control of the family."

"Very good," Eric says. "Well, everything changed after that. Where Castellano had been low-key, Gotti was flamboyant. He traveled with an entourage and wore two-thousand-dollar suits. His Mulberry Street headquarters became a fucking tourist attraction. He was begging to get nailed, and what finally made it possible was a set of obscure racketeering laws called R.I.C.O. statutes. They gave law enforcement leeway in terms of surveillance, and as a result, prosecutors indicted and eventually convicted most of the top guys in each family. It started a snowball effect. With each arrest, more chaos erupted—assassinations, turncoats, all the shit you see in movies—and it culminated in Gotti's 1992 conviction. Are you listening?"

"Yes."

"Because this is important. Two years before that, the feds busted Tommy and Joseph Gambino on extortion and corruption charges in connection with New York's garment-trucking industry. Tommy and Joe are the sons of Carlo Gambino, the family patriarch, and they've been involved on the crooked side of the fashion business for years. There are over two thousand sweatshops in the city, most of them in Chinatown. Every day, a fleet of trucks transports fabric and garments back and forth between these sweatshops and the showrooms farther uptown. Dozens of independent truckers used to share this business, but gradually Mafia-run trucking companies moved in. The biggest of these was Consolidated Carriers. *Write that down.* By the eighties, Consolidated and other 'connected' truckers had formed a cartel, pushing legitimate truckers out and raising prices more than double what sweatshop owners were used to paying. This went on for almost a decade, until the feds, armed with their R.I.C.O. laws, finally went after them. The D.A.'s office set up a phony sweatshop on Chrystie Street, then used independent truckers to move the finished garments. Sure enough, here come the Consolidated salesmen, demanding the owners switch truckers or face more *unattractive* alternatives. Problem was, everything they said was recorded.

"In the end, the government indicted a bunch of people, including the Gambino brothers. And the case was tight; they were going upstate for a long time. Still, everyone was worried—and rightly so—that nothing in the garment-trucking business would really change. The Mob would just replace their captured soldiers with fresh recruits. But then something revolutionary happened. The D.A.'s office came up with the concept of *monitoring*. Before they were convicted, the defendants were offered a choice: move forward with the trial, which meant conviction and a prison term, or *avoid* prison by pleading guilty, paying a twelve-million-dollar fine, and promising to stay out of the garment business for good. Faced with jail, they chose freedom and wrote the check."

"But couldn't the bad guys just start back up where they left off?"

"No, because the government used the twelve million to establish a garment-industry monitorship to make sure organized crime would stay away for good. And Kroll got chosen for the job. So now we send people down to Chinatown to canvass the area for signs of trouble, and we're in touch with the sweatshop owners to make sure they don't get 'visited.' We've set up a hotline and done background checks on all the truckers currently operating down there. And, of course, we have certain . . . assets in place, keeping us informed."

"Naturally."

"After two years, prices *are* going down. The monitorship has reintroduced competition and choice. And so far, the Mob has stayed away. It's incredible. I mean, we could be looking at the beginning of the end of organized crime as we know it."

"And you honestly think the Mob has just folded up its tent and gone home?"

"It's your job to find out," Eric says. "You start on Monday."

I STAYED AT SHELTON's for the first time last night and woke up to find three people I'd never seen before crashed out on the living room floor.

The dog was licking them. I left Shelton sleeping and walked downtown to clear my head and meet Gus for lunch.

P. J. Clarke's is a little red building with a big past. It was the Elaine's of the forties and fifties, the place where New York's well-heeled and well-known drank martinis at the front bar and finalized deals and divorces in the low-lit back room. It was the setting for Billy Wilder's *The Lost Weekend*, and a real-world haven for artists, ballplayers, and politicians. DiMaggio came here with Monroe; Sinatra came here with everyone. But these days Clarke's has about it an air of despondence. The Third Avenue El and the three-martini lunch are history, and the bar on most afternoons is littered with tourists and local drunks. It's like the last fading echo of a different city. Still, I'd wanted to come here since reading about it in an old Dan Jenkins book, and when Kroll turned out to be a block away, well . . .

I get to Clarke's just in time to see Gus pull up in front of a hydrant and stick his City Hall parking pass on the dashboard. When we walk in Frankie the bartender shakes his head and starts making two Bloody Marys. He's surly and slow moving, but he's taken to the two of us. I think we amuse him, in the way that pets amuse their owners.

He slides the bloodys our way, then throws the Metro Section of the *Times* at Gus. "Look at those crime numbers. You City Hall people are making that shit up. All I hear about in my neighborhood are muggings and robberies."

"Where do you live?" Gus asks. "The South Bronx?"

"You're paying for that drink."

"The mayor has cut violent crime by over thirty percent in a little over a year."

"Don't spin me like I'm one of your *Daily News* hacks. What do you know about crime? You're just a twenty-one-year-old kid from . . . where the hell are you from? Puerto Rico?"

"New Jersey. I'm a twenty-four-year-old Cuban-American from New Jersey."

"There was a civilized time when we wouldn't let people like you in here."

"Back when you had other customers?" I chime in.

"Well, if it's not our favorite private investigator. Tell us, what did you learn this week? How to call information?"

"I'm working on a Mafia case that I can't discuss with you."

"Great. We got a spic working for an Italian mayor and you, you liberal fraud, playing cowboys and Indians with the Mob."

"You should run for office," Gus says. "You really have a feel for the people, a Clinton-like charisma that gives hope to the downtrodden—"

"Don't say that fucking name in here! I can't stand that man."

"You can't stand anyone," Gus says. "You hate every ethnic and religious group, you hate blacks, whites, gays, politicians, women, kids, New Yorkers, tourists—"

"But I hate them all the same, so it's okay."

"Is there any group you do like?"

Frankie thinks for a moment. "Cheerleaders. I like cheerleaders."

An hour later, Gus announces he's meeting a girl on the West Side and wobbles out the front door. I don't know what girl he's talking about. They never last more than a week. Gus is as inept at relationships as I am. I've had only one real attempt—Emily Edson, an Arkansas tomboy I dated my senior year of high school. It was hopelessly innocent in the scheme of things, painfully serious and oddly detached in the way that all young romances are. College moved by without incident, or at least serious commitment, and now here I am in New York, with Shelton, pretending I know what I'm doing.

It's not that I expected to get swept off my feet. I'm a child of my generation, a legacy of divorce, a case study in reactionary living—reactionary because I've seen enough of my kind to know. When my parents split up they sent me away to boarding school while they ironed out the messy details. St. George's had a pristine campus overlooking the wide beaches of Newport, Rhode Island. Of course, I planned on hating it until I realized almost everyone else there was, if a bit wealthier, basically just like me. They didn't want to get sent away, either, but they had been, the young scions of the crumbling elite—shipped out, flown in, dropped off, and for a while forgotten. Their stories were all variations on the theme of disharmony. There had been a bad divorce and the mother broke down and moved to a friend's house in Vermont; or the father was drinking himself blind on Fishers Island; or maybe there were tax problems or drug problems or a suicide—everyone had a suicide story. Among these sagas my tale of woe

wasn't particularly memorable, but it was good enough to buy me member-
ship into the club of cynics and seen-it-alls that snuck around after lights-
out, rapping about everything from the grief of the wealthy to how the girls'
soccer uniforms were see-through this year. We were wannabe intellectuals who drank vodka but not beer, smoked pot but not cigarettes. But it was
the bond we shared as victims of our parents' great generational collapse
that kept our ranks close and led to a sense of entitlement born of misery.
Talk of prenuptial agreements, alimony payments, and family counseling
sessions can make any fifteen-year-old seem older and wiser than he is, and
over time a consensus formed around the flawed idea of commitment. Divorce, we decided, was the settling sediment of the sixties, an era when the
concept of devotion—to causes, to country, to *each other*—seemed so terribly important. Our parents had jumped at anything that held the potential for significance. Like love. Well, now look at them, rudderless in the still
waters of midlife. We vowed to learn from their mistakes, and the way to do
it, we were certain, was fierce individuality. We could afford to wait for what
mattered—commitment, careers, community—if it mattered at all. A lot
of pot and pretense went into these late-night conclusions, but in the
months and years that followed, there seemed something to them. The
coolest kids in high school, in college, were the ones who announced they'd
never get married.

But it's not so easy in the real world. I suddenly live with a thirty-year-
old lawyer and have a desk job at a major corporation. So maybe that's why
Shelton's such a good fit. She's becoming my girlfriend, sure, but it's not like
that. It's not *deep*. She's a sort of surface girl, gliding through her life and
mine without ever settling down. She gives me all the space I need, so I'll try
to keep that respectful distance, but honestly, if we move closer that's fine,
too, because I think I want to know her.

Frankie makes me another Bloody Mary, says it's on him. The TV in the
corner is replaying Hugh Grant's *Tonight Show* mea culpa. I finish my
drink, leave a twenty, and walk unsteadily out the door, wondering where
Shelton is.

CANAL STREET IN THE heat of summer smells raw and unprocessed.
While the rest of Manhattan shines with a smooth coat of confidence,

Chinatown bustles with the manic energy of immigrants. There are different codes down here, ways of looking and living that remain pure, uninfluenced by the morass of the surrounding city.

I'm meeting my new partner, Russell, at the Holiday Inn on the corner of Lafayette and Howard. I get there early but he's already sitting on a couch in the second-floor lobby, sipping coffee and circling addresses on a printout. Russell is an ex–beat cop who had enough connections to land himself a job at Kroll. Most law enforcement types who make the lucrative jump to the private sector shed their old skins quickly: they shave their mustaches and dye their hair, tone down their accents and lose their attitudes. But Russell still has the crude, washed-out look of a career cop, a time-clock guy who always gets passed over for detective. He's lanky and balding. His face is sallow, his mustache gray. He's wearing a cheap dress shirt, already sweated through to the tank top underneath, and his pants are dark and shapeless—just there to cover his legs and hide his gun. He shakes my hand indifferently, like this is another in a long line of chores.

I'm expecting a quick training session or strategy meeting—*something*—but Russell just says, "I guess we should go," and starts dragging his feet toward the escalator. Outside, the fruit stands and fish stalls on Canal are buzzing like hives. It's only 9:00 A.M. but the sun is already relentless. We trudge along, taking it in. I'm trying to play it cool, be nonchalant, but I have so many questions. We're about to spend the day tracking the Mafia through decaying buildings, and I thought there would be some attempt at being *partners*. We'd have a cup of bad coffee and chat idly about wives, girlfriends, and coworkers. But there's none of that. Russell's been assigned to this case for a few months now. He's visited hundreds of sweatshops, knows this beat like the back of his hand, and that's what starts to worry me. He's so obviously a cop, he may as well be in uniform. What if people are watching him? Watching *us*? So much of life in Chinatown is lived on the open street, but the sense that a secret city exists behind the markets and the mayhem is unmistakable, and it gives the neighborhood a claustrophobic vibe. We turn onto Baxter and I start glancing up at open windows, down cobblestone side streets, faces lurking in shadows—

"Take it easy," Russell says, looking at me.

"I'm fine," I tell him. "But I was just wondering, like, how dangerous is this? I mean, what if we run into mobsters in one of the sweatshops or—?"

"That's why there's two of us."

"Oh."

We turn into an alley and stop in front of what looks like an abandoned building. Then Russell opens a heavy door and we start up a dark staircase, the steps creaking out warnings beneath our feet. We pass old Asian ladies coming down in single file. They move in eerie silence, like apparitions.

Somewhere up ahead, Russell says, "It must be lunch time."

"But it's only nine-thirty."

"The workers get here early."

We climb to the top floor, then make our way through a thick fire door and into a room as bright as the stairwell was dark. Before me sit rows and rows of women pushing fabric through industrial-size sewing machines. It looks like a converted wartime factory. They are all very young or very old, and their lilting voices rise above the dull roar of machines like songbirds drowning out crickets. Under the tables, almost hidden, small children play amid the cutwork. In the corner closest to me, partly obscured by clothing racks, an assortment of oranges lies beside a shrine of small Buddhas. I turn to ask Russell what the fruit is for, but he's speaking to a man in the doorway of the only office, so I just stand there watching the kids, who look up at me with big eyes, then look quickly away.

Russell comes over after a minute, shaking his head. "The owner's not here."

"So what do we do?"

"Nothing. We check it off the list and move on."

"What do we do when the owner *is* here?"

My partner looks at me as if I've just told him I'm a transsexual. "What do you think we do? We talk to him."

The whole way down, all I can think about is getting back outside. There was something forbidding about the sweatshop. I feel like I've been living in a nice house down the street from a prison and now I've just gotten my first tour of the cell block. The fresh air of the street lasts only a minute before we open another door and wedge ourselves into a cramped elevator with women who smell of mandarin and lilac perfume, women who stand dead still with the patience of the long-suffering as we groan our way skyward. We visit six more sweatshops before a fast-food lunch, and ten more in the sweltering afternoon. Often we get to an address only to find an abandoned room, a dead space, where shirts with one arm or blouses with no buttons lie scattered across the floor or discarded in corners.

"These damn sweatshops change names and locations all the time," Russell says. "Amazing we find any at all."

When we do hit our mark, when, say, A & G Fashions on the sixth floor of a crumbling warehouse building on Hester Street really is there, we're often held at the door while a manager goes off to look for his boss. It's obvious they're stalling, and I keep thinking Russell will storm in to see what the hell is going on. Instead we wait in the hallway, watching roaches work their way up walls.

"What do you think they're doing in there?" I finally ask, as we wait outside a basement space on Lispenard Street.

"They think we're INS here to check papers," Russell says, laughing. "Probably fifty women running out the back door right now."

We stop at six thirty, and I walk through SoHo stuck with the lingering image of women racing down fire escapes. I'm meeting Shelton and some of her girlfriends for drinks at Casa La Femme. It's become a routine, meeting Shelton after work at some fabulous new lounge or club. And I love it, being part of her traveling fashion circus, lapping up her downtown lifestyle. Tonight, when I get to the restaurant, everyone is drinking cosmos and discussing Issac Mizrahi's lightweight fall skirts. I try to keep up for a while, try to be something more than a boyfriend in a bad suit, but my mind keeps going back to the sweatshops, where women are making three and four dollars an hour, working twelve-hour days six days a week, and running away like rats when white men appear at the door. Shelton's friends are F.I.T. students wearing asymmetrical clothes, actresses waiting for callbacks, models with states for names. Drinks turn to dinner, people come and go, a stream of boyfriends and roommates and relatives, and everyone is beautiful and stylish, and any other night I'd be wondering how I got a seat at this table of young glamour. But tonight I'm stuck on circles and geography and how a paradise like this can be just a few blocks away from Third World desolation. At some point Shelton and I move to the back, a private table with a curtain, and someone's playing sitar music and I take a long slow hit off a joint, then lean back and kiss my new girlfriend. A waitress appears and takes our drink order.

"I love your top," she tells Shelton. "Who makes it?"

"Galliano," Shelton says, but I know different.

THEY'VE REACHED A VERDICT in the O. J. trial, and everyone has migrated to the large conference room to watch the big-screen TV. I'm in the office today because I hit a home run last night, batting cleanup for the Kroll softball team, and Jeffries, in the afterglow of a stirring come-from-behind victory, told me to take a break from Chinatown and spend the day relaxing at a Bloomberg training seminar. Now Jeffries is in the front of the room, remote in hand, flipping from network to network, as if that might speed things up. I'm standing next to Eric, who's complaining about the awful sordidness that has pervaded every pore of the trial. When he realizes no one's listening, he turns to me:

"How's Chinatown?"

"I don't know. It's not really what I thought."

"What's the problem? Let me guess: Not exciting enough. No wild street chases or secret meetings with Mafia stool pigeons. . . ."

"Not a lot, no."

"At least you're out of the office."

"Well, it's not exactly a promotion. I feel like filler, like I'm the backup guy, there to bill more hours."

"But you're actually doing something worthwhile," Eric says. "You're contributing to the greater good."

"I guess, but I'm not sure how much *good* we're doing. When we question the sweatshop owners, they act like they've never had any Mob problems and we're doing all this for nothing. And everything down there is so dreary. I feel like a beat cop, drinking black coffee, eating donuts, checking out chicks. . . . It's been weeks of the same thing over and over. I wake up every day thinking it will rain."

Jeffries is still changing the channels—Brokaw to Jennings to Rather, media stars at their practiced best, fat with frenzied speculation, loving every minute of it.

"Maybe you should try something else."

"Another case?" I say, perking up.

"Another job."

"But I've only been here nine months."

"Is that all?"

Judge Ito is calling the court to order. The conference room falls silent. The camera pans the courtroom, catching this year's bumper crop of celebrities in a rare moment of unrehearsed apprehension. Then, quickly and efficiently, the verdicts are read. Eric says, "Oh, fuck." Two black employees let out a quickly stifled cheer. On the screen, O. J. is hugging Johnny Cochran as the prosecutors solemnly gather their papers. They cut to Denise Brown, who's already sobbing (there's nothing worse than a relative who comes to love the limelight). Someone turns off the TV. Phones start ringing in the offices down the hall. And the air . . . it feels heavy, funereal. I wish Gus were here to do a play-by-play, because this sure does feel like a defining moment of our age.

Eric slaps my back, says he was just kidding, but I know he's not. And I know he's right. The precision required, the attention to detail, the automatic stifling of every creative impulse. It sounds fascinating, being a private investigator, but it's monotonous as hell. And for a business predicated on finding answers, there seems to be a disturbing lack of them.

Or maybe it's just me.

Six

ON A CHILLY SATURDAY on one of the last days of fall, I walk across Fifty-eighth Street trying very hard to remember the end of the night before. The garbage trucks are out in force, grinding away at leaking black bags like children chewing broccoli. My street is a kind of support road for Central Park South; all the service entrances to the big hotels empty out here, and on mornings like this the sidewalk is filled with cooks on smoking breaks, busboys buying lottery tickets, and fanny-pack-wearing foreigners who took a wrong turn in the lobby. But the sun comes out beyond the Plaza, where the city opens up to the north, and the sounds and smells of waste management are replaced by the heartening sights of Christmas. The lamp posts are glittering with wreaths and a man is ringing a Salvation Army bell outside Bergdorf's. I reach into my pocket and pull out several rolled-up bills along with a dime bag of cocaine, which immediately explains both my headache and the memory problem. I suppose the cash is more appropriate than the coke, so I drop a dollar in the red pot and put the powder away.

I remember that Gus and I were trying to get in to Spy some time after midnight. We stood outside arguing with some mammoth doorman named King, as runway models and poster couples moved past us through the velvet ropes. Gus even tried the badge, but that only sealed our fate. So we drove aimlessly east until I suggested Save the Robots on Avenue B. It's one of my favorite clubs, a last vestige of some darker, untamed New York, where strangers are friends and anything still goes if you know who or what to look for. Ten minutes later, we were slipping in and out of unlit rooms where figures lurked in corners and a tribal beat was piping in from somewhere. This is when my memory becomes patchy. Gus faded away. I have a dim recollection of a bald man with pills and plastic bags, and a goth girl hoovering up lines with rare intensity. I don't know how long I was there or how I got home, but I woke up in my bed (and, thankfully, in my clothes), and now, standing outside Hermès on Fifty-seventh Street, the whole affair hardly seems real.

I'm meeting Shelton for brunch at Clarke's. We were supposed to see each other last night, but she never left a message on my machine. I still have time to kill, so I duck inside the store to buy my father a Christmas present. The tie racks are a rainbow of bold patterns and blending colors, watched over by two aging saleswomen in signature scarves. Places like this always remind me of London. Maybe it's the customers, the Upper East Side ladies who conjure images of their English counterparts carefully perusing the great Harrod's food halls, or the men, in dandy hats and three-piece suits, feeling fabric the way a tailor might.

My father was once stylish; we all were. In London my parents made a striking pair. My mother was young and reed thin, with long red hair and a pretty face of freckles. The men all loved her. They treated her like the darling girl of the embassy set, but my father wasn't around enough to notice. With thick glasses and dignified gray hair, he looked like a Hollywood producer—Robert Evans, maybe, circa Ali McGraw. He was handsome, athletic, and becoming successful, a corporate lawyer with a large American firm, sent to the capitals of Europe on a mission of expansion. But it was the rest of the world—the Middle East, Africa, India—where he spent most of his time. I used to stay up late, waiting for him to come home, aping my mother's habit of reading on the couch until I heard the door open and ran down the stairs into his tired arms. And he'd always have something for me, a British Airways key chain or date book, and I'd be thrilled, even though I had no keys or pending appointments. As he kissed my mother and poured himself a drink, I'd get the globe from the living room and make him point to the places he'd been. Then I'd spin it around to America, lost and lonely between the two oceans, and ask him when we were going home.

We lived among the Crescents and Squares of Knightsbridge. These were the days of coal strikes and energy shortages, and one night, as my brother and I settled in to watch *Dr. Who* on the BBC, all the lights went out. My parents were at a party and the sitter was asleep. What followed was a short and peaceful silence, interrupted after a few minutes by the far-off wails of a hundred two-tone sirens. All of London had gone dark, and my brother

and I huddled in my parents' bed until they found their way home, well after midnight. Buoyed by the blackout, by the closeness at hand, we asked
them questions we'd never asked before, about the people and things we
saw in the news: the IRA and the PLO and the punks . . . and what were the
Sex Pistols and who was The Who, and on like that into the black night, until my brother was asleep and my parents had nodded off in the candlelight.
When the real lights came back on sometime close to morning, I opened
my eyes and the four of us were all curled up together, keeping the world
away.

Some time later my mother drove me to the King's Road to see the
punks. I hung out the car window and stared at them, pale young men with
colorful Mohawks and black leather jackets adorned with patches that read
Clash Always or Bowie Is a Man, and I pointed and laughed as if I was at the
circus. But my mother's smile was wan and weak. She said something about
disaffection being a disease. I asked what she meant, but she changed the
subject. It stuck with me, though, her expression more than her words, and
later, by myself, I wondered for the first time if there might be a more private world behind the first one, behind all the furniture and the people, a
second, more complicated world where lots of things were thought but left
unsaid.

I'd heard of The Who because their manager lived next door. For three
years long-haired men and stick-thin women slinked in and out of that
house until one day I came home from school and it was burning down.
Word was someone fell asleep with a lit cigarette, but I didn't believe that.
The truth had to be far more glamorous—these were glamorous times. I
thought of all those nights I'd lain in bed as the sound of acoustic guitars
made its way through the thin walls, like rock-and-roll lullabies, and helped
me fall asleep.

Daytime was for school, Young England Kindergarten, where a ruddy-
cheeked princess-to-be named Diana was everyone's favorite teacher; then
Hill House, the famed preparatory school for boys. In red corduroy knicker-
bockers and yellow jumpers, my classmates and I walked double file down
the streets, and everywhere we went the ladies of London would smile because we were all so right and proper, so very *English*. But then something
changed. It was a slight shift in the air, a straining at the edges that appeared

on the few nights when everyone was home, my parents off in another room, their angry, muted words spreading under the door like a low-level poison. And always, after a time, one or the other would come upstairs to the playroom, where I was racing toy cars or whacking my brother with a light-saber, and I'd ask what was happening. They would sigh and tell me not to worry. I was a young boy. And so I didn't.

That seems ages ago.

I've been in Hermès for too long; I'm going to be late for Shelton. I find a green tie adorned with tiny golfers in plus fours. It's a new pattern, or at least one I've never seen my father wear, so for the fourth year in a row I shell out $130 and watch the cashier wrap the tie in a tasteful orange box. I'd get my father something different, but he always wants ties. Ties and books on tape. He's a long way from London now.

I GET TO CLARKE'S as it's opening, along with two beefy women from Germany. They're leafing through a book on historic bars. Shelton's not here yet.

"Fucking tourists," Frankie sniffs, throwing me the *Post*. "You here by yourself or is that fat Cuban fraud about to show up?"

"I'm meeting Shelton."

"She's a nice broad. What she's doing with you?"

The German women want a drink. With a great show of effort, Frankie makes his way over to serve them, leaving me alone with the paper. A couple drifts in; the man wants to sit at the bar, the woman at a table in the back. The sun begins reflecting off the building across the street, and soon the old wooden bar is bathed in rays of light. Frankie turns on the TV above the waiter's station and there's Princess Diana herself, in a low-cut black dress, outside the Hilton a few blocks across town. She looks tan and beautiful, like an actress playing a princess.

"Nobody says that anymore," I tell him.

"What?"

"'Broad.' You sound like Dean Martin."

Someone puts Louis Armstrong on the jukebox. Frankie makes me another drink, then catches me glancing at the clock on the wall.

"Don't worry," he says. "The best ones are always late."

When Shelton does finally walk in, a few minutes before one, it's an entrance worth waiting for. I can tell she's stoned, but she looks beautiful anyway. She takes her coat off to reveal a low-cut wrap-around shirt and vintage Levis. It's effortless. She never dresses like anyone else. When we walk the streets together, men look at her and women look at her clothes. I always hold her hand, trying not to be forgotten.

"Sorry, sorry, sorry," she says, breathlessly. She kisses me, waves to Frankie, lights a cigarette, and puts her shoulder bag under the barstool, all at the same time. "I so can't deal with my apartment right now. It's ridiculous. Last night there were these guys hanging out who are friends with Johnny the party promoter who lives next door and I was about to call to see if you wanted to spend like a mellow night and have dinner somewhere and get some low-key drinks but these guys were all in the living room doing lines and Shannon was making margaritas and one of them, I think it was Sean who's opening a Moroccan restaurant in the East Village which we should go to by the way, convinced us to come with him to Spy, which is this new—"

"You went to Spy last night?"

"Yes, you should have come. Anyway, we were all in the VIP room and Sean and Shannon started hooking up and some cheesy guy was doing magic tricks and Bijou Phillips was dancing on the tables with her pants half off and everyone was staring at her ass and I'm like so over that shit because that girl is so obnoxious so like twenty of us went down to this huge loft on Broome Street and there was this fountain in the middle of the room and Alexa, you remember her, was so coked up that she totally jumped in and the rest of the night her shirt was see-through which she totally meant to do and I think she has a problem because she's doing coke like all the time and sure enough she went downstairs with some Italian guy while the rest of us went up to the roof and watched the sun come up over Brooklyn and a boy named Laurent rolled these joints which were half tobacco which is cool because it's really smooth that way and you save so much pot—"

"*Shelton!* Stop for a second! You can't just launch into a story about all these people I've never met."

"But that's the point: I want you to meet them."

"Did you ever go home?"

"Of course I went home, and when I got there the dog had licked up the lines we left on the table so Shannon and I tried to make him throw up but then we figured one of the guys next door had come in and done them because we left the door open so . . . anyway . . . what did you do?"

It's so exasperating, all these people I don't know, these nights I'm not there, and sometimes I can't help thinking her freewheeling lifestyle is as endangering as it is endearing. Because we're involved now. It kind of happened when I wasn't looking.

Clarke's is filling up. Two rough-looking men in T-shirts are sitting at the far end of the bar. One of the Germans snaps Frankie's picture with a disposable camera. Frankie walks past the register and adds a drink to their tab.

"I went out with Gus," I say.

"Are you mad at me?"

"Well, it's a bit disconcerting knowing your girlfriend is out in VIP rooms every night with a bunch of coked-up Euros."

"You're being silly. We'll go to Spy tonight if you want. Just me and you."

"I've already been there."

"You have?"

"Sure. I even know King."

"Isn't he great?"

There's a commotion right behind us, someone running past.

"HEY, HE'S GOT HER BAG!" Frankie shouts. "THE BASTARD JUST STOLE IT!" The two men from the far end of the bar jump up and run out the front door, chasing a figure across Third Avenue.

"What's going on?"

"Oh, my God," Shelton says. "He has *my* bag!"

We all move toward the front. The men from the end of the bar are across the street now. They've stopped running and one is fishing through a trash can on the corner.

"Don't worry. Those guys are cops," Frankie says, as the German woman snaps another picture.

"My wallet's in there," Shelton says. "All my money, my passport . . ."

Frankie looks at me. "Did you see anything?"

"No. I missed him."

"How could you not see *anything*?"

A crowd of curious back-room diners is gathering near the waiter's stand, and when the two off-duty cops walk back through the doors holding up my girlfriend's purse, it must be close to thirty people who break into spontaneous applause.

One of them walks up and hands it to Shelton. "Might want to check to see that everything is in there, Miss. The kid threw it in the trash as he ran away."

"Thank you so much," Shelton says, beaming. She opens her arms and hugs them both, and everyone claps again.

"He must have been hiding in the bathroom," Frankie says. "When he came out I think everyone saw him . . . except the boyfriend here. Hey, Magnum, how come you're the only one in the room who missed it?"

"My back was to the—"

"Hey, Jimmy. Guess what Romeo here does."

"What's that?"

"Fucking private investigator."

"Everything's here," Shelton says, closing her bag.

"For who?" Jimmy asks, hopping back up on his barstool.

"That place Kroll," Frankie says. "It's just down the street."

"No shit. I know some guys from the force who work there." He leans over the bar and looks at me. "You might want to think about another line of work, my friend."

"I've been telling him that for months!" Frankie says, laughing.

The German women start laughing, too. Frankie pours me a beer, and I down it in one long swig. Shelton looks at me and gives me a quick kiss. "I hate to say it, babe, but I think they might be right."

An hour later I put my girlfriend in a cab and walk over to the office, marginally drunk. The weekend guard barely looks up from his wall of monitors. I sign in, then walk down the dark, empty halls, past rooms stacked high with documents bearing the world's latest secrets. When I get to my cubicle, I keep the overhead lights off, opting instead for the eerie green glow of the monitor. I slip in a disk I haven't touched in a year, and as my fledgling résumé appears on the screen, I look up at the camera recording silently in the corner. For once, I don't care who's watching.

PART THREE

Failing Upward

"Reality is the best possible cure for dreams."

—ROGER STARR, *The Rise and Fall of New York City*

Seven

THE BLIZZARD BUILDS for three days. By Monday morning the wind is a gale and the snow—being measured in feet now, not inches—is falling like rain, sweeping sideways down the narrow corridors of the city. When it finally ends around noon, records have been set and New York is a modernist's view of urban beauty, all white on white, deep and paralyzing. The streets are deserted, businesses are closed, and there's no sign of the citizenry.

But here comes Gus through the drifts like Santa, complete with round belly and a sack slung over his shoulder. The doorman lets him up and in he walks, praising the response time of city services, then dumping a large duffel bag on the floor.

"How did you get here?" I ask, looking out the window.

"It wasn't easy. Now, when does your roommate get back from . . ."

"Budapest. I think he's in Budapest. A few weeks."

"So he won't mind if I stay here temporarily, until things get sorted out."

"What things?" I ask, but he's already in James's bedroom, unpacking.

THE SUN COMES OUT in the early afternoon, and soon people are taking their first tentative steps outside. From the fire escape we watch the city slowly waking from its coma. A young couple with cross-country skis makes first tracks up Sixth Avenue. Boys in snowsuits shuffle toward the Park, dragging Rosebud sleds behind them.

Gus emerges from James's closet wearing a Yale sweater under a Yale windbreaker, and soon we're outside, too, making our way down Fifth Avenue. A gusty breeze is blowing snow back up into the air, and as it comes down for the second time, it catches the light and everything glistens. We're walking with no real destination, the way people have always done on luminous days in New York, and it's moments like this when we realize our relationship with this metropolis is personal. New Yorkers become vested, and the payoff comes in sporadic moments of ecstasy—or beauty. And today it *is* beautiful, all of it: the Christmas windows at Saks, framed now in powder white; the sleepy lions posing as if for a portrait outside the public library; even the grungy garment district lurking behind Lord & Taylor, usually dirty and dark, looks this afternoon like a present wrapped with care.

We buy the *Post* and dust off a bench near the dog run in Madison Square Park. I tell Gus I'm looking for another job; he says it's about time. While he checks out the movie section, I watch a girl with golden hair, wearing cords and a sweater and a vintage green vest, play fetch with a black lab.

"I'm sick of reading about Sundance," Gus says. "Look at this shit. Redford's complaining about the commercial nature of this year's films, how Sundance is . . . what's he say here: 'losing its independent roots.' They've got this other festival right across the street, this anti-Sundance called Slamdance. But apparently even that's been tainted with impurity, so another group has gone and set up *Slumdance*. It's ridiculous. No one wants to see all those films. There's not enough time. There aren't enough *people*."

We're up and walking again, through a narrow pedestrian snow trench with walls as high as parking meters. Past the Flatiron Building, a city snowplow comes lumbering by and Gus gives the driver a thumbs-up.

"Sorry, but I don't see an excess of art topping the list of the world's problems. So not every movie gets seen. Maybe you need bad art to help the good stuff stand out."

"No, no, no," Gus says, stopping outside the Barnes & Noble on the corner of Sixteenth Street. "There's too much product, too much *content*. Too many magazines and bands and books and designers and stores. At some point the audience runs out. And what happens then? People resort to gimmicks: soft openings, fake tits, lip synching . . ." He points at the B & N window, where *Primary Colors* is prominently displayed. "Or books with no authors. And suddenly nothing is authentic because authenticity is boring; it isn't real enough anymore."

"And that's how we end up with Tina Brown firing George Trow?"

"Exactly. I still need to give you Trow's book, by the way. It's all in there, the overexposure of everything. I have it at home."

"Whose home? Mine or yours?"

"Mine. Although you bring up a good point. I need to find a new place soon. One of my roommates wants his girlfriend to move in, and there are some . . . *issues* with the rent, and I want to move downtown anyway. What do you think?"

"Are you asking me to live with you?"

"You can't still want to live with James. He's never even there."

"Which you should be thankful for."

"Well, think about it," Gus says. "It would be great."

But I don't need to. "Let's do it, then, in a few months, when my lease is up."

We keep walking, past the handsome prewar buildings on lower Fifth, until we reach the grand arch at the end of the avenue. Washington Square is alive with flying snowballs, professors wearing L. L. Bean, dealers hawking tinfoil packets of oregano.

My parents lived down here as newlyweds, in the years before London, before life caught up, with its moves and children and responsibilities. They never talk about it now. I found out by accident, when I discovered their record collection. I must have been thirteen or fourteen, that curious, painful age. It was like finding gold but being too young to realize its value. There were fifty or sixty albums, stacked underneath an RCA record player in a dusty corner of my father's study. I was a cassette kid, so these LPs were like dinosaur bones, old but intriguing, and the names on the covers only enhanced that image. Joni Mitchell, Phil Ochs, Bob Dylan, Joan Baez, Leonard Cohen . . . Looking back now, of course, it's a common lot for the time, but when you've never heard those names, those songs, when you're just becoming aware that eras other than your own did exist (and not long ago), then the records have resonance. They suddenly *mean* something. I placed the needle on the worn grooves and what came out of the speakers was a sound with weight. And as I listened to the lyrics—the names of bars and streets and lovers—it seemed as if this whole new world emanated from the cobbled streets surrounding Washington Square. When I asked my mother about the Village in the sixties, she said they had lived there back when it was the place to be. "But did you hear these people play? Were you part of the *movement*?" She said they'd been at this place or that, the

Village Gate or the Bitter End, but that no, my father was in law school and she was at Barnard and when you live through times like that, you don't think they're memorable because it's just your life, a kind of endless present, one day after the next. The sense of place or history or legacy gets attached later, she said, like a price tag.

But it wasn't long before I was hopping the DeCamp bus to the gloomy Port Authority, spending my allowance on cabs downtown, and sneaking into the Bleecker Street bars from the songs. Most were still there, but just holding on. A year later, when I went off to boarding school, I imagined late-night gatherings and organized protests and the background sounds of strumming guitars. I took the albums with me, set up the old stereo, and waited. But no one showed up. They were all down the hall trading Dead bootlegs and smoking pot to Bob Marley. Time makes a mockery of revolutions, and privilege adds the final insult. But those albums still spoke to me, even if their hard meanings had mellowed, so I listened alone, and at some point, through those songs of the past, downtown New York City became my version of the future. And the girl to whom all others would be compared existed in black and white on the back cover of Leonard Cohen's *Songs from a Room*. She was a radiant blonde, a *writer*, sitting alone at a typewriter in a bare white room at what I'd hoped was the Chelsea Hotel. In the photograph she's looking up from her work, caught slightly off-guard, but smiling and expectant, all innocence and brightness, and she's so beautiful, so *out front*, that I've always wished I were in that room, that time, that city, with her.

Gus isn't much for coffee-shop poets and antiwar protests. He doesn't care for young men walking cold streets with guitars strapped to their backs, or smart girls with long hair and books full of rhymes. He believes in the Rat Pack, in local politics, in knowing the outcome. So I keep certain thoughts to myself.

An old man shuffles through the snow wrapped in a scarf and blanket, verbally sparring with his other half.

"Have you noticed how many people stagger around talking to themselves?"

"The mayor is doing his best to find everyone a suitable living situation."

"It's like they're in a lifelong fight with a city that keeps knocking them out."

Gus looks at the paper again. "We've got *Kids* or *The Brothers McMullen*. And don't say *The Brothers McMullen*. I saw it last month. It's all grainy and low budget. That guy Ed Burns introduces characters in the beginning that never make it to the end."

"That happens sometimes."

"And now every idiot with a camera will be trying to make features."

"Have you heard of *Nico Icon*? I think it's playing at the Film Forum."

"Who's Nico?" Gus asks, watching two skiers slide their way down Waverly.

"She was the singer for the Velvet Underground. Andy Warhol discovered her. She was this icily beautiful . . . what's the word . . ."

"Chanteuse."

"Chanteuse, right. For a while, she was the It Girl of the Factory scene. Everyone hated her and wanted her at the same time."

"Let me guess: she got all drugged up, then disappeared, only to be discovered years later living in Reykjavik with a man named Otto."

"Come on. I've been reading about it, the whole Warhol scene. You know, okay, you know how he had his Factory in Union Square?"

"I thought it was on Madison in the thirties."

"Maybe, I don't know, but it was this place where completely implausible people came and went all day and night—junkies and rock stars and painters and patrons and models and filmmakers—and Warhol was the ringleader, the wizard who pulled the strings. And it was really fucked up. The walls were covered in foil. People were always shooting movies, shooting drugs, appearing and disappearing. There was this one guy, I forget his name, but he was a photographer who lived in one of the closets. Every once in a while someone would be sitting around thinking they were alone and then they'd hear a voice inside the wall. Shit like that. And another guy, Ondine, one day he shot heroin into his eyeball and no one even thought it was a big deal because they were too fucked up to notice."

Gus shakes his head. "Didn't Warhol film the Empire State Building for, like, seven hours straight, and then release it? Talk about too much content."

"But the point is, people watched it. He got an audience to sit there and watch day turn to night, and he made them think they were seeing something important. If you get enough people thinking that, then it *is* important. That's Warhol's greatness. He had all this nonsense going on around him, but instead of letting it distract him, he fed off it. Think about that. He puts a building on film and it becomes art, but if you go there in person it's tourism. In the right context it's not absurd at all. In the right context it becomes a major artistic achievement."

Gus is looking down Sullivan Street. "When did all these people get cross-country skis? Do they keep them in their closets for that once-a-decade storm?"

In the end, we see *Nico Icon*. And Gus is right: She does drop out. She leaves New York at the height of her fame and lives a life of slow junkie decline in England, before dying in Ibiza, of all places. As if there's nowhere left to go after here.

Outside the theater, roads are being cleared, restaurants are slowly opening. New York is preparing for tomorrow, when we'll all wake up and that great process of living will begin anew. Here, we have the chance to be anyone we want—a mayoral staffer, a private investigator, a Warhol superstar. Or, like Nico, we can lose our way. New York is full of people shuffling past, muttering about what could have been.

TWO WEEKS HAVE PASSED since the blizzard crippled the city, and now you'd never know it happened. A year has passed since I moved here to write, and you'd never know that, either, judging by output. I'm sitting in a downtown wine bar with the "Help Wanted" section of the Sunday *Times*, clueless but oddly confident, as if just the act of looking is in itself some small victory. There must be something out there: New York is the publishing capital of the world.

I miss the "Writer" listings the first time through. Then I find them: a few small ads wedged between Word Processor Repair and X-Ray Technician.

COMPUTER SOFTWARE DOCUMENTATION SPECIALIST
L.I. firm specializing in Software Development/Network Integration seeks doc spec w/min 2 yrs writing users manuals for commercial software applications. Ms Word/Win background pref'd.

I don't know what any of that means. And the others—"multimedia authoring tools," "pension investment strategy," "online help packages"—are just as confusing. So I flip to "Editorial":

EDITORIAL OPPORTUNITIES
Publisher of special interest magazines seeks experienced editors
for *Kitchen Garden*, a new bi-monthly vegetable gardening
magazine with slant on cooking & garden design.

EXP'D MAGAZINE WRITER
Enthusiasm/knowledge of soap operas a must.
Send clips & resume listing salary req's.

It's the middle of the afternoon, but when the waitress appears I order a bottle of red. I've never published an article, never written a story. I have no "clips" or, for that matter, "salary req's." Soap operas and vegetable gardens . . .

"There's never anything in there," the waitress says. "Jobs, I mean."

"Really? Even for writers?"

"Is that what you are? I'm a writer, too. But I write in the dark when no one's looking. It's easier that way."

She walks off. I watch her open the wine, then I start writing numbers on a soggy napkin. Last week I had my performance review at Kroll. I sat there as Jeffries rattled off a long list of "areas for improvement." Then he offered me a year-end bonus of $1,000 and a salary increase of five percent. He said both were more than I deserved. At the top of the napkin I write my new salary, $26,250. Then I deduct taxes, $1,000 a month for rent and utilities, and $700 a month spending money. At year-end I'm left with a negative number.

The obvious problem (unless you work in finance) is that living in Manhattan, even frugally, necessitates a higher salary than people in their midtwenties are likely to make. This is where the tricky issue of assistance comes in. I'm not talking about inheritances; those are easy to spot. (Trust-fund kids have jobs but approach them in an abstract, sweeping sense, and when pressed, it turns out they're applying to grad school or starting a hedge fund or moving to London in the fall. They do their best work at night. Rich kids run the club scene, where money buys friends and no one has to be up at 7 A.M. They live in walk-up lofts on SoHo side streets, and that sounds amazing until you show up for a party and the place has no furniture. The more time I spend with wealthy friends, the more appropriate empty space becomes as a metaphor. They're always searching for something—fixtures, lovers, drugs, meaning—because there's nothing to struggle for. Some ancestor already found the answers.) The assistance I'm talking about is settling-in money, a modest allowance or a small loan that really does have to be paid back. Most people get help from home, but no one discusses it. It's the myth of making it on your own. My father gave me that graduation money—now gone—then supplemented my first year with a few hundred dollars a month. It was enough to live on. But now it's up to me. There's no trust fund waiting, no inheritance, no loaner cars or family apartments. I need to find a career. I'm ready to knock on doors even if I don't know where to find them. I don't want the big hollow loft, just a small apartment filled with furniture I bought on my own.

But finding a creative job that pays well is like finding a Playmate alone at the local bar. I study my paper and drink my wine in gulps, like beer. Moving backward from Editorial, the listings only get worse: Driver, Doorman, Dispatcher, Dietitian, Design—Footwear, Delivery, Data Entry, Customer Service, Credit—Collections, Cosmetics . . . And then something, a small ad nestled between Correspondence Clerk and Controller:

> COPYWRITER
>
> Leland's, the nation's leading sports memorabilia auction house, seeks prof'l with interest in the field to write catalog copy, mag columns & newsletters. We offer a competitive salary & flex hrs. Send resume and writing samples to: 245 Fifth Ave, Suite 902, NY, NY, 10016; Fax 212-545-0713.

I circle it, close the paper, open it back up to make sure the ad is still there, then finish the bottle and leave the waitress a big tip.

Eight

LELAND'S AUCTION HOUSE occupies a cluttered suite in a crumbling Flatiron District building. In a small room full of equipment from every conceivable sport, I sit down to interview with Michael Puzzo, the company's PR director. He's wearing a bowling shirt and jeans and has a script in his hand, like he wants me to know this is just a part-time gig. Perched on the back of the chair, his feet on the seat, he explains that Leland's holds two or three live sports-memorabilia auctions a year, each of which nets upwards of three million dollars. What they need is someone who knows sports, writes quickly, and doesn't ask questions.

"How do you get all the stuff you sell?"

"We put ads in papers across the country offering appraisal services, then set up in hotel conference rooms and people just show up with stuff. Most isn't worth much: it's in bad condition or it's a replica or an outright forgery. But occasionally you get the real thing—the grandmother with a ball Babe Ruth signed when she was twelve, or the collector with a tobacco card worth a hundred thousand . . ."

There's noise coming from the next room, someone yelling loudly into a phone. We can hear the words clearly through the wall.

"You can't fucking *do* that to me! How many years have we been doing business? It's not my fault you didn't have a chance to see the piece . . . *No* . . . You bid it up four times and scared everyone away and now it's yours—"

"Here we go," Michael says calmly, highlighting lines of dialogue.

"—But you bought it . . . What? Who told you that? That's bullshit. Of course it's real. I got letters from the family, from teammates, from, from the fucking trainer. If he told you it's fake he's got his head up his ass. Why didn't you—*Will you just shut up for a minute?* Why didn't you preview the piece before the sale if you had questions about it? . . . I don't care where you live . . . Don't talk to you like what? . . . No, *you* lower *your* voice . . . *Of course* I want to work this out, I want you to send me my *check. . . .*"

The voice trails off and Michael shrugs. "That's Josh. He's the owner."

"Is he always like *that*?"

"He's a challenge. But he's also the smartest guy in the business. Actually, he pretty much invented the business. He was the first person to understand there was a market for sports memorabilia. In the eighties rare baseball cards started selling for absurd amounts of money, and Josh figured out that if little pieces of colored cardboard were worth so much, what about a jersey worn by Mickey Mantle, or the ball Hank Aaron hit for his five hundredth home run—the stuff the players actually used or signed. He's got a keen eye for value and a . . . *tireless* will to negotiate—he'll wear you down until you agree with him just so he'll leave you alone. In the mideighties he started buying everything he could get his hands on, and a few years later, largely because of him, the industry took off. In the last decade all the major auction houses have gotten involved, and every weekend card dealer has started his own catalog business. But we still get the best stuff. Last year we sold the ball that went through Bill Buckner's legs for ninety-three thousand dollars."

"Jesus. Who bought it?"

"Charlie Sheen."

"I thought he spent all his money on hookers and drugs."

"And baseball memorabilia."

"You know, I was at that game."

"Sure you were," Michael says.

"No, I really . . . How much did Leland's pay for the ball?"

"We didn't buy it, we took it on consignment. We do that with the really valuable pieces—that way, if they don't sell, we're not stuck with them."

"So you charge a commission to both the buyer *and* seller?"

"As many people as we can."

"What if something sells for a really low price? Doesn't the owner get mad?"

"You don't know much about auctions, do you? We put a secret reserve price on every lot, and if the bidding doesn't reach that price, then the owner gets it back."

The argument next door is flaring up again, something about ambulance chasing and the FBI. Michael rolls his eyes. "Genius takes all forms," he says, looking down at my résumé. "You know, you don't strike me as the private investigator type."

"That's why I'm here."

"Well, Josh liked your baseball background. So the job is yours if you want it."

"That's it? Don't I need to meet him first?"

"Probably not the best time."

"What about salary and benefits?"

"What are you making now?"

"Thirty thousand, so I'd need a bit of a—"

"How's thirty-five plus health?"

"I guess that's fine."

"Good. Then we're done."

"What if I had said forty?"

"You didn't," he says, looking back down at his script. "You said thirty."

I get up and put my coat on. "I take it you're an actor."

"Yeah, theater mostly. Off off *off* Broadway. I was in one movie, with Sandra Bullock, called *Who Shot Patakango*. It was one of the worst films ever made. When Sandy made it big, the first thing she did was get it buried. It vanished from video stores overnight. Do you know what that's like, finally getting a big part and then having the movie disappear? People think I'm lying when I tell "

"MICHAEL!" Josh yells.

"I'll see you in a week," Michael says. Then he walks down the hall and slips into Josh's office. I can hear them as I wait for the elevator.

"Can you calm down for a minute? I was interviewing our new copywriter. He's probably scared shitless because you're in here yelling like a maniac."

"Well, if he can't handle it, he's in the wrong business. How much did you offer him? It better not have been more than—"

The door slams shut, and the eavesdropping, the whole investigative life, comes to an end.

• • •

My fabulous Kroll good-bye party turns out to be a half-hearted gathering of junior investigators and administrative staff, half of whom I've never met. We're all crowded into a smoky happy-hour bar on Second Avenue, among the usual assortment of young stockbrokers and the raspy-voiced girls who love them. I was thinking one or two senior staffers might show up for the event, but no such luck. Instead we have a chubby receptionist with painted eyebrows; two recently hired investigators discussing their first cases with the same mix of audacity and propriety that I once had (when I walk by they change the subject); and Simon, drinking Diet Coke and checking his beeper. It's been a year since we joined the company together, and Simon is already running his own investigations. But he deserves it. We're getting a bit sentimental, when I feel a slap on my back and look up to find Eric grinning at me. I wasn't sure he'd show up. We do a shot together. He tells me I'm making a mistake, that I could have had a good run if I'd stayed. He says this with a straight face. Then he hands me a note from Jim Hawthorne: *I'd be there to see you off, but I'm traveling. I wish you the best of luck in your literary endeavors. Hope you've found a few intriguing tidbits to jot down sometime.*

A half hour later I say the necessary good-byes, then sneak out. The drinks have gone to my head. I walk a few blocks, then check my messages from a pay phone on Park:

Friday, 7:44 P.M.—Hey, baby . . . I was going to stop by your work party but I have to go to this thing for John Bartlett in SoHo which starts at like nine so come meet me after if you get done early, so okay ciao for now love you bye.

Friday, 8:06 P.M.—What's up? Meeting some City Hall people for a drink over at Rudy's around nine. Come by when you're done and I'll get rid of the work guys. Feel free to bring any of those Bond girls from Kroll. Peace.

Friday, 8:12 P.M.—Hello . . . James . . . in from Budapest, though I'm sure you'll be . . . catch up later . . .

I can't understand the rest of my (official) roommate's message. It must be the middle of the night in Eastern Europe. I hope it's nothing serious.

RUDY'S IS A theater-district dive packed with chain-smoking stage-hands, aging jazz musicians, and the type of actor who looks too much like every other actor to get any good parts. The bartenders wear bow ties and the jukebox is superb, but the best thing about the place is the free hot dogs. Gus is in a booth toward the back, sitting with two wormy-looking men in dark suits and round glasses.

"This is my liberal friend I was telling you about," he says, as I walk up.

They both say, "Hey," then look down at their drinks. I leave them to their tax cuts and wander over to the bar, order a beer and a dog, and start feeding the jukebox money even though I'd have to stay for hours to hear my songs. When his two sidekicks have put on their overcoats and gone, Gus comes over to join me.

"Fun guys," I say.

"They don't get out much."

"You'd have thought I was Abbie Hoffman."

"Where's Shelton?"

"She didn't show up. She's going to—what was it?—a Helmut Lang party, I think."

"Maybe we should drop by."

"She didn't say where it was."

"On purpose?"

"I don't know."

An hour, three beers, and two hot dogs later, my songs still haven't played. We tip the barman and start walking uptown. I keep reading about Hell's Kitchen shedding its seedy, Guardian Angels image and becoming the new East Village—it even has a new name: Clinton. Tonight, though, all we find is an empty tourist lounge called Revolution, so we make our way over to Eighth and start back south, past second-rate hotels and empty comedy clubs, and soon we're dangerously close to Times Square. I've learned that no one who lives in New York actually goes to Times Square unless they work at Viacom or have relatives in town (the kind who drag you to Les Misérables because Rent is too racy, then get up early to stand outside the Today show and wave to everyone back home). We got here too late, missed the Vegas years of sex shows and streetwalkers, afroed pimps and Irish street gangs, jazz clubs and sidewalk card scams.

But just as I'm complaining about Times Square's new Disney image, we come upon a lone vestige of the past—a rundown former theater called Show World. The neon signs in the window offer "XXX Movies," "Private Video Booths," and the slippery promise of "Live Girls." I'm not sure why—maybe we're drunk or wistful—but we walk in. I'm hoping for a vintage burlesque show with girls in garters, but there's no stage. The first floor has walls of videos up front and a corridor in the back lined with coin-operated machines showing black-and-white snippets of lust. The live girls are upstairs, past the magazines and sex toys, in a glass bubble surrounded by private viewing booths.

Gus walks into one and slides the curtain shut. I pick a booth on the other side, a dim, discolored seat smelling of stale Lysol. Without touching anything, I drop a coin into the slot and a panel slides open to reveal two naked women sitting in the center of the circle, sagging into middle age. There must be a signal because they both get up at the same time and walk in different directions. The one coming toward me is a bottle blonde with skin so translucent I can see her blue veins at a distance. She looks like a (somewhat) younger Tammy Faye Bakker without all the makeup. She comes up to the glass and crouches, then raises herself slowly, becoming visible in pieces—hair, neck, back, and finally her ass, moored like a cruise ship to its wide berth of hips. The other woman is doing some kind of tap dance in front of Gus's window, but my view is soon obscured completely by an onslaught of skin, inches from my face, bunching up and folding into itself. She bends dexterously at the waist, her hair scraping the filthy floor, until she's looking back at me from between her knees, and before she can kiss the glass, before she can open up completely, I back out of the booth and, gasping for air, practically fall into Gus's arms. He grabs my shoulders and shakes them.

"Are you okay? What the fuck took you so long?"

"That's the worst thing I've ever seen," I stammer.

"At least you didn't have Mrs. Bojangles jiggling in front of your face."

"These girls are not for you," says a Russian-accented voice somewhere behind us. We turn around and standing there is a pony-tailed man dressed in black leather pants and a matching jacket. "Come with me. The girls for you are one more flight up."

There's not one reason we should follow him. But we do. We follow him upstairs like eager children to a low-lit lounge. A few girls are sitting vapidly on bar stools. They're young and willowy and wearing bright cocktail dresses with spaghetti straps. "This is better," the Russian says, slapping Gus's back. On cue, two girls make their way over and we shake their limp hands. They're stunning in the way that strippers are always stunning in dark rooms, at late hours, to unclear minds. They have long, arching backs and pumped up breasts and plastic heels embedded with specks of glitter. I'm suddenly too timid to talk to them, which is funny considering their job is to smile and say yes. But it's too late to say anything anyway, because one of them is leading Gus to a room with a neon champagne glass above the entrance. She playfully pushes him onto a couch, then closes the curtain.

"What's the deal up here?" I ask. I have a sinking feeling that whatever the deal *was*, it's much worse now that Gus is in that room.

"You do whatever you want," the Russian says, "but you must have champagne. The girls, they like champagne. I give you a deal: hundred dollars for half hour, plus hundred fifty for champagne, the best kind." He winks like we're in this together. "You have credit card?" The remaining girl puts her arms around my neck and starts doing something with my ear. I produce an AmEx.

"For your friend, too, yes?"

"*No!* God, no. We're separate. Totally separate."

"Okay, no problem," the Russian says, sweeping his arm toward the room next to Gus's. And then I'm in there with the curtain drawn, sitting on a surprisingly lush couch, and this girl is pushing my legs apart with hers, slipping rhythmically out of her dress as soft techno spills from the speaker on the wall behind us. She's tall and has olive skin and long hair that falls in fraying knots over her breasts.

"My name is—"

"Shhh," she purrs, the *H*'s lingering on her lips.

She rests her hands on the wall behind my head and stays there, swaying hypnotically, persuasively, her nipples lightly brushing my cheeks. She sighs in my ear, and it sounds like a moan. Then she moves even closer; her skin smells like scented sawdust. She puts her hand on my shoulder, then slowly moves it down to my chest, kissing my ear, and then down to my side, sighing still, sighing and—

The Russian comes bursting through the curtain, followed by a second man wheeling in a table with champagne and glasses. The girl doesn't stop, doesn't even look up, as the bottle is uncorked.

"Sign, my friend, sign," he says, waving a pen in the air.

Her hand is on my thigh, her mouth on my neck. I feel for the pen and try to lean forward to see the number on the receipt, but she's draped over me and I don't want her to move. It's dark but I can make out the number 250, so with a firm breast in my face, I sign my name and the two men go away.

"You like, no?" the girl says, speaking for the first time.

"You're Russian too?"

"No, Ukraine. Tell me, you have wife?"

"I'm a bit young for that."

"I am eighteen," she says.

"Really." Jesus. I try to think of something else to say, something normal, maybe ask where she lives, if she's in school, what else she does—I don't know, stripper small talk—but she's taking a little packet out of the depths of her dress, a clear zip bag, and she dumps a small hill of powder onto the table between the cheap stemware.

"So . . . how long have you worked—"

"You have money?" she asks, expertly carving out two lines with the edge of the yellow customer receipt.

"That's okay, I don't think I want to buy any—"

"No, darling, not for buying, for . . . you know . . ." She points to her nose. I give her my biggest bill, a crisp fifty. She rolls it tightly, then bends down on all fours and inhales a line in one smooth, well-practiced motion.

"What if that guy walks in again?"

"Is okay." She hands me the fifty and kisses my neck. "So you go."

I lean over and as I start snorting I hear the Russian shouting outside. The girl is still on all fours beside me. I do half the line and stop. But her hands are wandering again and she nods at the table, so I lean back down because it would be rude not to finish, and as I do the rest, my eyes glance at the credit card receipt an inch from my nose, and *fuck*, it says *$750*, not

$250. Her hands are roaming inside my shirt, and she purrs again, "Is sooo goood . . . ," and it is good, was good. Her breath is warm and we fall back into the couch, her fingers nimbly unbuttoning my shirt, and this is no time to bring up a billing dispute, so I let her professional hands massage my shoulders while I stare at her taut stomach . . . but something's going on. I can hear Gus shouting, but the music is drowning him out and I've never seen a stomach this . . . inspirational . . . the first level of a flawless three-level torso—

"YOU PAY! YOU PAY!" the Russian shouts, storming into our love nest again. The girl rolls off me gracefully, like a gymnast in a floor routine.

"What the fuck? Will you stop barging in like this?"

"YOU PAY!"

"That's all I've been doing since I got here."

"For your friend! He has no money."

"That's between you and him."

"No, no, no! He tells me you pay."

"This is bullshit. You already charged me five hundred bucks for nothing. We agreed on two fifty, and look what you did. You fucking charged me—"

"Look what *you* did," he says, picking up the little bag of coke lying on the table. "You take drugs into my club."

"I didn't take any drugs into your club," I say, looking around for the girl. But she's gone.

"You pay for your friend and you pay for the girl."

"But nothing even happened. You kept barging—"

"No more talk!" He's blocking the door, and there's another guy, the champagne guy, looming behind him.

"I need to speak to my friend. It's the only way you might get any money."

He thinks about this for a moment, then lets me sidestep around him into the room next door. I close the curtain behind me. Gus looks scared.

"Are you okay? What the fuck's going on?"

"I only have, like, a hundred and twenty in cash," Gus says, his voice shaking. "I didn't know how much it—"

"Well, *ask* next time."

"Next time."

"I'm not paying any more. He already charged my card seven hundred and fifty, so let's just leave."

"I don't think it's that easy. He has a gun under his jacket."

"Oh, come on. How do you know?"

"He showed it to me."

"This is Show World, for Christ's sake."

"Look," Gus says. "Tell him the extra five hundred bucks covers me."

"I can't. He's got leverage."

"Your credit card?"

"My cocaine."

"You have coke?"

"It's not *my*—"

"Did you do some?"

"It's *hers*."

"Did *she* do some?"

I can hear the Russian outside, getting restless. "Why don't you tell him you work for the mayor? Maybe he'll let us off."

Gus ignores me. "I think I have seven hundred in my account, if I can get to an ATM."

"That's how much you owe? What were you doing in here?"

"Let's just say it was worth it." Gus opens the curtain to find our leather-clad nemesis waiting on the other side. "I'll give you the money but I need a cash machine."

"No."

"And my friend will stay here until I give you the money."

"The fuck I will," I say.

"Come on."

"Fine, we go," the Russian says. Then he points at me: "But you wait here. With Boris."

So I do. I take a seat at the bar. Except for Boris, who is large enough to count twice, the room has completely emptied out. The girls have vanished into the fake wood paneling. Then I remember the rolled-up fifty sitting on the table in the champagne room. I hurry over to get it, but of course that's disappeared, too. Even Boris stops staring at me and eventually wanders off.

When I'm sure he's gone I bound downstairs, to semicivilization. I pass the peep show, which now seems quaint, almost Rockwellian, then run down another flight and out to the front entrance where people, normal oblivious people, are walking up and down the wide sidewalk. There's no sign of Gus. It's been almost twenty minutes; he must have left after handing over the money and these idiot Russians just forgot to let their captive go. I start walking outside, but then an apelike doorman wearing a headset and a shiny tuxedo stops me with a straight-arm to the chest.

He says, "Wait here until they get back."

"Are you serious? You can't make me stay."

"I suggest you do for your friend's sake," he says, in a way that makes me believe him. So I stand there beside the Live Girls sign, a prisoner in public.

"Where did they go?"

"The Milford Plaza."

"*The Lullaby of Broadway*. Perfect. Nice scam you're running upstairs."

His headset crackles and he puts a hand to his ear. I think about making a run for it, but if the Russian really does have a gun . . .

"Okay. Get out of here," the doorman says. "Now."

"Where's my friend?"

"Fuck if I know. But he paid his money, so go, and don't come back."

"Oh, no, *please* don't ban me. I wanted to come back tomorrow with a big group so we could all get screwed over by you assholes." But he's not listening.

I find Gus sitting on my front steps, looking exhausted. We ride the elevator in silence, not sure where to start. I open the door and the message light on the answering machine is blinking.

"You should get a cell phone," Gus says.

"I thought they don't work."

"But it's like a status thing," Gus says, falling into the futon. "You know, he put a gun in my side."

"Come on."

"We started walking up Eighth Avenue and he was, like, three steps behind me, with his right hand under his jacket. And there were all these people around but no one even gave us a second look, which is strange considering I was shaking the whole time. It's funny what you don't see when you're not looking. He stood right behind me while I got money out. I could see his reflection in the mirror above the machine. He kept saying, 'You better hope your friend is still sitting with Boris.'"

"I thought about splitting."

"Thanks."

"So how much did you give him?"

"Like four hundred bucks. It's all I had. Hey, what was the deal with that coke?"

"She started laying down lines. What was I supposed to say?"

"I guess, 'Thank you.'"

"Well, she wasn't much for talking."

"She isn't paid to talk."

I turn the TV on. It's almost four, but I'm too worked up to sleep. The garbage trucks are groaning, and the dim light that pervades New York in even its darkest hours is sneaking through the blinds. Despite losing all that money, I don't feel angry. Actually, I feel like I've gained awareness, like Gus and I have come through the other side and now have this shared experience, this foolish night where everything went wrong. Somehow it all seems worthwhile.

Gus goes to bed. He shuffles his slumping shoulders into James's room and closes the door. I flip through the channels and land on NY1, where an overnight news anchor is flipping through pages on his desk. As he starts reading the teleprompter, he lifts one of the pages too high and I can see that it's blank.

Time in the city moves forward in sporadic chapters. It's not knowing what comes next that either scares people off or makes them never leave. At first that was what I'd liked about Shelton. She thrives on chance, on moving haphazardly from one scene to the next, as if every encounter is an opportunity. There are no anxious what-ifs, no big-picture meltdowns. But now, as the months have moved us closer, those same qualities are eating at me. A few weeks ago Gus said that Shelton reminded him of Gloria Wandrous, that fast-living party girl in *Butterfield 8*. He was talking about her late-night proclivities, but then I read the book and started worrying about depth. How do you become intimate with a girl who lives for the moment, in the moment, every moment? And why do I suddenly care so much?

What happened to the kid who so proudly declared commitment a dead idea? That's the problem with declarations; when the world changes, they come back to haunt you. Its such a sobering realization, that second you realize you care. But do I? Club-hopping your way through life isn't the best way to sustain a relationship, though neither is being knee deep in strippers and coke. But if Shelton had just told me where to meet her, I never would have gone to that neon money pit. I'd have spent the rest of the night with her, I'd spend every night with her, if it could just be the two of us, away from temptations, the urges that keep us from being honest. . . .

I WAKE UP TO the sound of keys jingling in the door. "Hello?"

"Hello, David? Are you still awake?" James is walking in carrying two garment bags and a suitcase.

"James!" *Fuck.* "How are you? I didn't realize you were coming back today, tonight, this morning."

"I left two messages on the machine for you, one from the airport in Budapest, and one about an hour ago from JFK."

"Sorry, I just got in a little while ago. Uh . . . how was your flight?"

"Long. Very long. We were delayed three hours, so I'm pretty beat."

"You must be." He starts walking down the hallway toward his bedroom. I think about saying something, warning him, but—

"Oh! Hello . . . Excuse me. *David?*"

"Yes?"

"There's someone in here."

"Where?"

"In my bed."

"Oh, right. Sorry about that. It's my friend Gus. He's . . . well, he's homeless at the moment. Here, we can move him to the futon."

There's a commotion in the room, a rustling of sheets, a clearing of throats. Then I hear James say, "Are you wearing any clothes?"

"Great to meet you," Gus says. "David's told me so much. Here, I'll just get out of your way. We didn't know—"

"*David?* He's not wearing any clothes!"

I can't bring myself to go back there. "I know. Sorry. It was only one night . . ."

"He has suitcases in here."

"Oh, those are nothing," Gus says. "You caught me in between, uh . . . I saw your golf clubs in the corner . . . Do you play golf?"

"Please, *just go!*" With that, the bedroom door slams shut and Gus emerges in a blanket, looking miserable. He ambles over to the futon.

"James is right," I say. "But I think we both need to go."

As Gus tosses and turns in the living room, I walk over and play the new messages.

Saturday, 2:54 A.M.—Hello, David, it's James calling. Just landed at JFK and should be back in an hour. Look forward to sleeping in my own bed for the first time in weeks. If you're still awake, let's have a scotch and catch up. Cheers.

Saturday, 3:15 A.M.—Hey, sweetie, I'm at Wax on Mercer and I hope you can hear me because it's loud but I just wanted to say I miss you and that if you're still out you should come down and meet me because I'm with some really fun people and I've . . . hold on. . . . No, I don't have any more I don't think but check my purse . . . Sorry . . . anyway I've been talking about you all night so if you get this Wax is between Prince and Spring and give the doorman my name and he'll let you right in and if you don't come down leave a message and maybe I'll come up and stay at your place later if you want, so okay that's all . . . love you love you bye.

Nine

MY DESK IS IN the back of the storage room, surrounded by the history of American culture: millions of dollars' worth of uniforms, movie props, artwork, instruments, and sporting equipment of every conceivable sort. Every day I come in with my coffee and start typing away. I still haven't met Josh—he's on a buying trip in New England—but everything is already tagged with descriptions and estimated prices and there's a small library of reference books nearby if I have any questions. By the end of the first week I've written up twelve pieces, including O. J. Simpson's 1971 MVP trophy (estimated at $5,000 to $10,000), a 1961 Yankees World Series ring ($2,000–$2,500), a John Lennon and Yoko Ono signed photo ($2,500–$3,000), a 1995 Barry Bonds game-worn jersey ($1,500–$2,000), and a JFK signed White House Christmas card ($400–$600). I go home Friday afternoon looking forward to meeting my new boss next week.

But there's no sign of Josh on Monday morning, so I pick up where I left off, with Willie Mays's 1954 World Series bat ($5,000–$6,000). It's cracked but not badly, and I stand up and take a few swings in the middle of the room. It's heavy, in a genuine, substantial way, and the ball marks covering the barrel make it easy to picture Mays swinging it at the Polo Grounds on a misty autumn night forty-two years ago. With the bat on my lap I write a lucid biography of Mays: his early days on the broken-down buses of the Negro leagues, his rise to stardom in New York, and the climax, the 1954 Series, when Mays strapped the Giants onto his broad shoulders and carried them past Cleveland to a championship no one thought they could win. The World Series—the whole decade, really—was highlighted by Mays's stunning over-the-shoulder catch in game one, when he raced to deepest center field and tracked down a ball no other man could have caught. It was baseball's greatest player making baseball's greatest play, and here, incredibly, is the very bat he used then, a powerful relic, an instrument of perfection.

Next is a sepia-tone photograph of Babe Ruth and Lou Gehrig clowning around on the deck of a fishing boat, with two giant fish hanging from their straining rods. On the face of things it's just a picture capturing two close friends taking a time-out from fame, but I know it's so much more. It speaks for an entire era, when ballplayers led real *lives*, when they were more than just men playing on diamonds, when they fished and hunted and drank and caroused but were still role models the next afternoon.

When I'm done the photograph has become a symbol of all that was once good and pure. It's almost seven and my four coworkers have left for the day, but I'm staying late. It takes time to bring history back to life. There's a whole century of stories on these shelves, and someone needs to write them down.

THE PEOPLE AT LELAND'S deal in the market of memory. They recycle the past, give it a value, and offer it up to those who remember. Josh and his buyers spend their days in the attics and basements of America, hunting down history and paying in cash. When they finally roll back into town halfway through my second week, the spoils are unpacked and inventoried. An hour later Michael opens the door and says Josh wants to meet me.

"Bring everything you've written so far. And bring one of those helmets, too," he says, pointing to the football shelf. "He's in one of his moods."

I print out my descriptions and walk down the hall. I've seen Josh interviewed on TV (Michael gave me some tapes to watch), but it doesn't prepare me for the real thing. In person, he's huge, maybe six foot three, an intimidating bear of a man.

"So you're the baseball-playing spy," he says, shaking my hand. "Have a seat. I take it Michael's told you what we do around here."

"He did, thanks," I say, handing him a printout. "These are the pieces I've written up so far."

"*Lots*. We call them *lots*," Josh says, flipping slowly through the pages.

"I tried to add some real context, you know, full biographical backgrounds . . ."

"How many lots have you written?"

"Maybe like fifteen."

"So around three a day. Have you seen any of our catalogs?"

"I have. They're wonderful. The layout is—"

"And how many lots are there in each catalog?"

"I don't know," I say, shifting in my chair. "Maybe . . . eight hundred?"

"You're close. Usually between eight and twelve hundred. Now, we have three large sales a year, so how many lots would that be in total?"

I think I know where he's going with this. "Around three thousand."

"And with previews, auctions, traveling, vacations, let's say you're left with a hundred and fifty days a year for writing copy. How many lots is that per day?"

"Twenty."

"Twenty. And you're averaging three."

"But it takes a while to write each piece, or *lot*, sorry. I want to describe—"

"Let's see," Josh says, magnanimously. He starts reading aloud:

"'Willie Mays brought music with him on the road, filling the sagging hallways of old hotels with the midnight songs of Nat King Cole. He was like that, Willie was, bringing teams and towns to life, a universal hero in a segregated world. In 1954, while Ted Williams was earning $100,000 a year, Mays hit .345, won the MVP award, and was paid $17,500 for his efforts, most of which he sent back to his ten half-brothers and sisters in Alabama. On days off, while his teammates drank or hustled women at Toots Shoor's, Mays played stickball with his fans on the streets of Harlem, using brooms for bats and manhole covers for bases.'"

Josh looks up at me. "The midnight songs of Nat King Cole?"

"I was providing flavor."

"I don't give a fuck about Willie Mays or the music he listened to. Our job is to sell his bat, and your job is to describe that bat. The type of person who bids thousands of dollars on baseball memorabilia either knows everything about Willie Mays already or doesn't give a shit."

"But wouldn't some eloquent writing set the tone, make the bat more attractive?"

"We don't have room for stories in the catalog, and you don't have time to write them. You should be writing twenty-five lots a day and you're currently averaging *three*."

"I don't think twenty-five is possible."

"That's what our last copywriter said. It is possible, I promise. I can write fifty."

"In a *day*? But don't you need to research each piece?"

"Is this research?" Josh says, picking up my printout again. " 'So that the ocean itself becomes docile, complicit, parting in places as if to deliver the two great sluggers, the two heroes, the two friends, quickly and safely to shore.' This is a sports catalog, not *Moby Dick*. Besides, Ruth and Gehrig despised each other. Ruth was drunk one night and called Gehrig's wife a sow and that was it, they didn't speak for three years. That fishing photo was staged to make it look like they were buddies."

"I've never read that before, that they hated each other."

"Of course not. Sportswriters are failed historians with a hero-worship problem. They trade in the truth at the locker room door and create noble legacies for flawed men. Never believe what you read in the sports pages. Joe DiMaggio, Ted Williams, Reggie Jackson, Barry Bonds . . . all assholes. Even Mays has his share of detractors. Stick to describing the lots. If something really valuable comes up—say, ten thousand dollars or more—then sure, throw in some scenery, but not at the expense of time."

"If you don't mind my asking, how do you put a price on the past?"

"It's arbitrary, like assigning a value to paintings, or sex. The estimates in the catalog are educated guesses, although we err on the low side because we want people bidding. If I think a lot is worth, say, five thousand dollars, I'll estimate it at two to four thousand to get paddles in the air. Because once people start, they get caught up in the drama; adrenaline takes over and a minute later they've bought a baseball for seven grand when their budget was three. And the best part is they're not pissed off; they're ecstatic!"

Josh's eyes are dancing. It's clear he loves this game of buying and selling. He may be intimidating but his energy is contagious, and when he's finished his pep talk and shooed me away, I head back to my hovel ready to write better, faster, *more*. If Josh can write fifty lots a day, then surely I can, too. And I'll still make them sound like poetry. I'll write up every piece on

every shelf, keep Josh and his boys out on the road for weeks at a time, buying everything they can find. We'll hold more auctions, make more money.
Here, finally, is a job I can do.

LIKE THE FIFTH AVENUE Christmas windows, Fashion Week in
New York arrives earlier every season. The shows are held twice a year in
Bryant Park, and this spring, as every spring, the city's tabloids and magazines have put aside the real news—the Unabomber, the presidential pri-
maries—to focus on far more pressing stories. Today it's backstabbing in
the house of Gucci. The gossipy coverage is breathless. There's barely any
mention of the actual clothing.

When I first moved here, I could never make the connection between the
fantasy of fashion and the reality of clothing. The reality, of course, is everywhere—on racks in malls and closets in Queens, on everyday people walking drearily to work. America doesn't wear labels. It wears tank tops and
tracksuits and T-shirts from Fort Lauderdale. Sometimes I look at the models plastered across the sides of city buses, and then I look at the people
waiting at the bus stops and nine in ten aren't wearing anything "fashionable" at all. They're wearing *clothing*, everyday coverings—pants and shirts,
belts and shoes—and I wonder who's buying the gowns with the plunging
necklines from the fall collections? Who's paying for the Armani super-
stores, the Prada parties, the Helmut Lang campaigns?

I think I'm figuring it out. Their profits come from basics and acces-
sories. Prada sells shoes, Calvin sells underwear, Helmut sells cologne. But
Fashion Week is still the hottest act in town. And for one reason: the girls.
This is the second great age of the supermodel. The good few—Cindy
Crawford, Elle McPherson, Christie Brinkley—have been replaced by the
naughty many. Amber Valletta and Shalom Harlow mug on MTV, Kate
Moss trashes hotel rooms, Christy Turlington prances around NYU, Naomi
Campbell throws tantrums at restaurants. . . . They're the most beautiful
women in the world, and the clothes they model on their flawless bodies
end up lost in the shuffle. But nobody cares. Fashion isn't about clothes
anyway.

Still, it's had an effect. For the first time in my life, I've started caring
about what I wear. So when Shelton comes up for air toward the end of

Fashion Week and tells me to meet her at the new Diesel store on Lexington, I head over. It's a Saturday and I haven't seen her all week. She's talked her way into a marketing job for a hip sportswear line, and in a few short months it seems she knows everyone in the business. This week she's been to four or five shows, along with every party and after-party in Manhattan. She's perfect at those big fashion events, but I'm not. I never feel comfortable. All anyone talks about is this name and that store, as if we could all just go on indefinitely, sipping martinis and rolling our eyes, and no one would notice the world beyond the windows, getting light and dark and light again, an everyday place where people get up for work and slip on the same suit, wear the same shade of lipstick as the day before. In New York we spend a lot of time dismissing the small cities that dot the flyover states, but when I go to these places to visit friends, everyone is involved, engaged. They're talking about foreign policy and health care and how sales is such a tough gig. . . . I'll show up for a weekend in Chicago wearing a slim-cut shirt with a wide collar and cuffs that Shelton gave me, or pants with no pleats from Theory, and my old friends, in jeans and gray T-shirts—the stuff I once wore—will look me up and down and wonder what's happened. New York, I want to tell them, but they wouldn't understand. I'm not sure I do.

Diesel is one of those airy, modern stores with barely anything actually for sale. There's a DJ playing techno and Shelton dances her way over with a few things for me to try on. We make our way to a dressing room in the back and close the door, and now, up close, I can tell Fashion Week has taken its toll. Shelton looks like she's been through a war but is putting on a happy face for the homecoming. She hands me a green shirt and says it's all about snap buttons. I watch her take her jeans off to try on a skirt.

A few months ago we would have already been up against the wall, tearing at each other's clothing, but today, like every other day for the last month, I can't stop thinking of the issues that are accumulating between us. It usually starts with a late-night phone call. There's always that first jolt of noise and then Shelton's voice rising almost inaudibly above the din, saying she wants me to come down to so-and-so's opening in the meat-packing district, and I'll ask her what the scene is even though the scene never changes, and I'll be torn because I want to go meet her and I don't, as well.

And then, inevitably, there'll be a voice in the background, a girl saying, "Are you calling him again?" or worse, some guy, slurring through his Italian accent, saying, "Come on Shellltonnn, sweetheart, get off the phone. . . ." So I've stopped meeting her as much and she's stopped calling as much, and the gray area between days and nights has widened, New York's slender enticements swallowing us up with ease, like afterthoughts. And we're too young to spend our time patching up the damage. So when she hands me a pair of summer trousers, I tell her we need some time apart. At first she doesn't hear me, but when I say it more forcefully, she stops and looks at me with a puzzled expression, as if the lights have come up hours too early. There are tears and a small scene. She calls me emotionally unavailable. She says she's tired of people who don't know what they want. And then she storms off, waving to the DJ as she disappears down the escalator, looking as fabulous from afar as she did the day I first saw her.

I grab the clothes she picked out for me and make my way to the counter. She's always had great taste.

IN APRIL GUS and I start looking for an apartment. We want an exposed-brick loft in SoHo or a sunny two-bedroom with a fireplace and balcony in a West Village brownstone. We can pay sixteen hundred a month if there's no broker's fee. We search for weeks. I study the *Voice* on Tuesday nights; Gus checks the *Times*. We see a place without a kitchen, another with a communal bathroom in the hallway. We hike up six-floor walk-ups and consider meeting with a landlord who rents only to gay couples. (Me: "We need to hold hands in the interview." Gus: "I'd rather live in Gowanus.") We see a duplex that's recently been broken into and has glass scattered across the living room; a ground-floor apartment on Avenue D with a back garden occupied by squatters; a studio in Gramercy with a sleeping loft too small to fit a double bed. ("But it comes with a key to the park." "Good, that's where you can sleep.")

We finally settle on a one-and-a-half-bedroom shoebox overlooking a twenty-four-hour parking lot. It's on Thirty-second, just east of Fifth, a block away from the Empire State Building. On the colorful taxicab maps of Manhattan, ours is the only neighborhood without a name. It's just a bland place in the middle, a hodgepodge of rug merchants, Korean massage parlors, and tourists. We have no fireplace, no bricks, no balcony. The rent is eighteen hundred dollars a month and the broker's fee is 15 percent. But we do have a staircase, a rickety flight of steps leading up to a windowless cave that Gus immediately claims as his. The other room—mine, I guess— is reachable only by a narrow catwalk that branches off Gus's room. It's an attic-like annex directly above the living room, barely big enough for a desk and bed. The ceiling hovers a foot above me, like a threat.

There's nothing worse than two straight men on a flimsy budget trying to decorate a New York apartment, but we do our best. Our plan is to cover as much as we can. We throw a synthetic Oriental rug over the brown wall-to-wall carpet, find a secondhand slipcover for the secondhand couch, and put a blanket over a cardboard box and call it a TV stand. A weathered door begins life anew as my desk, and Gus sticks a mattress in the back of his cave and buys the wrong size sheets. We hang pictures and a shower curtain, clean the oven, set a mousetrap, order in from the liquor store, and decide to throw a party. We dial friends and then dealers, and comment with some pride that the two are still distinct and separate groups.

Half an hour later I'm outside waiting for Victor and his lime-green low-rider Cadillac. I hear him before I see him. He turns the corner and puts on a hydraulics show, lurching up and then down and then back up again. I got Victor's number through Shelton, and when I hop in he goes through a complex handshake and asks how the Fly Girl is doing. I say she's doing good. He lays a few zip bags of coke on the center console. I'm not into comparison shopping, so I take the first two and fish out some twenties as we bounce our way around the block.

Back upstairs, Gus untangles speaker wires while I chop up the coke on a glass-covered chessboard atop our coffee-table trunk. The chessboard is handmade and features ornate red and black squares painted directly onto the bottom of the glass. The borders are decorated with vintage hook-and-ladder trucks and a Chicago fireman's badge. Gus, who doesn't do coke himself but doesn't like to ruin a party, either, leans over to read the inscription.

"It was made for my great-grandfather," I tell him.

"Was he a fireman?"

"No, but he lived right next to a firehouse on the south side of Chicago. He was one of those fire junkies—"

"We call them arsonists."

"No, he didn't *set* them, you fool, he *followed* them. He'd hear the stationhouse alarm go off, and when it was a three or four alarmer he'd jump in his car and follow the trucks all over the city. I guess he got to know the guys real well, because they made him an honorary firefighter and gave him this board."

"How did you end up with it?"

"It was one of my father's favorite things when I was growing up. The summer after high school, after everything had happened, I found the board in the attic, so I took it with me when I went to college and I've had it ever since. The sad part is, I don't think my father's even noticed it's gone."

"Well, it serves a good purpose now," Gus says, returning to the stereo. He presses the power button and it comes to life just as a DJ is introducing the day's most requested song. It's familiar but I can't place it . . . until I hear the soaring voice. We sit in silence as Jewel's "Who Will Save Your Soul" comes at us through the air.

By MIDNIGHT THE TEN people we invited have turned into forty. My roommate's vision of a swank martini party with Sinatra crooning in the background has been ratcheted up a few levels, and now intriguing strangers are dancing to Joy Division and The Stone Roses. More people are walking in. There's a line for the bathroom. The kitchen is trashed and we're out of ice.

Our filmmaker friend, Ken Hamm, is holding court in the kitchen. He's about to start shooting his first film, *Moving In/Moving Out*. It's an East Village love story concerning two neighbors, an artist and a poet, who secretly lust after each other. They spend most of the script following each other around the garbage-strewn streets of Alphabet City, going through the painful stages of lust without ever meeting. "It's a simple story of love among the ruins," Ken said, when I told him I didn't really get it. "You'll see." I guess I will, because most people seem to think it's brilliant. Ken's become the budding celebrity of our little group, our first great hope, and now everyone is listening like they're at an Actor's Studio lecture as Ken weighs in on the opening sequence of Robert Altman's *Nashville*. He moves his hands like a camera, fingers framing the scene, and talks about the advantages of spontaneous continuity.

Someone puts Blondie on. People are upstairs in the bedrooms, outside in the hallway, but it's the bathroom that's still the focal point. The night moves along to the pace of the powder: faster and faster and faster. By 4:00 A.M. only a few of us are left. The drugs have moved out into the open, the lines laid out on the chessboard like hors d'oeurves. Shelton would love this; she'd light up the room if she were here. But I can't call her yet. I tried my cousin Deliah earlier, figuring she's always up for a big night, but her number was disconnected. Someone who knew her said she'd moved back home. She'd been living too fast.

A song ends. Ken's fan club is gone but he's still here, discussing B-movie actors with Ian, a gay banker who lives on Avenue C. Gus comes charging down the stairs, waving the George Trow book at Ken and jabbering on about the idea of independence being sucked up into the vast spreadsheet of America. Ken stands up and announces that he alone is a storyteller, struggling to be heard above the cratered landscape, and nothing, he says, almost shouting now, is more noble than staying true to invention, to ideas, to yourself. Ian and I are applauding through the laughter, because it really is quite a speech, and maybe it's the various ingested toxins, but I suddenly and quite acutely want to be part of Ken's world. I think briefly of grabbing a pen and jotting all this down, because late-night brilliance so often goes unrecorded, but Gus holds up his hand. He has an announcement.

"I'd like you all to know I've officially resigned from my position as a mayoral press officer and am leaving City Hall effective next week."

"Going back to Cuba?" Ken asks. "Fight those Commies?"

"I *will* be fighting pinkos like you, but not in Cuba. I'll be doing it from Police Headquarters right here in New York City."

"What?" we all say.

"I've joined the NYPD's press office. As I'm sure you're all aware, there's a new police commissioner in town, and we're dedicated to continuing the astounding citywide decrease in crime that all of you have been enjoying without bothering to say thank—"

"Does that include a crackdown on drugs?" I ask, rerolling a dollar bill.

"Yes, David, it does." And with that, Gus heads off to make himself a drink, leaving us all in stunned silence.

Ian and Ken make a concerted effort to discuss the Tompkins Square squatters, but they're too fucked up to give it more than a cursory effort. I wander over to the window, where the darkness is easing up and a slice of the Empire State—Warhol's stoic actor—is becoming visible. It's dull silver in the semidark, the color of coming down.

By six o'clock it's just Gus and me again, on the couch where we started.

"Are you serious about this police department deal?"

"Afraid so."

We swallow some Xanax and sink into the cushions. I'm exhausted but still a bit wired. Gus starts flipping through channels. I'm dozing off when he says he's been thinking about something.

"What?"

"That you need to be more careful."

Ten

I START WITH A pack of condoms (unopened) endorsed by Ted Williams ($100–$200), then move on to Muhammed Ali signed boxing gloves ($1,000–$1,500), a football signed by Nixon, Ford, Carter, and Reagan ($1,000–$1,500), a piece of Fenway Park's Green Monster ($300–$400), Gary Cooper's jersey from *Pride of the Yankees* ($6,000–$8,000), and a collection of Martin Luther King signed programs ($800–$1,000). By noon I've written ten lots, my best morning yet. For the last month I've been steadily increasing my output and now I'm averaging between fifteen and twenty a day. I won't win any Pulitzers, but it's better than what they had before.

I've grown to like working in the storage room, among the helmets and hockey sticks. I go for hours without speaking to anyone, and the chaos of the auction house stays on the other side of the wall. I scan the shelves for one more lot before lunch and settle on a figural-sided box seat from the Polo Grounds. I'm taking it down from its perch on a high shelf when something comes down with it. It looks like a piece of tile from the ceiling, but when I pick it up off the floor it feels different, smoother: older. There's no tag on it, so it's probably junk, but junk can be valuable around here, so just to be sure, I walk down the hall and knock on Josh's door. *"What!"* he shouts, which is his version of "Come in." I push the door open to find him examining an old baseball with a large magnifying glass.

"Take a look," he says.

Like all antiques and collectibles, the value of autographed memorabilia depends on condition and age. Exact age. A team-signed baseball from the 1927 Yankees (perhaps baseball's greatest team) can be worth thousands of dollars more than a Yankee ball signed in 1926 or 1928, even though the signatures will be almost identical. Dating, then, becomes an integral part of the research process. Usually it's as simple as locating the least-known names on the ball and looking up the years they played. But on older base-balls, where names are obscured or illegible, that doesn't always work, so Josh has been teaching me about the baseballs themselves—the different types of labels and inks and protectants used over the years. Now he's test-ing me.

Through the magnifying glass the ball looks yellow and glossy, courtesy of a decades-old coat of shellacking. The black ink signatures have faded and only a few are even partially legible: "Chick Gandil," "—— Cicotte," "Swede Risberg," and what looks like "E—— Collins." The names sound vaguely familiar. Holding the red stitches delicately with the tips of my fingers, I turn the ball around slowly, looking for the league president's name, which, in the first decades of the century, was stamped next to the label. I find it right where it's supposed to be, a faint "B.B. Johnson." I've memorized the list and know that Ban Johnson was the American League president from 1901 to 1927. But I still need more. I turn the ball over so the sweet spot, the area where the stitching is closest together, is facing me. There's room for one signature here, and for as long as baseballs have been signed, it's been saved for the manager. The ink has run across the stained leather surface, but I can still make out the name Gleason. Kid Gleason managed the Chicago White Sox in the years after World War One . . . and then it hits me: Chicago! Of course! This must be a ball signed by the infamous 1919 "Black Sox." If that's true, then this is the oldest team-signed baseball I've ever seen. More important though, there should be another signature. . . . I start over, checking every surface care-fully, precisely, like a diamond merchant. And on the very last panel, I find it: the slightest whisper of a name, shakier and more forced than the others, barely there at all. The ink has completely vanished in places, leav-ing only an indentation, the hint of a man, powerful and mysterious. The remaining letters spell "J_e Ja_kso_."

I look up at Josh like a boy who has just seen his first shooting star. "Is it real?"

"Yes," he says, slowly. "The great Shoeless Joe Jackson."

"But I thought he was illiterate, that his wife signed everything for him."

"That's true, but there are a few instances—mostly on legal docu-ments—where he signed, himself, by copying his wife's 'Joe Jackson' signa-ture. Though this is the first time I've seen it on a baseball."

"But how do you *know*? You can barely even see it."

"That makes it even more legitimate. A forger would have made it readable."

"And there's that much of a difference between his handwriting and his wife's?"

"Enough so that I can tell. Don't forget, I've spent my life doing this."

"But it's just a few faded letters on a baseball that's seventy-five years old."

"And those few letters are worth a *fortune*, maybe hundreds of thousands. I wouldn't be surprised if this is the most valuable baseball in the world. And I don't want you talking about it with anyone. Not yet. Now get out of here."

I'm almost out the door when I remember my original question. I hold up the small piece of tile. "I just wanted to make sure this isn't anything important—"

"God, be careful with that!"

"But it looks like deformed ceiling tile."

"That's exactly what it is—ceiling tile from Nagasaki, Japan, deformed by the three-hundred-thousand degree heat of a nuclear explosion. August 9, 1945. The Japs literally picked up the pieces and sold them as souvenirs. Put a five-hundred-to-one-thousand-dollar estimate on it."

"How do you find these . . . Never mind."

ONE MORNING IN JUNE I walk into work ready to pack boxes all day. We've just had our first auction of the year, in the ballroom of a hotel near Madison Square Garden. It was the same weekend as the Westminster Dog Show, and all these odd-looking four-legged creatures kept barking in the lobby, peeing in the elevators, and running around the auction room while people were trying to bid. The two-legged crowd wasn't much better, though. I thought the place would be filled with nostalgic fathers and their sons, maybe some old-time Dodgers fans who still remembered Ebbets Field; instead the first ten rows were all fat memorabilia dealers. We grossed almost two million dollars, although I'm not sure the catalog copy made any difference. Josh has winnowed my writing down to bare essentials, and my once lengthy descriptions have become more like "Brown Louisville Slugger, 34", cracked and in shitty condition." "It's an auction house, not Random House," he keeps telling me, and since it's *his* auction house, I listen. But it's frustrating, being so reigned in. And now I've been put on shipping detail. Hundreds of lots need to be sent out to successful bidders the world over, and I spend the morning giving myself paper cuts on box edges. I'm about to grab lunch with Michael to hear about his latest audition horrors when Josh appears:

"You need to go pack. We're going to Boston, and you're staying up there."

"For how long?"

"All summer."

TWO HOURS LATER, on the short flight to Logan, he tells me why: Leland's has won the job of auctioning off America's most fabled arena, the venerable Boston Garden. We're flying up to meet executives from the Bruins and Celtics, and once the details are ironed out, I'm going to stay up there and write the catalog. Josh explains how it all happened, how Leland's beat out Sotheby's and Christie's by playing up its focus on sports, by promising a portion of the proceeds to charity, by being flexible. "That's the key to life," Josh says. "Flexibility."

The Garden is only a ten-minute ride from the airport, but a half hour later we're still in the cab. Josh has failed to factor in the Big Dig, the largest public-works project in the history of Massachusetts. The North End is inundated with earth-moving vehicles, towering cranes, and drills the size of rockets. Traffic is at a standstill. Josh demands we take another route, but there are no other routes. We're inching up on Quincy Market when he boils over. He gets out and starts yelling at the hard hats, but no one can hear him. The cabbie and I can't help laughing. So much for flexibility.

It's not a fun walk. I carry all the bags and we get there almost an hour late. We're met by a team of executives who lead us through North Station and into the deserted arena. I've never been to the Boston Garden before, and now, standing on the floor, I look around in awe. Even empty, the place seems crowded and claustrophobic. Rows of yellow seats spill onto each other like breaking waves, and the championship banners hanging from the rafters seem almost low enough to touch. As we start walking around, a Bruins official gives us a brief history of the sixty-eight-year-old arena—the early boxing matches, the rodeos, the concerts, and, of course, the hockey and basketball. On the eve of his 1960 election, John F. Kennedy threw a rally here. Then along came the Beatles and Bobby Orr and Larry Bird, and it wasn't long before it had become the most famous arena in the world. Now, though, the place is undersize and falling apart. The futuristic Fleet Center, with its luxury boxes and luxury prices, stands ready right next door. We're here a few months ahead of the wrecking ball.

"This auction is about giving our building a proper burial," our guide says.

"Which would make you the obituary writer," Josh whispers in my ear. But I feel more like an imposter. I never even saw the place alive.

Soon Josh takes over. He starts walking around haphazardly, pointing out potential auction lots: basketball baskets, scorer's tables, twenty-four-second clocks . . . "We'll cut up the hockey boards, sell each section individually. And the penalty boxes: they'll go for thousands."

"How about the seats?" someone asks. "How do we sell fourteen thousand seats?"

"We'll auction off the best ones—the owner's seats, the front row, the last row, a few deuces and triples—then have a giant yard sale the next day right here on the floor. We'll slap a price on whatever's left, say, a couple hundred bucks per seat."

Smiles slowly break out as our hosts do the math. Josh moves off down a tunnel that leads under the stands, and we all follow close behind, ready for more. He points at turnstiles, ticket boxes, seating maps, and dozens of fixtures no one has ever put a price on before. Keys are produced, doors unlocked. Soon we're in the Bruins' locker room, where jerseys still hang in lockers and mismatched equipment lies scattered across the rubber floor. Josh rattles off more lots: the uniforms, the whirlpool, the lockers . . . He stops in his tracks: "Imagine having Bobby Orr's locker in your basement?" And for a moment we all stand there dreamily, imagining just that, until Josh brings us back to earth by asking how we get to the roof. A moment later we're in an old service elevator, making our way to the top of the building. We get out, climb a steep set of stairs, and come out onto a narrow ledge. We're so high that the legendary Boston Garden rafters are actually below us. Josh points at Bruins championship banners, the retired numbers, the American flag, and I write it all down as fast as I can.

"Where are the Celtics banners?" Josh asks.

"That's something we need to discuss," says an older man in a brown suit. "The Celtics, um, don't want to be part of the auction. They think it's, you know . . ."

"I don't know," Josh says.

"They think it's tacky."

"Well, that's a major problem. That means we can't sell any of their banners or equipment. What about the parquet floor?"

"Afraid not."

"The most famous floor in American sports. It's worth a fortune!"

"Maybe we should go back downstairs."

"No," Josh says, annoyed. He points across the arena, toward the giant hanging scoreboard in the center. "I want to go out there."

Our hosts look at each other uneasily, but Josh is already making his way across a rickety catwalk that runs the length of the arena. No one follows him except me, one foot in front of the other until I'm directly above the floor. The catwalk hangs suspended from above, and it sways with every step Josh makes. I'm afraid to look down, so I focus on my boss instead, his substantial torso grazing the rails on each side. I start thinking of corpulent Ignatius J. Reilly from *A Confederacy of Dunces*, who kept leading everyone into ridiculous situations. Up ahead Josh is barking about mercury vapor TV lights and Super Trooper carbon spotlights, and the last thing I want to do is let go of the rails and start taking notes, so his words are falling away into the air on all sides. He stops directly above the massive scoreboard, waiting for me to catch up. His hands are on his hips, his feet apart, like the giant on those cans of corn.

"Look at all these lights; they're fifty years old. I bet no one's been up here in decades."

"For good reason."

"Come on, where's your sense of adventure? Remember you asked me how I find things. This is the answer. You look in places no one else would dare." He peers over the side and the catwalk starts swinging like a heavy pendulum. "Check out this scoreboard," he says, grabbing one of the wires that supports it. "We can take it apart and sell it to some developer as a centerpiece for a shopping mall."

"Can we get down?"

"And the Zamboni, the organ. Remind me to ask about those," he says, moving back toward me. I stand sideways to let him past, and as he edges by me, his belly grazing mine, I hang on for dear life, praying those architects back in 1928 envisioned this weighty future. When I get back to the platform, it's like getting back to land after being seasick for a week.

"I'm going back to New York tonight," Josh says, as we start the journey down, "but you're going to stay here and scour the arena for the next few months, looking for anything valuable and writing it up. I'll tell these guys to build a security cage where we'll assemble all the potential lots."

"What are you going to do about the Celtics?"

"Leave that to me. You have enough to worry about. I hope you realize this is your big shot. America's greatest arena—don't fuck it up."

IN THE SPRING of my senior year of high school, on a rocky point overlooking a beach in Newport, I professed my love to a girl named Emily Edson. It was windy and cold, and Emily, fresh from her lacrosse game, had her long legs drawn in against her chest. She showed me a bruise, the result of a cross-check by some brute of a girl from Groton. Emily was always showing me bruises and scars, the accumulated trophies of a tomboy childhood spent on diving boards and backyard trampolines. It was getting dark and we were late for dinner, and Emily was talking nonstop about how stupid girls' lacrosse was because they blew the whistle so much. We had been dating almost a year, and as we sat there shivering, the surf pounding the rocks below, I told her I loved her. The words tumbled out as if they'd been trying to escape since the day I met her. And they had: I did. I had never said them before, and (with the exception of one or two drunken nights with Shelton) I haven't said them since. Maybe that's because Emily started laughing. "You shouldn't be so serious," she said. "We're only in high school." And then she kissed me quickly and skipped off to dinner.

We broke up after graduation—eighteen was no age for a long-distance relationship. In college Emily became a two-sport All-American and a dead ringer for Mariel Hemingway. Now she works for the World Peace Foundation in Cambridge. To her, the world has always been more important than any one person in it.

EMILY PICKS UP the phone on the first ring. "World Peace," she says, breathlessly, as if she's working incredibly hard just now and if people would stop interrupting her she could have the planet in order by sundown.

"Hey, I'm in Boston."

"It sounds like you're in an echo chamber."

"More like the penalty box at the Boston Garden."

"You do the strangest things."

Two hours later I'm at her Beacon Hill apartment, waiting in her cramped living room while she changes. On her coffee table there's a copy of *Rolling Stone* with Jewel on the cover. Her breasts are spilling out of her shirt, and the teaser reads "Girl from the North Country: How did Jewel do it?" I'm flipping to the article when Emily reappears wearing a summer dress, a narrow headband, and flip-flops. She looks like a flapper lost at the wrong end of the century.

"Isn't that Jewel girl hot?" she says. "I wonder if she can really sing."

We walk two blocks to a small Italian restaurant, where the owner gives Emily a kiss on each cheek, then shows us to a candlelit table. "I come here a lot," Emily says, sitting down. She starts fidgeting, like she's not used to wearing a dress, then looks half-heartedly at the menu. "So last time we talked you were chasing the Mob in Chinatown, and now . . . are you working for the Bruins or something?"

I tell her about the upcoming auction, but she's not really listening. We order pasta and I point to the second-cheapest Chianti on the list. The owner smiles and hustles off toward the bar.

"How's your mom?" Emily asks.

"Good, I guess. I mean, she's settled down since . . ."

Since Emily last saw her, when the two of us were still in school, climbing rocks and dancing around love. My family was a mess back then, and it was Emily I always turned to.

MY FATHER WAS CALLED back to the States in the early eighties, so we hopped an ocean and put down in leafy Montclair, New Jersey, in an old house with a yard, on top of the first hill west of New York City. From my bedroom I could see the lights of the skyline through the trees, and though I was only nine, I wondered what might be happening in that big place, if it might be anything like London, where every day was the first day of some wonderful new adventure. Because Montclair wasn't like that.

My mother went to law school. She took night classes in Newark and my brother and I saw her even less than we saw our father, who still traveled like an airline pilot, flying to meetings in Saudi Arabia, dinners in Brussels. We all kept separate hours, and it soon became a different life, a life of keys left under mats, scribbled notes on tables. We traveled in car pools and cooked by microwave. What had started in London got worse here, back home. Family life became a charged thing, brief arguments followed by days of silence. When Reagan got shot, when the space shuttle exploded, what I remember is being alone. But there were reprieves: every few months an old family friend from Europe would stay the weekend, and for a short time my parents' lives—my life—would return to how they were before: the sound of ice in cocktails, the long dinners, the missing smiles. The past trailed into the house with these people and lingered, so I did, too, at the head of the stairs, well after midnight, listening to the stories that framed my childhood, and to the laughter, growing louder and more honest with the hours, where there hadn't been any in quite some time.

What Emily knew so well was what happened next. It was 1986, the year the Mets won. I watched the opening games of the World Series on a small TV in the kitchen, keeping meticulous score on my mother's yellow legal pads. The family didn't eat there anymore. We'd long since started taking our meals to go, and the kitchen table had become my mother's office, piled high with sketches and sheets of numbers, the beginnings of a small business—some kind of Oriental furniture/sculpture scheme she was starting with a woman named Sydney. Sydney had short gray hair and a gap in her teeth and was nice in that cursory way that people who need to be nice sometimes can be. She came over a lot when my father was away, and she and my mother worked together at the kitchen table with a brisk, happy sense of purpose. So I moved to the living room and watched the Mets slug it out with Boston, until my father appeared one night with tickets to game six, the Bill Buckner game. We saw it all it from seats behind third base. It was the most thrilling comeback of the century, and much needed, because everything else came apart.

The meetings in the kitchen became daily events. I'd get home from school and my mother and Sydney would be huddled over their plans. When they saw me they'd move away instinctively, like teenagers. My father became more distracted than ever. He started running at night; he spent hours in his study with the door closed; and he played golf—two, three, even four rounds a weekend. Then, one crisp Saturday morning, he canceled his tee time and dragged me off to see a professional school counselor. Odd, I thought: school was the only thing that was going well. The woman asked a few questions, then dumped a dozen boarding-school brochures on my lap. Trips were scheduled, first with one parent, then the other. My father drove me up to Deerfield, his alma mater. It was the first time we had been alone together in months, and I wanted to ask what was going on at home, but I just couldn't broach it. Entire states passed in steely silence.

Deerfield, still all boys, seemed harsh and cold. It rained all weekend. Back in the car, my father asked what I thought. I told him I didn't want to go away.

"I'd love you to stay, too," he said, "but that's not an option." Then he put in a book on tape, some James Michener saga, that conveniently lasted all the way home.

The following weekend it was St. Mark's and St. George's with my mother. At least these schools had girls, and St. George's was pretty and overlooked the ocean. But it didn't change my mind. Driving back to Montclair, I tried the same tack with her.

"Boarding school would be best for everyone," she responded, and when I asked why, why, *why*, she changed lanes and drove faster.

It all came clear—or came out, at least—a month later. Sitting next to my brother, Douglas, on the living room sofa, I listened as my parents *announced* their separation—*announced* because it was an announcement, a dispassionate statement of fact. *This is happening and now your life will change.* It wasn't that they had no emotion but, rather, had no emotion left. It had been drained by whatever long and painful process had led to that moment. And so they became mortals. For the first time I realized that they were people, with lives and longings that didn't necessarily revolve around me. I knew something had been going on, but I'd never envisioned that scene in the living room, my parents sitting in opposing chairs, separated by a coffee table but already miles apart from each other. My father was staring at the painting over my head, of a couple walking hand-in-hand down an empty beach in Europe. Once it had been my favorite piece of art, but now it seemed a particularly sad canvas of browns. Gently, my mother explained that she'd be moving to a smaller house on the other side of town, the bottom of the hill. Douglas got up and hugged her. And then he hugged my father. And then he hugged me. Tears streamed down his twelve-year-old face as he started asking questions. His voice was high pitched, heart-breaking: *Why is this happening? It just is, honey, we need to be alone for a while. . . . Who will we live with? Both of us, baby, and it'll be fine. . . . Is this because of Sydney? No, of course not. . . . Is it because of us? No, no, no, don't ever think it has anything to do with you, we just . . . we need to sort some things out is all. . . . Well, it's only for a little while, right . . . ?*

My mother's new house looked just like the houses on either side of it, and with my father gone so much, that was where I spent the following spring. Sydney became a fixture, and so did the two ceramic "pillows" in the backyard.

"They're prototypes," my mother said, when I asked her.

I considered them again. Each pillow was actually three pillows stacked one on top of the other, largest to smallest, like the base of a pyramid.

"Are they seats or sculptures?"

She looked at them and cocked her head to one side, like she wasn't quite sure herself. What I was asking, politely, is if they served some practical function, but the answer, like the real pillows, never came, leaving us with the two hollow prototypes sitting side by side, not quite right for the space they were in.

A few months later my mother sat Douglas and me down again. This time Sydney was moving in. The news wasn't a shock because she'd spent the night before, but it raised more questions—the kind I didn't know how to ask. No matter. It was all kind of exciting, this household-building business, this starting over.

Up in the house on the hill, my father kept living his work-loaded American midlife, but he slowly started *making time* as well. I'd go to stay with him and he'd be there to greet me with a hearty handshake at the door, smiling, energetic, *younger.* But his transformation wasn't so predictable. He didn't go out and buy a Harley or a sailboat. He didn't start wearing wide chalk pinstripes or seek therapy or dive with desperation into the New York society scene. Still, it was clear that my mother's leaving shook him up and now he was looking for answers, poking and prodding the boundaries of traditionalism, the limits of a lifestyle based on a previous America, where dinner was on the table at 7:00, where men went to work in the morning without feelings of wanderlust and women measured success through the accomplishments of their children. He dated a few divorcées. He started taking me to comedy clubs, to ballgames, to *bars*. He said nice things about Mario Cuomo. And the handshakes at the front door turned into hugs.

Moving back and forth between houses became an electric experience. Everything was now so *possible* that I couldn't help but wonder how these two suddenly fascinating people had stayed married so long. At some point the separation became a divorce, and still they managed to make the house-hopping work. Or maybe Douglas and I did. We learned to accept the end of a normal upbringing. Having a gay mother started sounding kind of cool. And a father on his own became someone we could hang out with. Our parents' lives had come apart, and watching them scramble to start over was like watching a sitcom in its final season: the plotlines had become implausible and the show was barely holding together, but still you watched, because anything could happen next.

WHAT HAPPENED NEXT for me was boarding school, with its late-night dorm sessions and, soon enough, its love interests. Emily lived through the divorce and its immediate aftermath with me, and though I never took sides, Emily identified with my mother. I guess it makes sense: they share a kind of raw independence. Now, in the candlelit restaurant, Emily leans in close as I catch her up on the latest family plotlines. I tell her my mother moved south a few years back. She packed us all into the family station wagon (the one I later sold to that farmer in Ohio) and headed down I-95. She made it a contest: whoever figured out where we were going would get first choice of the bedrooms in the new home. With Sydney following in her own car, we came up on the New York skyline. I was sure that's where we were headed. It was where I'd have gone if I were her, running off to start a new life with a woman. She could set up shop in an apartment near Central

Park, in a building with an old elevator, the kind with crisscrossing gates that rattled when they closed. Yes, we were a ragtag crew, the great hope of postmodern America, an eclectic band pieced together from the ruins of older, less imaginative unions. There were no rules anymore, no ties strong enough to bind, and so New York—

"But I thought you said she moved south," Emily says.

"Well, she did. She drove right past the Lincoln Tunnel and kept going. Turns out she'd already accepted a job as a criminal district attorney in Baltimore."

"Wow. An inner-city prosecutor," Emily says.

"She and Sydney bought a row house in Bolton Hill, one of those neighborhoods that was up and coming for a while. Except it went, and so did Sydney. She moved out after two years. I think the idea of Sydney was a bit more palatable than the woman in the flesh."

"So to speak," Emily says, grinning.

"So to speak. Sydney was one of those sad radicals who ran out of causes. She had that chip on her shoulder, the whole I've-been-wronged thing. I was willing to give her the benefit of the doubt. But I don't think my mother was. Sydney was trying to mold her, shepherd her along the path to some drastic new identity."

"She may be liberal and lesbian, but I don't think your mom's a radical feminist."

"No, I agree. Now she's living alone in her Baltimore brownstone, stuck somewhere between conformity and its opposite."

"Nonconformity," Emily says. "It's not that hard a word."

The restaurant is filling up with older couples—bearded men in corduroy jackets, women in long summer skirts. Emily watches a waiter pour our wine.

"Your mom is the only person I know who got divorced for the right reasons."

"There is no right reason," I say.

"But she was pursuing something . . . I don't know . . . *more*. Remember in school when we'd all sneak down to the beach and talk about the future and everyone said they wanted to be an archeologist or a painter or the ambassador to Argentina—"

"I was going to play baseball."

"No, you were going to be a writer."

"I was?"

"That's what you used to say."

"Well, I do write. I write *rapaciously*."

"Really. That means to take by force. I think you mean voraciously."

"Oh."

"—And now everyone's working in finance. Even our most artistic friends, the ones who had the best answers, are either biding their time in weird niche jobs or happily buzzing along in advertising."

"I'm *trying* to write," I say, ignoring the "weird niche" comment.

"Are you, though?" Emily asks, but I don't answer. I sip my wine, and she changes the subject. "Remember Trevor Collins? The guy who used to go on endlessly about the lack of art in modern architecture? We'd all walk around Newport together, and the whole time he'd be staring at pillars and balconies and making passionate speeches about changing the way people looked at the world by changing the way the world looked."

The owner comes over and tops off our glasses. He gives Emily a toothy smile, then walks off humming.

"I met him for drinks at a bar on Newberry a few weeks ago," Emily says.

"The owner?"

"No, Trevor Collins. And to be honest with you, I was excited. I kept grinning at the thought of him walking around with his head in the clouds. When I got there he was sitting at the bar in these handsome thick-framed glasses. We talked for a while, but then, when I asked him how the buildings looked these days, he didn't get it. He said he was working for Fleet Bank, analyzing long-term interest rates for commercial lenders. I asked if he was still into architecture, and he shrugged and said Fleet was a good company, a 'more viable option.' I got up and went to the bathroom, and when I came back he was still sitting there, except now he looked like every other guy in Boston—badly dressed and three inches too short."

"You should come to New York," I say.

"I want to go to Bosnia. Or Rwanda. Countries where civil wars are raging, where entire races are being wiped out, *ethnically cleansed*. And most of the Western world doesn't even know about it because our government pretends it's not happening."

I'm trying desperately to remember the details of a recent *New Yorker* article on Bosnia, but nothing's coming back. "Milosevic's a bad guy," I say, awkwardly.

"It's more complicated than that. The conflict goes back centuries and the consequences are devastating. The war has created an entire generation of refugees. I've applied to the Red Cross and the U.N., but I haven't heard back, so maybe I'll go to law school for a while, study human rights. I guess I just feel shiftless here, you know?"

"I do."

"I get up in the morning, go for a run along the river, then come home and watch Cary Grant movies. And even the World Peace Foundation—it sounds prestigious but really it's just a think tank. They have long lunches and discuss the wording of position papers no one ever reads. Peace is such a bureaucratic business. It makes me wonder if there's anything left worth doing."

WORKING AT THE Boston Garden is like working on an archaeological dig. Days are spent searching, sifting, and recording, alone with a flashlight, in dark corners and closets. In the basement I find an ushers' changing room, with dusty red uniforms from the 1950s still hanging in their lockers; and further on, a secret card room near the boiler, where poker chips and Schaeffer bottles lie scattered across a fold-up card table. Upstairs, an old Western Union telegraph center; an equipment closet with primitive shot clocks; and a darkroom filled with vintage photographs— yesterday's heroes, scattered ankle deep across the floor.

One morning I come across a storage room near the roof. It's dark but I can make out a wooden trunk in a corner, partially hidden by a pair of wall sconces. The trunk is marked BG Originals. I open it to find a series of giant canvas concert banners: Tom Petty, Plant & Page, Aerosmith. . . . I'm rolling them back up when I notice something else in the trunk, a thick cylinder filled with onionskin sheets. I carefully peel away the top sheet and lay it flat. It's an architectural rendering of the arena's upper deck, with a handwritten date in the lower right corner: March, 1928. My God. These must be the original plans for the arena, the blueprint for Boston sports. Why does history always end up stuffed in corners?

The architectural plans join the Stanley Cup banners ($3,000–$5,000 each), the Zamboni ($3,000–$5,000), Bobby Orr's 1972 jersey ($15,000–$20,000), and the overhead scoreboard ($40,000–$50,000) as the major lots of the auction. I write the copy and fax it to New York, where Josh puts the catalog in order. He also sends up several boxes of new property to round out the sale. It's all Celtics-related, of course. The team refused to take part in the auction, so Josh found his own basketball memorabilia, including a 1987 Larry Bird game-worn jersey ($1,500–$2,000), a Red Auerbach half-smoked cigar ($100–$200), and signed pieces of the parquet floor ($500–$1,000). I don't know how he does it.

The catalog comes out a few weeks before the auction, under less than ideal conditions. The Celtics have threatened to sue; a photographer is claiming rights to the photos we found in the darkroom; a rumor is spreading about the banners from the rafters being replicas; and the fire department has said they'll close down the building unless they're *taken care of*. Josh and Michael fly up to deal with everything, while I organize the exhibition on the Garden floor. The *Herald* and the *Globe* have been publicizing the auction heavily, and when the doors open for previews, thousands of people stream in. After years of watching from the cheap seats, they walk around the floor like trespassers expecting to get caught. It must be strange to see their arena barren like this, and I wonder if they're experiencing that same sad feeling of ending that I've felt for the past three months. A few ask where they might find one thing or another, but it's pretty clear that most aren't here to buy but to pay their respects, to take one last look.

The networks are here, as well, and Josh happily hops from one interview to the next while I hold up lots for the cameras. A father and son from Brockton ask me about the wall sconces. The father says he remembers when they hung outside, their yellow lights glowing through the snow like beacons. He obviously loves the place, so I tell him about the crawlspaces in the basement, the catwalks hanging from the ceiling. . . .

"Let's talk to this kid," says a reporter, standing nearby.

Soon I'm surrounded by cameras and engulfed by questions. I look at the red lights and answer everything I'm asked. When they've gotten their sound bites and the arena lights have gone low, Michael and I walk through the brisk autumn night to a bar across Causeway Street.

"Where's Josh?" I ask.

"I don't know; he's been in one of his moods all month. It started when the FBI showed up at the office."

"Are we the good guys or the bad guys?"

"We're not forging signatures in the back room, if that's what you're asking. We're the good guys. The entire sports-memorabilia industry is under investigation, and they've come to Josh for help. He's one of the few who can tell instinctively what's real and what isn't. And he's almost never wrong. Still, sometimes I feel like I'm doing PR for William Morris."

"How's the acting?"

"Oh, that. . . ."

We drink for a while but we're both exhausted, so we call it a night sometime after midnight. When I wake up six hours later, there I am on the morning news, talking about mice in the Western Union room. It's unnerving, watching myself, so I walk across the street and start setting up folding chairs.

Four thousand people come to the auction, though only a few hundred register to bid. Almost everything sells, but with few high rollers, the bidding is sporadic and uneventful. Emily shows up halfway through. I put my best spin on things, but she says the scene seems melancholy, like the drawn-out sickness of a distant relative. I try to introduce her to Josh but he ignores me. I give her a tour but there's nothing left to see. Toward the end of the night Emily takes off to work on her law-school applications. She's writing an essay about America's subtle but steady campaign to keep Africa mired in the Third World. And she's not the only one leaving early. Hundreds of downcast New Englanders are making their way to the exits. Some look around one last time, but most walk out with hanging heads, too heartbroken to see another ending, another concession to the future. An hour later, when a shopping-mall magnate buys the Boston Garden scoreboard and the gavel comes down with a muted thud, there's almost no one left to watch it happen.

PART FOUR

Publish or Perish

"There is, I believe now, a force in stories, words in motion, that either drives them forward past things into feelings, or doesn't."

—ADAM GOPNIK, *Paris to the Moon*

Eleven

". . . AND AT SOME POINT," Ken says, "you get tired of talking and you make the decision. At first you think there's an easier way. In New York, you see all these people who have made it and their lives look so painless, so comfortable. Comfort is a well-funded missionary sent to convert the slightest hint of artistic ambition. Comfort points you down a smooth highway where it's always sunny up ahead. Like California. But have you ever been to California? It's not a real place. And if you're smart, you realize that before it's too late. Before the wife and kids, before they dangle Managing Director in front of you like a hidden prison sentence. You realize you need something more than a *career*. And that's when you notice the exits snaking off that highway to riches. They don't have signs, only ramps leading into the unknown distance. But if those exits nag at you, then you still have a chance. It's a cold, isolating decision, turning off that highway. Your life becomes defined by one goal, and everything in it before—your jobs, your friends, your family—gets recast, reevaluated, and if it doesn't move you forward, removed. You stop reading profiles and biographies, stop going to premieres and openings, because other people's artistic success only makes you question your lack of it. And anyway, the story is always the same. You don't need some kid with concealer telling you how hard it *was*, because you know how hard it *is*. *Right now*. You're in that room, staring at that page, all alone, and Ed Burns or Harmony Korine or . . . or that singer you're always talking about . . . never had it as hard as you. They've all compromised and so should be ignored. You *have* to think like that. You have to hate everyone. It's how you need to live—with that creative chip on your slumping, debt-ridden shoulders, and it's so fucking lonely you forget how to act around people. You forget how to have a normal relationship. It's just you and your art. But you know what? You're finally living with no regrets. And you know that your day is coming soon."

"So how much do you need?"

"Eleven thousand five hundred to finish the film."

"And how exactly do independent film investors make money?"

"It's like any other investment. You own a percentage, and when the film sells you share in the profits. And this *will* sell—believe me. Everyone's looking for quality: Miramax, New Line, The Shooting Gallery . . . And *Moving In/Moving Out* is exactly the kind of gritty, urban love story these people go for."

"Does it have as many clichés as your speeches?"

"The history of art is in the retelling, my friend. I'm taking young love and turning it on its side. And the response has been incredible. We haven't even finished shooting yet, and we're getting into festivals based on the trailer alone. We're doing exteriors on Fifth Street in a few weeks. You should come down and be an extra. Bring Shelton. The two of you can be in a scene together."

"How did you know we were dating again?"

"It's in your eyes. You like to hang on. Don't worry, I'm in the same rut. At least *you* don't live and work with her."

Ken and I are sitting in a booth at Blue & Gold, an East Village dive with a battle-scarred pool table and an unreliable jukebox. The bartender and owner is a wide-bodied Polish woman with a permanent scowl. People try to make her laugh, but it never works. Right now The Rake's Progress is playing; it's their semihit "I'll Talk My Way Out of This One." I thought they were still under the radar, but half the bar is singing along.

"Let me get this round," Ken says, jumping up to do battle.

I want to help him out with the movie. No, I want to make money, and help him in the process. Ken is becoming a close friend, and if his little pep talks are longwinded, they're also sincere. I mean, who talks about the inherent selfishness of being an artist unless they really are one? He's a working-class kid from a mill town in Massachusetts who has come to New York to make movies. He's organized his life around this film, and everything he says or does is an extension of it. I think he's pretty brave.

I've saved almost $10,000, which I've invested in the market. Some awful broker woman at Merrill Lynch took on my account in an effort to get my father's business, and as soon as that didn't work out, I stopped hearing from her. But before the phone went dead I did manage to invest $5,000 in Merrill's Asian fund (I liked the idea of emerging markets, and I found out only afterward that Asia's markets aren't emerging at all, but are, like ours, already well established), and the rest in a small company called Oracle because I liked the name.

Ken comes back with two longnecks. Spacehog's "In the Meantime" comes on, and everyone knows this song, too.

"How long before I'd see a return on my investment?" It's a grown-up question. I feel like we're role-playing.

"We should definitely sell at least the American rights by next spring."

"Then I'll invest five thousand. It's all I can afford. It's more than half my money."

"You don't know what this means."

"It means I'll have to get rid of either Oracle or my Asian mutual fund."

"Keep Oracle," Ken says. "It's a tech company." He raises his glass, looks me in the eye. "I won't let you down. This is only the beginning. For both of us."

I almost believe him.

It's an Indian summer day in early November and I wake up feeling anxious. I was at Leland's until almost eleven last night, trying to catch up on a summer's worth of accumulation. The boys were buying while I was in Boston, and now the back room looks like one of those garage storage units that's packed so tight that just opening the door sets off a violent chain reaction of falling debris. Everywhere I look: Castro signed baseballs ($1,000–$1,500), Munich Olympics torches ($1,200–$1,500), Amelia Earhart signed photographs ($600–$800), Jim Morrison signed checks ($1,000–$1,500) . . .

I've started doing lines in the bathroom, small ones, once or twice a week. It helps me focus. I can sit back down and write like a machine, ten lots an hour, type without pausing, without thinking, like a courtroom stenographer. But a week straight and I start feeling the way I do now, nervous and jumpy, high and low, tired and restless, all at once. I can't face that room again, those endless shelves. "To be written": The three worst words in the language.

I call the office but Josh isn't in yet, so I leave a message with the receptionist, tell her I'm sick, spinal meningitis ("Oh, okay, well, feel better"), then take the F train to Central Park. I walk past the bandshell and the boathouse and along the narrow gravel running path that rings the reservoir. Maybe it's those Woody Allen films they shot up here that give this place its seventies feel. Or maybe it's the people—gray-haired Upper West Siders in short shorts and classical-music T-shirts, working their way around the water on tired, straining legs. When I get to the Great Lawn I sprawl on the grass and open *The New Yorker*. Clinton has just been reelected and the magazine, like everyone else, is full of hopeful predictions for his second term. The world can look dreamy when gifted writers spin their fantasies, and on this sunny patch of lawn, populated by ballplayers and guitarists and readers like me, the future does seem bright. Nearby a man with John Lennon hair is quietly strumming chord progressions. His guitar is beautiful, a gold-colored Martin with a studded strap, and I lie back and listen while he sings.

It's time to move on again. I've got that same feeling I had at Kroll, of days too similar to separate or characterize. Last week I started writing about a Brooklyn Dodgers team-signed baseball. I was halfway through when it started looking familiar—the signatures, the inks, the colors—and I realized I'd written it up before. We had sold it in the spring, and now the buyer was consigning it back. Leland's was becoming a recycling plant, an endless circle with no finish line, nothing built or made or completed, just a paycheck and a place to speed through another day without looking up. Does anyone stop and think anymore? Writers, maybe, and musicians. Except the man with the guitar has started playing "Imagine." I guess it was only a matter of time. If I ever get around to putting pen to paper, these are exactly the stupid New York allusions I'll stay away from.

I GET TO LELAND'S in midafternoon, just as Michael is leaving.

"I have an audition, otherwise I'd love to stick around and watch the fireworks."

"How do you know there'll be fireworks?"

"Spinal meningitis? The natives don't come down with something like that unless they're really getting restless."

Josh is on the phone in his office. He points to an empty chair, but I remain standing while he finishes his conversation, something about hand-gun laws. When he hangs up, he looks me up and down.

"Thank *God* you're okay. I was *really* worried."

"I quit."

Josh leans back and laughs. "You can't quit. What are you going to do?"

"Write."

"Write what?"

"Sentences. Paragraphs. Stories. Anything but this. I can't do it anymore. I'm writing up the same lots I wrote in the spring."

"That's called making money, selling the same thing more than once."

"Except I'm not seeing any of it."

"You'd rather write short stories where you'll make nothing at all? Where you'll end up temping or waiting tables again or crawling out to the suburbs and begging for money when it doesn't work out? You don't just wake up and decide to write and then drop everything else. No, you write late at night, early in the morning, in the hard hours that make it mean something. Start small, be realistic. Stephen King wrote in his laundry room at midnight."

"I don't want to be Stephen King."

"Fine. Don DeLillo. He started as an advertising copywriter."

"Really?"

"Yes, really. Look, we've invested a lot of time in you, and even though you spend half the day on the phone, you're finally coming around."

"There's so much shit on my desk, I can't even find the phone."

"All right, here's what I'll do. You can make your own schedule and I'll pay you by the lot. That way it's all on your head. You can make as much or as little as you want. You get your freedom and we get our copywriter."

"What would be a fair—"

"Give me a number."

"No. You taught me that game. You say a number first."

"Fine. Four dollars per lot. All cash."

"Five," I say, because it's the next number.

"Four-fifty."

"No fractions. We'll be here forever."

Josh looks at me in a fatherly way. "No fractions. I like that. Five it is." We shake hands and then he reaches into a drawer and pulls out a gun. It's a silver pistol and for a second it scares the hell out of me. "Calm down, it's not loaded. Do you know anything about guns?"

"I've been learning."

"Well, here's your first five-dollar lot," he says, handing it to me. "It was Al Capone's. It's a twenty-five-caliber nickel-plated Colt. In 1929 Capone presented it to his friend Kiki Cuyler, the Hall of Fame outfielder for the Cubs. There's an inscription on the side. Go write a nice long story about it, and make the estimate seventy-five to a hundred thousand."

"I see. Now that we're operating per lot, you want more substance."

"Careful what you wish for, kid."

WE'RE SUPPOSED TO WALK down the street arm in arm, grinning, laughing, mouthing small talk—be seen but not *seen*. The real action will be in front of us, where the two leads are finally meeting. It's a pivotal moment. The script says it's summer but actually it's freezing, so we wait until the last possible second to take our coats off. "I hope they don't mind a little nipple," Shelton says. She's wearing a white tank top and a vintage A-line skirt, East Village all the way. We got back together a few weeks ago, after running into each other at a club called Chaos. She came twirling up to me like an Arabian belly dancer, and in the low lighting she looked positively radiant. I had no chance. But soon the old problems started creeping back. Gus called it the seminal rule of dating: that relationships never work the second time around. And he's right: the second act *is* different. We're both so aware of what happened the first time that we tiptoe around each other, playing nice, playing dead. It's been two weeks of superficial smiles.

I rub her goose-bumped arms as the overhead lights come on. The assistant director shouts, "ROLLING!" then Ken shouts, "ACTION!" and suddenly the sidewalk is alive with pretty faces, precise movements. Shelton and I start walking. I have a vague sense of the action to my right, lines being spoken, but I'm focused on acting natural. Shelton says something in my ear. I squeeze her hand to remind her to mouth words, not actually say them. She turns and shoots me a look, then pulls her hand away. Then Ken yells, "CUT!" and everyone stops, exhales, and waits to see what's wrong. I hear someone complaining. Then Ken's AD appears in front of us.

"Why the fuck were you guys talking? The mike picks up everything. You have *one* job—to move from here to there. We don't have the time or money for more than a few takes, so please shut up and act like you're in love. If you can't do it we'll find someone else who can."

Shelton glares at him, then she turns to me. "I'm doing this as a favor, you know. I don't have to be here getting yelled at by some attitudinal film student."

"PLACES, PLEASE. LET'S DO THIS AGAIN."

"Shelton, it's only ten seconds. Can you not talk for *ten seconds*?"

"I can not talk for a lot longer than that."

We do it again, and this time we make it to the other side without incident. Then twice more, until we hear, "THAT'S A WRAP," and everyone starts packing up. Ken comes over as Shelton's looking for her coat. She doesn't want to talk to him, either.

"How did we look?" I ask.

"Okay," Ken says, "but it wasn't too natural."

"Your idiot assistant told us to act like we were in love," Shelton says. "I guess it was too much of a stretch."

Half an hour later, on a graffiti-covered stoop that may or may not be part of the set, we break up again. This time it's more depressing than emotional. As Shelton walks away she doesn't look back. I don't think either of us will.

MAYBE IT WAS the energy of the film set. Or the staleness of the auction house. Or maybe it was the realization, a few days ago, that I've been living in Manhattan for two years—living as a *writer*, claiming that mantle, that world—without writing one creative word.

In my claustrophobic closet of a room, I separate magazines into piles: sports, politics, men's, women's, arts, lifestyle, entertainment, culture. . . . Then I scour the mastheads, looking for New York offices and lenient submission policies. The piles start dwindling. I throw out the women's magazines, the health magazines, the politics and science, and sports—no more sports. What I'm left with is an eclectic assortment of fringe publications (*Paper, Interview, Cover*), mainstream titles (*Esquire, New York, Spin*) and free weeklies (*The Village Voice, NY Press, Manhattan Spirit*). I don't have any experience to tout or clips to include, so my pitch letter gets right to it:

an insider's look at the making of next year's independent film phenomenon, Ken Hamm's *Moving In/Moving Out*. I call it "a compelling downtown love story for our time," and promise "an intimate account of low-budget film-making in a highbrow city." I sign my name, throw in some Leland's catalogs, drop the packets in the mail, and hope for the best.

KEN'S GIRLFRIEND, ANNE, knows a woman who is looking for a writer. Her name is Camille and it's a TV project. Somehow my name came up and now I'm off to meet her at a West Side coffee shop. I'm wearing charcoal pants and a striped Agnes B shirt. On my way out the door I ask Gus if I look like a professional TV writer.

"No, you look confused."

I've never been in a coffee shop at night. I walk in and look around, wondering if someone named Camille would be blonde or brunette, but all I see are goateed men speed-typing on laptops and women flipping magazine pages without reading. It's a scary, caffeinated subculture. Even the babies seem hyper, like they've been rocked too quickly. I try to order some regular coffee with milk but immediately get swept into an alternate universe of exotic flavors and Italian sizes. I look at the chalkboard menu for an explanation, but I can't read the writing, and as the chubby girl behind the counter prattles on about cinnamon soys and white mocha lattes, I back away, past the shaking babies, the glowing Mac screens, all the way out the door and on to Columbus Avenue.

A woman in a low-cut leotard top approaches me. "Aren't you supposed to have a writer's bag?" she says. She has dark hair and eyes that are too far apart. The leotard is more like a cat suit, the bottom half of which is obscured by a long black skirt. It would be a dancer's outfit on a different body, but hers is too voluptuous, too straining. I can't tell how old she is, except that she's older than she wants to be.

"I don't know," I say. "Probably. How did you know—"

"Anne told me what you looked like. Have you ordered something? Because if not, let's go to that new place, Rain. I hate coffee shops."

We walk a few blocks to a spacious Asian restaurant with bamboo decor. It looks like an upscale tiki lounge. Camille orders us colorful drinks that come with umbrellas, then she starts talking. And talking. I think the gist of what she's saying is that she's a producer with several projects in various stages of development, and that she *might* need a writer for any one of them. She orders more drinks, blue this time, and frothy. Her cell phone rings, loudly, and I sink into the banquette. When she hangs up, she puts a fifty on the table and says she wants me to come meet some friends, so I down the rest of my potion and follow her out to a waiting livery car. In the backseat, lighting Camille's cigarette, I ask where we're going, but instead of answering she climbs on top of me. The driver doesn't turn around. Camille straddles my legs and puts my hands on her tits, her fingers in my mouth, and her phone starts ringing again but this time she doesn't answer—her hands are already busy. I don't stop her. I haven't reached the age where I might say no to gratuitous surprises, where I might consider the long term over the short, the getting out to the getting in.

The car takes us to a private party in the basement of the Blue Water Grill, but we're barely there long enough to order drinks before we're off to the upstairs bar at 13. Camille tells me things, but it's too loud and I can't hear. When we end up at Wax, it's all becoming too familiar. But this isn't Shelton's crowd. These people are older, wealthier, more drunk. There's a wisp of desperation to their actions, as if these nights are numbered. But the drinks keep coming, and I, knowing no one, keep drinking them, one after another, as Camille's hands wander around below sea level. No one asks who I am or why I'm here—except me.

WHEN I WAKE UP, the sun is streaming through the window beside the bed, so I know I'm not at home. And I'm not wearing any clothes. Camille is on the phone in another room, pacing back and forth across a hardwood floor. She's talking about patents. I can't remember if we had sex or not, so I look for evidence. But there isn't any—only a headache and my boxers, under a desk across the room. I'm about to retrieve them when she walks in, looking incredibly put together in a chocolate-colored suit and high heels. She's still got the phone to her ear, but she waves and points to her watch and mouths the words, "I have to go, honey." Honey? I stay in bed because I don't want her to see me naked. Again. When she hangs up she smiles a toothy smile and sits down beside me.

"I want to keep you on a weekly retainer," she says. Before I can protest, before I can even say good morning, she hands me a check for $500 and kisses me with lipstick lips. "I'll call you soon. Be a doll and lock the door when you go."

But I don't even know where I am.

Twelve

MY FATHER WANTS TO meet for dinner. He does this sometimes, rolls into town and sounds his trumpet, and I come running. I'd never see him if I didn't. He's busy, but he's also involved again, remarried, removed.

He stayed single for a few years after the divorce, became the cause célèbre of the country-club set — the most eligible man in town, the perfect paper husband in a currency community. Women *felt* for him. Twenty years, then the wife up and splits. Sure, no one really knows what happens behind closed doors, but how bad could it have been? Speculation is the heartbeat of every commuter town, and Montclair had no shortage of it. My parents' lives were inspected like supermarket produce: the outer skin studied for signs of inner damage. And when no deep bruises were found, the available women lined up at my father's front door. He, being a man and all, chose the prettiest one of the lot.

Cynthia — women like this are always named Cynthia — Pederson was a pretty blond widow with four blond children and a large fortune, the legacy of a husband who died on a beach in Hawaii and left her holding the reins of a private company worth millions. I know all this because my parents were friends with the Pedersons. And Douglas played hockey with their son. But now, in this new warped reality, I came home and Cynthia was suddenly everywhere — planning vacations, taking golf lessons, *redecorating*. . . . And her children came and went like beautiful amoebas, attired in the various phases of youth. Sensing trouble, I asked around, and the bio came back quickly, second- and thirdhand. It was a wholly American story — the worst kind.

Bare bones version: Cynthia grows up in a middle-class suburb of Houston; she's a popular girl, a high school cheerleader, but forgoes a college degree to become a stewardess for TWA; she meets her meal ticket in first class, a married millionaire playboy who inherited a successful company from his father; he leaves his wife, and she leaves the airline and starts a new life of private jets, sailboats, and houses in Nantucket, Hawaii, Aspen; and then kids and country clubs, and just as it's all fully in place, it comes crashing down on an empty beach in the Pacific. Now here she is, a few tumultuous years later, in the living room, shimmering in diamonds, dating my dad.

There are a thousand takeoff points to this saga, but it's a story for someone else. It is enough to say that the Pederson family is an extraordinary family. They are the type of people who are talked about out of envy, admiration, disgust, wonder . . . and out of earshot. There was a legal battle after Conrad Pederson's death, a family vs. spouse money grab that played out in the business section of the *Times*, and Cynthia held her own. She became a local celebrity. Part of it was the rags-to-riches thing, but a lot of it was sheer appearance. She's an attractive woman, and her kids look like angels. Every one of them has the chiseled features of a child star. The year before my parents separated, Cynthia threw a sweet-sixteen party for her eldest daughter, Ashley, at a swank Mob hangout in West Orange. Conrad had just died and the party was as much a reemergence for Cynthia as it was a coming out for Ashley. My parents were there—it may have been their final public appearance together—and so was I, invited at the last second as an extra male body in the face of too many girls. Except Ashley and her friends were out of my league. They were actresses and models from New York City, older and more beautiful than anyone I associated with. One of them, a tall, dark-haired creature named Jennifer Connelly, had been in a *movie*. I sat in a corner by myself, fifteen years old, my eyes glued to her. She was so pretty I shuddered when she floated past. But Cynthia owned the night. She was the one wearing white, the one all the adults were watching. She was taking flight. I'd have never guessed she'd land in my father's bed.

It was weird watching my father *courting* someone, laboring in jewelry stores, buying tickets to musicals. My father's friends pulled me aside and asked, gravely, quietly, how serious he was about Cynthia. Douglas told me he got a creepy feeling every time the woman smiled. But when I complained to my mother, hoping for a sympathetic ear, she explained how much the Pedersons had suffered, then asked me to imagine what it was like to lose a father, a husband. She told me how wonderful it was that my father has found someone special, and so soon.

They got married in 1989 on a beach in Nantucket. Cynthia looked beautiful. Her kids were resplendent. And Douglas and I, forced to wear pink and white, looked as pathetic and miserable as we felt. It was quite a party, I heard later, but I spent it in an upstairs room, sulking. As a wedding present, I had taken a dozen of my father's old albums—the ones I stole when I went away to school—and recorded them onto cassettes so he could listen to music in his car. It took me three days of sitting in front of my stereo, and when I gave him the tapes the day before the wedding, he stuck Dylan's *John Wesley Harding* into his Blaupunkt and . . . nothing. No sound. Apparently I had failed to push the record button, and what my father now owned were twenty-four neatly labeled sides of static silence. I told him it was an omen. He didn't think it was funny. But I wasn't joking.

After the divorce, in the rubble of his life, I felt that I had found my father. Now, in his joyful resurrection, I'd lost him. Two families—six kids— were merging, and Douglas and I fell into the background. My father moved into *her* house, where pictures of *her* kids adorned every surface, covered every wall. Her kids had trust funds and fast cars and . . . and no father of their own. So when, after two years there still wasn't one photograph of us anywhere in the house, when her kids seemed to take up all my father's time, when Cynthia's ugly "incidents" had piled high enough to leave permanent scarring, I reminded myself what my mother had told me: These people lost a father, a husband. And the resentment they showed us was the pent-up by-product of that loss.

Now, more than seven years later, it isn't much better. But I've learned to choose my battles, and I've learned to let things go. I see my father when I can. These days we stick to the safe subjects: girlfriends and golf. We sit there and sip our drinks and maybe he'll make some crack about my politics, but we always run out of things to say after ten or fifteen minutes. Yet there's everything to say, the million things between a father and son. I want to know what he's up to, how he's *doing*. Does he really love his second wife? Does he ever think of his first one? Is there anything he'd still like to do or see, aspirations dangling in some corner of his busy mind? And what *I* want to tell *him* . . . the life I'd love to lead, beyond this current state of youthful decadence. I want to spill my dreams, explain these thoughts I can't cut loose. *I'd like to be a writer, Dad.* Why can't I look him in the eye and say that? Because I already know the answer, can envision the rolling eyes and the speech about the world not working that way. I haven't proved anything to him—haven't given him one thing to read—so he's only being practical, the way fathers are. But doesn't he know how far a little encouragement could take me? Doesn't he understand the power of words?

I TAKE A CAB up to the Four Seasons restaurant on Fifty-second. It's one of those rare nights when Cynthia's traveling and my father is here. I haven't seen him in weeks, and I want so badly to impress him with news of some success or other, but there's nothing much to say. Stuck at a light near the Condé Nast building on Madison, I bend down and key up a few quick bumps, hoping they'll mask any hints of despair. When we pull up to the restaurant a few minutes later, I feel like I'm flying.

The faces in the Grill Room look like caricatures, all noses and chins— tables full of fossils eating bones. I've forgotten a jacket, so the maitre d' gives me a blazer that's two sizes too small and tells me to follow him. I don't want to sit down; I want to walk around, up and down stairs, a few laps around the bar just checking people out. I did enough coke to feel my heart, the beats, one after another, rush hour. Come down a level, I tell myself. Act ordinary, bored . . . predictable. Be predictable.

I'm being led down a short hallway to the Pool Room, past tables spaced discreetly apart. Everything in this room is discreet, the glances, the unsaid words, the way people move. We walk by Donald Trump, and even he's being discreet. At the moment when I pass, he's pulling apart a piece of bread. He's at a table full of men, all of whom are watching him pull apart the bread, as if being taught, finally, after many years, how to do it right. My father is sitting at a table near the pool in the center of the room. Every year or two I read about a woman—a socialite, no doubt flapping her tightened wings—who ends up creating some unfortunate scene involving the pool—a dare, perhaps, or more likely too much wine—but tonight the water is serene, and even in my heightened state I can't imagine anyone jumping in.

"Is that the best jacket you've got?" my father asks, getting up to hug me.

"They gave it to me at the door. Considering the venue, I thought they might do a little better myself."

"You're supposed to bring your own."

There's an Absolut and tonic waiting for me on the table. My father sits back down, picks up the wine list.

"You don't look well," he says. "Are you sick?"

"Coming down with something."

"You should get more sleep."

"Did you see Donald Trump over there? Something's wrong with his hair. It's orange." My father takes his reading glasses off and turns around, discreetly. He never notices famous people unless someone points them out. It's an attractive quality.

"People like that always end up looking strange," he says, flipping through the Burgundies. I take a sip of vodka. It has the dull taste of a secondary vice. The sommelier drifts over as my father runs his index finger down the laminated page and settles on a 1990 Beaune. My legs are bouncing. The napkin falls off my lap.

"What's this about you quitting? You haven't even been there a year."

"I'm trying to write for magazines. Freelance stuff."

"About what?"

"About whatever."

"And how's that going?"

"I haven't heard from any yet."

"Well, you need more of a plan than that."

"I'm still working at Leland's part time."

"That's not good enough. You need to be getting on with a career, not scraping along on the underside of commerce. Writing isn't a life. It's a hobby. Have you given any thought to business school? You know your brother Douglas has already—"

"Dad, I don't care."

"Look, all I'm saying is that you're on your own now."

"Fine. I haven't asked you for help."

I watch the waiters circle the room like large cats, gracefully pouncing, then retreating. The great thing about cocaine is that it offers, at its best, the isolation of experiences, the breaking down of the whole into comprehensible parts—instruments otherwise unheard, fleeting thoughts allowed to develop, a petri dish of senses distilled to their essence. Right now it's the elegant waiters, as removed from the wider context of the restaurant as goldfish swimming in air. My father is talking, but I can't hear him. I don't know what he's saying. Or maybe I do. Maybe I know exactly what he's saying. I could give the speech for him.

The sommelier arrives, dignified, calm, separated from the separated: twice removed. My father begins his ritual, feels the bottle, checks the year. I take a long sip of my vodka tonic. It still tastes diminished. I put the glass down and notice for the first time that they put cranberry in it. Strange. On the other side of the table, the sniffing and swilling is reaching a crescendo. The sommelier says, "A good year after a bad one." I look back down at my drink. The cranberry is still dissolving, like . . . blood. *Fuck.* Instinctively, I wipe my nose and a few drops seep into the white cotton napkin. I sniffle a few times and now I can feel it, a buildup back there, my first nosebleed in years coming on—and *here.* I need to get to the bathroom, but my drink is still sitting there, looking more and more like fruit punch. I pick it up as my father picks up his glass, and I swallow the Absolut and blood in three quick gulps. Then I wipe my nose again, snort to stem the mounting tide, and stuffing my napkin in my jacket pocket, excuse myself.

There are always people in bathrooms when I need to be alone. The napkin is saturated, deep red on starched white, so I throw it out and press my nose with toilet paper. A man at the sink is fiddling with a contact lens, trying to see straight. And I'm starting to feel straight. I wait a minute for the bleeding to stop. Then, on a toilet in a stall, I key up a small line and snort it up the backup nostril. I sit and wait for the man by the sink to regain his focus and leave, then make one last check. All is in order; the dam should hold. I bound back up the stairs, two at a time.

There's a crisp new napkin folded on my plate.

"Sorry."

"You disappeared."

"I was—"

"See what you think," my father says, nodding at my oversize wine glass. Our waiter is hovering nearby, making me nervous. I taste the wine, linger over it like I know I should, and of course it tastes all wrong, like juice after toothpaste.

"It's wonderful—fruity, woody . . ."

"Nineteen-ninety was a great year across Europe, across the world. Keep that in mind when you're looking for a nice red with some age to it."

"Thanks, but I'm broke. I buy the stuff on sale next to the register."

"What happened to your savings?"

"I invested most of it in my friend Ken's film. It should be really good. Actually, he still needs another five or six grand to finish it off. You should—"

"Don't you know that films rank right up there with restaurants in the annals of bad investments?"

"Not this one."

"Who's in it? Anyone I know?"

"*I* make a cameo."

"Jesus."

I'm suddenly feeling much better, and the restaurant is humming right along with me. Except for the waiter. He's eyeing me suspiciously. I wipe my mouth (my nose) to make sure everything is okay. But he's looking down around my feet. Then I figure it out: He's looking for the *old* napkin. They don't just vanish at a place like this.

"I have a client I want you to meet," my father says. "He runs a company that owns oil-processing facilities. Do you know anything about oil?"

"The Alaska Pipeline is eight hundred miles long and runs from Prudhoe down to Valdez."

"I'm talking big-time—lightering points, offshore transfer stations. . . ."

"And what should I do when I meet him?"

"Dress well and sound intelligent."

"Dad, do you honestly see me as an oil man?"

"Honestly? No."

"Well, then."

"But I don't see you as anything else, either."

"Thanks. Can we move on?"

"Sure. How's your love life?"

CAMILLE CALLED LAST NIGHT and told me to meet her outside my building at noon today. Another $500 check appeared in the mail yesterday, the third in as many weeks, and I still haven't written anything for her. I'm sure it's just a matter of time. Gus and I have been debating her age, and we've narrowed it down to between twenty-eight and thirty-eight, but he wants to see for himself, so he just happens to be walking by as a white limo pulls up and she gets out, champagne glass in hand, still speaking to someone inside. Camille's scene transitions always overlap.

". . . because you can tell if she's had Botox when she frowns. Everyone wrinkles when they frown . . . so tell her that Tom has herpes and then watch her reaction. That's how you'll know. . . . *Boys! Good morning!*" Camille opens her arms and lands a kiss on my mouth. She's wearing a leather coat and a short black skirt with fishnet stockings. She looks like a groupie with a spending problem. "We've got quite a little day planned for you, sweetie."

"This is my friend Gus."

"A pleasure," Camille says, holding out her hand, which Gus suavely takes and kisses. "And this is *my* friend," she says, extending her arm toward the limo door like an emcee introducing the main event. There's a dramatic pause and then the main event emerges from the depths of the limo, in stages—legs, waist, breast, breast, head—until all of her magnificent parts have reassembled in front of us, covered in painted-on pants and a plunging pink top with feathery frills.

"I'm Daisy," she says. Gus stares at her, at a loss, for once, for words.

Camille smiles and pulls me toward the car. "Gus, we'll try to get your little friend back to you in one piece." I land in the back seat, sandwiched between body parts. As we start moving away, it's all I can do to turn around and look out the rear window. Gus is still standing there, in the middle of Thirty-second Street, watching us. He looks bewildered, like he's just seen something he can't quite believe. I know how he feels.

WHAT I LEARN in the afternoon is how smoothly a certain type of woman moves through Manhattan. It is a Saturday in December, and the midtown stores are mobbed. With anyone else, getting around would be a logistical nightmare, but Daisy and Camille are whisked past people, through places, with slight nods and silent gestures. As I trail behind, Camille and Daisy cut through the heart of the high life in Blahnik stilettos—Bendel's, Bergdorf's, Takashimaya—and everywhere we go, we're met at the door and led quickly to the upper floors reserved for private clients, where champagne is served and the Christmas crowds and perfume sprayers are pleasantly absent. Up here the air smells expensive, like fine suede and fur. Dresses appear with the drinks and are changed into and out of. I nod my approval and do what I'm told because that's what hangers-on, escorts, boy toys—whatever it is that I am—are trained to do. Flattery, like the dollar, is accepted everywhere.

Back in the limo, shopping bags strewn about, Daisy is talking business on her cell phone. With her leather pants and cleavage she looks like a movie star playing a stylish hooker, but listening to her now, discussing strike prices, liquidation preferences, and Series B financings, it's becoming very hard to pin her down. It's hard to reconcile any of this. Camille knocks on the glass partition and it swiftly comes down. Leaning into the front seat, giving me a full view of the garters holding up her stockings, she says, "Take us to the St. Regis." The driver nods and glances back at me. He must be wondering how I won the lottery. Daisy puts her phone away, adjusts her bra, and asks if she has lipstick on her teeth.

"No," I say.

"Thanks, baby. Where does Camille find boys like you?"

THEY'RE STAYING IN a suite littered with lingerie, high-heeled boots, and empty champagne bottles. Daisy is in the shower. Camille is lying across a couch. Trying desperately to sound normal, I say, "How long have you guys been staying here?"

"Since yesterday. Daisy's only in town for the weekend."

I've held off on the questions all day, but there are just too many.

"Where's Daisy from?"

"D.C.," Camille says. I'm not sure I believe her. Girls in D.C. don't look like that.

"Is Daisy her real name?"

"Does it matter?"

"It's just that—"

"Pour us some champagne and we'll talk. Do you like Xanax?" she asks, picking up and swallowing a pill from a small bowl on the coffee table in front of her. "Really, there's no reason not to. It's much better than Valium. It floats you around more. . . ."

I pour two glasses of champagne from a bottle lying in an ice bucket on the bar. The mirror on the wall shows Camille behind me, still lounging on the couch, her skirt riding up her thigh. I move to the left and she disappears and is replaced by another mirror against the far wall. Mirror on mirror and now the room goes on forever. It's better that way, with no people.

"Can you cancel your plans tonight? Daisy's boyfriend is having a little party."

"She has a boyfriend?"

"Of course, darling. What, did you think we asked you up here for a little threesome?"

"*Can* I have one of those Xanax?" I ask, walking over with the drinks.

"So, my favorite writer likes pills after all," she says, popping one into my mouth.

"Will you tell me what I'm supposed to be writing?"

Camille looks at me for a moment, thinking. "Will you sign something?"

I shrug and say, "Sure," then follow her to a table in the living room, or the drawing room—whatever you call the room in a hotel suite that doesn't have a bed.

"Here's the deal," Camille says, sliding a confidentiality agreement in front of me. "Daisy and I are partners in a production company. One of our *many* current projects is a TV show called—Have you signed that thing yet?"

"Yes."

"—called *Extreme Planet.* Unless you can come up with something better. Anyway, we need you to write a treatment. It's an adventure travel show, to be shot on location in the world's most exhilarating places—skiing in avalanche country, swimming with sharks . . . You know, real hair-raising stuff. The hosts will be sexy, and the cast will be composed of young celebrities—actors, models, musicians. . . . Imagine Donovan Leitch cliff-diving in New Zealand or Bijou Phillips rock-climbing in—"

"Please, not Bijou Phillips."

"Okay, I agree with you there."

Daisy walks out of the bathroom wearing only a bra and towel.

"Dais, I'm telling him about the show."

"Which one?"

"EP."

"That's my favorite," she says, bending over to shake her hair out.

I try to stay focused. "How many projects do you have?" I ask, casually.

"Let's see . . . ," Daisy says. "There's *Extreme Planet, Earthwatchers* . . ."

"We just got the rights to the Texas teen murder story."

"We're opening a chain of American-style coffee bars in London . . ."

"And don't forget the toothbrush invention."

"Oh, yeah," Daisy says, sliding into a black party dress. "Camille invented this toothbrush holder thingy. We're trying to get it patented. Will you be a doll and zip me up?"

I pretend not to notice the red thong peeking out just above where the zipper begins. Moving behind her, I can smell her neck. It's fresh, a mix of soap and cinnamon. Everything about these two is fresh. In a way, they are like so many other ambitious souls in New York—passionate filmmakers, political spin doctors, singers playing chords to match majestic voices. Except Daisy and Camille are playing on a higher level, with riskier weapons.

Zipped up slowly and carefully, Daisy hikes up her breasts with her hands and looks around for the champagne.

"If you don't mind my asking, how do you guys fund all these projects?"

They look at each other, giggling. "You'll see tonight," Camille says.

WE MOVE EVER UPWARD, to another, bigger suite, the presidential suite at the Four Seasons hotel. When we walk in, everyone turns to look. Considering my dates, I'm expecting DJs and dancing, disco balls and glittering people. Instead we're met by a group of men, maybe forty of them, all wearing bad casual-Friday outfits—blazers with gold buttons, khakis with pleats, belts with whale patterns—and there's no music, none at all. The few women are bony, thin-lipped, shoulder-padded. The party seems to have arrived with me, and people start crowding around to say hello. I step away and wander down an empty hallway. The presidential suite takes up almost an entire floor, so I do the whole loop, taking in the views of the city, the lighted kingdom below. I walk through bedrooms and bathrooms, but no one's back here—no locked doors, no naked couples, no drug dens.

In the main room Daisy and Camille are still surrounded, so I head to the bar. The man in front of me orders a Diet Coke. He smiles at me, raises his glass.

"Work for the company?" he asks.

"Here with friends, actually."

"Who?"

"The two girls over there."

"Really? Daisy and Camille?"

"You know them?"

"Of course. We all know them."

I'm not sure what to say to this, so I nod and order a vodka tonic.

"So what do you do, then?"

"I'm a writer," I say, wincing.

"Smart man. Content is king. *Slate? Salon?*"

"Excuse me?"

"Who do you write for?"

"I kind of freelance."

"Getting in early but keeping your options open. I like that. How does it work? You guys charging for online subscriptions or working off banner revenues?"

"I'm not sure you understand. I'm talking about real magazines. The kind you buy in a store."

"Oh," he says. He shuffles his feet from side to side, like he's having trouble with the concept of a concrete world. "Well, good luck." He waves to someone who's not there, then excuses himself and walks away.

I make my way across the room, catching snippets of conversations, "proxy servers" and "parallel platforms," "cryptosystems" and "coaxial connections." And I hear the phrase "irrational exuberance" repeated again and again, like a mantra, and always followed by laughter, the easy noise of those who know better. It's like an antitrade show up here, where instead of publicly flaunting the latest invention, these people are hoarding it, reveling in their exclusiveness. This is a new type of club, whose members have, not sterling pasts, but promising futures. Whatever's happening in this room hasn't spread to the greater, lesser world.

Daisy is in a corner with her arms around some guy in a Polo shirt.

Camille is entertaining a group of men near the window; they're trying hard to keep their eyes above her chest. When I finally manage to pull her away, I lead her back to one of the empty bedrooms.

"You want to do it in here?" she says. "Right now?"

"I'm leaving."

"*That's* what you dragged me back here to say?"

"These people are all—"

"Rich? Yes. You should get to know a few of them."

"Who the fuck are they? What is this?"

"You really don't know? This is an AOL company party, a *private* company party—only executives and the venture capitalists who love them. America Online is the future, baby. And these people are the new aristocracy. I know, I wish they dressed better, too."

"What's your connection?"

"The guy kissing Daisy is the son of one of the founders."

"And Daisy is dating him?"

"*He* thinks so."

Gus is on the couch, watching CNN, when I get home.

"Midthirties," he says, without looking over. "But who's her friend? She's incredible."

"Daisy? She *is* incredible."

"So what happened to you? Couldn't keep up?"

"Guess where I was tonight."

"No."

"A private AOL Christmas party in the presidential suite at the Four Seasons."

"Incredible views from up there. Did you walk all the way around?"

"Daisy's dating the founder's son."

"Damn, that's tough to compete with. What was it like? A bunch of tech guys speaking in code?"

"They were speaking a different language all right, but they weren't tech guys. They were management, but young, a few years older than us. Except they all dressed and talked the same, like they were trying to convince each other."

"Of what?"

"I don't know. I don't even know what AOL does."

"They're a cult," Gus says.

"They just assumed I was one of them, that I got it."

"But you don't get it."

"At least now I know there's something *to* get."

"You and the rest of the world. Look at the market: It's absurd. The whole country is riding on the back of technology no one understands. Don't you find it strange that America is bumping along for decades, minding its own business, and then, all of a sudden, half the country is either inventing or investing in technology?"

CNN is showing a clip of Alan Greenspan, and Gus turns up the volume: *"But how do we know when irrational exuberance has unduly escalated asset values . . ."*

"See?" Gus says, "They've been showing that speech all night. Even Greenspan, that hydrocephalic faith healer, thinks the whole game is rigged."

"No. Those people tonight were *joking* about his speech."

"That's because they've already made their millions and gotten out, and before anyone else even figured out what a modem was."

"I still don't know."

"Well, either way, it doesn't matter to us. We don't have any money."

"Funny how modern revolutions leave out the masses."

Gus shakes his head. "It's too late for your leftist political pronouncements. I'm crashing. Oh, Ken called an hour ago. He wanted you to call him back."

"Maybe he sold the movie."

"Maybe Uma Thurman's upstairs in my bed," Gus says, heading up that way.

It's 3:00 A.M., but I call Ken anyway and, sure enough, he picks right up.

"I'm watching the dailies," he says, sounding drained. "I think I screwed up some of the casting."

"Hey, what exactly is a treatment?"

Ken starts laughing. "Has Camille roped you into one of her TV shows?"

"She's been paying me for weeks to do nothing."

"At the risk of sounding like your father, *there's no such thing as a free lunch.* Remember that. And speaking of your dad, he just sent me a check for six thousand dollars, along with a note that says 'Don't disappoint!' What a cool thing. That pretty much gets the rest of the movie made. I wanted to tell you before I call him tomorrow."

"You're kidding. He did that?"

"Everyone wants to be involved in movies these days. Except *you* won't be, at least on-screen. I had to edit out your scene with Shelton. It was a continuity issue."

"How art imitates life."

Before hanging up, Ken promises to drop a few examples of movie treatments in the mail. Which reminds me. I walk over to the pile of bills amassing on the kitchen counter. It's the usual fare: Con Ed, NYNEX, and Visa. There's a well-timed CD-ROM from AOL, and an ominous "Eviction Warning" from the landlord (it must be some mistake; the one thing we do manage to pay is the rent). Then, at the very bottom, what I've been looking for: two thin letters from *Paper* and *Black Book* magazines. I tear open the former and the word *Sorry* stares back at me from the top of the page. They've turned the *Moving In/Moving Out* story down flat: *It's been done before, but try us again* . . . The second, from *Black Book*, is actually my original proposal, sent back to me, with the words *Call Us* scrawled hurriedly above a number. That's all: a two-word beginning.

Thirteen

ANOTHER HOLIDAY SEASON comes and goes in a blur of clubs and cocktails. At Leland's I write the bare essentials in drug-fueled bursts, then run home to check a mailbox devoid of personal correspondence. I keep calling *Black Book*, but I'm not sure whom I should ask for. When I tell them I'm a writer they put me on hold. It's tough, that moment you realize no one is going to pick back up.

Camille's weekly checks keep arriving, like unemployment. I'm working on the *Extreme Planet* treatment, but the real work is being done after dark, at swank restaurants and crowded dinner parties. The nights have become freight trains of stamina, moving from one neon station to the next, letting people on and off until the last blurry stop uptown, in Camille's bed.

When, at Pravda, I do finally hand over the *Extreme Planet* treatment, Camille flips through the seven pages of exotic adjectives, far-flung locales, and B-list celebrities, then shakes her head. "Oh, baby," she says, "there's nothing in here about *money*. Sure the show is important, but the whole point is merchandising. Think in terms of target audiences. We're going after MTV, VH1, USA, E! . . . Jenny McCarthy, Daisy Fuentes . . . Play up the sex, the danger, and most of all the marketing potential. Think of this as a cross between *The Real World* and *Baywatch*. This is a gold mine if we do it right. I think there's a future for real-life shows, *reality television*. Just you watch."

I'm writing as much as I can on a wet napkin, the ink running, making a blur of the word *Baywatch*, but after another round of martinis I put the pen down. And then I stop listening. In this crowd no one notices when you tune out. They're too busy talking.

WHEN I GET HOME there's an eviction notice glued to the door. Staring at me, at eye level, is the foreboding figure of $3,600. I read the small print, which states that Gus and I, the two leaseholders, have been officially evicted due to lack of payment, and that right now, in some housing court in a cruel corner of Manhattan island, proceedings are already under way to remove us, because despite repeated attempts to contact us, we haven't responded, haven't paid, haven't done anything except cheat our friendly landlord out of two months' rent. But this doesn't make sense. I don't exactly balance my checkbook, but I usually know about what I've got in my account. And every time I get below three hundred, I hustle down to Leland's and type until my fingers hurt. I haven't missed any of my rent payments, so that leaves only one other person. If this figure is accurate, he's bounced four rent checks in a row. And he hasn't said a word. The eviction notice is affixed to the door with superglue. I can't tear it down without chipping the paint off, so I leave it up there. Gus has always admired his own handiwork.

Phone messages: Camille sounding frantic (*Meet me at the Royalton for drinks at eight, just you and me, I want to see you . . .*); my mother sounding annoyed (*You're never home, sweetie, is everything okay?*).

I turn on the TV to get my mind off the fucking eviction notice. Jewel is reciting a poem on VH1. She's been nominated for two Grammys, including Best New Artist, and watching her now, she looks thinner, shinier, stripped of edges. She's been put on the MTV diet, streamlined and mainstreamed. Only the crooked teeth are still the same.

I leave a message on Camille's cell phone, telling her I'll be there. I'm getting used to answering machines and voice mail. Sometimes you can converse for days without speaking to someone. And that has its plusses.

THE SUNKEN LOUNGE at the Royalton on Forty-fourth Street is the meeting place of choice for the foot soldiers of the glamour business. I immediately spot Camille checking her messages on a couch across the room. I walk toward her, past young men and women so accented and accessorized they look like they're here for a Versace casting call. And Camille, in a short black bias-cut dress, is setting the pace. She looks lovely tonight, and has that outward glow that New York girls manage to muster even in the dead of winter. Women always look their best when you're about to leave them.

"You look like you need a drink, baby."

"I'm fine," I say, as a blonde with ironed hair arrives with two martinis.

"Well, I got you one anyway," she says. I sit down and take a sip. Two women are sitting behind Camille and one of them looks exactly—I think—like Gloria Steinem: right age, right hair, right glasses. It looks like she's being interviewed; there's a tape recorder on the table between them. But it's not possible; no one's that unlucky. Breaking up with a girl with Gloria Steinem sitting next to you would be like trying to negotiate a cease-fire with General Patton watching over your shoulder.

"Look," I start, "I want to talk to you about—"

"*Extreme Planet.* I know. You're being so patient—"

"But I have no idea what's going on. I've written one minor treatment for you, and you keep sending me checks. You're paying me for nothing."

"I could think of worse arrangements."

"Well, I don't think it's working out."

"Is it the money? Do you want more money?"

"No, that's not it at all. It's like all you and your friends do is glide around town from party to party, and you never stay in one place long enough to enjoy where you are. Don't you ever want to talk about something besides money and technology and . . . *reality television*? I . . . This just isn't my scene right now."

"Parties, paychecks, and pussy: it sounds like a pretty good scene to me."

Gloria Steinem turns around.

"Camille," I say.

"What! What is it?" she says, blowing strands of hair out of her face. "Tell me, what is your *scene*? Sitting in that shitty apartment all night, *talking* about New York society with that roommate of yours? Or the tortured-artist thing—you know, the world owes you something because you know how to suffer, because you make the valiant decision to . . . to what? You haven't done anything. You don't even have a real job. Get over yourself. There's nothing more pathetic than someone who is scared to"— Gloria is watching us. I wonder if the tape recorder is catching all this. I can just imagine some Condé Nast exposé on thankless men with no spine—"take risks, scared to throw themselves into the mix and see what the fuck happens. And I gave you *access*, introduced you to all these people who could help you. But you don't follow up. You don't *engage* . . ." Camille stops, looks around. She takes a tissue from her Fendi bag and wipes her eyes, but I can't tell if the problem is tears or too much makeup. "This is a new low: being dumped by an unemployed, coked-up child."

"But we're barely even dating. We've never even talked about it. For all I know, you could be fucking five other guys at the same time as—"

"*What?*"

"No, no, I know you're not—or weren't—but . . ."

"You're one to talk. You stare at every girl who walks by. How do you think that makes me feel?"

"I didn't know you had feelings."

"Fuck this," she says, standing up to put her coat on. I get up to help her, but she storms away. I sit back down and finish my drink. Gloria gives me a look, then turns back around. I want to ask her if she really is Gloria Steinem, because Gus would love the post-postwhatever of the whole situation, but suddenly Camille materializes in front of me and throws down a twenty.

"God forbid you pay for anything."

ON MY WAY HOME I think about a comment I overheard at one of Camille's VIP-room soirées. An Internet millionaire was celebrating because he'd finally achieved the New York trifecta: perfect job, perfect girlfriend, perfect apartment. Most people, he said, end up with one, or two if they're lucky. All three, though, all three was the ultimate success. But what happened to the means that got you those ends? People are skipping an entire step of the process—the whole idea of doing something worthwhile, being with someone who matters. Camille never did. I used her like she used me. And the only good thing I can say about the experience is that it won't take long to get over it. It must get better than this. Yet I'm so far away from anything I'd like to call a life. Even the concept of being a writer is still an idle one. When I sit down at my desk, all I can do is think of how I have absolutely nothing original to say. Am I supposed to wait for stories to come or just grab at loose thoughts and try to force them together? Is there a process I don't know about? Maybe that's what they learn in all those writing schools.

So I end up reading instead. I read articles by Adam Gopnik and John

Cassidy and Phil Gourevitch. I read fiction by a roll call of well-known writers, and I realize they can say more in one sentence than I could in a page. I try to take my mind off it. I watch baseball with Gus and wonder about paths not taken. The season has just started and the announcers are full of optimism. In early April every team is still in the race and someone is always hitting .700 or has five home runs after only three games, and I want to see how long they can keep it up. And then I go to parties, bars, clubs. I fill my head with liquids and pills and powders to make me forget I even thought about anything meaningful in the first place.

WHEN I WALK PAST the eviction notice and into our apartment, I find Gus watching *Das Boot*. He's vacated his usual spot on the couch and is in a chair up near the screen, squinting to read the subtitles.

"Hey," I say.

"Hey," he says.

I open the icebox and grab a beer.

"You notice anything different about the front door?"

"Yes, what's up with that?"

"I was going to ask *you*."

Gus takes his shoes off and rubs his feet. "It must be a mistake."

"It's our second notice. It's two months' worth of rent."

"There's no way I've bounced *four* rent checks, if that's what you're getting at."

"Could you stop watching the movie for a second?"

"*All right.* I'll call the landlord tomorrow."

"Good, because we're about to get kicked out of here. What the hell are you doing with your money?"

"I'm a fucking civil servant. I'm not exactly pulling down six figures."

"You're making a lot more than I am, and I still manage to—"

"It's not the same. If you must know, I'm helping my mom. She's raising my sister all by herself, and sometimes I send her extra cash."

As close as we've become, Gus has never talked to me about his family, his other life, the one he's been trying to shed. What little I know I learned from mutual friends.

"What about your dad? Is he around at all?"

"I think he's in Miami. He left when I was a kid . . ." Gus pauses and is about to say something further, but he stops. "Look. I'm sorry about the eviction notice. I'm sure it's just a scare tactic. Don't worry, I'll take care of it."

He turns back to the gloom of the German submarine.

"I just broke up with Camille."

"It's about time."

Fourteen

THE DOOR BUZZER JOLTS me out of my bed. I can hear Gus in the shower, so it must be a workday. Monday, I think. I amble down the stairs and am confronted by a living room littered with remains. Fruit flies hover over beer bottles, cigarette butts lie stubbed out on plates, and the bookcase has fallen over. The buzzer sounds again, louder.

"Can you get that?" Gus shouts from the bathroom. "It's the dry-cleaning guy."

It's been a few weeks since the Camille debacle, weeks of excess on all fronts. But how the hell did everything go so sideways on a Sunday night? I remember I was at that new club, Life, and then . . . shit . . . I invited the whole crowd back here. It's always a great idea until everyone is actually *at* your place, throwing CDs around, laying out lines, burning holes in the car-pet. I remember Gus came home in the middle of it and hung out for a while, but it wasn't his scene, these creatures of the night, the guys with ponytails and beepers, the girls with runny noses and names that end in *I*. He asked us to keep it down, then went upstairs to bed.

I scare up some small bills for the dry cleaner and walk over to the door (the eviction notice is still up, more of a joke now, like a college rejection letter taped to a dorm-room wall), but instead of a deliveryman with starched white shirts, it's Victor, the coke dealer, in a starched white suit.

"Hey, man," I say, trying not to look surprised.

"You just waking up?" Victor asks, grinning. He has a new gold tooth. We've become chummy in that fake dealer-and-customer way, chummy enough that he now offers door service. I beep him and he's here within the hour—except I haven't beeped him today.

"Did I . . . ?"

"Last night, man. At one, at two, at two thirty. Remember? I said I couldn't come until now and you said fine. So here I am. Guess I missed the party."

Gus turns the shower off and shouts, "How much was it?"

"You still want some?" Victor asks. I can't imagine doing any; my head feels like it's in a vise. Still, there's always later.

"I'll take two," I tell him, then run back upstairs to find bigger bills. When I come back down, the dry-cleaning guy is here, as well, speaking with Victor in Spanish. Gus walks out of the bathroom with a towel around his waist as I'm paying for our shirts, and for a moment the various transactions are paused as the four of us take one another in—it's another Monday morning in New York. Then Gus walks away. I give the dry cleaner twenty dollars, give the drug dealer a hundred. As he turns to leave, Victor eyes the eviction notice, then looks over my shoulder into the chaos of the living room. He slaps me on the shoulder: "You doing okay, my friend?"

I take a long shower, then put on one of the clean shirts and the same jeans I've been wearing for days. Gus has left for work, so I grab his blue police windbreaker from the coatrack. It has an NYPD patch on the shoulder and the letters *ESU* in bright yellow across the back. The Emergency Services Unit is some kind of elite task force; Gus borrowed it at a potentially volatile rally and has forgotten to return it. Even in my dark mood, I can't help but chuckle at the thought of Josh's face when I walk into Leland's, in my current condition, wearing a police jacket. One more look in the bathroom mirror, a final attempt at passable, at normal. But I can't do anything about the inside, the various poundings, the thoughts that won't come in order: I keep starting tasks and then forgetting, moving on and then remembering a minute later. I walk over to the coffee table to make sure there are no drugs still . . . Oh, God. The chessboard—it's *broken*. It's been fractured like a windshield, cracks emanating from the center like sunrays on a child's drawing. I pick up a piece of the jagged glass puzzle; it's painted fire-truck red on the bottom. Cocaine has spilled into the cracks; the whole glass painting is ruined. I shovel what's left of the powder onto a piece of aluminum foil and put it in my pocket. I'm tired of looking at it, tired of nights that end like this or don't end at all. I feel like I'm in one of those sleep-deprivation studies, where they screw around with time until you don't know where you are or how long you've been there. You can't sleep, can't stay awake and instead exist in some dark limbo where things happen and you react slower and slower until nothing matters anymore—not failure, not love, not living.

Outside it's a bright, breezy spring day. Women are strolling down the wide sidewalks, pretending their skirts aren't as short as they are; men are standing in line at hog dog stands, waiting for gyros and cold knishes, watching the women walk by. The air feels good, smells good, and for a minute I feel okay again, safely anonymous, a regular guy heading back to the office after lunch. There's a double-decker tourist bus idling at the light on Thirty-first and Fifth, full on top and empty below, and kids are pointing in every direction and parents are recording it all on shaky handheld video cameras. The bus pulls over, yielding to a white police van racing downtown. Then, without warning, the van veers sideways across lanes and pulls up dramatically onto the crowded sidewalk twenty yards ahead of me. I've seen this before, the undercover bust. These cops in street clothes will swoop down, badges dangling around their necks, and suddenly two shady-looking guys you hadn't noticed are being cuffed right in front of you. The cops will throw them in the back of the van, then drive off like nothing's happened. It's all a bit Gestapo-like. And sure enough, here they come, three of them, in jeans and blue windbreakers, jumping out of the van like soldiers spilling from a hovering helicopter. I look around to see who's running away, but no one is running. Then one of the cops points at me and, resting his other hand on his gun, shouts, "IDENTIFY YOURSELF!"

I start reaching for my wallet.

"HANDS UP! AWAY FROM YOUR BODY!" He draws his gun but doesn't point it, just lets it hang loosely at his side. I raise my hands and his two partners, one with a ponytail, the other overdoing it with a McEnroe headband, run past him and grab me. I let myself go limp as they drag me over to the side of a building and slam my hands against the concrete wall above my head. One of them kicks my legs apart, really kicks them hard when he could have just asked. It is now, on display for all of Fifth Avenue, that I realize we are all dressed alike. Like a Western-movie sheriff, the first cop holsters his gun and walks up to me slowly, milking the moment. He comes right up to my face. "Tell me where you got the jacket," he says.

"I just put it on," I stammer, turning my head toward him. "I didn't know—"

"WHO THE FUCK GAVE IT TO YOU?"

"A friend."

"Is he a cop, your friend? He better be a cop, because if I find out this thing is stolen, we're putting you away. You don't wear an ESU jacket unless you're an on-duty officer. How fucking stupid do"—*Oh, God.* I think I have cocaine in my pocket—"because impersonating an officer is a serious fucking crime. You could get shot wearing this thing. Now start talking."

"It's my roommate's jacket. He works downtown, One Police Plaza. He doesn't know I'm wearing it. I was late for work and it was hanging there—"

"What's his name?"

"Look, it's my fault. He told me not to wear it and I didn't listen."

"Put him in the wagon," the lead cop says. And with that, McEnroe forces me up and onto a bench inside, then handcuffs me to a pole. Pain shoots through my right shoulder, and for a moment it feels like I'm at a baseball tryout again, trying to ignore my throbbing arm. I try to adjust, but the cuffs are cutting into my wrists. "We're taking a trip downtown," one of them says, "see if we can find your friend." I see a group of people standing around the van; then the doors slam shut and it all goes dark.

The three cops sit up front, separated by a metal grille. I can hear their radios squawking on and off, arbitrarily, like in-laws. Bending at the waist, I scrape my left arm against my thigh and *fuck*, I can feel it, nestled snuggly in the denim—the folded-up foil. I've watched enough cop shows to know these guys are screwing around; they'd have already arrested me if they were serious, read me my rights, acted out their parts. I'd be fine if I didn't have this coke on me. But now all they need to do is pat me down and this becomes a very different game.

"Hey," I shout, toward the front. As my eyes adjust I can make out the back of their heads, but no one turns around. "Hey, my roommate's name is Gus—Gustavo Chavez. He works in the press department. You can call him and—"

"SHUT UP BACK THERE!" McEnroe shouts.

Minutes go by. There are no windows, so I try to figure out where we are by the sounds outside—the traffic, the construction, the stops and starts— but that works only in movies. Finally, the long-haired cop—Borg—turns around.

"We got Gus on the phone. He says he doesn't know you and has no idea how you got his jacket. Sorry, buddy, but we're taking you in."

I start protesting, so he closes the divider between the front and back, leaving me alone with the bumps in the road. We're moving slowly through traffic, no siren, so there's plenty of time for reflection. Aside from the immediate imposition of not allowing me to reach into my pocket—to do what: Throw the tinfoil across the van? Dump the coke out on the dark floor? Snort it?—the handcuffs bring with them a certain clarity. I am no longer hungover. I feel sharp, and suddenly it's not hard to see a time line of events leading up to now. I try to pinpoint a moment when things turned, when dreams and ambitions gave way to darker, more pressing needs. I feel that deciding to be a writer has put me in some holding pattern. I thought I could just start typing and stories would come. But I don't know anything about writing, and it's not coming easily. And so I've drifted away from the larger plot as well. I know that lives are not bottled, like perfume; you don't wake up one morning having found some sweeping answer to the questions of the night before. I know that goals get set and that the living is done along the way, but the route isn't supposed to spiral downward; it isn't supposed to lead to this, being handcuffed to a paddy-wagon pole with hard drugs hidden in my pocket like Easter eggs just waiting to be found. Now, in the blackness, my stomach churning, my wrists sliced like ripe fruit, my life seems too far away to find.

We stop. I can hear noise outside and then the van doors open up to daylight, and through it, shining, laughing, sweating in his mismatched suit, is Gus. He looks as beautiful as a centerfold. The cops are standing on either side of him, laughing as well. It's almost as if Gus is in charge. McEnroe uncuffs me, slaps me on the back.

"Shoulda seen him, Gus. Took him all of five minutes to give you up."

"Figures," Gus says, nodding. "Sorry about this, guys. I'll try to keep the department stuff in the office from now on."

"No big deal," Borg says. Then he looks at me: "And no hard feelings."

The three of them wave and walk off toward police headquarters. I hop down from the van, rubbing my wrists.

"What the fuck was that?"

"Sorry," Gus says. "Those guys can be assholes. But what were you thinking?"

"After last night? Not much."

"I think you need to regroup," Gus says. "Like, in the larger sense. And you can start by taking that jacket off before they arrest you for real."

I do what he says. I take the police jacket off and hand it to him. Then I reach into my pocket and discreetly take out the packet of foil.

"And one more thing," I say, handing him the coke before he realizes what it is. "I think I'm done with this, as well."

Fifteen

AT THE END OF APRIL the baseball coach at Kenyon invites me out to lecture his young troops as they gear up for the stretch run. My brother, Douglas, is the starting shortstop now. I haven't seen him play in years, so I jump on the offer. A weekend in the heartland could do me some good.

Alumni have a brief window, about three years, when they can still come back to campus as minor celebrities. Teachers like tales of the real world (especially from people who aren't making millions), and current students, sick of the same faces, gravitate to the returning ones, their bridges to bright futures.

I fly to Kenyon on Friday afternoon and make it to the baseball field in time for practice. I give a rousing sermon about running everything out and never knowing who might be watching, then hang around the cage and give hitting pointers. After practice the guys start asking me questions, but almost none are about baseball. They want to know about New York ("Is it true that chicks there like going to museums?"), about writing ("Are you doing, like, books and shit?"), about Gus ("Dude, is that guy still alive?"). They invite me to a frat party later, a Spring Fling out at one of the lodges ("*Six* kegs," the catcher says, earnestly).

With darkness descending I make my way to the campus bookstore. It is here, while idly chatting with a former professor, that I spot Claire Davis. From the corner of my eye I see her pour milk into a coffee mug, then sit on a couch and open *The New York Times*. Claire is in my brother's class. She was a freshman when I was a senior, and back then she had very blond hair that framed high cheekbones, and sleepy Susan Sarandon eyes that made me lose my concentration every time they fell on me. The girl I'm watching now is even more beautiful, if that's possible; the hair is longer and the Andover tennis jacket and jeans of three years ago have been replaced by a leather coat, snug-fitting cords, and sunglasses.

I ran into Claire last winter, at a holiday party on the Upper East Side. We talked for a while then, and though it was just a short conversation, I remember everything about her—the way she laughed, the birthmark near her collarbone . . . and I distinctly recall her saying she was moving to New York after school.

Now she sees me walking over and jumps up to hug me, as if we're better friends than we are. She invites me to sit down, and soon we've picked up where we left off last December. We move from bookstore to coffeehouse to campus bar, from afternoon to evening and on into night. Over pints of beer we tell our stories, and after a while familiar names and common experiences give way to more personal yearnings. Claire grew up in New York. She's an English major with notions of writing, but when she mentions this, it's with humility, as if she already knows how tough it is. We talk about books, lovers, families. I'm vaguely aware I'm supposed to be meeting my brother somewhere, but only vaguely. Claire is halfway through telling me about her parents—some great story about her male friends always falling for her mother—when I realize how completely *enamored* I am. Enamored with a girl who is still twenty-one, a girl who eats in cafeterias and listens to Steely Dan. I barely know her, but it doesn't matter. We talk until closing, then kiss on a dewy lawn, and if a kiss can be loaded with auspicious beginnings, this one is. We spend the rest of the weekend together, hopping from frat parties to baseball games. And the whole time the words come out in bunches, like there isn't enough time to get them all in. When we do run into my brother on Sunday afternoon, he looks at us and tells us to stop acting weird. "Everyone's talking," he says, but Claire and I aren't listening.

WHEN I GET BACK to New York there's a message on my machine from an editor named Kevin at *Black Book*. Finally! I run upstairs and grab their premiere issue from last fall. It's a terrific mix of investigative journalism, gritty Nan Goldin photographs, and outlandish fashion spreads. And it's the first magazine I've read in a long time that *feels* like New York, the city I knew.

Kevin's name is near the top of the masthead. I dial the number, give the receptionist my name, and am put on hold. I've memorized the music, but this time it barely starts playing before Kevin picks up. I can hear giggling in the background. "Tell me something," he says. "Is that really your last name? Because it's too perfect. Listen, we hadn't heard from you so I wanted to give you a call. I think the indie film thing is over, man, so we can't do your *Moving In/Moving Out* piece, but if you've got any other—"

"Actually, I'm working on a bigger story," I say, quickly. "I've been talking to other magazines, but come to think of it, the story might be a good fit for you guys."

"I'm listening."

"It's the inside story of the Mafia's hold over the New York fashion industry." There's silence at the other end of the line, so I go on to describe the sweatshops, the truckers, the private investigators, the whole concept of monitorships. I tell him about my background, about long days on the streets of Chinatown, endless flights of stairs, hollow immigrant eyes. It's a cautionary tale of modern capitalism and crime, a sweeping epic, and when I'm done, there's another pause, a seemingly endless silence. . . .

"Well, it might be right for us. Meet me at our offices at noon tomorrow."

I PACE UP AND DOWN Prince Street for fifteen minutes, then ring the Black Book buzzer at 12:05. Kevin greets me at the door. He's my age, maybe a little older, and has perfected the British rock-star look—the Gauloise cigarettes, the shaggy hair, and the vintage Pumas, retrofitted for a more colorful age. We walk to a coffee shop across from Raoul's and situate ourselves at a table near the window, surrounded on all sides by tall girls picking at croissants and thumbing through portfolios. We order coffee and make small talk. Kevin waves to a model at the counter who I think might be Amber Valletta. I'm so nervous I ask for one of his cigarettes, then can't light it.

"I *love* your idea," Kevin says. "We've been looking for a hard-hitting story like this. But if we're going to do it, let's really *do* it. I want a major exposé—five thousand words, undercover reporting, hidden microphones, grainy photos, interviews with sweatshop owners and investigators and maybe even the Mob. I mean, why not get their side, right? It's perfect. Here we are in the fashion capital of the world, at the dawn of the information age, and we've still got Third World factories controlled by organized crime right under our noses!"

"That's what I was thinking."

"We can call it 'The Fashion Police.' You said you were shopping it around. Have you actually spoken to anyone else?"

"The *Times Magazine*," I say. It rolls off the tongue easily, like most lies.

"We want it exclusively. Let's go back to the office right now, get it in writing."

"How much do you pay?"

"How's fifty cents a word?"

"Fine, but I want the rights back after a year."

"You're thinking about the movie already," he says, grinning. "Nice."

IT'S BEEN A YEAR and a half since I walked the halls of Kroll, but nothing has changed. The same faces look up from the same desks, and I wave to a few as I walk by. I think briefly of dropping in on Eric and Simon, the old crew over in Investigations, but I want this to be as professional as possible. Besides, I'm an outsider now, looking for information, and people around here don't like the tables turned.

I wasn't thinking about a movie at all. I just didn't know what else to ask for, and the rights sounded as good as anything. Kevin said he needed the story for their next issue, which is closing in less than three weeks. So I've gotten to work. I've been reading books on organized crime and going through public records from old court cases. And when I sat down to list potential interview subjects, the first name I wrote was Robert McGuire, the president of Kroll.

McGuire ushers me into his corner office and points to a seat. He's a tall, angular, well-dressed man who moves smoothly and speaks in measured clips. He looks like he's operating at half speed, like an executive with a golden parachute. But it's more likely he's still recovering from his former life. From 1978 through 1983 McGuire was commissioner of the New York City police department. I was scared of him when I worked here, thinking of what the man had *seen*, the secrets he kept, but now, as I ask routine questions about the origins of the monitoring program, those fears fall away. He looks at the tape recorder and speaks deliberately. His answers are upbeat and general, the clichés of corporate achievement. Even as I try to probe below the glossy surface of the garment trucking case, he stays the course, delivers the company line in a voice so even and assuring I almost start believing it: "I leave it to other people to say whether the monitorship was a success because I don't want to toot our own horn. . . ."

I wonder how he really feels. The city, when it was his, was dirty, industrial, broke. The streets were violent; there were strikes and blackouts. And organized crime held New York in a chokehold. Today, of course, the city is clean and the subways run and no one I know has been mugged in years. And here's McGuire, who held the keys to New York in its darkest years, watching the turnaround from his corner office, where yesterday's failures are easily forgotten and today's victories celebrated, even if they are hollow ones. Maybe the man deserves some easy living.

As he works through his sound bites, I think back on my version of the monitorship, the dance we did through those sweatshops, that hot summer of lip service, and I want to challenge his answers, but I can't. McGuire's just too nice, his résumé too long. And anyway, I have no idea what I'm doing.

DOWNTOWN, AS ALWAYS, it's a different story. I pay an unannounced visit to one of the sweatshops on the old Chinatown route. I picked it because of the owner; he's younger than the others, and I figured he might talk. I hide a tape recorder in my jacket pocket and press Record.

I find the owner right where I left him two years ago: peering over women's shoulders. When he sees me walk in, he waves his arm in a big rainbow as if he's been expecting me. He shakes my hand firmly, then leads me into his office and closes the door. But as I start to tell him about the article, he stops me and lowers the window shades until they're hovering a half inch above the bottom of the frame.

"Who saw you come in?"

"No one."

"In your book, you don't use my name."

"It's not a book; it's just a magazine article. And I'll call you . . . Johnny Chang. How about that?"

"I like that. Sounds very American, very cowboy." He sits in the chair and puts his sneakers up on his desk, like boots. I ask if he thinks the recently ended monitorship really has kept the Mafia away, and if so, whether they'll stay away.

He looks at me, then past me onto the factory floor. "In the beginning the Mafia wouldn't let go. They kept coming here, even when you people were coming here. They just come at different times."

"What would they do?"

He gets up, walks around his desk, grabs my jacket, and cocks a fist. For a second, I think he's found the tape recorder and is about to hit me, but then he lets go and laughs. "They scare you like that," he says. "And then, for a while they leave. But only for a while. When the monitors stop, the Mafia comes again and tells us to use only *their* truckers. They always come back to people like us. Be careful when you write your story. Because I tell you for sure, they're not so nice."

When Claire moves back to New York after graduation, I keep my distance. She's staying with her parents on the Upper East Side, and the last thing she needs is an older and mostly unemployed boyfriend latching onto her. My relationships have the nasty habit of dying young, and I like Claire too much to lead her into that trap. But what if she leads me? Soon drinks are turning into dinners. Innocent midnight phone calls are becoming less-than-innocent late-night cab rides. And one thing is very definitely leading to another.

In early summer she takes an apartment in a prewar building near the entrance to the Fifty-ninth Street Bridge. The traffic outside provides steady background noise, an urban soundtrack of revving engines, piercing horns, and curses, delivered in heated outer-borough accents, like parodies of themselves. Here I am in her sun-streaked living room, moving her furniture and hammering nails into thick brick walls. I open a box filled with hardcover books—Fitzgerald, Vonnegut, Pynchon, Plath, Amis (*père et fils*), and so many others I don't even know. These aren't books she was assigned; these are books she bought, on her own, a literary trail of interests and inquiry, and she handles each one gently, like they're worth all that weight. Here's a girl who was taught at some early age that books make people more whole. And she *is* whole, intact, well rounded in everything but her physique, which is already city slim. And she's so young and impressionable. She hasn't yet lived those first years on her own, where the safety net slips away and life becomes elusive. She's still blissfully unaware of all that, and it's exhilarating to watch her run around placing things on shelves, in cupboards, in corners, as she unpacks her young life in front of me. I can't help but feel like I'm starting over, too, that the last three years in New York—the first three years in New York—were only a teaser, just false starts and folly. Here, with Claire, all those wasted nights and game-show after-noons don't matter anymore.

We open a cheap bottle of wine and find some cigarettes and the unpack-ing process quickly comes apart. We sit in the center of the hardwood floor, surrounded by clothing and accumulation, talking about art as if it means something, as if it matters that people try.

"Can you come to dinner at my parents' apartment tomorrow night?" she asks. "You can talk writing with my dad. He reads everything."

"I'd love to," I say. And I would. We don't discuss books at my family table(s). Actually, it's been a long time since I was around a family that's still together. Claire restores all kinds of hope. We start kissing, then move to the couch, unfastening buttons and belts, my hands running over her smooth Nordic skin, her broad shoulders, her small, firm breasts. Then I take her by the hand to her bedroom, bare but for the bed, the first thing I'd set up.

GUS GETS ME A PHONE interview with a friend of his from Elaine's, the NBC reporter John Miller. Miller made his name in the 1980s, cover-ing the various trials of John Gotti. For years the government tried to con-vict the Gambino family boss of various organized crimes, but Gotti always won in court. The press took to calling him the "Teflon Don" because noth-ing ever stuck. Except John Miller. Out of a tenacity bordering on stupidity, Miller stuck to Gotti like glue, tailing him through the streets of Howard Beach and staking out the Ravenite Social Club on Mulberry Street. Miller may have had the most dangerous job in America. But Gotti liked the atten-tion, thrived on it, and soon Miller became an emissary of sorts between Gotti and the public, *his* public. But then, in 1992, the Teflon finally wore off, and Gotti was put away for life.

I've already spoken with several off-the-record sources concerning Mafia activity in the fashion industry, and the same names have started surfac-ing—made guys who still hang around the garment business. I want Miller's take, but more than that, I want to get inside, like he was. I want to talk to the Mob myself.

I get Miller on his cell phone, at an airport, and fill him in on the article. Then I start asking questions—off the record, of course.

"This is the first time you've done a piece like this," Miller says.

"How do you know?"

"Because you should never offer to keep an interview off the record unless it's absolutely the only way to get someone to talk. Now tell me, are you using an alias?"

"I wasn't planning on it."

"Then be careful. These people you're writing about, they don't enjoy reading about themselves. The Mob may be diminished, but it's still active. I don't know what those desk jockeys at Kroll think, but sending a few *investigators* downtown with a checklist and a bunch of brochures about the monitoring program doesn't exactly scare anyone away."

And then, just like that, Miller starts naming names, connecting dots, until his flight gets called and the lesson ends.

"Any chance I can talk to one of these guys, maybe get his perspective on—"

"You want to talk to a *made* guy? They don't exactly have spokespeople, you know. Why don't you stick with what you've got? You're already in pretty deep."

"So can I use your name on the record?"

"Sure," he says, before hanging up. "It's using yours I'm worried about."

I put the phone down and walk over to the living room, where Gus is watching replays of Farrah Fawcett's meltdown on Letterman.

"Look at this shit," he says. "She was definitely on something. She thought his set background was the real city skyline. How do people get that fucked up?"

"Miller was great."

"I know. He's a badass."

"He's flying to Europe to investigate a story on Islamic fundamentalists."

"I think he's chasing the people who bombed the World Trade Center in ninety-three."

"Well, I'd love to stay here and watch *Extra!* with you, but I'm having dinner with Claire and her parents at their apartment uptown."

"And I'm going downstairs to White Castle," Gus says, standing up with some slight effort, then grabbing his wallet and keys. "I swear I could eat twenty of those burgers at a time. By the way, don't wear any of your weird Diesel shit."

"Thanks. I was *hoping* for your fashion input."

"Because their apartment is really nice."

He's out the door before I realize what he's just said.

CLAIRE GREETS ME at the door looking absolutely lovely in a simple black cocktail dress. She gives me a quick kiss and leads me into her family's apartment. I briefly met Mr. and Mrs. Davis at Claire's (and my brother's) graduation, and they left an impression of warmth and repose, of earned ease. While my parents circled each other at a safe distance, like tired heavyweights, the Davises sat happily in the sun, enjoying the day. And tonight, seated in their living room, surrounded by framed family photographs and leather-backed books, they are even more striking. They look like poster children for tasteful urban middle age.

John Davis is a handsome man, maybe a decade older than my father. He's thin and tan and well turned-out in a sports jacket and tailored slacks. Claire's mother, in an untucked white blouse and black leggings, looks chic and alluring. She comes over and kisses me warmly on both cheeks, like I've just flown in from Paris.

"I love your apartment," I say.

"DeLillo had a wonderful expression about people's homes," Mr. Davis says. "He called them 'complex boxes where people do their living.' I've always thought that's about right."

"Dad, come on."

"Claire tells me you're doing some writing."

"A few articles for magazines, but I'm really just starting out."

"I think it's a noble pursuit, that life, because it's exactly that—a *pursuit*, the whole way along. The cold days and dead nights, the time spent alone, with your thoughts, yourself. I wish I had the strength to—"

"*Dad!*"

"Claire, I was just saying courage sometimes needs caressing. It's not easy finding your own voice, believe me."

It shapes up as that kind of evening, the talk floating from books to politics, celebrities to sports. We dissect the Paltrow–Pitt breakup, Princess Diana's upcoming auction at Christie's, and, of course, baseball, the great American middle ground. When the candles are low and the wine bottles have outnumbered the courses, Claire taps me under the table. We leave her parents framed in the front doorway, their arms around each other. Walking home, I tell Claire how lucky she is to have parents who are happy together, but she just shrugs and changes the subject. We're almost at her door when I remember something.

"Hey, has Gus ever been to your parents' apartment?"

"Why?"

"Because he said something about it. Have you thrown parties there before?"

"Do you really want to get into this now?"

"Get into what?"

She sighs and looks out toward the bridge. "We dated for a little while, Gus and I, before you two were friends. I was going to tell you, but . . ."

"Did . . . did you guys—"

"Look, it was a while ago, and it just wasn't a big deal. *At all.* I wanted to tell you but I didn't want to ruin anything with us. I *don't* want to ruin anything with us. Believe me, if I could change what happened, I would."

I've stopped walking. She tugs my arm but I don't move. She kisses me and I kiss her back, but all I can think about is my best friend and my girlfriend in some happy earlier incarnation, laughing and drinking and

"I think I'm going back to my place tonight," I say.

I'LL START THE ARTICLE the way it started in real life, with oily streets and foreboding alleys. I've gotten all the interviews professionally transcribed and now the pile of words is sitting on my desk, a foot high, along with various notes and articles. I spend the morning separating the big pile into smaller piles. I'm scared to start writing. I've got all these different accounts of the same story, and it takes a while for me to realize this is a good thing. I'll lay out all the evidence and let the reader decide what to believe.

Gus gets home from work around seven. I hear him come through the door like my father used to, with a loud exhale and the sound of keys thrown on a table. Two months ago I would have jumped up to greet him, but it's different these days. After a third eviction notice, Gus finally came clean and admitted he had no money. He had gotten behind, and now he owed people and couldn't see a way out. There is nothing more sobering than a man who has run out of options, and watching him confess was hard. I didn't want to get kicked out of my apartment—every day I was coming home half expecting a bar across the door—and I wanted to help him, too. There are only a few times in a friendship when you can step up and prove yourself, and this, surely, was one of them. So I loaned him money, and so did my father, who charged interest (parents love charging interest; the world has been doing it to them for decades). The crisis passed, at least temporarily, but the situation has changed. The balance of power that keeps friendships in sync has subtly shifted. Gus has retreated and so have I. The parties have stopped and the debates have ended and we've regressed into polite camaraderie—quick greetings and obvious jokes, sent out like test balloons to fill the space between us. And now comes the issue of Claire. And that might not be as fixable.

"Are you in there?" Gus calls out, opening my door before I can answer.

"Hey," I say, not quite looking up.

"Working on the article? Read me the first paragraph."

"Okay. 'It's a brisk spring day in Chinatown. The cold gray clouds that have hovered for weeks over New York have finally lifted to reveal the beginnings of a fragile new season, a—'"

"You can't start with the weather. Everyone does that."

"Thanks. Anything else?"

"Just this." He throws me a magazine with Jewel on the cover. It's *Time*.

Sixteen

WHEN I FIRST STARTED at Leland's, Josh told me the auction world revolved around three things: debt, divorce, and death. Recently, I've added another *D*: disappointment. The disappointment of finding out your heroes aren't who they seem. The other day, one of them—his poster once hung above my bed—showed up to sell his World Series ring for cash. Last spring my father's favorite ballplayer called to consign some old signed checks he'd found in his attic. But nothing prepared me for this morning. There on my crowded desk was a small plastic bag filled with Mickey Mantle's hair, dyed brown to hide the gray. And more: his passport, reading glasses, credit and casino cards, bathrobe, golf clubs, hotel keys (?), neck brace, and a collection of his prescription medicine bottles. These aren't an icon's memorabilia; they're a man's remains.

Josh is eating breakfast in his office, and he grins when I walk in: "You're too predictable."

"We can't sell Mickey Mantle's *hair*. Isn't there some line, somewhere, that we can proudly say we won't cross?"

"I didn't hire you for your critical commentary."

"How do we even know it's—"

"Because it all comes from his agent, who just happened to be his live-in girlfriend, as well."

"Convenient."

"We're selling his boat and his condo in Georgia, too. Along with the rest of the shit he had lying around when he died. Don't worry, she's giving a bunch of the proceeds to charity, so just go back to your hole and start working."

I try to write about Mantle for a while, but it's too depressing. What is there to say about an American idol who spent the last half of his life reliving the first half, night after night, in one barroom after another? There was an evening, maybe fifteen years ago, when my parents came home late from the city and said they'd seen Mickey Mantle walking down the street. My mother was tucking me into bed, gushing like a schoolgirl as she told me how he'd smiled when he caught her staring, and I fell asleep with the warm knowledge that my parents had heroes, too. But now his hair is on my desk. The century's most gifted ballplayer drank himself to death, but apparently not before leaving his wife and kids in Texas and moving to some prefab golf community with his agent, who managed to keep him sober enough to sign baseballs and bats at $300 to $500 apiece, until the pen ran out of ink. If only we never knew the other side. If only the memories meant more than the merchandise. But we do it to ourselves. Needing heroes, we give them too much, then watch them slowly strangle themselves with all the rope.

I exercise my freelancer rights and leave. The *Black Book* article is due in two days and I want to write one more draft—my fifth—because I don't know how to tell if it's done. I walk home and spend the day fine-tuning my story, happy to be creating, not recycling, and hoping this bright future of words might open up to me, if only so I can stop recounting sad pasts.

TOWARD THE END of August, Claire and I drive up to spend a long weekend with her parents at their summer home on Cape Cod. It's an attractive, understated house wedged between sprawling compounds—the Bingham publishing family on one side, the Johnson (& Johnson) clan on the other. Claire and I hit tennis balls back and forth, watch cloudless sunsets, and talk nonstop of the city we've left behind. Last week, after two months spent searching for a job in publishing, Claire interviewed with a top buyer for Bergdorf's, an older gay man with framed photographs of trophy boys littering his office. She must have been wearing something great, because he offered her a job right away. She thought about it—the clothes, the discounts, the whole allure of high fashion—and quickly said yes. She'd try publishing in a year or two, when she'd gained some experience, made some money. She sounded so sensible, taking life as it came, and as another sun disappeared below the horizon, I wondered if my lack of literary output was a result of putting too much pressure on myself. No, I decided, it was more a question of confidence.

On Saturday we walk over to the Johnson house for lunch. It's an old-world estate with a wide back lawn that rolls down to a bay. Children are everywhere, bounding around semiforgotten, like pets. It's barely noon but wine is being poured and sandwiches nibbled, and people with ruddy cheeks and wealthy voices wander in and out of the screened-in porch, serving themselves and saying, "Hello, great to see you," just in case I'm a relative. I stick by Claire, whom everyone loves because she's *not* related, not tangled up in whatever generational complications burden families like these. The older set switches to liquor around two. The women stir their unmixed drinks and ask Claire wistful questions about New York, while the men, in plaid shirts and knee-length shorts, leer too long at her tanned torso. Some of the Johnson kids are selling lemonade at the end of the driveway, so I wander between the houses and across the yard and give fifty cents to a girl with a trust fund the size of Kansas.

I handed in "The Fashion Police" the day before I came up here. It was almost 5,000 words long and I couldn't let it go. I kept making changes, words here and there, but soon the many small edits started requiring larger ones. I was working backward. Finally Claire put me in a cab and sent me down to Prince Street, where I nervously gave it to Kevin, then went to Fanelli's and drank shots at the bar. I *think* it was well written. I think it was hard-hitting and fair. It was full of lurid detail and sensory description, and the accompanying photos were grainy black-and-white street shots taken by a professional photographer using a fish-eye lens.

I wander back past the house and down to the water lapping peacefully against a weathered dock. Two clam diggers are raking the bottom of the bay, and I wave to them because everyone waves when they're near water. As I watch them work I imagine the impending media sensation as "The Fashion Police" gets picked up by more mainstream outlets, then afforded a second life of NPR interviews and TV talk shows and—

"Are you with someone, dear, or just lost?" It's one of the ladies from the porch. I didn't hear her walk up.

"I'm sorry," I say. "I'm Claire Davis's boyfriend." It feels strange defining myself like that, so *completely*. "We're up from New York."

"And what does one do in New York these days?"

"One tries to write."

"Ahhh," she says. "We have plenty of those around here. At some point families with money become families with artists. You must know my nephew Robert Bingham."

"I don't think so."

"He's our best hope at the moment. He lives in TriBeCa, above a burlesque club. That's the way to do it: Stay close to the edge or you begin to lose it. Anyway, he runs a wonderful literary journal called *Open City*. You should send him a story to publish."

"I'm sure it's not that easy," I say, wondering how this older woman knows more about the downtown literary scene than I do.

"You'd be surprised. Robert fretted for years about people reading his stories, and when he finally sent them out everyone loved them. Even *The New Yorker* published a few. You should buy his book, *Pure Slaughter Value*. It's a tawdry little collection, filled with addiction, infidelity, and a proclivity for failure. He mined the family, of course, stripped us bare, but I suppose that's inevitable. At least he changed our names."

"I'll look him up," I tell her, as she ambles off to join the array of bodies migrating toward boats. For a few minutes I watch drunk men tangle themselves in ropes and sails, then make my way back up the lawn, where I run into Claire.

"Where have you been?" she asks. "I had to get out of that house. Everyone's hammered and it's not even four o'clock. And one of the Johnson kids was crying because he sliced his finger open and couldn't find a Band-Aid."

"Didn't that family, like, invent Band-Aids?"

"Does everything always have to *mean* something with you?"

Dinner: Nantucket bay scallops and finely seared tuna and white wine served two bottles at a time. Mrs. Davis keeps shuttling back and forth to the kitchen, and every time she sits down or gets up, Mr. Davis stands until she's either settled or gone. The first few times I'm caught off-guard and manage to stand only as he is sitting back down, but now I'm on the edge of my chair, anticipating moves from the female side.

"How did the crime article turn out?" Mr. Davis asks, filling our glasses again.

"I'm not sure. I kept thinking I had to get it perfect."

"Did you use a nom de guerre?"

"Pardon?"

"A pseudonym."

"A fake name," Claire says. "No, he didn't. And he didn't change any of the Mafia people's names either."

"I think the bad guys have bigger things to worry about," I say. "The Giuliani era hasn't been too good for business."

"That reminds me," Mr. Davis says. "There's an interesting story in this month's *Vanity Fair* about the mayor having an affair with one of his—"

"Oh, John, everyone has affairs," Mrs. Davis says, cutting in casually.

"I think the mayor is weird and asexual," Claire says.

Mrs. Davis leans in toward me. "What does Gus say? Don't you live with him?" I glance over at Claire, who is staring at her mother.

"He works for the police department now, but he's mentioned it before . . . the affair. He was surprised the press didn't pick up on it sooner."

"Maybe they don't like messing with people's private lives," Claire says.

"How is Gus?" her mother asks. "He's so funny. John, do you remember—"

"Dear, let's drop it."

"Thank you, dad," Claire says, standing up to clear the plates. Her father stands just before I do, and I gather what's left and join my girlfriend in the kitchen.

"I don't know what she's doing," Claire says.

"How well do they know Gus?"

"He had dinner with them a few times, but my dad thinks he's shady."

"He is shady."

"I thought he was your best friend."

"Has he been up to *this* house?"

"*No.* Here, take some ice cream with you, and watch out. My mother is getting drunk."

I rejoin Mr. and Mrs. Davis sitting in silence at opposite ends of the table. She's looking out the window, though it's too dark to see the water. Mr. Davis stands as Claire comes in to sit, then sits down and is about to start eating when his wife asks if I'd like to join her on the patio for a cigarette. I'm not sure how to play this one, but a cigarette sounds good, and having her on the patio might allow her husband to eat his dessert in peace, so I follow her outside.

"How are *your* parents?" she asks.

"Well, they're divorced, but otherwise I think they're fine."

"Claire told me about them. I think your mother is very brave to walk away from everything like that."

"I suppose so," I say, warily.

"John and I were separated once, for over a year, but I didn't have the courage to leave for good." She hands me a cigarette, then takes one for herself.

"Well, there's something to be said for staying together."

"Like what?"

"Can I light that for you?"

Mrs. Davis takes a drag, then walks over to a bench and picks up a book I brought up with me. It's a novel about the East Village in the eighties, peopled with squatters, street artists, and heroin dealers—not exactly the sort of book you'd like your girlfriend's mother leafing through on a soft summer night.

"This reminds me of the Mudd Club," she says. "And Max's Kansas City."

"You went to Max's Kansas City?"

"Everyone used to go there. We'd get a table in the back, a big group of us, drinking and smoking and waving to Warhol. Claire was still a baby and back then John liked to do things. Now it's all so . . . inane."

I'm not sure if she's talking about the New York social scene or her marriage. I can see Claire and her father through the window. She's pulled her chair over by his, and has her hand on his arm. Mrs. Davis finishes the rest of her drink, stubs out her cigarette, and starts blowing out bug candles. Then I follow her inside and there's another series of ups and downs as Mrs. Davis sits and Claire goes back to the kitchen.

"I didn't know you were smoking again," Mr. Davis says.

"Oh, John, stop it."

I pour more wine (the fourth bottle?) and swirl it in my glass.

"Why don't you take David golfing tomorrow?"

"*Mom!*" Claire shouts from the kitchen.

"Or go water skiing or play tennis. Isn't that what most families do on vacation? All we do is sit around reading and—"

"Drinking," Mr. Davis says.

His wife gets up and walks out of the room, not defiantly, not gracefully, not slowly. She just leaves. For the first time since I've met him, John Davis stays seated. He looks tired of being polite.

Claire finishes the dishes, kisses her father good night, and goes upstairs. I join Mr. Davis in the living room for a nightcap. He pours two glasses of tawny port and we sink into the comfortable white couches, surrounded by books and model boats and the sound of wind whipping through screens. I'd been looking forward to a moment like this since I met him, a late-night drink in the drawing room with a real man of letters, a man who understands the choices to be made. But we've mistimed it and life has intervened.

Mr. Davis asks about baseball again. I describe the overnight bus rides and Appalachian ghost towns. I tell him about the long hours spent at the ends of dugouts, my eyes roaming half-filled bleachers, my thoughts leaking toward the future, New York and the life that might be mine if I would just get on with it. I'm thinking he'll say something clever about romantic notions or frivolous youth, but he just nods and lets the words settle. Then he stands up, says good night, and walks down the hall toward his bedroom, his head held high in uxorious optimism, hoping, I suppose, for the best.

Upstairs Claire is curled up on the bed, still in her clothes. Her tears have dried and the makeup under her eyes has run. I lie down beside her, wrap my arm around her shoulder. I'm almost asleep when she takes my hand in hers.

"I told you," she whispers. "They're just as messed up as everyone else."

"They're fine."

"My mother can't watch him get old."

"You never told me they separated."

"She told you that?" Claire says, sitting up.

"Right before telling me about Warhol and the Mudd Club."

"Oh, God. It's her way of saying she married too early. Sometimes I think they shouldn't have gotten back together, that they'd both be happier apart, like your parents."

We take our clothes off and hold each other under sheets that smell fresh, like they've been dried outdoors.

I used to think things would be different if I came from a family like this one, where parents quote DeLillo at dinner and see art as a kind of ultimate achievement. But trouble, it seems, lurks behind every sturdy door, and more and more it's Tolstoy who comes to mind. If every unhappy family is indeed unhappy in its own way, as a whole they've become sadly ubiquitous. What if we actually had it right back in boarding school? What if commitment to anything more than oneself really is a failed concept? Certainly I've been living that way. But where is it getting me? Sometimes I look around and wonder if we're all headed for our own generational failure, a kind of reactionary idleness. We're all trying so hard not to be our parents that we're backing ourselves into isolated corners. But I don't want to be alone.

Claire shudders as she falls asleep. For the first time, I think I belong with someone. I've fallen in love with her, and not just for her mind or looks, but because of how she makes me feel—about myself, about the world. It seems a better place these days. Up here on the second floor the cool breeze rattles the windows and the house creaks and cracks and settles in for the night. A complex box indeed.

IN MAGAZINE SHOPS in September it is possible to find Princess Diana's face on fifty different covers. Her death has set in motion the predictable media frenzy that accompanies disaster—the speculation and blame, the "royal experts," the secret boyfriends and unsavory relatives.

The fall issue of *Black Book*, with Fiona Apple sprawled across the cover, is a welcome diversion. It's prominently displayed beside *Vanity Fair*, and I tear through until I find my article. It's almost exactly as I'd envisioned. There's even a bio at the end: *New York writer David Goodwillie worked briefly as a private investigator for Kroll Associates. A former minor league baseball player, he is currently a contributing editor for* Black Book *magazine.* I'm on the masthead, too, alongside David Mamet, Robert Mapplethorpe, and Gerard Malanga. *New York writer David Goodwillie. . . .* I buy a bunch of copies and look around the store, dying to tell someone I'm out there now, viable, but everyone is busy reading about Diana.

I head downtown to celebrate with Ken because Claire is still at work. Ken lives with his girlfriend, Anne, in a one-bedroom walk-up on St. Marks between Second and Third. It's an all-day carnival of a block, the noisiest in Manhattan, and its vintage shops, tattoo parlors, and rock clubs attract a steady stream of blunt-smoking hip-hop kids, postpunk leather boys with Kings Road mohawks, and goth girls with jet-black hair and piercings that weren't worth the pain.

I buzz Ken's apartment and thirty seconds later he's bounding down the stairs.

"Just in time. I had to get out of there. That place is too small for both of us."

"It's going that well?"

"Never make a movie with someone you're supposed to still love afterward."

I give him a copy of *Black Book* and he flips to the story.

"Cool," he says, sticking it in his coat. But I want him to read it *now*; I want him to stop and read every word, absorb each one, linger over the language, its impact, its implications. . . .

"*Moving In/Moving Out* was accepted into the Mill Valley Film Festival in San Francisco. It's one of the best in the country, right up there with Sundance, and we have a feature slot. You should come out with us, leave New York for a few days."

"How about selling it to a studio?"

"That's what the festivals are for. We did sell the Hungarian rights to HBO, which is better than nothing. You might catch it if you're staying at a hotel in Budapest."

We make our way past the sidewalk vendors outside his front door and start walking down the Bowery, past Cooper Union and the *Village Voice* building, past modern-furniture shops and one-word lounges. There's a construction site on almost every corner. Gone are the flophouses and movie halls of Joseph Mitchell's day. The sailors and streetwalkers have been replaced by young professionals. Outside the Sunshine Hotel, a lone holdout where beds still rent for $13 a night, three old men on milk crates stare as a girl in a miniskirt walks past. She's wearing an "Edie" T-shirt and has an NYU book bag slung over her shoulder. She doesn't even notice them.

We walk to M&R on Elizabeth. It's six thirty, safely cocktail hour, so we grab a seat at the half-filled bar and order vodka tonics. A pretty DJ is spinning Oakenfold. I light a cigarette and watch as she sways to some back-beat we'll all be hearing a song from now. Ken starts railing against his latest adversaries: film producers.

"They're like leeches," he says. "They attach themselves to other people's stories and then don't let go. And they're *applauded* for it. Today, the reward comes not from creating something from nothing, but from adapting, making an art form economically viable. We've become a society that champions the second guy in. Do you know there are sixty-two new millionaires every day in Silicon Valley alone? *Sixty-two!* And every one of them is a potential producer. You help make a movie by funding it, and suddenly you're just as much an artist as the poor sap who wrote the screenplay. You're—" Ken stops and looks around. "I just remembered. I came here on my first date with Anne. Perfect. I've been trying to get away from her all day and I come to the bar where the whole thing started. That's how it always is: escape to a desert and the silence shouts in your ear."

"Who said that?"

"Who said what?"

"What you just said. About the desert." I remember it from somewhere, a book I've read—Graham Greene, maybe, or Maugham. Anyway, it's too good to have come from one of my friends.

Ken shrugs and finishes his drink. "Let's go to Max Fish," he says.

I think we're in for a long night.

KEN IS RIGHT: Somehow the main event in America has become what happens *after* the spectacle, after the home runs are hit, the movies made, the Band-Aids sold. We're a country that argues over remains, a sad lineup of lawyers and accountants and multiple spouses, of wealth managers and spin doctors and image consultants who always manage to drown out the original accomplishment. Maybe it's the ever rising tide of capitalism—the lure of bigger and better—that grabs us by the collar and shakes the innocence away, wedding ambition to success instead of achievement. Creation has become an introduction, a prelude to a lawsuit, an excuse for an entourage.

I want to write a morality tale about an artist who doesn't compromise, who creates for the challenge of the act itself, not the economic afterlife. I've been talking to my editor at *Black Book* about writing fiction, and for the last few weeks ideas have been gathering in my mind like mosquitoes before sleep, buzzing quite close but never long enough to be caught. I hear again and again that the best stories are just that: *stories*. But I still think writing, art, must *mean* something—to the audience *and* writer. It's a quaint notion, I know, especially these days, as we hurl ourselves toward the millennium . . . but is there a better challenge, a better life, than creating your version of the world in words? The beginning of every story is a blank screen with a faint reflection of the writer.

The following evening I start typing. Maybe all I needed was a takeoff point to help me focus: *an artist who doesn't compromise.* . . . Her name is Jensen Phipps. She's a young fashion designer struggling with illusions and compromises, the taints of her talent. The Empire State goes dark at midnight, but I press on, not caring that the words are poorly costumed personal experiences, blurred snapshots of the people who have passed through my life. I write until 3:00 A.M., write five, six, seven pages, a *first draft*, then bleary-eyed and feeling almost chemically euphoric, I save what I've got and slump into bed. It has taken three years to write my first New York story.

I'm thinking, maybe dreaming, about how I got so far off track when the phone rings. It's the middle of the night. It could be Claire, but she has work tomorrow. Or maybe it's for Gus, some late night police emergency.

"Hello?"

"Is this David Goodwillie?"

"Who's this?"

"We know where you live, you little fuck."

"Hello?"

"Why couldn't you just mind your own business?"

"Come on. Who is this?"

"Watch your fucking back."

THERE HAVE BEEN three more calls since that first one. More than a dozen if you count the hang ups. It's always the same outer-borough accent, warning me to be careful. Before he hung up the last time, there was a loud bashing sound, which must have been the receiver hitting the pay-phone wall. On my end it sounded like a sledgehammer. I haven't told anyone—not Claire or Gus or my editor at *Black Book*. Instead I pretend it isn't happening. But the calls keep coming and I've started lying awake, envisioning violent ends. I curse myself for using real names, then, bolstered by the daylight, congratulate myself in the morning for telling it like it is. Maybe it's a stupid prank, some idiot from Queens who read my article and is having a little fun. Why would the real Mafia screw with someone like me?

Still, I can't walk down the street without looking over my shoulder, so I visit a friend at Kroll, an operative who specializes in the more clandestine areas of the business—wiretapping, surveillance, Third World revolutions. . . . We meet in the back of a cop bar on Second Avenue, and though he says he's familiar with my article (everyone at Kroll has been reading it, with varying degrees of enthusiasm), he goes through it again, circling names, making margin notes.

"This really isn't bad," he says, when he's finished. "It's an interesting read, but the problem is you've mentioned names you shouldn't have mentioned. Including your own. It's fairly out of character for the Mob to go after the media, but it has been done before, and in situations like this. The general rule is it's acceptable to write about murder trials and all that glossed-up history—the John Gottis and Chin Gigantes—but exposing a source of revenue is asking for trouble."

"So what should I do? Should I call the cops or tap my phone or—"

"That won't do any good. If they wanted to get you they would. But I think they're just fucking with you. Try to ignore it. They'll move on eventually. One way or another."

I TAKE HIS ADVICE, but it doesn't work. Every day New York is becoming smaller and more amplified, threats hovering on every block, in doorways, on loading docks, in passing cars. Voices come up behind me, loud, close, and my heart pounds until they pass, harmlessly, just two old men in suspenders, talking of the weather.

At dinner with Claire at Odeon, at Rialto, at Bar Pitti, I sit against the wall, facing the door, so I can see the room, the people, the looming danger. We're doing well at playing grown-up. We eat out most nights after long days of working. Claire is always late, bustling in from Bergdorf's in her discounted designer suits and fresh makeup applied in the cab. There is nothing more attractive than energy, and Claire has it in spades. Her thoughts go deep and her ambitions are complex. There aren't enough hours for her, not enough stories, and so she talks, meaningfully, the way she should, the way couples do, except I'm looking around the room, studying faces—the loud group at the bar, the guy with the earring loitering near the hostess stand. I can't let my guard down, can't pretend for a second that the threat isn't real—

"Are you listening?" she asks, one night at Jules.

I can't focus on anything or anyone else. I feel like the next victim in a horror movie, hapless and pale, counting down the scenes. And so I tell her. I give her a watered-down version of events, mostly the hang ups and heavy breathing, and with eyes wide and suddenly very young, she starts asking tentative questions about a world that has never crossed her mind.

But it continues to cross my mind, to consume it. I try to stay busy. I work on my Jensen Phipps story. At Leland's the Mantle sale comes and goes in a predictable sea of bad press, and I start writing up the next auction. When the phone rings in the apartment, I let Gus get it, because they seem to recognize his voice and hang up. Maybe they know he works for the cops. Gus thinks it's some girl he's slighted, and I don't tell him otherwise. Instead I stay upstairs, hiding in fiction, and sometimes it works, until the phone rings again and that other world—the one where I cower in corners and take taxis even three blocks—comes swiftly back.

WHEN A FRIEND INVITES you to a film festival in California while the Mob is after you in New York, you pack your bags and go. I can't get on the plane fast enough. I'm traveling with a friend named Casey, who seems to think Ken Hamm is a young Spielberg. Casey is one of those tall, blond-haired Fifth Avenue kids who still have the shaggy hair and frayed wardrobe that give their prep-school background away. He talks quickly, in nervous fits and starts, and I've never seen him sit still—the result, perhaps, of his stressful job as a midlevel producer at HBO. Still, he's good-natured and friendly, and just the kind of person to disappear with.

I've never been to San Francisco. People out here live in houses with windows on all sides, offering views of wide bays and long bridges that reflect the sun. They run and surf and ride bicycles up and down trolley-car hills. They walk their dogs in clean parks and throw Frisbees higher and farther than anyone in New York. Casey and I descend upon our friend Lisa, a bohemian schoolteacher who lives in The Avenues near Golden Gate Park. We find bikes in her garage and set off across the city, hill-riding through Haight-Ashbury, now a touristy tribute to its former self; through the dilapidated Tenderloin, with its porn theaters and pawn shops; through the Mission, the Castro, Nob and Russian Hills, Market Street, North Beach . . . the whole city in a day. And everywhere we go one theme runs through the streets, the buildings, the billboards. It is, of course, the Internet, an omnipresent force hanging over this boomtown like a massive electric thunderhead, its size dwarfed only by its potential, the vibrant volts of energy that course its innards. Everywhere we look, people are carrying logo laptop bags, wearing company polo shirts, talking in bursts of evangelical zeal. Cybercafés are sprouting on every corner, bus stops tout Apple computers and Pentium processors; even the cars carry advertising, whizzing every which way in a blur of neon marketing.

"San Fran is a year and a half ahead of us," Casey says, authoritatively, answering a question I haven't asked. We're at the top of another hill, and the city stretches out before us in all directions. Casey points south, past Candlestick Park barely visible in the humid afternoon haze. "The real action is down there, in the Valley. Sun, Cisco, Intel, eBay . . . They're all there, stretched out like a rubber band along Highway 101 from Redwood City to San Jose."

"Is Oracle down there?"

"Sure. I think they have their own small city."

We stand there, on top of that hill, and look off into the distance like explorers happening upon some foreign civilization, the wired civilization, my so-called generation, exploding out here without me. On the tiring ride back to Lisa's house, Casey treats me to a rambling discourse about delivery platforms and streaming video and the imminent arrival of something called convergence. I try my best to listen.

Ken's screening is tonight. We get home and shower and Lisa drives us over the Golden Gate toward Mill Valley. Casey, riding shotgun, is still going strong, fogging up the windshield with talk of satellites and Web TV and a world without commercials.

"There's Alcatraz," Lisa says, hoping Casey might get the hint, but he doesn't stop until we're in the postcard suburbs of Marin County. The theater is on one of the main streets, and there's a crowd out front, velvet ropes, cars double-parked. It's kind of like the real thing. The marquee sparkles with the words *Moving In/Moving Out* and I'm briefly overwhelmed with pride for my long-suffering friend. As we walk up, he's doing an interview under the lights, and I pause to watch his dreams come true in real time.

From a seat in the VIP section (as yet the only return on my investment), I watch the theater fill with high-strung dot-commers. As the lights go down Ken slips into the seat next to me. "I bet most of these people moved out here from New York," he whispers. "Maybe they're here to remind themselves of the authenticity they left behind." For ninety minutes the hard streets of the East Village slide by on-screen. True believers with scarred hearts and tattooed arms hold forth on love and art and passion, and when the show is done a round of generous applause turns quickly into a standing ovation. The entire theater is clapping, whistling, turning toward Ken. His eyes well with tears and he stands and waves back. Bonnie Raitt, here with her film-producer husband, comes over and hugs him. The cheers of strangers must be the most honest of satisfactions, and yet I can't help thinking some of the applause is for New York as well, that forgone town that's a year and a half behind. It's still a real place, where I live, and sometimes, alone in their halogen cubicles, surrounded by business plans and wealth equations, these true-believing transplants must miss that.

Seventeen

AFTER A MONTH of writing, my flimsy ode to artistic expression has morphed into a sardonic, sexually charged cultural thriller. Jensen Phipps, my brave young heroine, shocks the fashion world by flying porn stars in from L.A. to model her skimpy couture dresses on the runways of Seventh on Sixth. Sure, it's a publicity stunt, but her real aim is pure. Jensen is trying to tear down the boundaries between the two worlds. She's been around long enough now to know that high fashion is just pornography dressed up. What she's fighting is hypocrisy.

The timing is right. This is the age of Courtney Love, of *Boogie Nights*. AIDS is out, sex is in, and Bill Clinton's America is ready to be liberated. In the story, Jensen befriends Mandy Mynx (naming porn stars is too easy), a beautiful, barely twenty adult-film star who dreamed of modeling in New York but took a wrong turn and found herself on the other coast, lending her body to far more explicit fantasies than Calvin and Giorgio could ever muster. Jensen and Mandy, the artists of the moment: their worlds collide under the bright lights and crowded tents of Bryant Park, and as both women's dreams are realized and the publicity engine ignites its firestorm, Jensen's brash act delivers its message and the culture shifts perceptibly.

I tinker and tamper and finally deliver my three-thousand-word tour de force to the *Black Book* offices in early December. I have no idea what they'll think. It's still a long shot, considering they've never published fiction before. And with the exception of the subjects themselves, "The Fashion Police" hasn't attracted any undue attention—no fan letters, no media mentions. It's just come and gone, leaving me with nothing but threatening phone calls and the fear that my writing might not be as enthralling as I'd imagined. It is a shock, then, a delightful shock, when Kevin calls back a few days later to say he loves the whole Jensen Phipps thing. He wants to publish it as *Black Book's* first short story. He offers only $200 but promises far greater riches in terms of exposure. And he's not lying. He says he's putting together a glossy photo shoot to accompany my words, a spread featuring real-life porn stars—all the big Valley names: Jenna Jameson, Juli Ashton, maybe even Chasey Lain—wearing racy evening wear straight from the runways of New York and Milan.

"Imagine it," he says. "How many writers see their stories played out in pictures? It's all too perfect: fashion and fiction, sex and style, New York and L.A. Everyone here loves the idea. We're booking the talent already, trying to get a shoot together in Hollywood in the next ten days. It's such a great synergy, a true merging of mediums."

"Do you need me to fly out for the—"

"No."

I'VE STARTED WRITING at Claire's apartment. I lie there half awake as she gets ready for work, watching her run around in a frenzy of activity—coffee, eyeliner, stockings, NPR, dry-cleaning receipts, missing hair ties, credit card left at the bar at Rosa Mexicana. . . . It's a dance of memory, these few minutes in the morning, and most things get only half done before something else is remembered, and the entire time she's groaning as she looks at her watch and thinks of her boss, there since 7:00 A.M., waiting to tell her about Luke or Cyril or Jason. It's like watching a private rehearsal, an actress alone with her talents, before the props and people swoon in and surround her. Here she is, naked, weary, indecisive, vain. And beautiful. Women are most beautiful in the morning, in the act of transformation. Occasionally I can coax her back to bed, and we'll have sex or just lie there for a few minutes, entwined, watching dust hang in the air while water runs in the bathroom or the coffee pot sizzles ominously, but we'll stay there, finish the moment. That's my definition of love.

I write in her living room, with the sun streaming in through the tall windows. The bridge traffic hums its urban chorus, the city version of those nature sounds people sleep to. One morning, toward the end of January, Claire calls from Bergdorf's and tells me to turn on the TV. She says something about the president.

This is the morning America first hears the name Monica Lewinsky.

Even in the early hours of the scandal it's easy to envision what's coming: O. J. was a primer. The hours become days; the days become weeks. The scandal outgrows itself, becomes a kind of cultural endgame, something akin to what George Trow promised two decades ago. The story splinters, the branches filling with opportunists: Ginsburgs and Goldbergs and high school drama teachers from back home. Villains emerge: the beastly Linda Tripp, trying to escape her own skin; the robotic Ken Starr, shuffling down his driveway with his coffee, denying the very existence of temptation. And then, finally, Clinton himself, ensnared in his own nets, grinning through his lies, winking at America. I watch news during the day; Claire watches with me at night. We gossip at dinner parties, trade rumors at bars. We become addicted to developments. Soon it's difficult to step back, to see past the headlines to the real story, America sinking into a crevice formed by aftershocks. Gus would see the big picture. He'd be running upstairs to find a quote from some book, prattling on about the disillusionment, impurity, and incontinence that make up our generation, a generation defined by cyberspace, a place that doesn't exist.

Or maybe I'm just putting words in his mouth. I don't know what he thinks anymore; I'm almost never home. It's not safe there. The threatening phone calls subsided around Christmas, and for a few weeks I thought it was over. Then I walked outside to grab a sandwich at the corner deli and I noticed a man watching me from behind the wheel of a sedan parked across the street. He got out and started following me. I was well aware that perceived threats breed unnecessary fear—I had been walking around the city for weeks with the shifty eyes of a parole jumper—and as I ducked into the deli, I thought deep down that he'd keep going, that this was only a coincidence. But he came inside; he *was* following me. I watched him in the round shoplifting mirror. He walked slowly up one aisle and I walked quickly down the other. I couldn't breathe. Phone calls were one thing, but a man following me around was quite another. I hurried outside and back around the corner toward my building. This whole situation was so absurd. I almost wanted to turn around and tell this guy how much of a nobody I was, tell him I was just a confused kid piecing together an existence, squiring dreams around town. And yet I still thought that maybe, somehow, this was all some horrid joke. When I reached my door, he was back across the street, standing next to his car. We looked at each other. He was short and had a big neck. He had marks on his face. His coat was black and his car was brown. This is what I remember. And then he pointed at me, made a gun with his thumb and index finger, and he fired. I walked inside and threw up in the stairwell. So much for journalistic stardom.

I still haven't told Gus. I've just bunkered down at Claire's and tried to forget about that face. I'm becoming fatalistic: I can't control whoever is out there, so what's the sense in worrying? Of course, that's easier said than done. But as the days have passed and the phone has stopped ringing, I've started to believe the whole thing may be over and that the man in the car was a kind of grand finale.

When I do go home, it's with reluctance. The rent crisis has passed—I write the monthly check for both of us and Gus leaves his half in cash—but the place is a mess. Chairs and couches are piled high with coats, sweaters, and unopened mail. The plates and bowls in the sink have become a playground for the mice. The carpet is gray and stained in places, like a sidewalk. And until last week, several months' worth of Gus's daily papers (he reads them all, every morning) were stacked in yellowing floor-to-ceiling piles near the front door. One night I told him the mice were attracted to the pulp, and it worked: a day later the piles were gone. The mice, of course, have stayed on, defiant, like tenants on rent control. For a while I kept thinking all this was just a phase, a pride thing, and that my old friend and I would head up to Clarke's on a blustery Saturday afternoon and air out our petty grievances over Frankie's Bloody Marys. It would be like it was before. Before it all came apart. Girls, money, jealousy, trust. And I always thought our problem would be politics.

ONE AFTERNOON KEN calls me at Leland's with a unique proposition. The last one cost me $5,000, so it is with trepidation that I inquire about the nature of this latest opportunity.

"We could share a writing office in SoHo. I've been working there on my new script for the last month, and I need someone to split the rent. It's a great space, only a hundred and fifty dollars each."

"How about selling the first movie before you write the second?"

"Soon. But the new script is even better. It's about a college football player who gets hooked on steroids. It's really dark, kind of a *Jacob's Ladder* meets *Apocalypse Now*, but on the gridiron."

"How come every new movie is a demented blend of two others?"

"Just get down here. It's called the Filmmaker's Collaborative and it's on Greene Street just south of Grand. I'll meet you outside at five."

On my way down, I stop by *Black Book* to go over a few changes to the Jensen Phipps story. Kevin's not there, but he's left an envelope for me. I open it outside, next to a confusing sculpture of a woman with sixteen breasts:

> D — What do you think of the title "Becoming X"? — It works on several levels.
>
> 1) Becoming X — As in beautiful X-rated starlets.
> 2) Becoming X — Malcolm X used the X because all other names marginalized him. The X is an identity starting at zero without judgments attached.
> 3) And, of course, a small minority of our audience will associate it with the title of the Sneaker Pimps record and KNOW we are cool.

I walk down Greene Street pondering this new batch of wisdom and find Ken sitting on the front steps of a recently renovated cast-iron building. I hand him Kevin's notes and ask him who the Sneaker Pimps are.

"I don't know," he says, skimming the page, "but this is just the title. Imagine what he'll do with the rest of the story."

"No, they're good like that. They barely changed a word of my Mafia article."

"We'll see," Ken says, standing up. We walk inside, past an unmanned reception desk, and down a flight of stairs to a damp basement. The office in question is at the end of a long hallway, past several spacious rooms filled with bleary-eyed people editing video on expensive-looking machines. Ken opens the door and turns on the light. The room is the size of a storage closet. Ken has wedged a small desk up against a windowless wall, and books and scripts are stacked precariously against one another. It's cold and wet and the carpet has water stains. It *is* the storage closet.

"I'm getting a space heater," Ken says. "It's really not bad for the price."

Someone's editing a scene on the other side of the wall and the words

Don't leave now, we can make this work drift through the wall on a seemingly endless loop.

"Shit," Kens says. "Reminds me of Anne."

"Not going so well?"

"I just can't *live* with her."

I think about that for a moment, about the days spent working at Claire's apartment and the slippery slide toward dependence, and suddenly this seems like some major moment. Claire and I are doing fine. We've learned to be a couple, to be comfortable in that second, blended life that relationships foster. We spend most nights together. We encourage each other. We take things seriously. But still, we're playing at being grown-ups, forcing ourselves to fit. The blended life is a settled life, and settled is not what I am. I still find myself clinging to pockets of freedom. And that tells me all I need to know.

"I think I'll join you down here," I say. "It'll be good for me."

I HAD ALWAYS vaguely trusted time, had believed that with enough of it, success as a writer would follow. Now, finally, I have it: two or three hard days at Leland's and I can spend the rest of the week typing away. But time is playing tricks. It's speeding up. I build sentences in the basement and the world flies past upstairs. I take the day shift; Ken comes in at night. And I quickly learn that writing stories isn't some glorious end; it's a lonely beginning. I sit in the cold and stare at the screen, trying to remember that perfect idea from late the night before, when I could in which I had written faces across a bar, fashion entire plots from the smallest bits of dialogue. But it's always different the next day. I write a paragraph, then delete it and start over. I want everything to be perfect, but I'm becoming increasingly aware that every thought can be written a hundred different ways. I'm learning not to trust myself. Even when an idea sticks around for a while, I'll write a few paragraphs and then stop, unable to continue for fear that these newly minted words—rife as they are with clichés, romance-novel descriptions, porn-level dialogue—are perhaps the worst yet conceived in the language. To continue would be more than a waste of time. It would be an insult to other writers, other noble beings sitting in rooms like this one, describing true and moving accounts of the human condition. How do people write *books*? How do they write fifty, one hundred, *two hundred* pages, without losing their nerve and turning back? Even "Becoming X" seems far away now, an unlikely exception that I can't recreate.

I start writing about an aging male model, washed up at twenty-eight and trying to reinvent himself in the nine-to-five world. But he's lived the high life for so long he can't come down, can't find himself beneath the chiseled exterior. It's based on a friend, of course, a former Boss model who plummeted from the runways of Milan to J. C. Penney shoots in Milwaukee. Now he's trying to catch on as a radio-station ad salesman. I like the idea of a model, the ultimate symbol of American materialism, reduced to hawking air, selling nothing. So I write scenes, labor over words, and sometimes, at the end of days, I think I might have something. Then I tear it all up the next morning—every last hackneyed sentence. Who am I kidding? A male fashion model searching for meaning? I become restless as the weeks go by, as the pages slowly pile up. Movies are being made in rooms down the hall, editors and producers moving in and out, starting and finishing. My magazine pieces were like that, supervised assignments with word counts, deadlines. There were boundaries and constraints. Here, alone, there is nothing but possibility, and that's too much to bear.

I learn to waste time. I spend hours leafing through screenplays Ken bought on the street. I fiddle with the space heater until it burns itself up. In the ensuing cold I become addicted to computer Solitaire, playing until I win, one, two, three, four games in a row. I read *The New Yorker* cover to cover, *voraciously*, like a born-again with a Bible. I call friends at work and keep them on the line for as long as possible. Some mornings, when I can see my breath, I get up and wander next door to warmer climes and watch the filmmakers in action. I sit with them as they argue and compromise, keep and cut, frame a story from raw footage. It's like writing: you find a voice, a style, a plot, and run with it, then cut off the rough edges until you're left with only the essence, the rounded center, wrinkle-free and ready-to-wear. Except *I* can't do that. I mix metaphors. I copy clichés. I say too much or too little. I show when I should tell, tell when I should just shut up.

When the weather warms up, my follies move outdoors. I spend hours browsing the used bookstores on West Broadway, the art galleries on

Broome. Sometimes I walk up to the Strand near Union Square and scour its dusty shelves for inspiration, for clues. I go to the fiction table toward the back, filled with paperback classics I should have read by now, and open to random pages, read sentences out of context. I want to know how stories work. I buy books and haul them back to the office like a squirrel gathering nuts for the hard times ahead. And I read them in the slow lost hours of early spring: McEwan's *Enduring Love*, DeLillo's *White Noise*, McInerney's *Brightness Falls*; short stories by Raymond Carver, Richard Ford, Louise Erdrich, Pam Houston. And at first, when I try to fill my own pages, I find myself imitating styles, bastardizing tempos and turns of phrase. But slowly, as the false starts pile up and one character after another dies a quick death of abandonment, I begin to find something like a rhythm. And so I keep at it, starting and stopping like the editors next door, until I can feel myself moving forward without looking back, without frowning at my reflection.

THE OFFICIAL END of my friendship with Gus comes in the form of a lease renewal that sits for weeks, unsigned and unmentioned, on the cluttered kitchen counter. But the real end came months ago, when life was piling up on us and we moved one way instead of another. Two years like brothers, and then when adversity struck, when the bond was finally tested, it dissolved like a bad chemistry experiment.

One last time we sit together in the living room, only now we're splitting up CDs and books and silverware and pretending we don't care. On MTV a VJ is talking out of the side of his mouth about Jewel's new book of poetry. I turn the channel. Friendships end in whimpers. On our last night together, I go up to Claire's. When I come back in the morning, Gus is gone. There's a check on the counter for everything he owed me. We never discussed his relationship with Claire.

Gus is moving into some huge place near Gramercy Park with people I don't know. I'm moving in with Ken Hamm. He broached the idea one night last month, when I was lamenting my imminent eviction. After a year of fighting, Anne was moving out. I could have the bedroom—their bedroom—and he would take the living room. It would be tight, but the combined rent was only $1,100. "Think about it," he said. "You can't even be homeless in New York for five fifty a month."

"But my bed won't even fit in that so-called bedroom."

"If Anne and I could do it—"

"But Anne and you couldn't do it."

"Well, the problem wasn't the apartment. . . ."

I knew it was a good idea, though. We both did. Sharing the basement office was working out well, so this was just a logical next step. Perhaps I should be wary of living with a good friend after what happened with Gus, but this is different. I think just being around Ken will be good for my writing, my *ethic*. And when it comes down to it, I can't beat the price . . . or the location.

Ken and I move Anne out on a rainy Saturday afternoon and replace her with a pared-down version of myself. The building, Ten St. Marks Place, is a filthy five-floor tenement the color of toxic smoke. A narrow hallway leads past my room, a miniature bathroom, and a refrigerator and sink and ends in the living room, Ken's room, the only place where I can stand with my arms outstretched and not touch a wall. There's a fireplace but it doesn't work, and anyway it's blocked by Ken's desk, a kind of cinematic shrine, covered with screenplay books and famous quotes jotted down on Post-its.

My new room is only big enough for a bed and an upright bureau, so I've given away my old furniture and the last of my Shelton-era clothing and am venturing forth with a capsule wardrobe of bare necessities. The room is four steps by three, and the floor slants severely. There is a window, but it's a bow-and-arrow slit that overlooks an airshaft, a black hole with no bottom. After a good deal of measuring it turns out the room *isn't* big enough for my bed, so I become a futon person. Every morning I fold the thing up so I have room to dress. I feel like I'm practicing for a motor home. I paint the walls and hang a few mirrors because I read in *Wallpaper** that mirrors make a room look bigger. But all they really do is magnify the smallness.

In the end, though, it's Ken's cat, a maniacal creature named Shakespeare, who makes life in my new home challenging. The thing has nails like knives. There'll be no sign of him for days (I think he lives inside the couch), and then, as I'm brushing my teeth or spreading cream cheese on a bagel, Shakespeare will come swooping down out of nowhere, like Cato in *The Pink Panther*, and attack. My arms and neck have become a landscape of wounds. I look like one of those people who cut themselves to excise the inner pain.

Like all scoundrels, Shakespeare acts like an angel when his meal ticket is around. He retreats to his hidden lair, and so does Ken, who buckles himself into his desk chair for the bumpy writing ahead. I say writing, but there really isn't much of that. He spends his time listing character traits on index cards, developing scenes on cardboard time lines, and underlining passages in his how-to books. He scowls and paces and usually, by the end, five or six hours in, he's worked himself into black exhaustion. I'd never seen this side of him before, the anguish taking over. Sometimes I hear shouting and cursing and I come running, thinking the cat has finally gotten him, too—pawed open a vein or scratched an eye—but Shakespeare is never around. It's just Ken, alone at his desk.

Then, a few days ago, he walled himself off. I came home and across from what had been open space between his room and the kitchen was a thin surface of Sheetrock. *Our* living room had become *his* bedroom. The tiny apartment had been halved, and my half was smaller. No more natural light, no more street noise. Ken was in there with the door locked. It was when I heard the shouting through the wall that I realized he wasn't locking me out. He was locking himself in.

ONE MORNING I WALK across the street to the magazine shop on the corner of St. Marks and Third. The spring issue of *Black Book* was supposed to hit the stands two weeks ago, and I've been diligently checking every day to no avail . . . until now! There it is, propped up in the front window, with Milla Jovovich staring out from the cover with searing blue eyes. I buy a bunch of copies and hurry back home. I turn the pages slowly, with reverence, until I come upon my story, on page ninety-one, opposite a close-up photo of a pouting Jenna Jameson, the most famous porn star in the world. "Becoming X": the first fiction piece in the magazine's brief history—not a bad launching pad for its clever young author. I imagine sending the story (and its accompanying pictures) out with my next effort, to editors at *The New Yorker*, *Atlantic Monthly*, *Harper's*. It certainly won't get lost in the slush pile. I flip the page and there's a naked girl named Janine, followed by Juli Ashton in a gold mesh dress (I remember her from

Playboy's *Night Calls*, an old 3:00 A.M. favorite when the drugs wouldn't
wear off). I turn the page again, hoping for Chasey Lain, but there's nothing else. No more pictures, no more words. That can't be it. There are only
two pages of writing. I flip back to the beginning and . . . and this is barely
my story at all. They've cut the thing in half. And someone's rewritten
what's left almost from scratch. The characters have the right names and
the scenes unfold more or less in sequence, but that's it. I start reading. I
feel lightheaded:

> The idea was out, and a fermata of silence hung in its place, during which
> the idea passed through each member of the Jensen Phipps inner circle.
> Some drew air through clenched teeth, some smiled, and those who were
> uncertain scanned the faces of the others, deciding where their allegiance
> would fall.
>
> Jensen shifted from leg to leg, twirling a piece of hair, playing the shy
> visionary part to perfection while waiting for her staff to accept the fact
> that instead of another brace of agency ciphers walking the runway this
> spring at Bryant Park, porn stars were going to model the Jensen Phipps
> couture line. . . .

The *shy visionary* thing is mine, but the rest . . . the rest is awful: . . . *another
brace of agency ciphers . . . a fermata of silence* . . . I don't even know what *fermata* means. I press on, feeling a slow burn in my chest. The story I slaved
over for weeks has been replaced by a jumbled mess of cheap literary money
shots: *swimming with the sharks on Seventh Avenue . . . stunning visage and
Damascus steel attitude . . . aware that this is not, as she thought, a case of
thrust, wipe and leave . . .* An entire plotline is missing. Someone named Ray
appears halfway through the second (and last) page. And the grammar: I
couldn't even send this to *Penthouse*.

The last time I spoke to Kevin, everything was fine. He said everyone was
behind "Becoming X" completely, that it was the kind of piece people
would be talking about for months. He told me they'd remember my name.
Well, there's my name all right, as bold as can be, attached to the worst short
story I've ever read.

I walk down the hall toward Ken's room, the only outside air.

"You find the magazine?" he asks, looking up from his monitor.

"Yes, but they fucked it all up."

"Let me see."

I give it to him, then walk over to the windows feeling cloudy. It's the same feeling I get at the end of a writing day, that transition between fiction and reality. Sometimes I can't tell the difference: My characters start walking the streets while my real friends litter the stories. I meet people for cocktails and am unable to think of words. One world saps energy from the other. I wonder if that's why so many novelists lead troubled lives.

"Shit," Ken says, shaking his head. "The first drink's on me."

AT 2:00 A.M. WE'RE STILL OUT. We've shifted gears and forgone the perils of art to focus on the hopelessness of relationships—Ken and Anne's in particular. He starts in on his emotional race to nowhere, a speed trial of intensity that ended the way they all end—with the inevitable crash. They had made a movie about love, Ken keeps saying, but couldn't get it right in real life because it was too hard to figure out where the acting stopped. On and on he goes, and I try to listen, I really do, but I keep thinking about Claire. We've been spending so much time together that it's disquieting when we're apart. A normal day spent alone or with other friends starts feeling unfulfilling or, worse, straining, as if one of us has done something wrong. And a night without at least a phone call suddenly carries hidden meanings.

A few weekends ago I was at a family wedding in Michigan, and after the ceremony I called Claire here in New York and she started crying. She told me she'd blacked out the night before after leaving a party and had woken up inside her apartment building, on the landing outside her front door, her dress only halfway on. A neighbor was shaking her awake. I was looking out over Lake Michigan as she spoke, staring at that great expanse of water and nursing my own hangover. I asked a few questions, but she couldn't answer them very well. She was at a party with friends and then she wasn't. Maybe someone slipped her a pill, but maybe she just drank too much. I didn't want to ask about the particulars—how she got back, who she was with, and how *on* the dress actually was—so I didn't. She was too upset. And so the incident has rested there, between us, unmentioned but not unremembered.

When Ken and I run out of money we stumble home, and soon I'm on the phone, calling Claire. Why isn't she picking up? Almost 3:00 A.M. and she's not answering. The phone is on her night table and she's a light sleeper and . . . Where the fuck is she? Probably out with her "New York" friends, former prep-school guys from Dalton or Holy Cross. They're always coming up to her when we're out, inviting her to some private club or dinner party—with me sitting right next to her. Maybe she's up at some First Avenue frat bar, laughing away with a tableful of overzealous lacrosse players, writing her number on the inside of match books and—

"Hello?"

"Where were you?"

"Right here," she says. "I was asleep in the living room. What time is it?"

"Are you sure?"

"What kind of question is that? Of course I'm sure. I fell asleep reading. Why aren't *you* asleep? Are you drunk?"

"Don't turn this around on me."

"Turn what around on you? It's the middle of the night and you just woke me up."

I try to explain the situation but I'm all muddled up. I start telling her about the *Black Book* debacle, but I can't make sense. I want to explain how worthless I feel. Some twenty-five-year-old British kid just published a novel called *The Beach*, and people everywhere are reading it, the entire city entranced, strangers sitting next to each other on subways, reading the same chapters, comparing page numbers, who's reading faster. I just turned twenty-six and I can't even publish a short story. I want to tell her so much, but I—

"Why don't you get some sleep," Claire says. "We can talk in the morning. I'll come down and see you after work tomorrow."

I can't help myself. Love impairs my judgment. "Are you telling the truth about that night a few weeks ago? I mean, how can you not remember *anything*?"

"Come on. Don't do this."

"Tell me."

"I was probably as drunk as you are right now."

"Why did you get so wasted when I was out of town?"

"Maybe so I could finally have a good time without having to look over my shoulder every ten minutes."

"So you could parade around for your sea of admirers."

"Is that what you think?"

"I think you're lying."

"I think you're an asshole."

"Sorry, I didn't mean it like—" But she's already hung up.

THE LATEST STORY, the heroic tale of a stripper who goes to NYU and the young writer who falls in love with her:

> *Like many girls of a certain beauty, Megan felt uneasy by herself. It's not that she was vain; she had just grown used to the attention. When she first started dancing, two months ago, she had relished this short commute, but it had since become like any other. More than the change in season, it was her change in attitude. The club no longer held the appeal of liberation, but rather the secular strains of routine . . .*

Or:

> *Will and his best friend, Eric, resided in what Will liked to call "the seeping void of creative life," a large undefined place where artistic ideals wrestled with economic realities, producing an uneasy compromise of art and commerce that barely kept them afloat . . .*

I stop writing, six pages in, just after the obligatory scene where Will falls in love as he watches her dance in the empty club on a sultry summer Tuesday, and undertakes, then and there, to save her. In real life I've been finding my inspiration at the Baby Doll Lounge, a topless joint a few blocks south of Canal. Just a beer or two in the late afternoon, when the dancers are still waking up, moving at half speed as if we're in New Orleans, and then I'll go back and write more. I chalk the lap dances up to research.

I print out my unfinished story and read it over slowly, looking for something I can salvage, a phrase or thought, an original description or a metaphor that holds up, one I didn't nick from someone else. But there aren't any, so I take the pages with me to the roof. There's a garden up here, a few plants and small trees waving languidly in the light wind. This is where they throw the PR events for the films being cut downstairs. Ken and I always try to show up for the open bar, and we listen for as long as we can to the high-pitched chatter of the New York independent film world. It usually takes a half hour and five plastic cups of wine before Ken threatens to jump. Now, in the working hours of midafternoon, the roof is empty. The sun keeps flashing off one of the loft windows across Greene Street in strange, well-timed intervals. Except it's not the sun: It's a flash from a photo shoot, someone else's New York debut.

Page one doesn't fly so well. It does a kind of spiraling nosedive, a death roll, and it lands in the gutter. I add flaps to page two, precision stabilizers on the end of each wing, and sure enough, the takeoff this time is smooth and the paper glider rides the prevailing winds south toward Canal. Three and four follow suit, although two holds the record at almost half a block. I launch a few off the other side of the building, toward the new SoHo Grand, but the buildings are blocking the breeze and the words fall lifelessly, just as they were created. And still, as I walk back downstairs to check my mail, I briefly imagine someone finding those pages, one by one, literally picking them up out of the gutter and reading them, liking them, wondering who wrote them. I don't know: I have a problem with hope. My mailbox is full of responses to the few stories I've managed to complete and send out. I've lost track of which ones went to which publications, but I don't think it matters. Today it's *Granta*, *The Paris Review*, *Ploughshares*, and as always, *The New Yorker*. I still get excited just looking at a *New Yorker* envelope in my hands. Rumor has it that one or two stories from their slush pile find their way into print every year. But not mine. Not yet. I open *The New Yorker* letter last, but it says the same thing as all the others: No, thanks.

WE'RE ON THE LARGE balcony of a friend's apartment on Twenty-third Street, drinking red wine and lighting each other's cigarettes at close intervals. It's a cocktail party, or is supposed to be, but Claire and I have broken away from everyone and are sitting with our feet dangling over the edge, talking. I've just apologized for the tenth time, and now we're looking down the street, where the black iron balconies of the Chelsea Hotel hang gracefully over the sidewalk below. It reminds me of Paris. I've been reading about the Chelsea and its rich history of troubled souls, suicidal poets, murderous rock stars. All that bleakness and misery: it makes me think the whole artist thing is just a dark exercise in despair that only gets worse once you've made it.

We agreed to spend some time apart after our lovely chat on the phone, a few weeks that have dragged into early summer. I spent a lot of time at Leland's after my Kitty Hawk experiments. I needed the money, but I needed people, as well, and even Josh breathing down my neck was better company than that horrid basement. Claire worked on her résumé and read *She's Come Undone*. And we called each other, tentatively, like eighth graders, to "check in." I think we both knew it was only a hiatus, and tonight, as we take a cab from Chelsea to a quiet restaurant in the East Village, we find our stride again. We've couched our love in a series of resolutions, the usual fare: we won't drink as much, won't put pressure on each other, won't get jealous, won't worry about the future. Claire is talking again about getting into publishing, and I want to warn her in advance, but I want to support her, too, so I don't say anything.

There is no better equation for sex than two familiar bodies that have been apart. And the word "love," in the right moments, with the right meaning, can put any problem in perspective. Afterward, when Claire is asleep, I lie awake and, as I'm so prone to do when the world seems right, start running through my various failures. This shot at writing could certainly line up next to those other disappointments, but it feels different, more vivid, more intense. And its setbacks leave me devastated. They pile up in a daily catalog of nonprogress, and when the reckoning comes at the end of every month and there's nothing to show for the effort, I have to turn away just to continue. Writing is like religion that way: both require blind faith and a certain ignorance of the obvious. I've watched Ken, in his zealot preacher mode, talk about making films with a fervor that drowns out the noise around him. He circles the wagons and backs into a personal space where obstinacy rules, and now I think I understand why. Armor keeps the world away, yes, but it protects what's inside as well—the little that hasn't been exposed. Truth is, I just don't think I'm good enough. Plus, I'm not sure I'm ready for that level of commitment. Money and career are words that still matter to me, however tenuously. And so does success—it's something I've never known.

Eighteen

I MAKE MY WAY over to the new Barnes & Noble on Union Square to see if I can find any magazines or literary journals I may have overlooked in my various mass mailings. I walk into the store and right in front of me, in the New and Noteworthy Paperbacks section, is a short story collection, *Pure Slaughter Value*. It's a slim white book with a burning Zippo lighter on the cover, but what gets my attention is the author's name: Robert Bingham. It takes a second, but then it all comes back: the lady in Cape Cod with the nephew in New York, the writer I was supposed to look up. He had the literary journal and the loft in TriBeCa. I buy the book and head upstairs.

The periodical racks are on the top floor near the coffee bar. Call it savvy retail architecture: try to lounge around reading our magazines for free and we'll still get you with a four-dollar mocha latte. I've become one of those people who crouch in aisles, studying mastheads, looking for pleasant-sounding associate editors to query—Sallys or Chloes or guys named Peter. I flip through titles, trying to match potential proposals to publications: perhaps a story on telemark skiing for *Outside* magazine; or a humor piece on straight men who live in Chelsea for *Time Out*. On the other side of the room fifty or sixty people are listening intently to a panel of writers reading from a collection of essays called *The Art of Fact*. The panel is a who's who of contemporary nonfiction, and I wander over and take a seat in the back row as Richard Ben Cramer answers a question concerning the subject of his latest book, the great Joe DiMaggio. I know the DiMaggio back story. It's not unlike Mantle's: just replace alcohol with greed. Cramer knows it, too, and the audience sits engrossed as he lifts the heavy veil of the DiMaggio mystique for a glance at the mess underneath. He outlines the complexities and contradictions of a shy man who shunned the spotlight, yet married Marilyn Monroe; a man who personified elegance and grace but could

never quite live up to his image; a man who spent his last empty decades selling his name to the highest bidder. It's a sad ode to talent. Cramer ends with
a story about DiMaggio and Paul Simon. In 1969 Simon sounded the call of
a generation's lost innocence in "Mrs. Robinson": *Where have you gone, Joe
DiMaggio? A nation turns its lonely eyes to you.* A decade passed before Simon
and DiMaggio met, by chance, in a New York restaurant. When they shook
hands, DiMaggio said, "I never understood why you asked where I've gone.
I haven't gone anywhere. I'm still right here. I do Mr. Coffee commercials
and I'm the spokesman for the Bowery Savings Bank." Paul Simon just
stood there and smiled. George Trow would have loved it.

Gay Talese starts speaking. I recognize him from the society pages. I'm
trying to remember what he actually wrote when a man sitting to my right
leans over and says something under his breath.

"Excuse me?" I say, noticing him for the first time. He's older and has a
warm, handsome, ruddy face.

"I said nonfiction can be so intriguing."

"Oh, sure," I say, not in the mood for small talk.

"What do you do, if I might ask?"

"I'm a writer."

"Books?"

"Working on a collection of short stories."

"That's wonderful," he says, cheerfully.

I know where this is headed. But in a bookstore? I need a prop. Reflexively, I pick up *The Art of Fiction* lying on the empty seat between us, and
start flipping through the pages. It's an impressive assemblage: Joseph
Mitchell, Tom Wolfe, Hunter S. Thompson, Ted Conover, Norman Mailer,
Bill Buford . . . Buford, that bastard. He's the fiction editor at *The New
Yorker*, the one I keep sending my stories to. I bet they haven't made it past
his intern.

"Have you sold your book?"

"It's not quite finished yet."

"Are you represented?"

"Not currently, no."

"My name is Jackson Schultz," he says. "I'm a literary agent, and if you're
interested, I'd be happy to take a look at a story or two."

I glance at his hand. Just what I thought: no wedding ring. Playing on a young writer's dreams—the New York version of the casting couch.

"Here's my card," he says. It's simple, white, with the words *Jackson Schultz Literary Agency* in black, above a West End Avenue address. It screams Kinko's.

I say thanks and make a show of putting it in my pocket. Gay Talese has finished and a pale B & N employee is leading the applause. People are getting up to leave. I tell Jackson I'll keep him in mind. He smiles and wishes me luck. I'm thinking of going up to introduce myself to Richard Ben Cramer. Maybe I could help him with his research, tell him how the great DiMaggio is living his last days surrounded by a sea of sycophants who make him sign so many baseballs he's flooded his own market and made his autograph almost worthless. *Where have you gone* indeed. I walk up to the stage, but it's too late: all the authors have slipped away. I turn to leave and that's when I see Cramer, standing back where I was just sitting, part of a gathering crowd that includes most of the other panelists. My God, they're all surrounding Jackson Schultz. I hurry back over, watching people shake his hand. Someone says, "This is the man who got the book done." Jackson looks embarrassed by the attention. What an asshole I am. No wonder I can't sell any stories. Fishing his card out of my pocket, I shoulder my way through the circle. Jackson is talking to the book's editors, but I jump in at the first chance and tell him my name, how I could send him a story early next week, could fax it or drop it off or—

"Slow down, slow down," he says, his grin widening. "Call tomorrow and we'll work it out." And then, surrounded by famous writers, Jackson Schultz walks away.

NEW YORK PAYS YOU back in funny ways. Years of loyal patronage, of anonymous toil, then you sit next to the right person. It's why so many people come here: that chance of discovery. It happens all the time. A former coat-check girl from Michael's is wearing a see-through dress on the cover of the new *Vanity Fair*. She's being touted as the starlet of the future, and she's never made a real movie. All she did was hang up the right coat.

I do some Kroll-style research and discover that Jackson Shultz has several high-profile clients, and two books on the current *Times* best-seller list.

He was an editor for years before becoming an agent and has a strong reputation for working closely with his clients. Most important, though, for reasons I can't fathom Jackson Schultz seems genuinely interested in me—as a *writer*. I call him the day after we meet—the way desperate people do—and we talk for a few minutes, abstractly, about selling short-story collections, about fees and rights and contracts, and then Jackson starts prodding me gently for more *concrete* information. How much have I actually written? And published? And when can he see a story? I tell him I'll have something to him in a week, a story I'm just finishing now.

"Take *two* weeks," he says, "and then we'll meet for lunch."

It's not a complete lie: I do have an *idea*, a beginning, a loose plot cultivated from the shards of others, the product of a dozen false starts. I lock myself in the basement office and get to work. No Starr report, no Leland's, no solitaire. Just the writing, mornings and afternoons. The new story centers around two friends at an exclusive boarding school—Charlie, the popular class clown, and his roommate, the shy and impressionable narrator. Their revered American history teacher was a marine in Vietnam, and for years rumors have circulated among students that something terrible happened while he was over there. As the Vietnam era approaches in class, Charlie announces he's going to find out the truth once and for all: he'll ask Professor Campbell point blank, in front of everyone, if he's ever killed a man. Campbell has a beautiful college-age daughter who comes home for weekends and parades around in short skirts, her blinking blue eyes and venerated father making her all but untouchable. Except Charlie does touch her: he campaigns hard and she finally succumbs. On the morning of the classroom showdown, he wakes up in her bed, in Campbell's house, a thin wall away from expulsion. The final scene in the classroom is a suspenseful battle of wills with an O. Henryesque twist. I write three drafts, revise until I can't stand the thing anymore, and when I've finally finished, I know for the first time that I really have something. "This Means War" holds together. It flows. And despite the title, the story doesn't aspire to more than it is—just a well-written narrative with characters, conflict, *resolution*.

I give it to Jackson Schultz during a wonderfully civilized lunch on Columbus Avenue. It's a perfect summer day, and we sit in the window overlooking the Museum of Natural History, talking books and baseball, commenting on the women who walk by. To the waiter we must look so gloriously typical: a writer and his agent lunching on the Upper West Side. I'm as happy as I've ever been.

I HAVE JUST DONE my best to describe an Indian headdress worn by someone named Chief Thunderthud. He was a character on the *Howdy Doody Show.* A few months ago Josh managed to sell one of the original Howdy Doody puppets, a creepy-looking marionette, for $113,000. I would call that absurd, except nothing in the world of collectibles surprises me anymore. Where once I saw Josh as a gluttonous salesman, I now see him as a prescient capitalist, a man who figures out what people want and then sells it to them. Now it's this godawful Howdy Doody crap. I don't know the first thing about Howdy Doody, and yet here I am, thinking up adjectives to describe an Air-O-Doodle Rocket Beanie, a Phineas T. Bluster painting, a Buffalo Bob cowboy costume. And other fine remembrances of things past: items belonging to Clarabell the clown, to Flub-a-Dub, to Dilly Dally.

I just can't do it. I take the whole big box of Doody, stick it in the corner, and turn instead to a 1960s Yogi Berra catcher's mitt, a 1985 Pete Rose serigraph by Andy Warhol, a photograph of the 1986 Mets meeting the president at the White House. That's how bad Howdy Doody is: I'd rather write about Ronald Reagan.

At dusk I walk down to the Old Town on Eighteenth Street to meet Ken. I don't see him when I walk in, so I lean against the long bar and order a beer. Only when I scan the room carefully do I spot him, alone at a table in the back, huddled over a script. He blends in with the stained wood surroundings. He's dressed in three shades of brown, his dark hair has grown long, and what was a trim goatee has ripened into a full beard. He looks like a student communist.

It's been almost a year since *Moving In/Moving Out* sparked up briefly and flickered out, six years since he moved to New York to make movies. He still says his film will sell, but it's clear that the time for that has come and gone. Sometimes, when he's especially low on funds, he temps at Citibank in Queens, but mostly he's down in that basement, working on his football script. His entire life is based on the belief that he'll make it, that success is just around the corner. Success and vindication. But he's changed. The optimism is more desperate, the setbacks more personal. He's slowly becoming a recluse. I order him a Maker's Mark and walk over to break up the party.

"Where's Claire?" he asks, as I sit down.

"She should be here. She was coming down after work."

"Is she still at that department store?"

"Yes, but she's been interviewing at literary agencies."

"Not to be your agent, I hope. Take it from me, that won't work."

"No, I'm long on agents, short on product. I need to sell a story badly."

"I take it the auction house isn't working out."

"I wrote up Howdy Doody dolls today."

"Mmm," Ken murmurs, drinking half his whiskey in one long sip. "You know, I didn't think you and Claire would last this long. I thought you guys were too young." He says this flippantly, like he could be saying anything, but he's really saying *everything*, everything I've been wondering myself, as Claire and I have pitched and heaved through our second summer.

I'm about to offer up my theory on generational commitment when Claire herself appears, radiant as always. I swear she can actually brighten a room. She settles in, orders a drink of her own, and almost immediately Ken asks about her job search. She says she can't decide if she should get into the world of books. Bergdorf's is giving her a raise and being a fashion buyer wouldn't be so bad—

"Retail is the horrid endgame of our culture," Ken says, a bit too loudly, "It's the shining goal of a million marketers. It's filled with people who wear masks. Go into any mall or department store in America and look around: no one wants to be who they are, not the customers or the salespeople or the managers. They're all running away from truth. Retail is the last stop on the elevator to hell. Any job that has an Employee of the Month award should be abandoned immediately."

"I work at Bergdorf's, not Wendy's," Claire says.

But he barely hears her. He's moved on to literature, the "goodness in books, the honesty of words." Soon he's pointing a finger in my girlfriend's face, practically shouting at her to stop lying to herself, to start living a life she can be proud of. An uptown girl at a table nearby looks over, intrigued.

I can imagine the story she'll tell her friends: slumming it downtown, she sat near a real artist, as loud and obnoxious and eccentric as they're rumored to be. When I turn back around, Claire is crying.

I RECEIVE "MY AGENT'S" comments on "This Means War" on a Saturday in early fall. I'm at the SoHo office, working on my latest effort, the cautionary tale of a middle-aged magazine columnist, a family man who writes about celebrities. He has a wife and two young kids and an apartment uptown, but his devotion to the zeitgeist—the nights, the music, the VIP rooms that become as addictive as the drugs in the bathrooms—is taking its toll. He chases stars. But he's too old and the sky falls in.

I check my mailbox at lunchtime. When I see Jackson's package I take it up to the roof, the place I now equate with launches both good and bad. I open the manuscript envelope, imagining these moments might be the last before my life takes a turn. I flip through the pages slowly, pages I've read a hundred times, paragraphs I can recite like poems. There aren't many comments, just a few circled mistakes, hovering question marks, underlined phrases. And then the last page, and four words in red ink, printed like a P.S. near the bottom: *GOOD; but develop ending.* The "good" is capitalized and underlined. But that's it. I'm not sure what I was expecting, but it was more than this. I was hoping for validation.

I call Jackson but there is no answer, so I start leaving a message. I thank him and start asking about the next step—

"This is the first rule: Never call your agent on a weekend."

"You're there. Sorry, I just . . . thanks . . . I mean . . . I just got your comments and wanted to know what—"

"I told you what I thought. My comments are the ones in red."

"I know, but I guess I was wondering if you think the story is . . . good *enough.*"

He doesn't answer. For a moment I think he's hung up. Then I hear him breathing and I get this image of him doing the crossword with the phone barely hanging on his shoulder. The most important question of my life and he didn't even hear—

"This is what I think. Short story collections are always a tough sell, *but.* If you put this type of effort into six or seven more stories, if the ideas keep coming, if you really want it badly enough . . . then we might have something."

"A collection we can sell?"

"A collection we can *try* to sell. Now, take a few days off and go earn some money at that auction house, because you'll need it. Then write one more draft and send it out to the magazines. Maybe you'll get lucky and catch someone on a good day."

There must be very few good days in the publishing world, judging from the responses that trickle in over the next month. *Esquire* comes first, a handwritten letter signed by someone named Jim Adams: "I enjoyed reading 'This Means War' and found it entertaining and well-observed. However . . ." *The Paris Review*: ". . . amusing but not right for us . . ." *Story*: "While 'This Means War' had many fine moments, I'm sorry to disappoint you on this one." *Quarterly West*: "Try us next spring." Robert Bingham's *Open City* doesn't respond at all.

Over lunch at King Crab, Jackson Schultz plays the shrink. "Look on the bright side," he says. "These are handwritten responses. Most writers get form rejections. That's all writing is: one failure after another. Success comes when you stop letting that bother you."

He manages to send me back downtown recharged, and when I see a letter from *The New Yorker* sticking out of my mailbox, I take a deep breath and brace for the disappointment. I can see the outline of the small rectangular rejection slip through the envelope. I know exactly what they look like: I have a collection of them. But this one is different. Under the form letter, in messy handwriting: "A lively, polished piece—Keep trying. B. Buford."

Nineteen

FOR A WHILE THE CITY maintains a kind of gravitational equilibrium.
The leaves fall and the stock market rises. The snow falls and the stock
market rises. Then, when nature has nothing left, the forces of the market
take over completely. The citizens of New York prosper on the strong back
of technology, and for the first time in my life, everyone is having the
same conversation. They talk of jobs that are everywhere, comparing offers and opportunities. They talk of the Dow, which has climbed above
nine thousand. And the NASDAQ, the electronic marketplace for the
electronic age. It's shooting up so quickly that the graph lines look more
like a jagged cliff face than an uphill incline. Friends of mine who a year
ago couldn't calculate tips are CFOs at Internet startups. Actors are running marketing departments. The formerly unemployed head up Human
Resources.

Even my cyber-free life is being affected. Leland's is starting an online
auction site. After a lengthy search, Claire has found an assistant's job at a
literary agency, and she shows up one night espousing the virtues of the
eBook, its accessibility, its weightlessness. And Ken, that most brick-and-
mortar of souls, has quit the bank (with its free copying, collating, tele-
phone, and Web services) and started freelancing at Agency.com. Within a
week he's in charge of redesigning the Concorde Web site, rejuvenating the
tired image of supersonic travel by bringing it up to Internet speed. Ken has
never worked in advertising before. He has never designed anything. And
yet here he is, embodying the era, happily taking what's handed to him.
Sure, he still sits in a room, working on his screenplay, but now mixed
among the film quotes are paper-towel sketches of cockpits and cabins. One
morning he announces he's going to do something about the diminishing
service on Air France, and in this strange new era, where seemingly any-

thing can happen and does, the statement doesn't sound so absurd. Why can't Ken revamp the Concorde? Experience these days is the only roadblock to imagination. I ask if he's ever flown on it before, and he looks at me and laughs. He says he's never even been to Europe.

IT's HARD TO BE financially invisible. It's hard to be alone in a basement, dancing with words, stepping on their toes. I write a story about a man who has ideas. He's a genius who rents his mind out to companies for $5,000 a day, and if you're lucky enough to have him on the payroll when inspiration strikes, then his concepts become yours. It's a depressing tale, but the idea of selling thoughts before they even occur seems more than a little bit relevant.

Today, Friday, I get through almost fifteen hundred words before packing it in. I walk up lower Broadway in the twilight. In the large-windowed lofts above me, I can make out squadrons of my caffeine-fueled peers, sitting like sweatshop workers at rows of temporary desks. They're all staring at glowing laptops. They are all wearing blue shirts. They have the same haircut, same glasses, same Manhattan Portage shoulder bags. I walk past Pseudo.com at the corner of Houston, in what is now called Silicon Alley. Casey keeps talking about Pseudo and the great parties they throw, but he never talks about what they do. It must be something fantastic. When he told me New York was a year and a half behind San Francisco, I remember thinking my city would never *really* get caught up in this Internet craze. That wasn't even twelve months ago.

I'm meeting Claire at my apartment. She'll come over with a satchel of manuscripts to read over the weekend. She loves her job so far, loves searching for that diamond in the rough. But it makes me uneasy, all those pages waiting to become books. She'll tell me how bad they are, how most are about working for Anna Wintour or losing one hundred pounds in six months, but still, just knowing thousands of other writers in every part of the land are tapping productively away, day after day, cramming coherent thoughts onto pages, is almost more than I can stand. I've been trying hard for more than a year now to make some headway as a writer, but it's becoming painfully clear that nothing is happening. The basement on Greene Street has become such an obvious symbol for my failings that when it flooded a few days ago with a surge of water from the bathroom next door, I almost had to laugh.

I turn onto St. Marks and walk past Dojo, an NYU dive that specializes in tofu and stir-fried vegetables. I've been eating there a lot recently, entire dinners for four dollars. I'll be out of money soon. I'll have to lock myself into the Leland's storage room for days just to pay the rent. I'd like to do what other people my age are doing: take my girlfriend to dinner at Gramercy Tavern, maybe travel somewhere, to Prague or St. Petersburg. But those people have jobs. I have three finished stories, and the only one that's seen print was so badly mangled it was unrecognizable. It's hard to believe I haven't just been fooling myself. Scared of diving into some kind of career, I've used writing—whatever that really is—as a crutch, an excuse, a line for the girls. It's almost 1999. The world is getting rich. And I feel like I'm missing a good life that's waiting out there somewhere.

My block is waking up. North Africans are selling bootleg cassettes and five-dollar sunglasses. Kids are loitering in groups, passing tall-boys, character acting. Across the street a half dozen middle-aged men are standing on the steps of a building that once housed the Dom. For a while in the mid-1960s, Andy Warhol's Velvet Underground was the house band at the Dom. It was a mecca for the stars of the counter culture. Today it's a community center where recovering addicts bare their souls in desperate circles of solidarity. That's what those chain-smoking men are doing—it's halftime at the AA meeting. They're out there every night, trading down addictions—heroin for methadone, booze for cigarettes—searching for simple routines. How thin the line is in New York between one sidewalk and another—a choice or two along the way. I don't like that side of the street.

I climb the stairs to my apartment and open the door carefully, bracing for Shakespeare, but there's no sign of him. Ken's door is closed but I know he's in there; I can sense the tension of an artist in residence. I put my bag down and am about to make myself a drink when the intercom buzzes. It must be Claire.

"I have your cat," says the voice on the other end. It's a girl, but not my girl.

"Well, come up," I say, holding down the Door button. Ken must have lent him to someone.

"He jumped," says the voice. "Right off the fire escape."

"The cat?"

"Yes, the cat. Just now. I was hanging out down here and I saw him jump off from the third-floor fire escape. He hit the ground right next to us with a thud."

"Did he jump or fall?" I ask the box on the wall.

"Don't you want to know if he's alive?"

"Is he?"

"Yes, but he's dazed. I'll bring him up." I hit the button again, then go knock on Ken's door. There's no answer. I open it slowly, wondering if he somehow *threw* Shakespeare out the window in a fit of rage, but Ken's sitting at his desk with his head in his hands. He has headphones on and the window is open and a screensaver image of DeNiro in *Raging Bull* is moving slowly across his monitor.

"Ken! I . . . I think Shakespeare took a nosedive out the window—"

There's a knock on the door, and I walk back down the hall and open it. Standing there, with a motionless cat in her arms, is a pretty girl with red hair and black eyeliner. She's wearing a plaid miniskirt and an "I fucked Tommy" T-shirt under a leather jacket. She's rocking the cat gently back and forth, like a baby.

She says, "I think he might be hurt."

Ken appears in the hallway, looking like he hasn't slept in days. He reaches for Shakespeare, but the cat burrows further into the girl's chest. "My God," he says, "What happened?"

The girl again explains what she saw.

"I thought cats always land on their feet," I say. They both shoot me a look. Slowly Ken takes the cat from the girl, but halfway through the hand-off, Shakespeare, in a sudden burst of energy, leaps out of their arms and darts down the hall and into the small area we call our kitchen. All three of us watch the thing go; then the girl shrugs and walks back downstairs. Ken ambles back to his room, muttering. First his girlfriend, then his pet. It must be really bad in there.

When Claire buzzes a few minutes later, I meet her downstairs and we walk to Sixth Street and try to choose between the dozen or so Indian restaurants that line the south side of the block. They all share the same kitchen, I say, but she's already heard that joke. We settle on the most crowded one. We sip bad wine and discuss the lure of the dot-com world. Claire thinks I should keep writing. She says every story is better than the last. I tell her I really need money, that Leland's is slowly killing me.

"Okay, so what would you do?" Claire asks.

The food arrives just in time.

THREE DAYS LATER, at 8:30 on a Monday morning in mid-November, Ken bangs on my door with the phone. "Some lady," he says, only partially covering the receiver with his hand. Claire is asleep on the futon beside me, so I take the phone into the bathroom, the only unoccupied room in the apartment. The woman on the other end of the line introduces herself as the head of Human Resources at Sotheby's. She says she'd like to ask me—

Shakespeare leaps down at me from a shelf high above the sink. I try to protect myself, but he's too quick, and as he slashes me across my neck, the phone, with my future in midsentence, flies out of my hand, hits the toilet seat, and falls in. I fish it out, but it's too late. The line is dead. The cat prances down the hall, his back arched, victorious.

I sit on the side of the tub and try to make sense of the world.

PART FIVE

High Art

"In the absence of adults, people came to put their trust in experts."

—George W. S. Trow, *Within the Context of No Context*

Twenty

ON THE PAY PHONE, on the corner of St. Marks and Third, I dial the Sotheby's main number as a street-cleaning truck rumbles past. It stops at the red light, idling like a jackhammer, while the Sotheby's switchboard operator puts me through to the woman I was speaking with not ten minutes before. When she answers, I try to apologize.

"It sounds like you're on the side of a highway," she shouts.

"Oh, no. I just live downtown."

I cover the bottom of the receiver and let her talk. I can only make out half of what she's saying, but it's something about a job in their sports department. She wants me to interview with David Redden, Sotheby's executive vice president, this coming Thursday morning. I start to ask where she got my name and number, but cabs are honking, and a voice starts demanding another quarter, so I say I'll be there, then shout a thank you and hang up.

Of course I'll be there. We're more than halfway through the month and I still can't pay my rent. Yesterday afternoon I walked over to the Strand and sold two dozen hardcover books for forty-five dollars. It was a humiliating experience, made worse when I ran into Gus perusing the cookbook section with a cute European girl on his arm. Gus looked at my stack of books piled high on the counter and asked how life was going. I said it was getting expensive. He introduced his girlfriend, said they were taking a cooking class together. She smiled at him lovingly, then wandered off toward the art books, leaving the two of us standing there. In a slightly condescending voice (the voice he once used with the press) Gus told me he was now working for a major PR firm in midtown. As he lavished praise on the private sector, I noticed how much he'd prospered in my absence. He was wearing yellow trousers and a Burberry coat. He was thinner these days, his skin clearer, his thick, dark hair slicked back with product. As his girlfriend rushed up with a photography book in her hands, Gus made a big show of handing her a fifty that he peeled off his money clip. I wished them luck.

It's difficult to live in New York for long without hearing about Sotheby's and its age-old rival, Christie's. With their celebrity sales and socialite parties, the two auction houses provide the city's tabloids with a steady stream of headlines. I have no idea what kind of job I'll be interviewing for, but it can't hurt to broaden my knowledge past "Page Six," so I head back to the Strand on Tuesday afternoon and start leafing through secondhand catalogs. There's an entire section devoted to them, hundreds of catalogs dating back more than a decade. And they're almost works of art in themselves—the carefully constructed photographs, the detailed descriptions, the endless trails of provenance . . . and the *prices!* Several catalogs from the major Impressionist sales have final prices scribbled in the margins, and at first I can't believe what I'm reading: "$49,000,000" for Van Gogh's *Irises* (Sotheby's, 1987), "$78,100,000" for Renoir's *Au Moulin de la Galette* (Sotheby's, 1990), and in a Christie's catalog from that same year, I find "$82,500,000!!!" scrawled excitedly beside Van Gogh's *Portrait of Dr. Gachet.* My God: $82 million for a painting. I can't help but think of Josh, slogging it out at Leland's amid $500 bats and $1,000 boxing gloves.

In a corner downstairs, I find a good book, Robert Lacey's *Sotheby's: Bidding for Class.* I buy it and head over to the Cedar Tavern, which at this time of day is dark and empty and smells of cleaning supplies. In the fifties, Keroauc had worked on his drinking problem at the long oak bar in front, while Ginsberg and his brethren gave impromptu poetry readings at the booths in back. Impressed by the lineage, I've started joining the young literati who fill this place most nights, and it wasn't until recently that I discovered this isn't the original Cedar Tavern. In typical New York fashion, the original burned down, so they built this one just up the street and transferred the history over.

Alone at the bar, I start in on Lacey's account of the world's largest auction house. The place sounds like a fantasyland of money and privilege, where the wealthy compete for the spoils of the wealthiest. It's the upper-class trickle-down effect, played out with paddles and proxies in sales rooms across the globe. And it's not just paintings. In this rarified world, anything belonging to royalty—European or American—can sell for tens of thousands. At the Jackie O. sale in 1996, Arnold Schwarzenegger bought JFK's golf clubs for $772,500. Last year, at the Duke of Windsor auction, a California couple flew in and "won" a piece of 1937 wedding cake for $29,900.

Of course, Sotheby's has its own royal family, and the king is Alfred Taubman, a self-made shopping-mall magnate from Detroit, who bought the company in the 1980s as a way to break into New York high society. It's the queen, though, who runs the place. Hard charging and charismatic, Dede Brooks is a CEO whose bottom-line approach has brought the company into the modern age and, more importantly, profitability. Then there's David Redden, the man I'm about to meet. He's the visionary, the P. T. Barnum of the operation, who in his twenty-five-year career has sold everything from a *Tyrannosaurus rex* named Sue ($8.36 million) to the original Declaration of Independence ($7.4 million). In 1993 he organized Sotheby's first space auction, where, among other things, he managed to sell a Russian moon rover, the Lunakhod 2, for $68,500—an impressive feat made far more startling by the fact that it's still on the moon. Now Redden is moving from space to cyberspace: he's the man charged with the development of sothebys.com, the art world's largest Web site.

Lacey's book details the other side of the business, as well: the European smuggling rings, the forgeries that slip past the experts, and the controversial loans Sotheby's routinely provides to its largest clients. The loans fuel the astronomical prices by allowing clients to bid more than they normally would, and somehow the ensuing defaults seem almost too predictable. *Irises, Moulin de la Galette,* and *Portrait of Dr. Gachet* were all repossessed due to bankruptcy. It may have a shiny veneer, but it sounds like a pretty ugly business. At one point Lacey compares auctioneers to undertakers: "They [both] offer rituals to help us through less happy practicalities—and the two trades frequently operate in tandem: bury the body, then lay out the goods for sale." It's Josh's "three *D*'s," played out on a world stage, where the prices have more zeros, and the names are all well known.

By my fourth drink I'm hooked. The irony is everywhere. What began in

1734 as an English bookshop in Covent Garden has, over three centuries of pawning off people's fortunes, evolved into the most American of companies: a publicly traded conglomerate, complete with its own nouveau-riche king and a castle under construction on the Upper East Side. It makes the English lords and viscounts on the advisory board (plainly printed in every catalog for all to admire) look like the butts of a cruel joke: Here, we took your company and stole your prestige, but we'll print your names and invite you to the parties so you can keep up appearances. The truth is, Sotheby's defines *American* society now—in as much as there is such a thing. And for someone who has been isolated in a basement for months, who lives on a fold-out futon in an East village tenement, whose girlfriend's $25,000 salary makes her the breadwinner, Sotheby's sounds like a fairy tale. But what could they possibly want with me?

THE NIGHT BEFORE MY interview, I call Claire's mother on my brand-new phone. Like most Upper East Side women, she worked at Sotheby's for a while, and when I tell her I'm interviewing with David Redden, she starts laughing.

"God, I haven't seen David in ages. You'll love his accent."

"Where's he from?"

"Oh, you'll find out soon enough. What have they told you about the job?"

"The lady on the phone said I'd be working in the sports department."

"I didn't know they had a sports department," Mrs. Davis says. "Unless she means polo or cricket collectibles, or maybe paintings of English pheasant shoots."

"I *thought* she said sports. I don't know. It was kind of a bad connection."

"You'll probably be a cataloger, which is one step above an intern. Unless you're a Phipps or a Frick or an Astor—and you're *not*—you'll need to work your way up from the bottom. Which is fine, except they don't pay much; they assume you already have money. For all its excess, Sotheby's is still a business first. That's the big difference between the two houses: Christie's is a group of aristocrats pretending to do business, and Sotheby's is a bunch of businessmen moonlighting as landed gentry. The end result being that half the people who work there truly love art, and the other half have a father who's the Earl of Nottingham or some Impressionist collector with a villa on Lake Geneva. Still, the place is great fun. Everyone runs around making a fuss over the auctions and parties, and everywhere you look coworkers are kissing in corners and . . . well . . . that's nothing you need to worry about. Anyway, tell me how it goes, and use my name during the interview. At Sotheby's, name-dropping is an art in itself."

SOTHEBY'S WORLDWIDE HEADQUARTERS takes up the entire block of York Avenue between Seventy-first and Seventy-second Streets. Business must be booming, because seven floors are being added on to the original three, and the construction is tying up traffic in all directions. I walk through the guarded glass doors and am greeted at reception by Redden's assistant, a tall preppy girl with Lisa Loeb glasses. I follow her down a maze of hallways and fire doors, past union hard hats and heiresses in bright sweater sets, to a makeshift office in the depths of the building. When he sees us, the small man behind the desk jumps up and practically runs over to shake my hand. He's impeccably dressed and his gray hair has a politician's coiff. And when he speaks, it's with the accent of British aristocracy.

"Where are you from?" I ask. "Because I grew up in London."

"Greenwich, Connecticut."

"Oh, I just thought—"

"Here, do sit down. I'm sorry if there's been a mystery surrounding this whole thing, but what we're doing is still something of a secret. And every-thing we discuss today is confidential." I nod as he searches his desk and locates a Leland's catalog under a pile of papers. It's the Mickey Mantle catalog from last year. "A colleague of ours, whose husband is a sports collector, told us about you, and now that our plans are in place we'd like to offer you the job of sports specialist in charge of our new sports-collectibles business. We realize you're a bit young to be a department expert—in fact, you might be our youngest ever—but sports has suddenly become a high priority for us, and we're impressed with your background. So here we are."

What does Redden think I do at Leland's? Does he know I'm just a freelance copywriter who works in the storage room? Someone must have gotten his wires crossed. *Sotheby's Sports Specialist*: it sounds regal. Instinctively, I try to be intelligent.

"Why, if I might ask, are you starting a sports department now?"

"We had one once, in the early nineteen nineties. We held a few sales, mostly baseball cards and such, and they did quite well. We actually sold the most valuable baseball card of all time, the . . . uh . . ."

"The T-two-oh-six Honus Wagner," I say. "It's an old tobacco card, circa nineteen eleven. They say there are only twenty or thirty extant." (I throw the "circa" and "extant" in there for effect; they sound like good Sotheby's words.) "I think it sold for more than six hundred thousand dollars, to a group led by Wayne Gretzky . . ."

"Very good," Redden says, once I've finished pulling shards of overheard conversations out of my ass. "Well, the market died down for us after that, and places like Leland's took up the slack. But now, with the increase in prices of memorabilia and the advent of the Internet, we stand on the *precipice* of a bold new era. As you may have heard, Sotheby's is embarking on a massive online venture that we believe will make us the preeminent place to buy high-end collectibles on the Web."

"Kind of the eBay of the art world?"

"NO! We're the anti-eBay. eBay is a frontier marketplace, an unpoliced community filled with hucksters and frauds. The Sotheby's site will be one hundred percent authentic. Our experts will screen every lot that goes up for sale, so buyers will know the items are real. Trust is half the battle when it comes to e-commerce, and the other half is volume. That's why eBay is so powerful. We've got to attract—what do they call them?—*eyeballs*, so we've partnered up with amazon-dot-com to create the ultimate online marketplace: sothebys-dot-amazon-dot-com. Think about it. We provide the items and the expertise, Amazon provides the technology and the bidders. It's a perfect marriage. Of course, we know people aren't going to bid millions of dollars for paintings online; that's what our live auctions are for. But the less expensive items, up to, say, five thousand dollars, there's no reason they can't be sold on the Web. Hence, sports collectibles. Sports has a . . . how do I put this . . . a certain *mass market* appeal that makes it Internet-friendly. Clients will bid on a baseball online before they'll bid on jewelry or art. *Plus* . . ." Redden stops talking and looks me in the eye, sizing me up. "Do you know who has the most valuable sports memorabilia collection in the world?"

"The Baseball Hall of Fame in Cooperstown, New York."

"I mean privately owned."

"Probably Barry Halper."

"Go on," Redden says, folding his arms.

"Halper is a part owner of the Yankees, and he's been collecting memorabilia since he was a kid. He used to hang around ballparks before and after games and players would give him jerseys, bats, signed balls, anything he wanted. When the market for memorabilia shot up in the late eighties, people realized he had all the best stuff. Dealers who've seen his basement in New Jersey say it's worth tens of millions. Josh talks about it incessantly. He's been after Halper for years, but rumor has it he'll never sell. Apparently he doesn't care about money."

"You're exactly right, up until the last part. Everyone cares about money. And everyone has a price. Including Halper. According to a recent appraisal his collection is worth forty million dollars. And it's not in his basement anymore. It's in our warehouse."

"Are you serious?"

"Barry Halper has decided to sell his entire collection through us. It will be the largest sports auction in history. *Thousands of lots. Tens of millions of dollars.* The most valuable pieces will be sold in a series of highly publicized live auctions here in New York. We want them to be the first auctions ever held in the new sales room upstairs. The rest, the thousands of smaller-dollar-value lots, will be sold over the Internet once the live auctions have finished. We think it's the perfect way to launch our Web site. And we think you're the perfect man for the job."

I'm with Redden for almost an hour. From there I'm led upstairs, through another series of busy hallways peopled by smooth-skinned women in pashminas and pearls, to meet Bill Ruprecht, Sotheby's executive vice president and managing director. Ruprecht is Dede's number-two man, and I sit in his office waiting to be exposed. I felt bold talking to Redden—like *he* was pitching Sotheby's to *me*—but Ruprecht is more grounded, more suspicious. His way of saying hello is to tell me that Sotheby's isn't in the practice of hiring "kids my age" to run departments, let alone create them from scratch. He says he started at Sotheby's as a junior cataloger in the rug department and, over years of toil, worked his way to the top, but that these are different times, and sports experts with

Internet savvy don't grow on trees. The fact that I am neither of these does not come up.

Then he asks that worst of all interview questions: "What's your greatest weakness?" It's hard to pick just one. I could say working with people. Or using computers. Or handling finances or being on time or daydreaming. Instead I say hitting left-handed pitching, and he smiles. When I shake his hand and make my way out of the building, I keep thinking I'll get tapped on the shoulder by a security guard and escorted to a safe room where Redden and Ruprecht will conference Josh in on the phone and the truth will come toppling out faster than I can apologize. I'll be laughed out of Sotheby's and then fired from Leland's. But none of that happens. Instead an impeccably dressed doorman thanks me for coming, tips his hat, and says, "Good day, sir."

IT ALL HAPPENS SO QUICKLY. The official offer comes the following day; the Human Resources woman calls and offers me $45,000, plus full benefits and an options package. She says the stock options will more than make up for the salary once Sotheby's becomes a major Web destination. I tell her I'll think about it, but there's really nothing to consider. It's been more than a year and a half since I've had a full-time job. Wake up enough times to a lover kissing you good-bye as she trots off to work, take enough 10:00 A.M. subway rides downtown with the second string, eat enough four-dollar dinners at Dojo, read enough stories about twenty-three-year-old millionaires, and suddenly a job offer becomes less like an alternative and more like a lifeline.

What I'll leave behind is a dream stalled in neutral. I feel like I've finally been gaining on clarity, on success—an agent (sort of), an almost steady stream of stories, encouraging notes from editors. . . . Taking a full-time job now would be an admission of failure, a shift from creating art to selling it. No one talks about that difference anymore. But New York is a city of compromises, of special arrangements and freelance gigs and temp work. I'll still write on the side: early mornings and weekends. I'll drain the clock of its available hours, the in-between time spent on couches, in record stores, online. They say the busier you are, the more you get done. So I'll just do it all.

I call back the following Monday and ask for $60,000. They counter with

$50,000. Before I can even say yes, I'm thinking of the look Josh will give me when I tell him I'm finally quitting. And why.

I GET MY CHANCE the next day.

"If this is about money—"

"It's not about money."

"Then stop bothering me."

"I'm leaving."

"Excuse me?"

"I've accepted an offer from Sotheby's."

"*Sotheby's?* They don't even *have* a sports department."

"I know. I'm starting it."

"YOU?" Josh shouts. "But you don't know *anything*! How are you going to find property? You don't know any of the dealers, you don't know how to set prices or—"

"They landed the Barry Halper collection."

"BULLSHIT! Halper won't sell. *Especially* through Sotheby's."

"Okay, you're right. I'm fucking with you."

"Well, tell me, who else are they hiring? They must be getting someone *knowledgeable*. Halper's collection is huge. And it's full of fakes—forged signatures, counterfeit nineteenth-century jerseys. . . . Halper's too trusting, so people take advantage of him."

"So why have you always wanted the collection so badly?"

"Because it's still the biggest and best in the world. And I'm one of the few who can spot those fakes. Let's be honest here. You've got some basic skills, but you're a catalog writer, not an appraiser, and certainly not an expert for a place like Sotheby's."

"I'll be the youngest they've ever had."

"Then you're in way over your head."

"Well, that's the job they offered me. What should I have said? 'Thanks, but I don't think I'm ready. I'd rather work part-time in the back of a storage room?' Come on, you'd have done the same thing. Opportunities come and you seize them."

"But you don't have to become a direct competitor."

"If I'm so inept, you won't have anything to worry about."

"Then get the fuck out of here."

BECAUSE OF CONSTRUCTION at the main building, Sotheby's has rented an old car garage four blocks north and converted it into temporary office space for the smaller (i.e., less profitable) departments: Books and Manuscripts, Photographs, Prints, Wine, Rugs, Coins, Fashion, Automobiles, and Collectibles. Which is where I land. Collectibles is the Sotheby's catch-all, a loose assemblage of one- and two-person departments, all of which share interns, catalogers, and assistants. Collectibles almost never turns a profit, but Sotheby's keeps it around because a full-service auction house needs experts in curious fields like toys, dolls, comic books, movie posters, music, and Hollywood. And it needs the press coverage that such sales generate. So add sports to this mélange.

My desk is tucked behind several rows of accumulated property—signed guitars, model trains, original Star Trek costumes . . . There's only one other desk back here and it belongs to Giles Moon, the rock-and-roll specialist. I see him talking on the phone and I like him right away. He's short and pale and very English, and he has a complicated mod haircut that's either impressively visionary or a complete mistake. And with his narrow black suit and tie, he looks like an early Beatles devotee. On the phone, he's trying to verify the authenticity of an Elvis autograph. He mentions ink types, then asks about analogous specimens on display at Graceland. He sounds like he knows what he's talking about. Maybe he can help me with sports signatures.

People come by to say hello: George Hanson, the portly, good-natured toy expert; Laura Woolley, the Collectibles cataloger and the niece of Sotheby's legendary auctioneer Robert Woolley; and Gabrielle, the department's comely twenty-three-year-old administrator. It's a motley crew, an intriguing mix of castoffs and fanatics that differs in every way from the patrician atmosphere down on Seventy-second Street. There are no sweater sets in Collectibles, no Carolina Herrera blouses or Beau Brummel suits. We're edgier than all that.

Giles hangs up and comes over to introduce himself. "Where have you been?" he asks, grinning. "We must get twenty sports calls a day."

"Nice to meet you. You're not related to Keith Moon, are you?"

"No, sorry, mate. Be nice, though, wouldn't it? How about you? Goodwillie can't be your real name."

Giles takes me on a tour of the building—the musty shelves of Books and Manuscripts, the naked mannequins striking crooked poses in Fashion, the magnums and methuselahs over in Wine. He points at an enormous bottle.

"It's called a nebuchadnezzar," he says. "Twenty bottles in one. That's the kind of worthless bollocks you learn around here. Someone dropped one at a wine sale last year and the whole front row got doused with eighty-five Margaux."

He leads me down a back stairwell and into a cavernous loftlike space with freshly painted white walls. The room is completely empty, like a Chelsea gallery between installations.

"This is where they're putting the Internet people. This entire floor will be filled with hundreds of bodies in a few months, at a cost of forty million dollars. Has anyone told you about the deal with Amazon? Supposed to make us a *dot-com*. Should be interesting, considering most of the old boys around here can't even use e-mail."

IT'S FRIDAY BEFORE I realize something is wrong. Four days spent poking around, meeting coworkers, studying collectibles books, and no one has told me to be anywhere. Sotheby's is one deadline after another, and everyone else is racing down hallways, shouting into phones, frantically typing copy. Except for me. I'm not sure what I should be doing, so I walk down to Redden's office to ask.

"How's the collection coming along?" he asks.

"The Halper collection?"

"Of course the Halper collection."

"That's what I came to see you about. Um. Where is it?"

"Where's what?"

"The collection."

"What do you mean, 'Where is it?' It's at the warehouse. Do you mean to tell me you haven't been up there yet?"

"No. I had no idea—"

"My God, it's been a week. What the devil have you been doing? No, never mind. Just get up there and start working. There's a whole team there already."

Five minutes later I'm in a cab heading uptown. Way uptown. We cross
Ninety-sixth Street and the neighborhood nosedives dramatically—trees
give way to sidewalk trash; Irish pubs become take-out chicken joints; modern high-rise apartments are replaced by empty blocks, decimated space,
nothing. We're in Spanish Harlem. I read the cabbie the address and soon
we're pulling up in front of a large brick storage building bordered by weed-
covered ball fields and graffiti-glazed projects. I'm thinking this can't be the
right place when I see a young white woman—very white—in a tan skirt,
an aqua sweater, and high heels standing in the loading bay, checking off
antique furniture as it's unloaded from a truck. In my short time here, I've
already heard the complaints. Sotheby's art handlers are union, and the rift
between blue collar and blueblood is substantial. The union guys are the
only people allowed to move the art, and since they don't take to being
bossed around by trust-funded art-history majors, the transporting side of
the business operates in slow motion. And that's what's happening here:
half a dozen guys are standing around, and our girl in aqua isn't about to
tell them to get back to work.

I walk up and ask if she knows anything about a baseball collection.

"I think it's up on ten," she says. "I don't know where the elevator man is,
but if he ever comes back, have him take you up there."

I stand by the freight elevator and wait. Above me bells are ringing from
the various floors, calling a lift that isn't moving. Finally an old man saunters slowly over from between two trucks and asks where I'm going.

"The baseball floor."

"You the guy they been waitin' for?"

"I think so."

"Man, you got your hands full," he says, motioning for me to get in. He
shakes his head, pulls a lever, and heads us skyward.

The doors open. Sprawled out in front of me—on shelves, on hangers,
in bins on the floor—lies the physical history of America's pastime. In
every direction, hundreds of bats and gloves and trophies, cases of baseballs, rows and rows of uniforms hanging on industrial-size racks, stadium
seats lined up against walls, a bank safe the size of a dresser, and in the center, waxed and painted and as large as life, Babe Ruth with bat in hand. The
giant warehouse space is one hundred times the size of the Leland's stor-

age room, and I stand there in awe, until the elevator behind me jerks back to life and disappears through the floor.

But I'm hardly alone. Three young Sotheby's women are leafing through what looks like a stack of baseball card albums, construction workers are erecting some kind of cage around the collection's perimeter, and off to one side two union workers are playing catch. I walk over to the women and introduce myself. One of them stands up and puts her hands on her hips.

"Where have you been? You were supposed to be up here on Monday."

"I didn't know—"

"Well, we've been moving forward without you."

She's the opposite of a classic Sotheby's girl: small and no-nonsense, the type that actually gets things done. She starts explaining the complex inventory system, but I'm too overwhelmed to listen to talk of item numbers and reference codes, so I tell her I need to walk around and get a feel for what's here. I have no idea whether I'm her boss or she's mine. I don't know anything that's going on—with two exceptions. I know the trove of sporting treasures surrounding me is worth tens of millions of dollars, and I'm pretty sure those union guys shouldn't be playing catch with autographed baseballs and swinging bats that belong in the Hall of Fame.

Within ten minutes I'm struck with complete paralysis. The enormity of the project—the identifying, cataloging, publicizing, and successful selling of what is easily the world's greatest privately owned sports collection—hits me all at once. My face is getting flushed, the blood rushing around too quickly, and I sit down to steady myself. This life of half truths has finally caught up with me. I can't do this. I don't know enough. How long before David Redden or Barry Halper or even this girl frowning at me from across the room reveals me as a fraud? I pick up a catcher's mitt lying on the shelf beside me. The pocket, once so carefully broken in, has stiffened with age, and the only thing that distinguishes it from the dozens of other nearby gloves is the number "8" written in faded marker near the thumb. Yogi Berra wore number 8, but so did a hundred other catchers. I have no idea whose mitt this was, and there's no way Barry Halper can know the history of every item in his collection. Even if he did, how do I prove his account? The auction business is all about convincing the public of a piece's value, but I don't even know what most of these pieces are—to say nothing of their worth. I'd better learn to fake it pretty fast.

Twenty-one

ON THE MORNING of the Sotheby's Christmas party, I wake up and, as I have for almost a month now, put on a suit, kiss Claire good-bye, and walk to the Astor Place subway. I buy the paper and take the 6 train up to Harlem, walk four long rundown blocks east, and make it to the warehouse just after nine. I've spoken to Barry Halper on the phone, and he seems surprisingly laid-back, considering what's at stake. He faxed me several inventory lists, and now we've managed to identify almost half of what's here. We've also gotten serious about security. The giant floor-to-ceiling cage is complete, cameras have been installed, and the union guys aren't allowed to touch anything without my permission. As we've moved closer to actually beginning the cataloging process, I've tried to hint to Redden that I need help, but I don't think he understands the gravity of the situation. He keeps smiling, saying everything will work out.

I work on what little I know. This morning it's baseball cards. I'd heard rumors that Barry Halper owned at least one of every baseball card ever made. Now, flipping through hundreds of albums dating back almost a century, I can believe it. When my family first moved back to the States, I collected cards. At the candy store in Montclair, I'd study the see-through Topps packs with the same steely determination that older customers lavished on lottery tickets. I forecasted favorite players during spring training, went to card shows with my friends, and assiduously affixed values to every card (most were three or four cents) in the ill-fated hope that I might turn a profit. That went on for two years. Halper's been doing it for fifty, and his cards, like everything else in the collection, are rare and exquisite. He has full sets of every issue from the thirties through the eighties, but it's the early tobacco cards, with their curious shapes and artistically rendered images, that are the real attraction. I don't know what they have up in Cooperstown, but it can't be any better than this. I look up from the albums and stare at the surrounding shelves. Barry Halper deserves a lot better than me.

Toward the end of the day, I make my way back down to Collectibles. Giles is watching streaming video replays of Manchester United and Chelsea, Gabrielle is cataloging vintage movie posters, and Laura is playing DJ, spinning a Morcheeba track she downloaded from Napster. I check my e-mail. All this time in New York and this is my very first e-mail account. The concept is still oddly foreign — every time I press Send I mentally trace the path of wires my message must be taking (but how does it get across oceans?). Redden has sent me the schedule for the live portion of the Halper auction, and it's even worse than I feared. It's slated as a week-long sale at the end of June, which means the catalog needs to be ready by the first week of March and in people's hands by mid-April. That leaves us just over two months — two months to identify, write up, and photograph four thousand lots.

It's just not possible.

Around 6:00 P.M. my coworkers start getting ready for the Christmas party. They disappear one at a time, emerging ten minutes later looking like debutantes and dandies. Everyone at Sotheby's keeps a change of clothes hanging on the back of their door, as you never know when a good party might materialize. Giles looks like a midseventies Roxy Music devotee. The girls all look like magic. Together we walk the few chilly blocks down to headquarters and take the elevator up to the main gallery, which tonight is decorated with blinking lights and glass ornaments hanging from Christmas trees. There's top-shelf liquor at the bar and catering stations overflowing with sushi, caviar, and lobster tails. This is no half-hearted corporate affair; it's a high-society celebration.

Claire is at her own office party. There was talk of going to one and then the other, uptown and then down, but it seemed too hard. We're suddenly running with different crowds: book readings and publishing parties for her, exhibitions and gallery openings for me. When we relate our various adventures, we listen a bit too closely to the names and descriptions of new friends. I think we're both looking for clues, hints of irregularity. We've been together almost two years, and still we're sorting through issues, processing jealousies, finding a level for our love. It's really hard to do.

And so tonight I'm dateless. I order a martini and set off with Giles and Laura on a tour of famous names and faces. Sotheby's is a Who's Who of young New York society, a kind of holding pen for the unmarried children of well-known families. I meet Serena Boardman and Lily Phipps, perennial party faces in Claire's beauty magazines, and then Tiffany Dubin, the well-connected fashion-department expert.

"The fashion department loses tens of thousands of dollars on every auction," Laura says, quietly, "but Tiffany gets so much press that Dede lets her keep doing it."

"It doesn't hurt that she's Taubman's stepdaughter," Giles adds.

Back at the bar I'm introduced to a dapper middle-aged man named Jamie Niven. He may be the best-dressed person I've ever seen. He shakes my hand warmly, then tells me to come by his office sometime for a chat.

"What was that about?" I ask, when he's gone.

"He runs client relations," Laura says, "so he probably wants to find out who you know. He's David Niven's son, so he grew up surrounded by royalty and privilege, and somehow he's managed to broker his connections into a career. His Rolodex is so valuable he keeps it in a locked drawer."

Giles joins us again a few minutes later with his nineteen-year-old Australian girlfriend, Jennie. She's flown in from London for the weekend, has come here straight from JFK, and Giles is trying to convince her to move here permanently. She's a healthy, busty blond from Perth, a real outback girl with a party glow I know all too well. Our man Giles has his hands full.

"See that woman?" Laura says, pointing toward the caviar station. "That's Serena Sutcliffe, the wine expert. They say her palate is insured by Lloyd's of London for a million dollars. And the two twins near the Christmas tree, they're the Keno brothers, the furniture experts on *Antiques Roadshow*. Everyone thinks they're gay because they wear makeup, but I've heard they have girls in every city."

That's how it is here; information comes second- and thirdhand. And I'm not immune. Strangers keep asking me about the baseball auction. One man wants to know if it's really worth $50 million. Another says he's heard the whole thing is being kept behind bars at a secret location. That's right, I tell him, doing my best to play the game.

By ten o'clock most of Sotheby's is on the dance floor. Near a small podium in front, I spot David Redden talking to Dede Brooks. Dede is tall and angular and her famous blond mane is even bigger in person than in magazines. She's wearing a bright green jacket and skirt, and the pearls around her neck are enormous. Which makes sense, I suppose. Laura has told me Dede either likes you or doesn't within the first minute of meeting you, so I try my luck and walk over to introduce myself. Redden sees me coming. He whispers something—my name, I suppose—into Dede's ear, then turns around, holds out his arms, and gives me a loud London "Helloooo!"

"So this is our new sports specialist," Dede says, shaking my hand firmly. "Welcome aboard. You have plenty of work ahead of you." Then she smiles and says, "I understand you're dating Claire Davis. She was a knockout when she was a little girl. Say hello to her mother for me. I haven't seen them in years."

I'm about to ask how she knew that, but she's called away before I can.

"Did you get my e-mail?" Redden asks.

"I did, but I think the timetable is a bit . . . aggressive. I . . . well, I've been meaning to talk to you about this. I think I might really need some help."

"You mean you can't handle the world's greatest sports collection all by yourself, dear boy?" And then he starts laughing, a great belly laugh. "Don't worry, help is on the way!" And with that he sashays off toward the dance floor.

A few minutes later Dede thanks everyone for "one of the greatest years in Sotheby's history." There are cheers and back slaps and toasts. She gives a rousing speech about sothebys.com, the company of tomorrow, lifting our lives seamlessly into the next century, and already I can see the rift, the younger people clapping, even whistling, while the old guard stir their drinks in silence. And then it's over. Dede leaves to an ovation, vanishes through a side door, trailed by an aping entourage clutching Kate Spade bags and Nokia cell phones.

And then the problem of where to go next. The Niven set is going to Doubles; the younger crowd is talking of Morgan's, Lot 61, the Mercer. Soon I'm swept up with a group from Catalog Production, a dozen girls, all drunk and climbing into the back of a limo pointed downtown. I think briefly of calling Claire, but only briefly. I'm sure she's out with her new agent friends—some "great guy named Devon who published a poem in *The New Yorker* and shows his paintings at galleries," or maybe the "cool Park Slope agent who loves to party, but has this, like, great yoga side to her"—so I'll embrace *my* new reality, as well. Everywhere we go, tables are reserved, bottles are on ice, and velvet ropes part with no problems. I keep trying to figure out who's paying. Upstairs in the VIP room at Moomba, as the familiar sounds of Duran Duran's "Rio" tumble from the speakers, the pashminas come off, and long legs with wobbly heels climb onto tables. I'm the only straight man in our merry group, and looking up, I see red lipstick, ultralight filters, and skirts suddenly shorter than they were at the Christmas party. This must be the other side of Sotheby's. I don't know what kind of cavalry Redden is sending me, but I hope they get here quickly, because I want to stick around awhile.

A LOT GOES ON *but nothing much happens.* . . . It's a Ben Lee song I can't get out of my head. The other night I tagged along to his show with some Sotheby's photographers. The photographers are as bohemian as Sotheby's gets, and as they quietly debated the return of real songwriting, I listened to Ben Lee sing those words over and over again. *A lot goes on but nothing much happens*: That's Sotheby's, where auctions come and go in frenzied cycles, but nothing changes except the descriptions in the catalogs; that's my writing career, which lies as stagnant as a cesspool in the corner of my mind; that's Claire and me, still in this thing together but clearly not progressing; and that's New York, with its soft openings and world premieres, its Madison Avenue glamour and underground styles. Here the latest trends are so fresh and original—bare legs, backless dresses, *beading*—you can almost forget they're all recycled from the twenties.

NOTHING MUCH HAS BEEN happening with the Halper sale, either. I've been here over a month and we're still doing inventory. But then, on a cold morning in January—just as I'm nearing occupational meltdown—Stephen Carson appears. He takes a look around, then comes over to introduce himself. I don't tell him but I already know who he is. Carson runs a north Jersey auction outfit that specializes in early baseball collectibles, niche stuff like cabinet cards and painted trophy balls. He doesn't have a

Web site or hold live auctions or employ a copywriter. He's got a reputation for being extremely smart, very focused on authenticity, and fiercely independent. Josh has never liked him very much, which means he's probably a good guy. I knew Redden was up to something.

We talk for a while, keeping things general, feeling each other out. I give him a tour of the collection—the parts I know. Stephen clearly doesn't want to step on my toes, but he keeps picking up pieces and explaining their history. I don't think he's rubbing it in; I think he's genuinely excited. I want to tell him I'm thrilled he's here, because I was coming up against some harsh realities. But I think he can see that.

Stephen tells me he's signed a one-year consulting contract and has no intention of working at Sotheby's thereafter. He doesn't like the place and doesn't trust the people. Stephen wears jeans and T-shirts; he prefers McDonald's to Mortimer's; and he wears suits only to funerals. I was right: he is doing this for love. But he's doing it more for money. Turns out one of Halper's conditions upon consigning the collection to Sotheby's was that Stephen be involved in putting the auction together. Sotheby's agreed but then couldn't come to terms on the contract. Stephen was asking for hundreds of thousands for the year, which must be why Sotheby's hired me. I was a ploy, leverage. Redden must have known I could never do all this by myself.

The day after I meet Carson, Redden sits me down and asks if I'm okay with his coming on board. "It's still your department. You'll be here long after he's gone. But I want someone who's worked with this collection before, and Halper says he's the man for the job."

I want to kiss his feet, but instead I just say, "Sure, no problem."

STEPHEN CARSON *IS* the right man for the job. Within a week he's come up with a complex system of sorting, authenticating, grading, and cataloging. Soon we have a fully staffed assembly line of interns, catalogers, editors, and photographers working late every night, grinding through thousands of balls and bats and gloves and caps and autographs and letters and cards and contracts and programs and photographs and pennants and uniforms and jackets and pieces of jewelry. It's almost too much, except now that we have some direction, we're beginning to get a sense of the project and the scope of what we could achieve.

One morning in late February, Stephen leads me over to a quiet corner of the cage, where he's spent the last few days assembling a stockpile of spoils.

"I've been talking to Barry," he says, "and together we've come up with the ten highest-priced lots in the sale. They're what I'd call the 'press pieces,' and I think each could sell for well into six figures. In other words, they'll make or break the auction."

We start going through them, and I can't believe what he's showing me: Ty Cobb's 1928 jersey, Mickey Mantle's 1956 Triple Crown award, Lou Gehrig's last glove, a Honus Wagner T206 card, and a collection of Yankees World Series rings spanning the years 1947–1964. Then he opens a box and pulls out a document protected by hard plastic. It's the 1920 agreement that sent Babe Ruth from the Red Sox to the Yankees and changed the history of American sport. I didn't even know this was in the collection.

"And last but not least. . . ." Stephen carefully hands me a piece of leather. Perhaps it used to be round, but now the stitching has split and the insides are coming out. "Do you know what it is?"

"It looks like a dog toy."

"Not quite," Stephen says. "It's the very first baseball . . . *ever*. Barry got it from the descendants of Alexander Cartwright, the man who invented the game."

"At Elysian Fields in Hoboken."

"Then you know the real story."

"Most of it, I guess. I know that the origins of baseball are one of America's greatest myths, that the history books all say a Civil War general named Abner Doubleday invented the game in Cooperstown, but really it was a blue-collar sport, adapted from the British, and first played in and around New York City."

"*That's right!*" Stephen exclaims. "They used to row across the Hudson and play in Hoboken. That's where Cartwright organized the first team and set down the rules—ninety feet between bases, nine innings, all the stuff that applies today. And our man Doubleday was nowhere in sight."

"So why isn't this . . . *ball* . . . in the Hall of Fame?"

"Because the Hall of Fame still perpetuates the Doubleday myth. If they admit the truth, that the game was invented in Hoboken, then Cooperstown as a location becomes irrelevant."

"But how can we know for certain that *this* is the actual ball?" It's the old Leland's question, the one I've asked a hundred times before without ever getting a concrete answer.

"We can't be positive," Stephen says. "All we can do is present the evidence, which is substantial: a letter from Cartwright saying he kept the ball for the rest of his life, along with other letters from family members written through the ensuing generations. But in the end, people will have to make up their own minds."

I try to imagine Josh saying something like that.

"So what do you think it might sell for?"

"Personally, I think this transcends sports. It's one of the most important cultural artifacts in the history of this country."

"And?"

"And I have no idea. Five hundred thousand? A million? Who knows?"

STEPHEN AND I COMPLEMENT each other well. I oversee the writing and editing of the catalog, and he does everything else. He works hard, he's efficient, and best of all, he's skeptical. The entire sports memorabilia business is under siege this year (thanks in part to a rash of high-profile forgeries that appeared in the aftermath of the McGuire–Sosa home-run race), and in the last few months the FBI has made headlines by busting several large counterfeiting rings. Despite what Josh says, Halper's collection has a good reputation because almost everything in it came directly from players or their families. Still, with the press we're starting to receive, one mistake could compromise the entire auction.

Which is where Stephen's skepticism comes in handy. He's on the phone with Halper several times a day, asking for evidence, for specific memories. Did you actually see DiMaggio sign the ball? Did Pete Rose tell you he used that bat in a game? When the answer's not good enough, the piece gets pulled. We also catch fakes ourselves. I find a Babe Ruth signature on a ball dating to the midfifties (Ruth died in 1948). Stephen compares a batch of handwritten Ty Cobb letters to other known samples and concludes that someone else has written them. And the nineteenth-century jerseys, the ones Josh warned me about—they're not right. The flannel is too thin, the stitching too even, and the tags aren't faded at all. Halper can't seem to remember where most of them came from, so we pull them all—tens of thousands of dollars worth of jerseys—and truck them back to Halper's basement. We're not *sure* they're fake; we just can't prove they're real.

And it doesn't stop there. Redden agrees to fly in outside authenticators, freelance experts, the best in the business: a handwriting analyst from Phoenix; a bat authenticator from Chicago; a uniform specialist from Long Island; and a professorial type from Brooklyn who looks like he hasn't been outside since the Dodgers moved West, though Stephen says the guy knows more about nineteenth-century baseball history than any man alive. Taken together, they are the strangest assortment of men I have ever seen, and every chance I get I wander over and watch them in action. They've brought their own tools—magnifying glasses, miniature scales, ink and fabric samples, and, of course, research books. It's an impressive show, but I still think it's just that. Like anyone else who hangs an Expert sign outside the door, these men spend a lot of their time guessing. I watch them go through their piles, giving each signature, each ball, each jersey their *patented inspection processes*, and soon it strikes me that the science of authentication isn't a science at all, it's performance art, and the best actors are the ones who can convince an audience of their talents. No one can trace the history of an object with absolute certainty, and that's what scares me. Come auction time, these freelance con men will be long gone, and if a mistake has been made and Stephen and I haven't caught the error, the blame will fall on the person listed in the catalog, the in-house "Specialist in Charge": me.

Twenty-two

THE INVITATIONS ARE MANY for a straight man in the art world—auction exhibitions, gallery openings, museum benefits, boutique launches. . . . Sometimes Claire comes, but more often she doesn't. We seem to have switched lives somewhere along the way. I now run with the Upper East Side socialites and wealthy Europeans whom I once actively campaigned against, while Claire surrounds herself with young literary lights, the stars of the downtown scene. We've stopped asking each other to events because the response is always tepid, as if facing our former selves is too difficult just now. So we've started down the path to resentment. We still have good days, perfect moments, but that desire to spend every waking minute together is gone. We're quickly growing out of dependence. Or slowly falling out of love. No, I still love her. It's been two years and I can't imagine life without her. We've been partners at an age and in a city where couples appear and evaporate like contrails, streaking across the nighttime scene, then dissolving in the rust of morning. I'd like to think we're stronger than that.

Tonight it's a Sotheby's Young Collectors party down on Seventy-second Street. I wanted Claire to come, but she was going to a reading at Housing Works, so I've convinced Giles to accompany me, and now we're surveying the art, admiring the crowd, and taking full advantage of the open bar. Sotheby's throws these swank affairs in hopes of diversifying its clientele, but the invitations rarely reach anyone outside the tight ranks of New York's young elite, so they end up being exclusive society functions, where the children of privilege drink and flirt surrounded by the paintings their parents are about to bid on.

Sotheby's is quickly becoming two different companies, and the line between them couldn't be clearer. In the retrofitted car garage on Seventy-sixth, sothebys.com has become a village of young Internet hopefuls, a promised cyberland already sixty strong. It looks a lot like any other dot-com startup. The white rooms are crammed full of desks and people, almost all under the age of forty, and the pace is not that of languid auction-house refinement but is instead intense, almost crazed: it's the manic pace of unrealistic deadlines and unachievable goals. There's an air of self-importance surrounding the whole Internet venture, and Dede and David Redden stop by daily to check on progress, as if the fate of the company—the fate of the art world itself—lies in the hands of these young men and women.

Down the road at headquarters, the traditional ways of buying and selling carry on unabated yet somehow diminished. There's a growing resentment amid these departments of the past, as if the new reality threatens to make the old ways obsolete. Auctions are scheduled and held, in real time, in physical space, but the imminence of change is everywhere—in the young clientele, heavy with new money and anxious to spend; in company trends, where the veterans are already being fired or retired, put out to art-world pasture; and in the building itself, rife with the hammering and drilling of never-ending construction, a facelift for a company turning younger.

But Seventy-second Street still carries Sotheby's forward. This is where the money is made, the exhibitions held, the paintings sold. Here I can wander through galleries filled with works of artistic genius, or find myself alone in an elevator with the world's foremost expert in Chinese porcelain or costume jewelry or Fabergé silver. Down here, the word *Sotheby's* still means something grand. Giles likes this world better, too. He's more a child of my generation than I am—he goes to raves, plays video games, listens to the latest British house mixes from Cream—but in that distinctively English way, there is something about change that unnerves him, something about tradition he respects. And so he's come here with me tonight to make sure the old auction business he learned in the wood-paneled halls of Sotheby's, London, still exists in modern New York.

The outfits are impressive, and so are the paintings, most of which are in the upcoming Spring Impressionist sale. Giles leads me over to a Cézanne still life, *Rideau, Cruchon et Compotier*. It's obviously a major piece, so I tilt my head sideways, the way everyone else around here does, trying to absorb the gems of brushstroke genius, but it just looks like what it is—a bunch of fruit spilling out of a bowl.

"They're talking fifty million," Giles says, sipping champagne.

"Jesus." I turn back to the fruit bowl, trying to think of something smart to say. "Isn't it weird how you could just ruin the canvas if you wanted? I mean . . . we're so close and there's no glass protection or anything."

Giles frowns. "That's the problem with inviting *sports* experts to nice soirées like this," he says, shaking his head, walking back toward the bar.

I catch up with him a few minutes later, entertaining a small contingent of pearl girls: a woman from Prints, another from Clocks, a pretty French girl from Arms & Armor. We all make small talk, but even small talk at Sotheby's is mostly *art* talk, so I stay quiet until the girls move on, or we do, hugging and kissing on both cheeks in the typical Sotheby's way. It's a holdover from the Bond Street days.

We take one last look around the room. "Look at that wanker in the white suit," Giles says. "Thinks he's Elton John. That's the problem with the auction world. After a while people start taking it seriously. Let's get out of here before it's too late."

In some ways it's already too late. For the last few months a sense of disillusionment has been creeping into the urban Eden that Claire and I have so carefully constructed. Our desire to be that dreamy New York couple of nods and knowing, the couple that blends in so easily at every party—and in doing so *stands out*, as exemplary, fabulous, *untouchable*—no longer exists. We've been beaten down by the city, wounded by its pleasures, ravaged by its setbacks. We've started competing with each other, comparing our lives instead of living them, intertwined.

Perhaps the new jobs were the death knell. She doesn't say it, but I know she liked it more when I was writing. And I . . . I find it hard to hang out with her new crowd, young agents and editors and writers, writers who have pressing things to say, plots and characters bursting from every story. Claire used to give me her favorite manuscripts to read, but she's stopped. Or maybe I've stopped asking. Somehow I've fallen onto the wrong side of the artistic equation. And Claire, she's talking seriously about writing, herself. So we've come full circle. She is where I was, not a year ago, and I'm wearing a suit and working uptown.

Breakups come in all forms: ours takes two hours. Claire comes down to 10 St. Marks, ostensibly to spend the night, but I think we both know what's about to happen. It's a fitting setting, this claustrophobic back room of mine, with the cat lurking and roaches scurrying across the walls. Claustrophobia has seeped into all facets of our relationship, turning everyday moments into intense battles of will, making trust, which we once breathed like air, an endangered commodity. I don't know why or how it's all become so hard. She appears at my door looking luminous, of course, and soon we're thrashing back and forth through a waterfall of tears, of youthful misery that knows no perspective. Even the cat catches the vibe and stays away. We both know we need to end this. We've been stuck for months, afraid or unable to move forward. But knowing we're doing the right thing doesn't matter in the moment, and it's so hard to sit there with her, running through the full course of emotions, holding her closely one moment and punching the door and spraining my hand the next. When she leaves, finally, too soon, she's a sobbing wreck. But I am destroyed. We hug but I can't feel anything. She says she's going to meet a friend on Second Avenue and with that she's down the stairs and gone.

Ken hears the door close and comes out to play the consoling friend, then takes one look at me and turns back around. He says he's ready to drink when I am. But I'm not ready for anything. What friend is she going to meet? I bet it's that agent guy, the poet/painter. She says he's gay, but I bet he'll straighten out pretty quickly now. Maybe he's the reason for all this, and I'm just fooling myself thinking the problem was something else. That's why she's been so distant. Asshole has a poem in *The New Yorker* and she falls for it. Doesn't she know that poets are doomed? They wreak havoc with their philosophical rants, their late-night mantras, but are always MIA when the real world appears again, as it tends to do, every morning. What am I doing? I need to go save her. I run down the stairs and onto the street. She'll be at the new bar on the corner of Second and Seventh, her latest favorite. To think she's meeting him tonight! It's like they're going off to celebrate her release from custody. I run all the way there, not noticing anything, anyone. And sure enough, I can see her through the front window, sitting in a booth along the wall. She still has tears in her eyes. She's looking into her drink and talking to someone I can't see.

I take a deep breath and walk in, walk right up to the table. Claire sees me coming and the look on her face turns to contempt. Her deep blue eyes become beads, darts. I turn to face my adversary and . . . it's a *girl*. She's sitting with a dark-haired twig of a thing with Dutch cheekbones and eyes dancing in amusement.

"This is Melissa. She's a friend from work."

"Hi."

"What's wrong? Were you expecting someone else?"

"Claire, we need to talk."

"No we don't. Not anymore. All you're doing is yelling."

"Maybe I'll let you two be alone," Melissa says, getting up. She has a yoga mat sticking out of her bag.

Claire protests but Melissa can't get out of the restaurant fast enough. I throw cash down on the table and beg Claire to walk back up to the apartment with me. I say I'm sorry, that I was expecting Devon or whatever his name is.

"You're one to talk," Claire says, "parading around town with half of Sotheby's. You hated that world when I first met you. Remember when you said you were allergic to the Upper East Side? Now you're like its fucking poster child."

"It's only a job."

"It's more like your life."

We walk back up to my building in silence. She doesn't want to come upstairs, so we sit on the stoop out front, watch the line form for a concert at Coney Island High. The nightly party on St. Marks is just picking up. Outside Dojo a parked car with Jersey plates is getting hitched to a tow truck, and a crowd of goth kids are cheering their approval. We sit there for a long time. I take her hand and hold it tightly. She wipes tears from my cheeks. Then she stands up and gives me one last hug. Good-bye.

"Let's try to be adults," she says, and then she turns, walks to Third Avenue, and hails a cab heading farther downtown.

• • •

THE WEEKS THAT FOLLOW are the worst of my life. I trudge back and forth to Harlem, hiding in the monotony of work. I want to meet someone else right away, a Lower East Side girl with dyed hair and tattoos, and at the same time I want to disappear, save myself from more inevitable misery. It's Claire I still think about every few minutes: where she is, what she's doing. I call her sometimes at night—two, three times—until I finally catch her at home. She says it's a bad idea to talk. It sounds like she's busy.

Ken picks me up off the futon and sets me down on a barstool at Holiday Cocktail, the last of the great neighborhood dives, where Buds are two bucks and advice is free. Ken talks about time. He says he went through all this last year and is only now coming out the other side.

"I finally learned to channel the anger and emotion into the screenplay," he says.

"Which is why it's two hundred pages and counting."

"Fuck you."

Yes, Ken knows. He tells me to take advantage of my freedom and I listen. I call old friends, the dangerous ones who drift away when the girlfriends get too serious but come back with a vengeance when the coast is clear. I venture out alone, to places I remember from earlier escapades—bodegas on Avenue C, Dominican bars near Houston. The city takes care of its wounded, and the same guys are still around, the kind of health-care providers you won't find on any insurance plan. They lurk in bathrooms, behind counters, flashing sly smiles and little packets of foil. Cocaine really can make you forget. Just pick your spots—a line at lunch, a gram to take out on the town. The same beeper numbers, the same names, the same way of life comes swiftly back, and the nights become familiar marathons of stamina.

Now I'm single again and women are everywhere, like dry cleaners and Chinese restaurants. I meet them (it's so much easier when you're high: you forget you're supposed to be scared) but don't ask them out. I just can't. Instead I end up wired and alone in the middle of the night. Sometimes the lights down the hall are still burning, and I know Ken is up, writing, excising his own demons, but that only makes me feel worse. Writing—or my lack of it—is what caused all this. I try to sleep but memories won't let me—the low-cut red shirt she always wore because I bought it for her; the way she wrote her name on her CDs; and her eyes, finding me across crowded rooms. So Xanax, Valium, pot . . . something to come down smoothly. There's always work tomorrow.

But work is adaptable as well. I start doing coke at the warehouse. Just a line here and there, and for the same old reasons: I can write copy faster and we're behind schedule. The bathroom on our floor has no door. It's on the other side of a cinder-block wall in a remote corner, and the women go in pairs so one can stand guard. There's no stall door, either, so I have to be quick. One day, just after lunch, I'm filling the grooves of my house key with powder when one of the union guys walks in as quiet as a ballerina and catches me cold.

"Shit, man."

"Sorry," I say, startled, fumbling around. "Here, let me get out of your way."

"Don't worry, it's cool . . . but as long as you got it out . . ."

"Sure, go for it." And he does. He pours out a mini-mountain and snorts it all at once, like an industrial-strength vacuum running over lint.

"Get this shit from Jimmy downstairs?"

I've never heard of Jimmy, but the idea of a Sotheby's drug ring sounds alluring.

"No, got a guy downtown."

"Well, be careful," he says. "You kid running his own department should be doing this shit anyway."

ONE LIFE AND THEN the other. Suits then sneakers. Dinners then drugs. At some point, in early summer, my father and Cynthia stage an intervention for Anna, my youngest stepsister. She's a twenty-one-year-old blonde, a knockout who can't say no to temptation. One hazy morning I make my way up to the Freedom Institute in Midtown, wondering not what Anna did to get herself in trouble, but what she did to get herself caught. I take an elevator to a high floor and am led to a room filled with family members sitting in a circle. I'm the last one to arrive, and suddenly I get the horrid idea that all of this is for me! They know! My God, I've been tricked. The whole Anna thing was just a ruse to get me here. I'm offered a seat and my father thanks us all for coming. He looks tired. He stares at me for a moment, then speaks: "We're here to save Anna from more serious trouble down the road. . . ." What wonderful words. I exhale, try to collect myself, and sit down to judge someone else.

Twenty-three

To COINCIDE WITH THE baseball play-offs, Sotheby's moves the Halper auction to September. Perfect timing, Redden says, but in reality the Internet department, now over one hundred strong, is spiraling out of control and isn't anywhere near ready to launch. The much publicized deal with Amazon is coming apart, and the Sotheby's Internet team is stuck in the middle, moving too slowly for Amazon but far too quickly for the staid auction house. Dede Brooks and Amazon CEO Jeff Bezos hold a joint press conference to squelch the rumors of discord. Bezos, hunched over and balding, is the unlikely poster boy of the Internet age; on the pedestal next to six-foot Dede, he looks like a turtle. They stand there side by side, like a touring sideshow act, begging the world to believe them.

At the warehouse we make the most of the extra time, a dozen of us working into the night, finalizing lots, laying out pages, proofing color and copy. And a month later we see the result: a spectacular three-volume catalog housed in a thick glossy case. It's a shrink-wrapped box set that weighs five pounds, contains 2,481 lots, and is so overwhelming that it comes with its own informational booklet complete with a historical time line and testimonials from Ted Williams and Yogi Berra. Almost by accident we've created the ultimate history of America's national pastime. Sotheby's orders a print run of forty thousand and sets the price at $100.

The first boxes vanish from my office in two days. Senior staffers send assistants over, and soon half of Sotheby's is calling to request free copies. When I see Dede Brooks one night at La Goulue, on Madison, she waves me over and proudly introduces me to her table of Park Avenue friends.

"This is our young sports expert. He's responsible for one of the greatest catalogs we've ever produced."

The ladies smile like they're supposed to, but Dede is hardly stretching the truth. Within two weeks of its release, the Barry Halper Collection of Baseball Memorabilia has become the coffee table book of the summer. Articles and interviews are scheduled. The Bergdorf men's store decorates its windows with highlights from the sale. Every major dealer and collector in the country, sports and nonsports alike, receives a complimentary catalog. And a major traveling exhibition is planned, starting in L.A. and ending in New York a week before the sale. Things are about to change.

SOME NIGHTS I DON'T REMEMBER. I wake up with pockets full of things that don't make sense—names and numbers scrawled on receipts, matchbooks from unfamiliar bars, pills with strange markings. My dealer gets busted. John Kennedy Jr. dies. I lust after a waitress at Indochine. I even kiss a waiflike hipster guy at a gay friend's party. When I pull away he tells me to calm down, that I'm too jumpy. And he's right.

My relationships have never grown from friendships; they've ignited from nowhere. But nowhere is mostly a lonely place. It's been almost six months, and the memories and mistakes I made with Claire still disturb me. So do thoughts of writing. I'm enjoying success for the first time in my life, but success tends to mask other failures, and I can't remember the last time I sat down at my computer. Jackson Schultz used to check in, but those calls have stopped. The Greene Street office lease has expired. And the thought of engaging in a few lonely hours of torture at my tiny bedroom desk seems nothing short of silly. There's too much going on.

One night, in midsummer, I come home and the apartment building smells like burning wire. There are roaches on the stairwell walls. Ken's door is closed, so I slump into my room, press the blinking message light on my answering machine, and fall onto my futon, exhausted.

Wednesday, 4:52 P.M. Hello? Hello? Okay, I don't even know if this is the right number, but if this is the David Goodwillie who sent a short story to Open City *a while back, well, this is Rob Bingham, the publisher. I know this is random but I liked—what's it called?—"This Means War" and I saw you lived on St. Marks, so I figured I'd see if you wanted to join me and a few friends tonight at Café Mogador down the street from you. I know it's last minute, but we'll be there around nine, so just show up.*

We'll be the drunk group in the corner. And if this is someone else, then come anyway, if you're bored or something. Bye.

Robert Bingham. His name has been everywhere recently: a profile in *New York* magazine, fiction in *The New Yorker*, and rave reviews for *Pure Slaughter Value*. His *Open City* parties have made him the face of the downtown literary scene. I sent my story to him almost a year ago, and *now* he's calling me. I'm not sure I am the David Goodwillie he's looking for anymore.

I GET TO CAFÉ Mogador at a calculated 9:20 and spot Bingham immediately. He looks just like the picture on his jacket cover. I walk over and tap him on the shoulder, not quite sure what to say, where to sit, who to be. He turns around and I say my name and he gives me a jovial greeting and points to a chair across from him. Quick introductions are made, and I catch a few names, the pretty girls, of course: Joanna Yas, the editor at *Open City*, and Robin Troy, a statuesque blonde, who, if it's the same girl I read about, won the MTV fiction award with her first novel, *Floating*.

Here I am, across from the man I've watched from afar, the man whose short stories I've read and reread, wondering how they work, how he works, who he is. Rob has unkempt dark hair and the mischievous eyes of a family troublemaker. He's pouring wine for the table, liberally filling already full glasses, laughing as he spills everywhere.

"I loved *Pure Slaughter Value*," I tell him, absent any intelligent thoughts.

"You read that thing!"

"I thought it was great."

"Then how come no one bought it?" he says, smiling. I take a sip of wine and try to fit in. The other end of the table is discussing Robin's book, or more accurately, the marketing of it. Writers, from what little I've seen, rarely talk of the books themselves, but focus instead on the industry, on deals and sales and figures, as if delving into the work itself is too painful.

I want to ask Rob about my story so badly, but I'm starstruck. It's a strange feeling, meeting the very person whose life you'd like to have. Someone asks him about how the editing of his latest novel, *Emperor of the Sun*, is going, but he shrugs the question off.

"Tell me what you're up to," he says to me.

"I was writing for a while, short stories as I guess you know, but then I got sidetracked."

"Internet?"

"Sotheby's."

"God, even worse."

"I run their—"

"I found your story at the office last week under a pile of shit. The one about the boarding school kid and the teacher's daughter."

"I figured you guys didn't even read it."

"Sorry it took so long. We're not too organized. But I thought it was great," he says, looking me straight in the eye. "I went to Groton, so the whole thing sort of hit home. And if you haven't already sold it to someone else, I'd like to publish it. Maybe we can get it into the spring issue if we—"

I can't hear anything else—just the noise of a new world roaring through my ears. I feel warm. The restaurant feels like a living room. And these people, the ones I just met, are all my best friends. So many dormant dreams come flooding back, all at once, and I can't remember why I ever gave them up.

At some point I leave, but it's hours later. Rob pays and we all stagger outside. He'll be in touch, he says, and then we shake hands and I stroll home, slowly, breathing in gulps.

The lights are out in the hallway, and the smell of burning wire has grown stronger. It's 2:00 a.m., and I don't want to wake Ken up, so I tiptoe in and collapse onto my futon. Even in the dark, I can see—I can feel—roaches climbing my walls, so I keep the lights off. I thought cats were supposed to take care of bugs.

I can't fall asleep. Rob Bingham liked the story. Why couldn't he have liked the story last year, when it was all I had? If I could just budget my time better, find the will it takes to—

"FIRE!"

I hear the word before I hear the front door come down, falling to the blow of an axe. Instinctively, I cover myself as a fireman rushes in, a hulking figure in black and yellow. Behind him smoke from the hallway, dark and surprisingly thick, quickly fills the apartment. And people are shouting in the stairwell.

"Get out *now*," the fireman says loudly, firmly. He scans the room, barely looking at me. "Take the stairs, stay low, and cover your mouth."

"My roommate's still asleep," I respond, jumping up, looking for pants.

"Then go wake him up, but *hurry*." And then he's off up the stairs. I grab my wallet and reach for a computer disc on my desk, then run down the hall and burst dramatically into Ken's room. There's something perversely amusing about shaking your roommate awake from a dead sleep to tell him the building is on fire, watching him register and react in a jolted sequence like a strip of pictures from a photo booth. But he must know I'm serious because he's up and moving in seconds, looking for shoes, a shirt, the cat. Outside in the stairwell, people I've never seen before are making their way downstairs as firemen rush past them on their way up. More doors come down. The smoke is thick enough that we really do need to stay low to get through it. I don't see any flames, but the smell is pungent.

Outside we're greeted by the usual punk suspects, watching the building, waiting for action. Fire trucks are parked at odd angles, blocking traffic.

"Couldn't find the cat," Ken says.

"So this isn't all bad."

"Fuck you." We watch a fireman unscrew a hydrant with giant pliers. "We had more time than I thought," Ken says. "I should have grabbed some stuff."

"I got my wallet and the disc with all my stories."

"That's a good sign. Your subconscious speaking."

A fireman comes up to us, winded, panting: "You guys know who lives in 2B?"

"An old guy," Ken says. "Really reclusive. I don't see him out here. Why?"

"Judging from his apartment, I don't think he's been around for a while. The place is a sludge canal." He pauses to catch his breath. "The asshole must have turned on the sink and left without turning it off. The water short-circuited the power and sparked wires somewhere. And that's not the half of it. His entire place is infested with roaches. I've never seen more in my life. They're crawling on top of each other because they've run out of wall space."

They let us back in a half hour later. The roaches are everywhere now, so I move into Ken's room, hoping the cat might keep them away. But I can't sleep. Instead I lie on the couch, listening to the fire trucks head home.

"Hey," Ken says, after a while. "You still awake?"

"Yes."

"I need to tell you something. I saw Claire a few nights ago, at a bar with some guy. She introduced me but I forgot his name. I think they work together. And, well, it looked like they were . . . you know. . . . I thought I'd tell you before you heard it somewhere else."

"His name is Devon. Claire said he was gay."

"Sorry, man," Ken says, into the darkness. Five minutes later he's snoring.

Tossing and turning, plots and stories, fiction and reality. At some point, near dawn, the cat curls up beside me. Protectively.

The L.A. exhibition: Sotheby's trucks a hundred lots across the country to our office in Beverly Hills, then flies me out to run the event. "It'll be a scene," Redden warns me before I leave. "Parties, client tours, press previews, and cameras. So know your stuff, and try not to fidget when they're filming."

I don't fidget. From our offices on Rodeo Drive, I do a half dozen TV interviews. I thought I'd be nervous, but I know this collection inside out: names, dates, prices. I take L.A.'s bronzed sports reporters on guided tours, one camera crew at a time, and though it's all being taped for later, we get everything right the first time.

Later, at the VIP reception, celebrities and their entourages circle like planets with moons. I race around shaking hands, chuckling at jokes I can only half hear. Billy Crystal introduces himself, then leads me over to a display case where Mickey Mantle's game-worn baseball glove lies under glass.

"What do you think?" he asks.

"It could go for at least a hundred thousand."

"For a shitty old glove?"

"Afraid so. Imagine what his liver would be worth." Billy Crystal laughs.

It's a dressy affair and photographers from the L.A. *Times* and *Beverly Hills [213]* keep pushing me together with people I don't know. Then we're off to dinner at Spago. As movie stars come and go, as the night moves on, as I talk and talk, I wonder what Rob Bingham would think of this scene. Would he have the same phony feeling I have?

REDDEN SAYS I NEED a new suit, but otherwise my performance in L.A. was good enough that I'll be handling all the New York press as well. For the next few weeks I'll be the public face of Sotheby's—its young, approachable expert.

Meanwhile Stephen Carson has been stuck in the Harlem warehouse, overseeing the Internet cataloging, the four-thousand-plus cheaper lots to be sold online after the live sale ends. Stephen's the one who really brought this whole auction together, and now Sotheby's is practically ignoring him. Well, not ignoring him. I learned a few weeks ago that Sotheby's is paying him in the mid six figures for his year of work, and it's my guess that whatever ill will emerged from those negotiations has lingered, on both parts, to the point of animosity. Sotheby's doesn't see Stephen, with his Cubs T-shirts and faded jeans, as their type. For his part, Stephen thinks Sotheby's is full of shit, which is why he likes the warehouse, where most of the people—and accents—are real. And he's right: Sotheby's will always be a rich-man's playground. Even now, plenty of old-line insiders are looking for the Halper sale to bust, mostly because of what might happen if it succeeds. There's still time to go back to selling Picassos and Renoirs and jewels the size of New Jersey.

THE NEW YORK EXHIBITION opens on Friday, September 17. In less than two weeks' time, Sotheby's has erected a stunning display, a miniature Cooperstown, laid out across two entire floors of the main building. The exhibition is arranged as a walking tour, a stroll through time, from baseball's humble Hoboken origins through last year's epic home-run race. Hundreds of uniformed mannequins stand atop rows of stadium bleachers; sparkling World Series rings lie in velvet cases; paintings of baseball royalty hang on walls usually reserved for portraits of real kings and princes; and running down the center of the room, a fiberglass divider displays every type of baseball card ever made.

The crowds rush in at 10:00 A.M. Friday and stay for a week. I do interviews with all the networks, take correspondents like ABC's Morton Dean on private tours—just the two of us . . . and the millions who are watching. I let them swing Babe Ruth's last bat, touch Ty Cobb's dentures. Exposure leads to more exposure; local becomes national and then international: *Time Out, Sports Illustrated,* Japanese *Playboy.* . . . I interview-hop like a Washington pundit on the Sunday morning circuit, developing talking points, repeating stories, plugging our Web site.

Nights are filled with VIP dinners. Collectors and dealers arrive from around the globe, expecting the white-glove treatment Sotheby's is famous for. And the auction house doesn't disappoint: the well-bred stable of client-services specialists are rolled out along with the red carpets, and it doesn't matter that the Sotheby's girls are in Chanel and the clients are in track suits and Mets jerseys. These people have money to spend, and we're ready to help them.

I get home most nights around two, to a list of phone messages Ken has kindly scribbled down—interview requests from radio stations, endless questions from potential bidders, even Josh, calling from Leland's, demanding VIP treatment. On the night before the auction starts, I come home exhausted, expecting a new notepad barrage. But there are no messages, and no roommate, either. Only a note, scrawled in Ken's messy hand: *Can't take it anymore—Fucking phone's been ringing off the hook—Staying with friends until this awful saga ends—I liked it a whole lot more when you were a writer—K.*

Twenty-four

THE LIGHTS GO DOWN and David Redden takes the podium to an ovation befitting a rock concert. With his Savile Row suit and matching accent, he's an auctioneer straight from Central Casting. "Let's wait until we sell something," he says, dipping and swooning, and the room laughs and then falls respectfully silent. The capacity crowd is seated between the press area, itself spilling over with cameras on tripods and reporters eagerly studying catalogs, and the phone bank, manned by operators dressed to the nines and already cradling receivers to their ears, buttering up bidders the world over.

Above the masses, in a VIP skybox with semitransparent curtains, Barry Halper paces nervously. I watch his broad silhouette as I take my seat at the phone bank. He runs his hands through his hair, then fumbles through his pockets. He looks like what he is: a man whose life's work is about to be judged. The other five skyboxes have been the subject of a cantankerous weeklong debate between the industry's major players. Everyone wanted one, and not just for symbolic reasons. Each skybox phone connects to a Sotheby's operator seated at the phone bank, thus allowing for anonymous bidding, a vital perk for serious spenders. I'm at the phone bank, bidding for Leland's. Josh called for weeks, politely campaigning, and when that didn't work, he threatened to boycott if he didn't get special treatment. In the end, for better or worse, I wouldn't be here without him, so after getting him to promise he'd spend money, I got him the last skybox.

Lot #1 (estimated at $6,000–$8,000) is a small bronze baseball statue dating to 1868, just the kind of obscurely valuable piece that could either take off or sink. As Redden opens the bidding, I look across the room at Stephen Carson. He's standing alone against the back wall with his eyes closed, biting his bottom lip. It's the first time I've seen him nervous.

"Do I hear four thousand dollars? Four thousand dollars? Anyone?"

No one. Not one paddle goes up. It occurs to me, as the silence becomes consuming, that Stephen and I may have made some epic mistake. Maybe no one is here to bid. They think everything is fake or that the prices are too high. I can just see the dozens of reporters—taking notes even now—gleefully proclaiming this so-called auction of the century the biggest bust of the year. Who do these British bluebloods think they are, angling their way into America's—

"Bid." It's Josh's voice coming through the phone, which I'm not even holding to my ear. I sneak a look up at his skybox and he nods. "Bid seven thousand."

"But it's only at four thousand dollars," I whisper.

"I don't care, jump it to seven."

"SEVEN THOUSAND!" I shout, raising my paddle, and every head in the room turns my way. Redden accepts the bid with a look of relief.

Now a paddle goes up on the aisle, and then another, a woman toward the back. A phone bidder a few seats down gets in on the action and soon four people are actively bidding and the price surges past the estimate to $8,500 and then $9,000. I ask Josh if he wants to bid again but he says no, and a minute later a man on the aisle takes it home for $11,000 ($12,650, including buyer's premium). We're off and running.

Up in his skybox, Josh leans back in his chair with a wide grin on his face.

"You didn't want it?" I ask, through the phone.

"God no, it's a piece of shit. Just thought I'd help get the bidding started."

"How did you know you wouldn't get stuck with it?"

"I've been doing this since I was five."

"Well . . . thanks."

An auction is like a first date: it always goes one way or the other. Momentum builds toward some frenzied climax or it wanes and the evening dies. Tonight the sparks fly early. Because of its sheer size, Stephen and I have split the live auction into sixteen sessions to be held over seven days, and the opening-night offerings are mostly big-ticket pieces meant to attract attention. And they do. As each lot is revealed on the revolving stage in front, paddles shoot into the air like trading tickets on a market floor. Sotheby's, whenever possible, ties auctions to big names. Names are marketable. And in this industry, Halper's is the biggest name of all. Over months of careful marketing, Sotheby's has managed to build a real mystique around his collection. It's a neat trick, promoting the provenance over the pieces themselves, and it works. The room is filled with people who are here just to watch history, but it's the looming battle of the serious bidders that is most intriguing. I can see it all, right in front of me: the aging Bill Blass aristocracy, the elegant husbands bidding with practiced reserve while the wives fan themselves with addendum sheets; and then the younger collectors, the venture capitalists and IPO superstars, dressed in turtlenecks and Banana Republic khakis. It's a contest, old money versus new, but the new money has a lot of it, and they're bidding on more than just bits of baseball history. They're bidding for a piece of society, and that's what Sotheby's is selling. Tonight, as the lots come and go and the price board flickers in a complex rush of numbers and currencies, the thirty-five-year-old paper millionaires fire their paddles into the air and the establishment wearily counters in defiance, taking one last stand before the raging world moves past them. Babe Ruth's wool cap ($3,000–$5,000) sells for more than $24,000, and two of his rotting leather suitcases ($1,500–$2,500) go for almost $15,000. A baseball signed by Marilyn Monroe and Joe DiMaggio ($20,000–$30,000) suddenly seems a relative bargain at $48,875.

The evening's featured lot is Babe Ruth's last bat, and when it appears in front of the room, the crowd literally gasps. In 1948 the Yankees retired Ruth's number in an emotional ceremony at Yankee Stadium, but Ruth was so sick that he used this very bat (which he later signed) as a cane to help him limp up to home plate to say good-bye. A photographer caught the moment in a Pulitzer Prize–winning snapshot that seeped its way into the American consciousness. A few months later Ruth was dead. Stephen and I were keenly aware of the bat's importance but were unsure how others would respond, so we put a wide $50,000 to $100,000 estimate on it. But we shouldn't have worried. The bidding starts with an increasingly familiar flurry of paddles as dozens of people join the fray, including Josh, who lobs in a few bids from on high. As the thousands tick by like seconds, Stephen and I try to maintain poker faces. But when the hammer comes down at $107,000 and the room breaks into applause, we're both laughing like lottery winners.

By the end of the night all 133 lots have sold. Dede Brooks comes over to hug me, and Redden, hoarse but happy, follows with a sturdy handshake. The take is over two million dollars—not bad for a bunch of old bats and balls. And this was just opening night: there are still fifteen sessions left.

We go out en masse, Sotheby's style, a dozen of us speeding down the FDR to the lounges of Nolita. It's a diverse crew, a perfect cross-section of Sotheby's past and future—Antiquities and Internet, Prints and Press—but tonight we're all celebrating one thing: my auction. I become the acting cruise director, ordering drinks and making introductions and generally steering the night along. And the action under the tables is as fast as the conversation above them. Though I'm trying to stop, this is a special occasion, and I keep disappearing to bathrooms with coworkers, sampling their wares on keys and countertops. Every time I come back out the night has turned more fabulous. And so we venture ever onward, to Lucky Strike and Veruka, drinking champagne and toasting each other, like we're the ones who did something special, like we're the real artists of the age.

THREE HOURS LATER I'm lying on my futon with a bandage on my arm from where the fucking cat got me when I stumbled in. It's almost 6:00 A.M. and I can't sleep. After my stepsister's intervention, I told myself I'd cut out the drugs, but here I am, in familiar territory. There are three sessions coming up tomorrow, *today*—a full day and night of auctions—and I need to close my eyes. These are always the worst hours, the late-night blocks of despair, the downtime when I'm still up. I used to leave the apartment and walk the streets alone, watching the rest of this sad, hustling, insomniac city slide by in street-lit shadows. Usually I was thinking about Claire or my writing or how being broke wasn't so glamorous anymore. I don't know, I get stuck on things. Now, though, I stay indoors, put Beth Orton on low, and start leafing through folders of old stories, words I wrote just last year but no longer recognize. I've tried to get back into some kind of artistic mind-set as I wait for Rob Bingham's imminent call, but Sotheby's is so all-consuming and the greater culture is so ardently charging ahead. All the creative types I once knew are sliding into the Internet vortex, and the thought of writing has become almost quaint. I flip through the pages I once struggled over so preciously, and now that whole portion of my life seems nothing more than a hobby, a phase, like stamp collecting or buying baseball memorabilia. No: baseball memorabilia has value.

THE PHONE'S BEEN ringing for a while when I finally give in, clear my throat, and answer it. The clock says 7:15 A.M. I feel like I've been run over by heavy machinery.

"It's Susan, David Redden's assistant. Hello?"

"Hey."

"Are you okay? Were you asleep?"

"Of course I was asleep."

"Well, the limo has been waiting outside your apartment for half an hour."

"For what?"

"For you."

"What are you talking about?"

"Hasn't anyone told you? You're doing CNN at eight thirty. Live to the world. Hello?"

"I can't."

"You have to. David is doing the show with you."

"Couldn't someone have told me this yesterday?"

"Are you sure you're okay?"

I cobble myself together, slowly, piece by piece, alert even in this diminished capacity to another feline attack, but all is quiet, inside and out. The limo—it's a car service, actually—is the only vehicle on the street. The driver is a woman. When I tell her where we're going, she looks at me in the rearview mirror.

"Honey, you don't look like you're ready for TV."

CNN's New York studios are on the upper floors of a dreary office building near Madison Square Garden. I get there with twenty minutes to spare and am hustled straight into hair and makeup, where Redden sits serenely, being dabbed with base. He looks more like a news anchor than the real news anchors I just passed in the hallway.

"It doesn't look like you've slept," he says.

"I'm fine."

"I'll do most of the talking. And remember, this is live. No starting over."

I'm still wired. My jaw feels tight. When Redden steps away to take a cell-phone call, I ask the poor woman working on my face for some aspirin. She looks concerned. A minute later I'm ushered into the studio and seated next to my boss at a flimsy desk facing a firing line of cameras. I don't see an anchorperson anywhere. A producer explains that the interviewer will be asking us questions via satellite from Atlanta. "Look into the center camera at all times. That's where Daryn is. Whatever you do, don't look at the monitors on the side. They're showing what's being aired." He says this, so of course I look at the monitors on the side, and there's Daryn Kagan, the dark-haired anchor who's always on when I'm flipping channels at home. The red light goes on and I can see Redden looking straight ahead, me slightly off to the side. For a moment, I get confused, watching myself, but then Kagan introduces us, calls us David and David, and I manage to focus on the right lens.

Her first question is about last night's sale. I wait for Redden to answer, but he kicks me under the table. So I start talking. I don't know what I'm saying, but it must be coherent because the smooth voice in my ear laughs and asks a follow-up question. I pause again, but Redden is just sitting there smiling, and that's when it hits me: he doesn't know anything about baseball. So I keep going: Babe Ruth, Lou Gehrig, Ty Cobb . . . even the much discussed "Cartwright baseball," which I carefully say "*may* have been the very first ball ever." Then Kagan says, "The other David: can you tell us who paid a hundred grand for Babe Ruth's bat?" Redden doesn't answer the question. Instead, he launches into a speech laced with PR words and baseball metaphors. I sneak another look at the monitors while he's talking, and my hair is sticking up. Maybe if the feed goes back to Kagan, I could try to mat it down, but no such luck. My boss says something about "a lot of home runs to come," and now I'm back on the hot seat, describing upcoming lots, plugging the Web site, and smiling as best I can, considering my head still hurts and the lights are making me sweat Ketel One.

THE RIDE UPTOWN IS QUIET. "The other David" doesn't speak until his cell phone rings and I'm freed to look out the window at Central Park. Back at Sotheby's an eager assemblage is waiting to be let inside for the morning session, and as I get out of the car several people call my name. I move through the crowd shaking hands, answering a few quick questions and, yes, signing an autograph—one—for a young kid with a pen and a catalog. He must be as confused as I am. Redden shakes his head and walks in unnoticed.

Today's auction sessions build on last night's fast start. Cy Young's glove ($3,000–$5,000) gets hammered down for an amazing $71,250, followed by his 1914 contract ($20,000–$30,000), which goes for $63,000. The bidding on the Cartwright ball soars past $100,000, perches here and there for rest, and finally settles at $129,000. It's not the hundreds of thousands we were hoping for, but considering it's a rotten piece of leather, literally coming apart at the seams, we can't be too disappointed.

Between the afternoon and evening sessions, I sneak up to my office for a nap. Tonight's sale, "The Yankees of the 1920s," will be one of the week's biggest, and it's no coincidence that Dede Brooks is the scheduled auctioneer. I'm exhausted. I need to find a corner in Collectibles where I can put one of the interns on guard and curl up for a few hours. But as soon as I walk in I know that won't happen. The phones are ringing off their hooks. Every line is flashing with someone on hold, and Laura, Gabrielle, and two interns are going from line to line scribbling down hurried messages and, God, putting them all in *my* box.

Giles strolls by amused. "That's what happens when you become a big TV star, mate. America wants to meet you."

"Don't you have any Monkees signatures to authenticate?"

I take a handful of messages and march back to my desk. Giles is right. People are reading about these absurd memorabilia prices in their morning papers and thinking they're next. Every man, woman, and child in America with a faded signature or an old bat in the attic is calling to consign it to me. And they'll almost all be disappointed. I guess it's my job to tell them that, one message at a time. I start making my way through the pile, but almost all the scribbling is incoherent. Some have brief descriptions ("Guy says he has Olympic torch from the Olympics" or "1950s baseball card from Kansas City") but most are just names and numbers. I don't even know where to start. Then I come across a message from my mother, and, a few more down, another from my father, and then Shelton and Ken and even Claire.

My mother answers on the second ring.

"I can't talk too long but—"

"What's wrong with you? Can't you tell your own mother when you're going to be on TV? I turned it on this morning and imagine my surprise seeing you on the screen. You looked wonderful but you were fidgeting. And there was something wrong with your hair."

"Thanks."

"And who was that strange English fellow you were with?"

"That's my boss. He's from Connecticut."

"He actually said, 'A lot of home runs to come.'"

"I know."

"Has he ever been to a baseball game?"

"Mom, I have to go."

"Well, I'm coming up to New York to see one of the sessions. Maybe the Mickey Mantle sale next Monday. I always had a thing for him."

An hour later it's time to head back down to Seventy-second Street. I can barely keep my eyes open. I take a stack of business cards to hand out to clients, but when I open my wallet to put them inside, a small packet of powder falls out onto my lap. The remnants of last night: exactly what I need. Except I don't *need* it. Not like that. What am I doing? This stuff isn't helping. Sure there's the initial flurry of insight, of momentum, but it's always downhill from there—nights ruined by wanting more; the days after, wiped out with headaches, with dreary numbness, being left out of your own life. And it makes me feel like shit. A few days straight and I always get sick. I'll get a Red Bull from the deli on my way down. That'll have to do.

When Dede Brooks stands at an auction podium in front of a crowded room, all conversation ceases. She's not the smooth, somber auctioneer Sotheby's typically trots out on these occasions; Dede mispronounces names, loses track of bids, and playfully insults bidders who drop out early. But it doesn't matter: it's her show and everyone is watching. Tonight they've added more chairs and the room is buzzing. Cameras start rolling as the skybox heavyweights slug it out for Ruth and Gehrig artifacts. The Babe's glove goes for $96,000, and the infamous 1920 contract that sent him from the Red Sox to the Yankees tops off at $189,500. But it's Lou Gehrig who owns the night. His very imperfect World Series ring ("diamond in center is chipped but intact") sells for $96,000, and his Yankees jersey from 1927 ($100,000–$150,000) fetches an astounding $305,000. So it's not surprising that all eyes fall on one of the evening's final offerings, Gehrig's faded blue Yankees cap. It's one of those bargain lots that everyone circles when they're scouring the catalog for something *affordable*. It's not a jersey or a ring or an autographed ball—just an old cap, the kind of thing people overlook. We've put a $15,000 to $20,000 estimate on it, but our estimates were long ago rendered meaningless. Dede opens the bidding and immediately the currency board moves rapidly north, from $20,000 to $25,000 to $30,000. Five paddles are in the air when Josh, who has been relatively quiet, signals me to pick up my phone. "Bid $100,000" he says.

I look up at the board. "But the bidding's only at $35,000."

"Jump it to a hundred."

"You know you have to pay for it if you win it."

"Just put your fucking hand in the air!"

I think I know what he's doing. Always furiously competitive, the major dealers have now turned on each other completely, running up the bids on lots they have no intention of buying, just so the guy who does want it has to pay more. In most high-end auctions, it works the other way—dealers form little cabals, keeping prices down by working out beforehand who will bid on what. But this group aren't that sophisticated, and it's costing them tens of thousands. Then again, maybe Josh really *does* want this cap and is firing off some kind of preemptive shot, trying to scare off the competition.

"*ONE HUNDRED THOUSAND DOLLARS!*" I shout, and the room goes stone silent.

Someday I'll look back on this moment and the idea of bidding $100,000 on a sweaty old Yankees cap when the current bid is only $35,000 will seem completely insane, but now, in the moment, it makes perfect sense. Dede looks over, delighted.

"Thank you," she gushes. "I have one hundred thousand dollars on the phone with David."

"One oh five!" shouts the phone bidder next to me, acting, I'm sure, on orders from a rival dealer. Up in his box, Josh nods, and so I raise my hand again.

"One ten with David," Dede says.

Then from next to me: "One *twenty*!" and off we go again. It's high-stakes poker with Monopoly money. But Josh, determined not to be outdone, wins out in the end—if you can call paying $151,000 for a baseball cap winning—and the night comes to a close with another rousing ovation.

"Congratulations," I say into the phone.

"For what? I can't believe I just got caught up in this bullshit. A hundred and fifty thousand bucks? I just took the most expensive fucking bath of my life."

At some point during the weekend the numbers lose all meaning. The press recounts the daily tally in a series of astonished headlines. David Redden has become a fixture in the auction room, not daring to leave lest he break the spell. Jamie Niven and Bill Ruprecht take successful turns at the podium. Dede glad-hands starstruck bidders like a campaign politician. And the veterans who spent the spring looking down their patrician noses at the little baseball sale now sit in the back rows, leafing gently through the catalog, *my* catalog, as if it contains the Fabergé eggs and Rodin sculptures they're used to. I take their presence as a subtle blessing, a soundless concession to change.

On Sunday afternoon, with the auction on autopilot, I try to make some headway on the piles of messages, letters, and packages that now cover every inch of my desk. Giles is there, as usual, reading the *Sun* online. We've become close in the last year, a friendship filled with clever barbs and good-natured insults. A few weeks ago he told me he was going to marry his young Aussie girlfriend next month at City Hall. He asked me to be his witness. I asked if it was a green-card thing. No, it was a love thing, he said. I wouldn't understand.

"Can you delete some of your e-mails?" he says, over the partition that separates our desks. "They've bollocksed up the server and now everything's taking ages."

"Football scores aren't downloading fast enough?"

"No, it's the porn that's the problem."

I haven't turned my computer on in days, and when I do, I find my in box overflowing with hundreds of e-mails, most with JPEG attachments picturing every conceivable collectible. They all want evaluations, assessments, appraisals.

"And a FedEx came in for you, as well," Giles says from the other side of the cubicle wall. "I signed for it and put it next to your desk."

On the floor I find a long skinny cylinder addressed to "The Baseball Expert." I open it to find a handwritten note attached to the handle of an old baseball bat:

> *Dear Expert. I saw you on TV and decided to send you this to sell. This was Babe Ruth's bat from back when he still played for the Yankees. He gave it to my Grandma when my Grandma was at Yankee Stadium one day and then he signed it for her and they went on a date that night to a place on 3rd Avenue near where the elevated train was. She told me the name of the restaurant one time—I think it was P. J. something—but I can't remember and she died so anyway can you tell me what the bat is worth and then sell it for me in this big auction you're having right now. Thank You. Gary.*

Is this a joke? P. J. something? The return address is a P.O. box in Springfield, Illinois. There's no last name or phone number. Just the bat. It looks like the right model but it's too clean. If Ruth really used it in a game, it should be cracked or have ball marks on the barrel. And the signature: it looks genuine, although it's faded and partly smudged. I pick it up and take a half swing. It feels too light to be the Babe's, but then again—

"Dreaming of past glory, are we?" Giles says, walking past.

"Isn't it tea time or something?"

"You're a very cynical man."

"Let me ask you something serious. How do you authenticate your autographs?"

"I know what I'm doing," Giles says.

"No, seriously. How hard is it to forge, say, John Lennon's signature?"

"Not hard at all."

"So there's no way to know for sure."

"Not unless you saw him sign it."

"And that doesn't bother you?"

"Does it bother a priest that he's never seen God?"

"What the hell does that mean?"

"It means you do your research, make your decision, then have faith. Of course it bothers me. I'm sure there are fakes in half the catalogs we produce. It's a reality every expert lives with: no matter how much you know, no matter how stringent your authenticity process, you're bound to be wrong occasionally. And that's why image is so important. Sotheby's has enjoyed centuries of success by perfecting the concept of expertise. If people believe they're dealing with a well-known authority on a subject, they won't ask questions. And the more they blindly trust your judgment, the more of an expert you become. The truth is that at this level, most of the fakes are so good we're not going to catch them, but neither will the clients. So the fakes become real by default. And our reputations grow to the point where people will pay the extra money to buy from Sotheby's or Christie's even though they could buy the same sculpture from a dealer or the same autograph from a collectibles kiosk at some dreadful shopping mall in the Midwest—"

"Owned by Alfred Taubman."

"Don't remind me."

Giles leaves on that lofty note. He heads off to plan his City Hall wedding, leaving me to tackle my overflowing in box. The e-mails are all the same: blurry photos and hazy stories. But I *need* consignments. When the Halper sale ends, I'll have to find a whole new auction's worth of memorabilia—this time, without Stephen Carson's help. Redden has promised I can hire a few staffers, have a real department, but still, it'll be on my head to find the best stuff. Scanning the in box, I realize that may take some time: quantity hardly means quality. I scroll down, opening e-mails and attachments arbitrarily. Halfway down page four, wedged between a worthless collection of press pins and an all-staff meeting reminder, I see a familiar name: Emily Edson.

I've been waiting to hear from her all summer. She's in the middle of a war zone.

After that summer in Boston, she left the World Peace Foundation—where *World Peace* too often bowed to *office politics*—and went off to law school to study human rights. This summer she was supposed to clerk for a judge in New York but, after reading an article about the refugee crisis in Bosnia decided that helping them might be a better use of her time. She applied for positions at the UN, the Red Cross, a whole list of international aid organizations, but no one wanted volunteers. Last I heard, she was flying over to Kosovo, a volunteer army of one.

Davey Boy—

Miss you, sweetie. How's life in NYC? Hard to imagine a normal American day anymore—reading the paper, commuting, going out at night, even dating. None of that stuff here. Arrived a few weeks ago. Flew to Greece then took a crowded train up to Macedonia and hitched a ride to the refugee camps along the Kosovo border. All the camps had guards, and none of them spoke English. All I had for credentials was an old ID from WPF in Cambridge so I figured I was screwed. All these people were trying to get in to the camps—a chaotic line of humanity with bulging sacks and broken suitcases stretching as far as I could see toward Kosovo. But I cut the line, told the guard I was a Red Cross doctor, and he believed it. He nodded and let me walk right in. I guess he figured no female Westerner in her right mind would be here unless she had to be. Anyway, I met an American aid worker who put me in touch with a Belgian who was working for the International War Crimes Tribunal, a UN group charged with gathering evidence against potential war criminals. It's funny, I wrote them a letter back in the spring and they wrote back saying they weren't hiring. And now I show up and they're completely overwhelmed. They're begging for help.

They put me to work in the camps, sprawling tent cities of muddy women and children (most of the men didn't make it). I'm sorry, I don't mean to sound so dour, but it is dour here. Actually, it's worse than that. It's a version of hell I had never considered. The refugees are all homeless. Most have been walking for months, aimlessly shuffling around in the dusk after war. The lucky ones have found this place. It's my job to write down their stories, almost all of them horrific descriptions of genocide not even the most twisted mind could ever conjure. It's tough, because all they really want to do is forget, so most don't talk at first. I sit with them, if they let me, sometimes for whole days, just sit and smoke (what a way to start smoking!) and try to gain their trust. What I need, of course, are names and descriptions, exacting accounts of brutalities: evidence. I need to build prosecutable cases (is that a word, writer boy?). Some of the evidence is right there in front of me—scars and bruises, missing fingers, broken toes—but mostly it's in their minds. And sometimes, after a while, it comes out. With a translator and tape recorder I sit and listen to these tired victims as they describe their tormentors and name their torturers.

It's amazing what stripping away basic human dignity does to a person's soul. I spent yesterday with a girl who was raped by the same soldier that killed her father. She was only twelve, *only twelve*, and now she won't speak, not even to her mother. She sat in the tent with her legs crossed and her arms folded, staring straight ahead as the pop pop pop of gunfire echoed through the hills across the border. The guns are our constant backdrops, our hourly reminders, just in case the memories start to slide away. I don't know, it's all so incomprehensible. It makes you wonder how it could all go so wrong. Sometimes I ask how the fighting started, but no one seems to understand the question. It's like they've never known peace.

Anyway, sorry. I'm sure this is the last thing you need to be hearing. I'm coming home in a few weeks for my second year of school, but after this, studying torts and listening to pompous professors seems a waste. I'm convinced now that experience—real life—has very little to do with routine and protocol (the schools and jobs that breed security) and everything to do with a true commitment to yourself, stripped of outside expectation and blind to popular culture. (What the hell is "Who Wants to Be a Millionaire"???) My advice, I suppose, would be not to follow anyone else's. I know that sounds naive, but seeing misery like this has sent me back to basics. If I stay in school I might try to transfer to Fordham or Columbia so at least I'll be in NYC. Are there any real men left in your city, or are they all getting manicures and shopping at Prada? And speaking of . . . how are the pearl girls at Sotheby's? Are you still selling that guy's baseball collection? Are you writing any new stories? And is it true the Internet is making everyone rich? (I'm currently typing at the only Internet station in this entire camp, and there's a line of people waiting behind me—I feel like a prisoner on a pay phone.) By the way, I'm glad you're still working in the old economy and not the new one. Something seems wrong with all that instant wealth. A rising tide lifts all boats, but it's still just a tide, my boy. It goes back out. Peace. E

I sit still for a long time. Then I look at the baseball bat with the Babe Ruth signature that may or may not be real. David Redden told me once that Sotheby's is in the business of making people happy: we offer them beautiful distractions from the ugly world, he said, and that sounded good then, and meaningful. Until moments like this, when the ugly world emerges with all its sores and reminds you that beautiful distractions never solve the problems underneath.

There are people who make the world better, and I'm not one of them.

My mother shows up for session ten on Monday night. She watches me deliver my nightly network sound bites and do a few quick print interviews. The auction has worked its way up to the 1950s, the golden years of New York baseball, and the room is packed again. Billy Crystal and Penny Marshall are here, and several major leaguers are bidding by phone. Tonight it's DiMaggio, Mays, Berra, and that great promise of a man, Mickey Mantle. Everything attached to Mantle soars: $123,500 for his 1956 World Series ring, then, three lots later, an astounding $211,500 for his 1956 Triple Crown Award.

Toward the end of the evening, Mantle's glove appears and the room instinctively quiets down out of some mix of reverence and anticipation. This is the glove Billy Crystal was asking about in L.A., and I think it's my favorite piece as well. It's a well-worn Rawlings outfielder's mitt with Mantle's famed "7" on the outside of the thumb. Every time I tried it on at the warehouse (which was a lot), I thought about how many children of the fifties must have solemnly written that same 7 on their gloves and headed off into the outfields of America to chase fly balls and dream of someday playing center field at Yankee Stadium. Mickey Mantle's glove: it's like Billy the Kid's gun or Elvis's guitar. And, like those, there is more than one. In fact, there are dozens of Mantle gloves kicking around museums and major collections, but tonight there is only this one, given to Barry Halper by Mantle himself, and as the bidding starts and the paddles shoot up, our modest $10,000 to $20,000 estimate is quickly blown away. The numbers move north of $50,000, then $100,000, then $150,000. By $170,000 only two bidders remain—a nervous but determined man in the center of the room, and a phone bidder who's represented by an icy Sotheby's blonde with hair pulled back so tight it looks like it hurts. Maybe ten of us in the room know that it's Billy Crystal on the other end of her line, giving orders from the skybox above her head. Crystal's in town shooting *61**, a movie about Mantle and Roger Maris's epic home-run chase, and he's made no secret of how much he wants this glove. In L.A. he told me Mantle was his boyhood idol, but as the bidding steams past $200,000, I begin to wonder where idolatry ends and insanity begins. His blond proxy nods again at $205,000 and all heads turn to the man in the middle of the room. He hesitates, then raises his paddle carefully, as if he's trying to stretch in class without getting called on. And so back to the phone, where the woman is in deep conversation with her comedian client. A minute goes by, people start murmuring, then as the auctioneer starts in with his "Going once . . ." routine, the curtain parts in the skybox above us and Billy Crystal himself sticks his head out.

"How high do you plan on going?" he shouts down to his competition. The whole room looks up at once, and the initial shock from the breach of etiquette turns quickly to howls of laughter as people realize who it is. Even the other bidder cracks a smile.

"Looking for two hundred fifteen thousand," the auctioneer says.

"Two hundred twelve thousand five hundred," Crystal shouts. Below him, the blonde puts her phone down.

The auctioneer accepts the half bid (rules are bendable at these amounts), then turns to the other man, who raises his paddle one last time—but it's more like a white flag. Crystal counters with $217,500, and as the gavel comes down the crowd roars. Including the buyer's premium, he has just bought a baseball glove for $239,000.

"Does anyone have a ball?" Crystal asks, leaning out from his perch. "May as well play a little catch." He's kidding, of course, but right now someone in Client Services is running off to find him one.

Two nights later the live portion of the Barry Halper auction comes to a close. After the crowds have filed out and the house lights have dimmed, David Redden gathers us by the podium, pops some champagne, and reads us the numbers: almost $22 million in sales; twelve lots that went for more than $100,000; and perhaps most staggering of all, every single piece sold. Redden says he's never seen anything like it. Dede looks like she wants to lead us in a cheer. And then Halper himself appears to offer his thanks. He gives a heartfelt speech, then pulls Stephen and me aside and almost starts crying.

It's ten thirty, time enough for one more drink, so I hop a cab down to Maya, on Sixty-fourth and First. I was here once before, two years ago, for dinner with Claire and her father. I remember, he ordered a Ketel One and tonic. I had never heard of Ketel One before, and it sounded, to me, from him, like the perfect drink, a movie line. Sometimes we all want to be grown-ups: I've been ordering Ketel One ever since.

Tonight, though, it's *my* parent I'm meeting, and when I walk in my mother is sitting at the bar, alone, with a glass of red wine. She hasn't seen me yet, so I stop and just watch her for a moment. She still looks young: fifty two and barely a wrinkle on her freckled face. Her hair is still quite red and her trim figure betrays none of the natural letting-go that often accompanies midlife. She's wearing black pants and a thin cashmere sweater, and she seems so at ease in these surroundings—in all surroundings—that it's hard to believe she's lived so . . . boldly.

A few years ago my mother fell in love with a woman again, a well-known—and wonderful—network news reporter. Soon thereafter she moved to Washington, D.C. It was good timing; Baltimore was turning ugly. There was no more room in the prisons. Criminals my mother had put in jail for life were getting right back out. And then one of them came looking for her.

Washington is so much safer. My mother and her partner have broken ground on a modern dream house just outside Georgetown. Together they're becoming something of a power couple: they cocktail with senators and go to parties at the White House. She has stopped practicing law. Now she mentors inner-city kids, takes cooking classes in the afternoons, and— inevitably—has started playing golf on weekends. If only she'd liked golf the first time around. . . .

For a long time, as I watched my mother move from one reality to the next, I admired what she was doing, even as I never quite understood it. Certainly she was looking for independence. She understood yearnings, she followed aspirations; so, naturally, she'd believe in my writing. She'd be the champion I've never had. But I've never managed to discuss it with her. I think I've been intimidated. She has so much to show for her various undertakings; I have only two readable stories after almost five years in New York. Even now, in this unfamiliar glow of achievement, I want to tell her that Sotheby's is just a phase, a way to make money, find the confidence for my real calling. I'd like to think she'd believe that. I'd like to believe it myself.

When I tap her on the shoulder, she turns around and smiles warmly. We hug and then I flop down onto the stool next to hers.

"Quite a week," she says.

For a while we sip wine and talk about the auction. She says I look nice in a suit, but I know that's not what she's thinking. She wants to know how I ended up here, among the Nivens and Reddens and Boardmans.

"Can you keep a secret?" she asks, leaning in close.

"Of course."

"I saw your father last night."

"What?"

"We had a drink together, at the bar at the St. Regis. Just the two of us. It had been . . . I don't know . . . more than ten years, so I called him up and he agreed to come meet me."

"*And?*"

"And it was nice. It was more than nice. It was really great to see him. We caught up on stuff, talked about you guys. He looked good."

"God, if Cynthia found out she'd kill him."

"Oh, come on. We're all past that, I hope."

"I'm still working on it."

"Do you know what I told him? I told him I thought you and Douglas had handled all this family stuff very well, all things considered."

"What did *he* say?"

"He said he was just glad you both had jobs."

"At least there's one constant in all this."

"Oh, I wouldn't be so sure. I think he'd support you no matter what you did. As long as you were serious about it."

"I don't know. It's kind of weird watching the two of you start over again so completely. It's like your former lives never happened."

"I've come to think of it more as an evolution in stages," she says. "People change, sweetie. They discover different interests, find new worlds. . . .

I hope the divorce wasn't all bad. Maybe it's naive, but I've always hoped that two such opposite living experiences might help you view things with a wider perspective, to realize there are so many things to do, ways to *live*."

I sip my drink and try to figure out what she means. Is she saying what I think she's saying? Should I be reading between lines? Most mothers would be thrilled to see their sons on TV, in the spotlight, *succeeding*, but she's talking about something else. Reinvention. She knows all this isn't me. She knows me better than I do.

Then she puts her glass down and swivels her stool around to face me directly.

"Tell me," she says. "What does the Sotheby's sports expert do after he's sold the world's greatest collection? I mean . . . Where does he go from here?"

Twenty-five

THE NASDAQ IS UP more than 35 percent since the beginning of 1999, and the Dow is doing its best to keep pace. Day traders, domain names, money honeys, launch parties, Kozmo, *Fast Company*, trust-fund venture capitalists—these are the words on the street. Sotheby's—my own dot-com—is launching its site next month with the lesser half of the Halper haul: four thousand or so lots in the $100 to $2,000 range. Dozens of top dealers have signed on to list their goods on sothebys.amazon.com, as well. So it should be a defining moment, this most traditional of companies becoming a new-economy giant almost overnight, but it doesn't feel that way. The testy relationship with Amazon has become an all-out war; morale among the hundred-plus Internet staffers is incredibly low; and worst of all, the company's stock price has fallen off a cliff amid rumors of a price-fixing investigation.

Word is Sotheby's and Christie's have been colluding on the fees they charge to buyers and sellers. When I first heard the whispers, it just didn't make sense: Dede Brooks is too intelligent and her hatred of Christie's too real. But the more I think about it, the more it seems possible. I imagine there was a time when the great auction-house rivalry was about pride more than profit, but that all ended when the two companies moved across the ocean. For years they've been undercutting each other to acquire collections, in much the same way bidders compete at the other end of the process. And once you get past their enchanting images, you begin to see the toll the rivalry has taken. These days the high-end auction business is barely a business at all. Even the Halper sale won't make much money. If the entire auction (including Internet sales) grosses $25 million, Sotheby's will receive only about 15 percent of that amount (almost all coming from the buyer's premium). That's less than $4 million to pay the salaries of dozens of people, including Stephen, who've been working full time for a year. Add the hefty costs of catalog production, marketing, outside experts, and exhibitions in three cities, and suddenly the net profit has dwindled to almost nothing. In the end, it always comes back to jewelry and Impressionist paintings (the Cézanne I saw at that party—the one with all the fruit— sold for over $60 million, which puts the Halper sale in perspective). But as more major paintings find their way into permanent museum collections, and the competition (Phillips, eBay, and a dozen other upstarts) for what's left becomes fierce, it's not hard to see how a little price fixing might serve to stem the bleeding.

UNDER THIS FORMING CLOUD I focus on starting a permanent sports department. Hoping to build on the momentum, I set up Tuesdays and Thursdays as appraisal days when people can come in with potential consignments. Seeing the real piece is so much better than JPEGs and FedExed photos, but with the client standing in front of me waiting for answers, there's no time for research and no margin for error.

Soon I'm handling almost fifteen appointments a day. They usually come in pairs—elderly couples, fathers and sons, two childhood friends hoping for a payday. They'll sit at the viewing table and say they saw me on TV or heard about Sotheby's through a friend who consigned a painting in the eighties. I'll take a close look at their piece as the inevitable provenance story begins, and usually, by the time they get to the part about the miraculous find at the yard sale or the discovery in some dead relative's closet, I already know they'll go home unhappy. So much memorabilia is more memorable than valuable. I'll tell them the card is too common or the autograph was signed by the clubhouse attendant or the bat is a store model that was never used in a game. It's hard to watch the faces, sliding downward from expectation to despair.

A few days ago I had to tell an elderly couple from Boston that the signatures on their 1947 Red Sox ball weren't real. I could tell how much the ball meant to them: it had been a comfort in the back of their minds all these years, a last memory of faded youth. And now here they were, making the long trip down to New York because they'd seen this Halper thing on TV and, well, to be honest they could use the money. . . .

"Mr. and Mrs. Sullivan," I said, "thanks so much for letting me see this, but I have some bad news. The signatures on the ball were applied by a stamping machine."

Mr. Sullivan shook his head. "But my father went to Fenway Park and got the ball signed himself. He used to tell me about it all the time, how Ted Williams looked up at him as he handed the ball back and said, 'Enjoy the game, sir.' And this was after the war, when Ted Williams never so much as smiled."

"I'm sorry," I said. "Maybe there was some kind of mix-up. Fifty-two years is a long time."

"There's been no mix-up, son."

"Here, I'll show you how you can tell it's a stamp."

"I don't have my glasses," he said, although it was only a minute ago that he'd been proudly showing me every signature.

"I'll have a look," his wife said.

"Okay, then. Notice how the ink fades at the extremes of every signature. That's because the stamping machines back then had a flat surface, and not every part could touch the rounded baseballs. And look at the spacing between the names; it's too perfect. When players sign a ball, they scribble their names quickly, then flip it to the guy at the next locker. These are far too neat, far too manufactured."

Mrs. Sullivan was interested now. "Is this type of thing common?"

"Teams do it all the time and plenty of people get fooled."

"And if it were genuine? How much might it be worth?"

"If the signatures were real and the ball was in good shape, it might get a thousand dollars."

She frowned. "But the things you sold on television sold for so much more."

"Yes, but—"

"Let's go," Mr. Sullivan said, standing up briskly.

"—they were all either very rare or very old. Most of the players on the 1947 Red Sox are still alive, including Ted Williams."

"So you're saying people are worth more when they're dead," Mrs. Sullivan said.

"Something like that."

"Come on, Helen. We're going. We'll get a second opinion somewhere else."

"George, be nice to the young man."

"These *experts* always think they know everything. If you spent any time in Boston, you'd know the Red Sox would never do anything crass like that."

"I have spent time in Boston," I said, quietly. "And every team does it."

"We'll find our own way out," he said, hustling his red-faced wife away.

And these are the easy appointments. It's when people show up with something valuable that things get dicey. I'll sit them down, study the piece, and listen to the story. Then I'll show them the Halper catalog, and as they're leafing through the pages, intrigued by the prices, I'll signal to Gabrielle or Laura and a moment later I'll have an important phone call on line two. It's all prearranged, of course, and after I excuse myself I'll race back to my growing library of reference books. I've got all the essentials: *Total Baseball*, autograph analysis books, team histories, card price guides, and dozens of auction catalogs. I'll tear through the pages looking for answers while one of the girls flirts with the client to buy me some time.

Today it's a small-time suburban dealer with a rare collection of autographed boxing photos from the turn of the century. We do the whole routine perfectly, and as the client ogles Gabrielle's fitted, *almost* see-through blouse, I try desperately to locate a "Gentleman Jim" Corbett signature dating to the 1890s. Giles peers around the corner.

"Thank God we've hired a real expert."

"Like you know all your shit."

"And will you stop telling people I'm Keith Moon's son? Some producer from VH1 just called to see if she could interview me."

"How do you know for sure that you're not?"

I find what I was looking for in an old Leland's catalog—a Corbett signature that matches the one I'm holding. I gather myself and walk into the viewing room portraying an air of gravitas, the way the painting experts do it down on Seventy-second Street.

"Excuse me," I say. "That was urgent. Now, you say these photos came from the estate of an early boxing promoter?"

"That's right. I have a bunch of ticket stubs and programs, as well."

"Well, I'd be happy to sell the collection on our new Web site. We'll put a four- to six-thousand-dollar estimate on it and sell the whole thing as one lot."

"Why can't we sell it in a live auction like Halper's?"

"Because the Internet's where it's happening."

"Christie's said it was worth ten thousand and that they'd put it in a real sale."

"You went to *Christie's*?"

"Yes, last week. They said the Internet is overrated."

"That's because Christie's doesn't have online auctions. Look, I'll raise the estimate to six to eight thousand, with a five-thousand-dollar reserve. That's the best I can do. It's a nice collection, but after our last sale, the whole country wants to sell through us, and—"

"I'll think about it," he says, getting up slowly.

"Don't wait too long."

"Please thank Gabrielle for me. She's quite a girl."

And so it goes: the endless dance of buying and selling. I'm starting to get the hang of it. Everything is negotiable; everyone has a price. As usual, Giles was right: being an expert is all about projecting an image, and right now I'm the young wunderkind. So what if it was Stephen who really made it happen? He's leaving soon, taking his money and going back to his basement business in New Jersey. And I'll be left alone, at the top of a field I still know nothing about.

As I walk back to my desk I see two new messages in my in box. One is from Michael Dell (the computer guy?). The other is from Rob Bingham. It must be some distant reflex that makes me call Bingham back first.

PART SIX

The Only Eloquence Left

"What we call the beginning is often the end. And to make an end is to make a beginning. The end is where we start from."

—T. S. ELIOT, *Four Quartets*

Twenty-six

"HELLO?"

"Hey, Rob. This is—"

"Where the fuck have you been? All this shit's piling up over here and I can't *find* anything. I keep trying to get Tom on the phone but he's out getting his picture taken with Parker fucking Posey, Malkmus says he's leaving Pavement—which I think is a mistake—and I can't find anyone who strings tennis racquets in this goddamn city."

"I think Paragon does."

"Wait. Who is this?"

"David Goodwillie. Calling from Sotheby's. I got a message that—"

"Oh, fuck! I thought you were someone else. . . ." His voice trails off. He sounds out of it. Way out of it. He's breathing hard, and the pauses keep coming at the wrong time. In the background I can hear traffic, large trucks chasing up city streets.

"Are you at home?" I ask, trying to focus him, keep the conversation together.

"I'm always at home. It's the curse of the life. You write to *engage* people, and you end up disengaging yourself. It's . . . it's very *dangerous.*"

He's slurring his words. And I don't know how he means anything. I haven't spoken with Rob Bingham since that dinner a few months ago, but I've been tracking his exploits in magazines and gossip columns. He's the kind of inside guy whose name gets dropped a lot, as a credential, a sign of status. He just got married to a gorgeous blonde and he's been finishing his much anticipated first novel, *Lightning on the Sun*, a literary thriller about Asian drug trafficking. He starts breathing into the phone again, then says something about the strip club he lives above, how it's gone to shit.

"You should come up to Sotheby's," I say. "Plenty of cute girls here."

Maybe it's the mention of my job that gets him looking through his sights again. "You got to get out of there," he says. "*That's* why I fucking called you. I want you to meet some people, friends of mine, editors and writers. I'm having a party next weekend and I think you should bring a few good stories down—the boarding school one, maybe, and whatever you've been working on recently. I . . . I don't want you stalling out on me."

"I'd love to. I'd—"

"Then I'll call you soon with the info," he says, and hangs up abruptly without saying good-bye—and without actually hanging up. He's put the phone down but I can still hear him, walking away across a wood floor, then coming back. He starts humming, then goes quiet. I think I hear the squeak of a chair and envision him sitting down at his desk in the late afternoon sun, trying to regain his composure in front of an ominous screen. It's the way writers should be captured in portraits: thinking, smoking, staring into nothing. Is he drunk, or high, or was he just lost in some stupor? God knows I've been there, that place where the mind goes fuzzy, where your head gets tired. Tired of *trying*. Listening to the silences of someone else's life brings it all back, those wasted days that never end—and then do, too quickly—and all those hours when thoughts fall flat and words won't surface. But Rob's probably not even at his desk; he's napping or reading *Harper's* or taking a shit—

"FUCK!" I hear him shout, at no one, at himself. "FUCKING DEAL WITH IT!" I hang up quickly, suddenly feeling like the intruder I am.

I'm so jazzed by the Bingham call, I almost forget the other message—a Jack Norton, calling from Michael Dell's office in New York ("*The* Michael Dell!" Laura has scrawled next to the number). Dell must be another one of these new-economy moguls who's starting a sports memorabilia collection. I'm not surprised; it's becoming the new contemporary art, with Babe Ruth as Jackson Pollock, the offbeat Honus Wagner as Andy Warhol. I've gotten calls from the offices of several Dell types in recent weeks, and as I dial the number and get put on hold, I sneak a peek at my schedule for tomorrow. It's completely filled with appointments.

Jack Norton comes on with the rushed tone of a man who spends his days moving from Line 1 to Line 2 to Line 3. He introduces himself as the managing director of MSD Capital, Dell's private investment firm.

"And are you calling on his behalf or yours?"

"I'm calling on *yours*," he says. "We'd like to take you to lunch tomorrow."

Now it hits me. Dell doesn't want to buy anything. He wants to *sell*. I've never seen his name on any major collectors lists, so it must be one or two pieces: a gift he got at a corporate getaway, or some stupid autographed ball he thinks is worth millions.

"We're pretty busy," I say, running with the pronoun. "Maybe we could help you over the phone, or book a time for—"

"I don't think you understand. We have an *opportunity* we'd like to discuss with you. It shouldn't take more than an hour." There's authority in his voice; he's not used to hearing no. And in this economy, when Michael Dell's people ask you to lunch, I suppose you have to go.

"Okay. I'll meet you guys tomorrow at Petaluma."

"Petaluma it is. Let's say one o'clock. The reservation will be under 'Sterling.'"

PETALUMA IS OVERPRICED and Italian: it's a Sotheby's favorite. On any given weekday, more high-end art deals are consummated at its back tables than perhaps anywhere else in the world. Today David Redden and Bill Ruprecht are both here, huddled with three lawyer types in dark suits. I'm led to a table in the center of the crowded room, where a man and woman stand up to greet me. His name is Fred Sterling. He's handsome, maybe five years older than me, and has dark hair and a trim beard. He's wearing a frayed shirt tucked haphazardly into pleated suit pants. I like him immediately. The woman is older, a mother, maybe. She says her name is Nancy Spielberg. We all sit back down. Fred checks his cell phone as Nancy looks for a waiter. It occurred to me on the way over that this might be some flank sales move, an ill-conceived attempt to get Sotheby's to use Dell computers. But these two aren't in sales, not that kind.

Fred snaps his Motorola shut. "I guess you're wondering what this is about."

"You could say that."

"We want to hire you. We're starting an Internet company called—"

"*Hold on*, that's my boss over there," I say, nodding over at Redden, two tables away. "So be careful."

"Did he see you come in?"

"I don't think so, but if he comes over here, pretend you're, I don't know, with the Yankees or something."

"How about the Mets?"

"Sure."

"Because we are . . . sort of. Their manager, Bobby Valentine, is the chairman of our company. I'm the CEO. And Nancy here is the executive VP in charge of entertainment. It's called A-bid-for-charity-dot-com," Fred says, pushing a business card across the table, "and we plan on being the premier portal for philanthropically oriented auctions on the Internet. A-bid-for-charity will leverage the Web's worldwide reach to revolutionize the dynamics of charitable giving by offering one-of-a-kind celebrity collectibles and experiences. We're creating an entirely new value proposition for the over one million U.S. charities, a streamlined, highly efficient market for giving—" Fred stops there, midsentence. "You don't want the road-show speech, do you?"

"You can keep going. I just won't understand any of it."

"I'm not sure *I* do," Fred says, laughing. "Let me try it in English. We're starting a Web site that will auction off high-end sports and entertainment memorabilia, along with 'dream experiences'—a round of golf with Tiger Woods, dinner with Heidi Klum, a walk-on sitcom role—and the proceeds will go to charity. We want you to run the auction side of the business, everything from procuring lots to overseeing fulfillment."

"Maybe there's something I'm missing here, but how am I supposed to get stuff for the site if all the proceeds go to charity? I mean, people don't just give stuff away."

"From the charities themselves. If, say, the American Heart Foundation has a celebrity they work with, we'll auction off his or her time. And individuals, pro teams, corporations, anyone who has access to goods and wants to raise money."

"And if this is a nonprofit, then how do *we* make money?"

"It's not a nonprofit. It's very much *for* profit. We'll charge a buyer's premium just like you do at Sotheby's. And we won't have any of the associated costs: no warehouses, no catalogs, no auctioneers, no unions. We'll be doing good and making money at the same time."

Nancy Spielberg's cell phone rings. It's the same shrill ring that Camille's phone had, a hideous noise I've never forgotten. She answers it a bit too loudly, then excuses herself. I turn around to check out the Redden–Ruprecht situation, but they're both gone.

Fred calls the waiter over and orders a bottle of Chardonnay. "The best part of the whole thing is the people. As you might imagine, Bobby Valentine and Nancy Spielberg are incredibly connected, and they'll be able to get the sports and entertainment industries involved—"

"I take it she's Stephen's sister."

"Of course she's Stephen's sister. And we've got MSD Capital backing us as well. We've already raised three million dollars in seed money and are going out for another ten million within two months. MSD manages most of Dell's money, and Jack, the guy you talked to on the phone, is in charge over there. I wish he could have come today, because you'd really like him. He's got me involved in all this. We went to Wharton together. He found you, too. Saw you on TV promoting some big sports auction last month."

"It all sounds wonderful, but I'm pretty happy at Sotheby's. That 'big sports auction' was actually the biggest ever, and I've just started my own department which will have its *own* Internet sales—"

"But Sotheby's isn't an Internet company. It's an old company. It's not *scalable*. There's no IPO, no exit strategy. It can't make you . . . *rich*."

Nancy reappears, saying she has to go, something about a babysitter. She walks out as the food arrives. Fred rolls his eyes. We split her pasta as the waiter fills our wine glasses.

"So what's your background," I ask, "if you don't mind my asking?"

"I guess you could say I'm a nontraditional investment banker. I leverage assets and—sorry, there I go again. I bring ideas, people, and capital together and form companies. We'll be sharing offices with one of them: RxCentric-dot-com. It's a Web-based pharmaceutical start-up. I think companies are kind of like kids: you should keep them all under one roof until they're ready for the real world."

"You mean an IPO?"

"That's always the goal."

Fred's cell phone rings again. The millennium is almost upon us and I still don't have one. I used to take pride in my small nod to the past, but now it just seems stubborn. As Fred discusses Web infrastructures and load-balancing solutions, I sip my wine and try to get my head around all this. It does sound enticing, starting a company from scratch, a company run by famous names and financed by one of America's richest men. And this guy Fred, furiously writing figures on a napkin, there's something incredibly alluring about him, a charisma to match his confidence. He's America's new man, the artistic businessman. I'd always believed people were one or the other. But the age of typecasting is over. Business has become an art, and the finished canvas is the successful start-up company.

"Would you stay for the long haul?" I ask, once his phone has gone silent.

"Certainly until we find a big-name CEO to take us public. The way the numbers work, we're looking at an IPO in less than twenty-four months."

"And let me guess. We're talking lots of stock options."

"Let me put it this way. If this thing works—and a lot of very smart people are betting that it will—anyone in on the ground floor will be able to put their feet up for a very long time. Would you at least like to hear the offer, or do you have baseball cards you need to get back to?"

"I can probably spare a few more minutes."

"What are you making right now?"

"Ninety thousand," I say, firmly.

"We'll match it," Fred says.

"That's not enough. Sotheby's may have been around forever, but that tends to bode well for job security."

"Job security these days means you're in the wrong business. Besides, I've heard a few rumors about . . . *issues* on the Sotheby's horizon."

"And the options?"

"Seventy thousand."

"How many shares does the company have outstanding?" I'm thrilled with this question. It may be the best question I've ever asked. (And I owe it all to my father. A week after the Halper sale, Redden raised my salary to $55,000 and granted me five hundred extra options. This seemed like half the company until my father—in a series of crayon pie charts drawn on the paper tablecloths at Café Un Deux Trois—explained that the number of options meant absolutely nothing by itself; they only became important in the context of an overall total. He said a company like Sotheby's probably had 40 or 50 million shares of outstanding stock, which meant that my five hundred shares, well . . .)

"Almost nine million," Fred says.

"So I wouldn't even own one percent."

"Almost one percent ownership of a company worth tens of million adds up quickly, believe me. Plus there'll be plenty of option grants along the way."

"As the shares become diluted."

"Right . . . as the shares become diluted. How'd you learn that? I thought you were a sports memorabilia expert. We already have a CFO—a very cute CFO, by the way. . . ."

The truth, of course, is that I've now reached the limit of my financial knowledge. And Fred knows that, too. But we're having a good time, and I suddenly don't care that my afternoon appointments are starting to stack up, adjusting their chairs for a better look at Gabrielle's legs.

"Look," Fred says, signaling for the check. "I don't want to fuck around. You're our man. And *this* is the time. I'll offer you a starting salary of a hundred thousand dollars a year. You can hire all the help you need. Steal people away from Sotheby's. Think about it and call me in the next few days." Fred puts down a corporate credit card without even looking at the bill. It reads aBid4Charity.com.

FRED STERLING MADE IT sound so logical: you've done well, here's your reward. A year ago I was dodging landlord phone calls and eating at Dojo. Now I could be checking the six-figures box on all those questionnaires. I could get my own apartment, eat out every night, go on *vacation*. And what if it hit? What if this auction site actually worked? I'd be rich in my twenties. But it doesn't feel quite right. That lunch was too easy. There were no questions about my background or my work at Sotheby's. Fred didn't even ask for a résumé. Is that what the economy has come to? I said $90,000 when I'm only making $55,000, and Fred didn't even flinch. I could have said anything.

When I get home Ken is still at it, slogging through the final round of another screenplay bout. He looks beaten up—wild-eyed and bloodied—and I feel guilty as I tell him about Fred; it's probably the last thing he needs to hear. I'm expecting his usual artistic integrity speech, but instead he seems happy for me, almost relieved.

"Look at you, man. Last night you come in here blabbering on like a starstruck teen about how this Rob Bingham guy is going to get you back on the literary fast track, and now, not twenty-four hours later, you're talking like the next Larry Ellison."

"What do you think?"

"A hundred thousand dollars?"

"Maybe more."

"You're fucking nuts if you don't take it."

     I JOIN SOME SOTHEBY's friends for drinks at Serena, the plush new lounge carved into the rock under the Chelsea Hotel. The girls are talking about Edie Sedgwick, Warhol's beautiful bad-luck muse. She almost burned this place down once, in the midsixties, after Warhol had given up on her and all the speed was taking its toll. She was a rich girl surrounded by artists, engulfed by the scene. Was it really all peace and love and anti-materialism back then, or were the drug dens and coffee shops filled with people struggling with the same eternal questions we struggle with today— the promise of art, the pull of commerce, the sly lure of involvement . . . ? Here we are, at century's end, taken by the sudden velocity of our lives, the way we're all *needed*. Art and commerce, meaning and money: "It's the enduring problem for people like you," Josh once told me, at Leland's. But people like me like money, too. People like me take advantage of opportunities. And so it is, in the cellars of the Chelsea Hotel, where I once imagined I'd write books, that I decide to join my generation, my prosperous comrades. The writing isn't working. People like me are realists, too.

     I CALL FRED the following Tuesday. "I can't do a hundred thousand," I say.

"Then what's your number?"

"One-fifteen, plus eighty-seven thousand shares, which I believe is one percent of the company."

"Done," Fred says. "When can you get out of there?"

"Are you serious? That's it?"

"That's it. Welcome aboard. I'll messenger a contract over this afternoon. And if you can, give one week's notice instead of two. We really need you down here."

I suppose I should celebrate, so I take myself out to lunch, to Hi-Life on First Avenue, and order a burger and a Bloody Mary and leaf idly through the *Times*. What I'm thinking about is something my father once said about careers, how they *develop* over time, like fine wine. I laughed. No one works at the same place for thirty years anymore. Just look at the paper today, exploding with stories of our new, fluid reality: a domain name selling for $7.5 million; a crackdown on opportunistic hackers; a piece on freelancers—the Ken Hamms of the world—striking Internet gold. This is a culture based not on solid careers but on daring ideas. It's the first day of the last month of the millennium. I flip to the Metro section, the New York stories of—

STARTLING ENDING FOR YOUNG WRITER OF PROMISE

As his first novel was being typeset, Robert Bingham, 33, was found dead in the bathroom of his TriBeCa home on Sunday. A law enforcement official said that the authorities believed that Mr. Bingham, the last male writer in the storied and contentious Kentucky newspaper family, had overdosed on heroin.

It was a startling ending to a writing career with auspicious beginnings. At 26, Mr. Bingham saw his first story published in *The New Yorker*. His first book, a collection of short stories, was well received, he married in May, and his novel *Lightning on the Sun* was being compared to those of F. Scott Fitzgerald. . . .

Oh, God. Is this right? Immediately I think back to last week's disjointed conversation and the ominous sounds of some inner struggle. But I never imagined the level of the fight. I read the article again and again, trying to reconcile the man I met, the figure I so wanted to be, with this senseless end. My burger arrives and sits there untouched. I feel sick. I need air.

I leave a twenty, leave the paper, leave my lunch, and walk west through the chilly midday streets, past restaurants and bars and office buildings that have hosted former versions of myself—a breakup here, a chaste kiss there, a corner where I once staked out the Mafia, another where I bought my first ecstasy. . . . If you live in New York long enough, the places become more important than the people. Geography is stationary, whereas the faces are always changing, fading in and out with seasons, fads, phases, friendships. I would have been like that for Rob Bingham, a new name in his urban periphery. I might have made some small contribution to his life—a decadent night, a loose friendship—but more likely he would have changed mine. He *has* changed mine. I knew he would. Only, he's brought it spiraling back to earth.

The park is bare. The leaves have all fallen and the colors are gone. I make my way toward Sheep's Meadow with my hands jammed in my pockets. In the back of my mind—in the *front* of it—I saw Robert Bingham as the mentor I've never had. He'd help me overcome all these swirling distractions, these New York sidelines, and show me what really mattered. But that won't happen now. What a fucking pointless end. I used to think sordid deaths were glamorous, but that was before I knew the dead.

When I get to the meadow it is closed, so I sit against the fence and put my head in my hands. A man I barely knew is gone. A dream I've always had seems lost. And I don't know which the tears are for.

THE YOUNGEST EXPERT ever hired by Sotheby's is also the youngest to quit. I send an e-mail to Redden and fifteen minutes later he appears at my desk like a reluctant prince visiting a third-world colony. He tells me I'm making the mistake of my life by leaving Sotheby's at a time like this. Then he says he'll match the offer, until I tell him what the offer is. For a moment his eyes widen, then they turn cold.

Officially I get two weeks to wind things up, but as word spreads that I'm decamping to a competitor (the only greater offense is going to Christie's— in which case they escort you out of the building), I'm soon being shut out of meetings. The lifers start treating me like a traitor, but the younger people—the Internet department, the catalogers, the assistants—see me as a way out. They come up, one by one, and ask me to keep them in mind. I'm not the only one who thinks the air at Sotheby's is growing stale.

aBid4Charity.com is located on a high floor of a prewar storage building below the Port Authority, in a giant one-room loft with fresh paint, new walls, and hundreds of wires, crisscrossing the room in a haphazard search for power strips. The place looks like a temporary military command-and-control center. Fred Sterling's other venture, RxCentric.com, is already up and running on one side of the room, and they've stolen anything worth stealing, leaving our side barren. Fred's desk is a door laid across two saw-horses. I set up shop on top of a defunct radiator. On my second visit, the office manager greets me with a new cell phone, Palm Pilot, laptop, and company credit card. I ask her what my spending limit is. She says there isn't one.

I meet my new coworkers at a strategy meeting with our Web designers. Still straddling two jobs, I rush down from Sotheby's in midafternoon and interrupt the meeting-in-progress. Bobby Valentine is sitting at the end of the conference table. His suit is perfect, his tan is dark, and his hair is coiffed like Trent Lott's. The last thing he looks like is a major league baseball man-ager. But I was expecting Bobby; it's Sarah Connelly who throws me off. Fred told me he'd hired Sarah away from Morgan Stanley to run business development and be an interim CFO, but he didn't *tell* me about her. Sarah is wearing a sleeveless white turtleneck that looks like body paint. I focus on her eyes and manage not to check her out until some Web guru with a pierced eyebrow has resumed his presentation on back-end fulfillment. Sarah has long gold hair that falls over her broad, bare shoulders in ironed strands. She's tall and lean and fit—almost too fit—and has a high nose and a small, accentuated chin, a movie star's chin. Perhaps it's the years she spent on Wall Street that make her seem tough and rigid, like a swimmer. She sits straight, her shoulders thrown back, her chest pushed enticingly forward. Sarah is the only one taking notes. She's the only one listening. Fred's hunched over his Blackberry and Bobby is doing what I'm doing: watching Sarah. People can't wear outfits like that to work—even here.

The meeting is vague and without structure. And so are the following weeks. I leave the Sotheby's sports department in disarray and spend the last days of the old century starting a business tailor-made for the new one. The hours are ridiculously long. Armed with a Bloomberg machine, Fred focuses on his mini-empire of investments while Sarah and I face the daily responsibilities of a multi-million-dollar corporation with no business plan, no Web site, no product. She works on financials for the next round of investors (the $10 million round); I work on the site itself. We hold dozens of meetings a day, with a torrent of Internet experts, Web designers, small-time charities, and potential employees, all of them sniffing around the edges, curious—with the big names involved—to see what we're up to. When we get stuck we call Fred in to lay on some jargon-heavy speech filled with big numbers and bigger forecasts, and always, when he's done, everyone in the room wants to be part of the team. Nancy Spielberg flutters in and out. She keeps calling her brother's office and getting put on hold. Bobby Valentine shows up every few days for a progress report. He gives me the numbers of famous athletes who might donate collectibles to the site. I call a dozen ballplayers. But everyone is busy playing golf in Florida. And we don't have a site yet anyway.

Sarah and I do our best, but there's some initial tension. She has come from the most competitive of environments into this free-form work-in-progress, and it takes her a while to stop worrying about titles and job descriptions and get into the rhythm of working amid chaos. I, of course, love it. We run around like Ritalin addicts from one crisis to the next, bathed in blind optimism. At the other end of the floor, the pale RxCentric people peek above their monitors with bemused expressions, as if they'd pictured a work life a lot more like ours but, after six months, have reached instead a kind of tedious, anxiety-riddled Internet midlife. Through it all, Fred Sterling sits there with a vague smile on his face, agreeing to all ideas, signing whatever we put in front of him, but never fully involved. He buys and sells and buys again as the market ends the century in a Web-fueled fury. The NASDAQ chart looks like a vapor trail after a shuttle launch. And Fred Sterling's expression says it all.

DECADES NEVER END on time: they roll up early or flicker out a few years too late. But this one feels right. The future has been brewing for a while now, readying itself in presidential suites and low-rise Silicon Valley buildings, and now we're here, in the fourth quarter of capitalism, and I've hung around long enough to share the wealth. What more could I ask for than to be where I am, in New York, making money, creating something from nothing. All those thoughts of literary grandeur, they seem so dated now, so blatantly naive. I was only being stubborn, refusing to join the festivities.

I spend the turn of the century at a loft party in TriBeCa. On a TV in the corner, it's already New Year's in Moscow, in Paris, in London, and nothing horrible has happened—no synchronized bombings, no Y2K blackouts, just millions of people celebrating in squares and parks around the globe. When the ball drops, a mile and a half uptown, I find myself kissing a pretty girl with dark hair and smooth, pale skin. She works for a start-up somewhere downtown but I can't remember its name, and as we untangle I get the sudden desire to be outside, in the cold air, alone. I climb the stairs near the elevator and open a fire door and here I am, twenty stories up, high enough to see the city, to hear the quiet, to conjure half-baked resolutions, all the brightness to come. But my thoughts move the wrong way, backward, not forward, and I think instead of Rob Bingham. I can't help it. Did he mean to kill himself, or did he just get careless? His writing could be dark. He seemed to thrive on the worst traits of his characters. But he wrote with a conscience, too, his stories serving as a warning cry to a generation losing its way. That's why I liked them so much. His writing served a purpose; it laid out a loose worldview, in equal parts bleak, hopeful, and haunted. I guess it mirrored his life.

ONE NIGHT A few years ago, Gus and I threw a party that got away from us. Around 4:00 A.M., as people were finally slinking home, these four kids from Brooklyn showed up, friends of friends. They rolled joints and sank into the couch and one of them started playing Leonard Cohen tunes on my guitar. They were incredibly laid-back. At some point I went to the bathroom. The door was closed, so I knocked, and when there was no response I opened it. One of the guys was sitting on the edge of the tub, holding a spoon filled with dark liquid. He looked at me but didn't say anything. Then he reached over to the sink and picked up a small syringe lying next to my toothbrush. I started backing out.

"It's cool," he said. "Just a skin shot."

I'd stayed away from heroin until then, or maybe heroin had stayed away from me. In any case, I hadn't been looking. But I'd read all the books, seen all the movies, and in real life I'd seen the people, stumbling across Tompkins Square, down side streets in Chelsea, their skin a colorless shade of caution. They were always walking around clutching at things, feeling for objects, for reminders of the physical world. And they were never dressed for the weather. That's how you know a junkie: he's bundled up when it's hot, stripped down in the cold, as if temperature doesn't matter anymore.

Beyond the messy needles and murmurs of easy addiction, I'd always liked the world I was in too much to seek out some temporary paradise. Still, I stayed in the doorway, even moved in a little, conspiratorially. He filled the syringe with water, squirted some onto the spoon, then pulled a lighter out of his pocket and started heating the spoon from underneath. Slowly he pulled the plunger from the syringe and used it to stir the murky concoction. When he was done, he looked up. His eyes were yellow.

"Want this one? I'll do you."

"I'm good. I just did some lines, so . . ."

"It's not the same thing."

"Maybe after."

He tied his shirt tightly around his upper arm, then took a cotton swab from his pocket, rolled it into a little ball, and dropped it onto the spoon. It puffed up like a blowfish. Then he sank the needle into the middle and sucked the heroin into the syringe.

"Filters it," he said.

In the living room the others were moving around, either laughing or arguing—I couldn't tell. I closed the door behind me. The kid sat down on the lip of the tub again. He put the end of his shirt in his mouth and pulled, and his arm tensed slightly. I wanted to ask what happened if he missed the vein and shot the stuff into tissue or muscle, but this wasn't the time. He bit his lip, slid the needle in just below the crook of his arm, and pulled the plunger back a little. Blood came swirling into the syringe. "That's how you know it's in," he said. Then, giving me one last look, he injected himself, pressing down with his thumb until all of it was gone. He waited, and so did I, maybe twenty seconds, and then he smiled, a stupid blow-job grin, and leaned back against the tile wall.

"I have a clean needle," he said, smoothly, pointing to his pocket. "You could just do a little. It's not like you think, man. It's just . . . a really good time."

The door was still closed. The living room had turned eerily quiet. I looked in the mirror. Then his hand went up in the air, like a stop sign. His eyes started watering. He suddenly looked bad, damp and dry at the same time. And then he clutched the toilet and threw up, or tried to throw up, his knuckles white, his skin a glazed surface of sweat.

"You okay?" I asked.

But he didn't answer—maybe he didn't hear me. The bathroom smelled clinical. I opened the door and backed out, figuring his friends would know what to do. But everyone was gone. Upstairs in his overhanging cave, Gus was snoring. How could these guys have left their friend? Did they know he was still here? I hurried back to the bathroom. Now I just wanted this kid to leave, but he was lying in the tub, sideways, feet dangling over the side. He looked up at me, past me. He was playing with the plug. Then he closed his eyes and started humming.

At some point he fell asleep. His pulse felt fine. He was breathing normally, too. I considered waking Gus, getting a second opinion, but I didn't want him involved. So I took a Xanax and stayed downstairs on the couch, nearby. I turned on the TV and there was Allen Ginsberg, and then Kerouac and Cassidy and, fittingly, William Burroughs. It looked like dusty Mexico, a collage of famous friends, no shirts, arms around women, around men, the frenzied images rolling into one another like beat prose itself. I'd stumbled on an early-morning documentary, perfect for coming down, for saying all this has been done before. Except a newsman came on, frowning, grave, and there was Ginsberg again, in a box in the upper right corner of the screen, with years under his name, a beginning and an end. I pressed Mute, listened for breathing from the bathroom, and hearing it, closed my eyes and tried to sleep.

He was gone when I woke (and Gus was never the wiser). For a while after, I kept thinking he could have died in there. Like Bingham did.

On the cold roof in TriBeCa, I think of Rob's phone call again. Why did he call me, not once but twice? Did he see something there, or was he just looking for a fast friend? I look uptown, at the giant spotlights roaming the skies above Times Square. The millennium is turning. The truth is, I feel like an impostor every time I think about Rob Bingham. He did everything for real.

Twenty-seven

Sarah finds two other start-ups, eSuperstars.com and UltimateBid .com, doing exactly what we're doing. She does this by reading the paper one morning. It seems no one has bothered to research the marketplace.

"There's nothing to worry about," Fred says, nonchalantly. "A little competition means we're on the right track."

I'm beginning to think Fred walks on water. Maybe it's the trust he shows in us, the way he casually green-lights even our most outlandish ideas. He tells us to hire anyone we want, and soon a stream of friends and friends of friends is bustling in and out. Everyone has Internet experience. Their résumés read like games of hopscotch, starting with a traditional job, then giving way to a series of quick, frantic dot-com leaps, the titles and salaries improving with every venture, every colorful company name. Even Giles makes his way down to investigate. We sit on a couch next to our fully stocked office kitchen and open some wine. It's two-thirty in the afternoon.

"I have a few questions about your résumé," I say.

"And I've got an answer: *Fuck off!* The only way I'm working for this tax write-off front company is if they pay me what they're paying you, then get me a green card."

"I can probably get you a hundred thousand and a shitload of stock options. And I'm sure we can do something about a green card."

"It'll be harder than you think."

"No, it's a great market opportunity, and the team we're assembling is—"

"I was talking about the green card," Giles says. "But listen to you. You sound like one of those nutters down in sothebys-dot-com."

"I heard the government announced their price-fixing investigation."

"We steal from the rich to give to the richer."

"It's a good time to get out."

"I told you what my—fucking hell, who's that?" He's looking at Sarah, who has just walked in wearing a halter top.

"She could be your coworker."

"I'll take ninety thousand," Giles says, only half joking.

ONE MORNING, IN A rare lull, Fred kneels down next to me. "I don't know what your situation is," he says, "but I've got something you might want to look at."

"Sure," I say, a little too eagerly.

"It's a company I helped finance a few years go: Inkine Pharmaceuticals. It went public, and now their lead drug, Visicol, is testing well and the stock has gone from one dollar to over five in just a few months. I think there's more ceiling there, especially if Visicol gets FDA approval."

"What does Visicol do?"

"It's a bowel evacuant. It's a pill that makes you shit. You used to have to drink this awful liquid before a colonoscopy, but now you can take these pills."

"Well, thanks, I'll look at the numbers."

Of course, I don't know how to look at numbers. I've never valued a stock. But does it really matter? All they do is go up—even bowel evacuants. At lunchtime I call my old broker at Merrill Lynch. We haven't spoken in more than three years, and predictably she has no idea who I am. It takes her five minutes to dig up my account.

"I was wondering if you could tell me my balance," I say.

"*That's* why you called? Don't you open your statements?"

"I don't get them anymore. I've moved a few times."

"Well, let's see. You bought almost five thousand dollars' worth of Oracle back in 1995, and . . . huh, guess how much it's worth now."

"I don't know. Eight thousand."

"Over forty thousand."

"You're *kidding.*"

"It's had a great run. I picked a winner for you."

I dimly remember her telling me not to buy it back then—when the stock was at three—because it was far too risky. But this is no time for semantics.

"I want you to sell ten thousand worth, and buy Inkine—INKP."

"What do they do?"

"Don't worry about it."

"Okay, let's see. INKP is at a little over five right now. I trust you know this is a risky small-cap play. Why don't you diversify a bit, spread the *wealth*."

"You mean, like, blue chips?"

"Oh, God no, you're too young for that. Other Internet stocks, maybe some tech. I'll put together a list and get back to you." And then the line goes dead.

IT'S TIME TO MOVE AGAIN. It's a combination of factors—the unexpected Oracle windfall, the roaches, Shakespeare—but mostly it's the need to get out on my own. Living with Ken makes me uneasy. It's been two years since *Moving In/Moving Out* died its lonely death, and Ken's been working on his new screenplay since then: the steroid-riddled football script *Endzone*. But he doesn't talk about it. We don't talk about writing at all.

Perhaps the only thing that's kept pace with the market is the price of real estate. It's tough to find something downtown for less than $2,000 a month. I see more than a dozen apartments before settling on a small one-bedroom on the ground floor of a Chelsea brownstone on Fifteenth Street. It has a big bathtub and a small backyard, and it's blissfully quiet. I sign the lease on a cold winter morning: $1,800 a month, plus $2,000 for a toothless Russian broker who spent a total of twenty minutes with me. He smiles, baring his gums, then wads up the cash and leaves me alone in the empty living room.

It's taken five years to find this silence, but like most things in New York, it's fleeting. I need to get back to the office for a meeting with our new Web development agency. We've hired them to give us an image overhaul, starting with our company name. In the early afternoon Fred leads us—Sarah, me, and the half dozen employees we've amassed in less than a month— over to their office for a brainstorming session. We march through the Flatiron district with our Starbucks coffees, our vibrating phones, our MP3 players, and make our way up futuristic elevators, around glass partitions, and are finally shown into a Lego-like conference room. The agency people come in dressed like rock stars, complete with pierced brows and Bono shades. Caterers appear with sandwiches and beer, and as we stuff our faces the agency people start throwing out names. "No idea is too stupid," they say, but of course all of them are: astonish.com, biduponastar.com, cause wecare.com, celebriceeds.com, itruistic.com, projectearth.com, starrystuff .com, wondersnevercease.com. . . . Three hours later, when we call it quits, the blackboards are littered with hundreds of possibilities, each worse than the one before.

"That sucked," Sarah announces, in the cab back uptown.

"The real problem," Fred says, "is that we still owe the old agency a hundred and ten thousand."

Sarah looks startled. "For what?"

"They came up with the original concept and navigation."

"But it was so bad we're not using any of it."

"Still . . . ," Fred says, gazing out the window.

Back at the office there's already a message waiting from the new agency. They've run a domain search on the company names we came up with, and as ridiculous as they are, almost every one is already taken.

ON THE LAST FRIDAY in January I come into the office early. The agency is making its final branding presentation this morning; we need to finalize our Web site infrastructure; and I'm interviewing two girls someone met at a bar the other night for a position we haven't invented yet. All this and I need to pack because I'm moving tomorrow. It's not even 8:00 A.M., but Fred is already at his desk.

"Any interest in going to the Super Bowl this weekend?" he asks.

"Are you kidding?"

"Just got tickets from one of our investors. You and Sarah can fly down to Atlanta this afternoon. I'll come down later tonight. We'll all stay with my friend Jerry."

When Sarah walks in, causing the usual stir on the RxCentric side, we all head over to the conference room. Our agency's project manager is standing in the corner next to an easel. When we're settled he starts in on a superlative-laced speech about our new reality, where image controls perception, and substance and quality no longer define success. His team has come up with a powerful branding solution designed to make us omnipresent, like eBay or Amazon. There's a dramatic pause—a magician's pause—as he flips the first page, and there, in big bold letters, is our electric future: DREAMGIANT.COM. Underneath the words is a squat little figure with spindly appendages, a flattened Humpty Dumpty with a thinking cap—a *dreaming* cap—on his head. It's the Dream Giant himself, our new company mascot.

"Isn't it great?" someone says. "Can you believe the name wasn't taken?"

"IT'S ABSURD," SARAH SAYS. "Dreamgiant-dot-com sounds like the tooth fairy on steroids. What's it have to do with an auction site?"

We're taxiing toward the Teterboro runway in Wayne Huizenga's Gulfstream IV. Huizenga owns Blockbuster Video and the Miami Dolphins. I have no idea how he's connected to us.

"Branding," I say, enthusiastically. "The physical representation of an idea. Think big. Dream giant! That's what our company lets people do."

"Except we don't. We don't do anything. We've been at it for over a month and we don't have a Web site, we don't have any charities on board, and we have no memorabilia or . . . *experiences* . . . whatever the hell they are. The only thing we do have is a burn rate. I figured it out the other day. It's like fifty-five thousand a month, and that's before we pay for this whole Dreamgiant thing."

"But Fred doesn't seem worried, and anyway, we're raising another ten million in the next few weeks."

"We're supposed to, but—" The engines drown out the rest of her thought. We start hurtling down the runway, and a few seconds later we're airborne, shooting acutely toward the clouds. We're on a couch without seatbelts, and Sarah falls into me as I brace myself against the armrest. All those years of buckling up on benign commercial takeoffs, and now, when seatbelts would actually help, there's nothing, no restraint at all.

When we've leveled off, a tan flight attendant in a black miniskirt comes by to take our drink order. Sarah orders us champagne, then takes her sweater off.

"You know, the more I study our business plan, the more holes I'm finding."

"So why did you take the job if you have all these questions about it?"

"Because everyone wants out of Wall Street. And when I first talked to

Fred he was so . . . convincing. He promised I could make strategic decisions that actually shape the company. They don't let people our age do that
in the real world. Plus . . ."

"What?"

"Well, what if it actually works?" she says, quietly.

"I know."

Turbulence arrives with the champagne, and I take a large sip so it won't
spill. In the back of the small cabin, two businessmen are discussing the
proposed AOL/Time-Warner merger. "I can't believe AOL would do it," one
of them says.

I lean back, close my eyes, and start thinking of . . . *Sarah*. I didn't like her
at first. I saw her as a preppy finance girl whose sex appeal was blunted by
a cold exterior. She's a perfect stereotype. She grew up in Greenwich, one of
three sisters in a conservative Catholic family, then went to Georgetown and
Columbia Business School. She lives on the Upper East Side, dates investment bankers, goes to church on Sundays, and idolizes Ronald Reagan. In
the 1980s Sarah would have worn a power suit with shoulder pads and
eaten at Bouley with the boys just to prove she could. Today, she works out
religiously and eats at the Rye Country Club so her food minimum won't
go to waste.

But I'm coming around. She may be analytical but she's *honest*. She's
come to this company expecting to make it work. She raises questions and
waits for answers, and her ability to stay grounded makes her a valuable
commodity in a helium environment. In meetings she shows up with a
copy of the latest financials and asks Fred or Jack Norton or even Bobby
Valentine why, say, the cost of sales in Q3, Y2, jumps up 25 percent. The
men in the room get these wry looks on their faces, not because they know
the answer—they don't; no one has thought that far ahead. No, they're
wondering how a realist slipped into this dot-com nirvana. And an attractive woman at that. As we begin our descent into Atlanta, one of the men in
the back walks past and says hello. He glances at Sarah's tits as he makes his
way to the bathroom. Sarah puts her sweater back on and looks out the
window.

"Can you feel how fast we're going?" she says.

. . .

IT STARTS SNOWING almost as soon as we get to Atlanta, and by Saturday morning the airports have shut down. But, for those who have beaten the weather, Super Bowl weekend is one long, disjointed celebration. Sarah and I follow Fred and his friend Jerry from one VIP event to the next. We go to superagent Leigh Steinberg's party, where aging quarterbacks hobble around looking for dot-com endorsement deals; we take a limo to an Elton John concert and sit next to Faith Hill, who, up close and despite her music, is one of the most beautiful women I've ever seen; we have dinner at a four-star steak house, an extravagant event featuring half a dozen bottles of Opus One; and then it's on to the Gold Club.

We walk into the legendary strip club and are immediately surrounded by a sea of silicone-enhanced women, writhing and stretching over men in green Masters golf shirts. I was coming to view my coworkers as something like a second family, but now I do my best to remember that Fred is indeed my CEO, and Sarah, even with a body that rivals the naked ones, is a conservative Catholic girl. Jerry follows Fred toward the bar, leaving Sarah and me in the middle of the floor, studying shapes and sizes. Sarah stops a curvy blonde in a plastic dress, and incredibly, they start climbing on top of one another. The plastic tears away like Velcro and they start rubbing against each other, skin on skin. I look around for Fred, wanting him to see his CFO in action, but he and Jerry have both vanished. When the show ends—and it's some time—Sarah sticks a twenty in the stripper's thong like she's done all this before. "Your turn," Sarah says, pulling herself together, and for a second I think she's going to hop on top of *me*, but she gets up and starts leading me around the place.

We walk slowly across the main floor, then make our way up to a balcony lined with curtained-off VIP rooms. Sarah walks down the row, making eyes at passing girls. I start thinking about the constraints of Catholicism. Up ahead there's a commotion, a crowd of strippers loitering around the last two rooms. A waiter pushes past us with a trolley of champagne. Sarah follows him as he moves a curtain aside, and there, naked but for a cowboy hat, is my CEO, spanking an equally naked Naomi Campbell look-alike. Jerry, who is at least partially clothed, has a girl on his lap. When he looks up at us, he raises his arms as if for a group hug. "Where the hell have you two been?"

"We've been waiting for you," Fred says, administering more punishment.

"What's up with the crowd outside?" I ask.

"Dennis Rodman's in the next room," Jerry says.

Sarah's eyes get big: "Really? I've always wanted to kiss Dennis Rodman." She looks at Fred — all of him — then smiles and adjusts her top. "I'll be back soon."

There are drugs on the table, but I'm not interested. Any lingering chemical desires died along with Rob Bingham. In the far corner it's Fred's turn to pay for his sins. He bends over and Naomi winds up with a paddle. I look away.

At some point the music stops, the girls give up, and we're herded toward the exit. I look around for Sarah. Fred looks around for his clothes. There's a bottleneck by the door, and as we slowly move closer, we see Rodman surrounded by a harem. And there, in the center of his parade, is Sarah. Rodman has his arm around her. She whispers something into his ear. Then he bends over, all six feet six inches of him, and kisses her. Fred cheers.

Outside in the snow, our CEO tries to flag down cars by waving money in the wind, but in the end we're forced to call Jerry's pregnant wife, who shows up twenty frozen minutes later in a mood that can only be called dark. We pile in and drive away in silence.

At the house Fred and I have one last drink as Jerry and his wife argue upstairs. Jerry has left his credit card in the VIP room. His wife, of course, wants to know what the hell he was doing in a VIP room, and on it goes from there, until the sun comes up on Super Bowl Sunday and I climb up-stairs to my assigned bed, an air mattress on the guest-room floor. Sarah's in the real bed. I'm almost asleep when I feel Sarah lie down next to me. "The bed's too hard," she whispers. Her body is warm. The morning is young. And Sarah has a boyfriend who works for Goldman Sachs. That's all I'm sure of anymore. I roll over and close my eyes. It's like some last grasp at decency.

"Who's playing?" Sarah says, as I fade out.

"What?"

"In the game."

"Does it really matter?"

Twenty-eight

THINGS HAPPEN QUICKLY. The NASDAQ hits 4,500. Inkine hits 8.75. And Sarah breaks up with her boyfriend. Turns out Goldman Sachs fired the guy weeks ago but he didn't tell anyone. He kept getting up in the morning, putting on a suit, and walking out the door. He fooled Sarah until she dropped by his office to surprise him.

So we commiserate and curse the thought of love. Life has become too fluid for real feelings. Our hearts belong to the company, and we're finally getting somewhere. The new agency is building our Web site; Sarah has the business plan ready for the road show; and I've secured a few large memorabilia collections for the launch. We're coming together—all twelve, then fourteen, then sixteen of us—in the name of charity. Sometimes, when I don't think about it too much, I can actually believe that.

We're ready to launch the site, raise some money—*open for business!*—but then Fred starts stalling. He tells us to be patient, wait a few days. He takes phone calls behind closed doors. And he disappears for hours. Sarah and I suddenly have nothing to do. We send each other frustrated e-mails. Sarah starts a market research project, an Excel spreadsheet listing hundreds of venture capitalists and well-funded startups—a kind of social registry for the new business century. I get into the domain-name business. I buy trytohelp.com and a half dozen other monikers, hoping to build an online real estate empire. The rest of the company begins to follow our lead. They take three-hour lunch breaks; they have online chess matches with people in Finland; they play baseball with the memorabilia. And I can't really blame them.

Sarah and I start flirting. Heavily. In our boredom, our hurry-up-and-wait downtime, she writes me provocative e-mails and waits for the reaction. I try to take my mind off her by opening an E-Trade account and buy-ing more Inkine. The NASDAQ climbs to 5,000. INKP reaches ten. Then Fred walks in for the first time in three days and calls Sarah and me into the conference room.

"It's official," he says, "so I thought you two should be the first to know—we just merged with eSuperstars. We're on our way."

ESUPERSTARS IS A twenty-person outfit with a business plan simi-lar to ours—except they don't have a charity angle. Their idea is to auction off one-of-a-kind celebrity experiences and sell a few collectibles on the side.

Sarah and I take the subway to their offices in the Colgate-Palmolive Building on Park Avenue to meet their founders—our new CEOs—Vince Rubinstein and Jordan Marsh. Vince is a large, fast-talking marketing type with reddish hair and pock-marked skin. Jordan is tall and thin and blond. He's the "talent" behind the operation, having written "Go New York Go," the awful theme song that plays incessantly at Knicks games. Fred says they're great guys. He's gotten to know them over the last month as they've secretly put this deal together, the contents of which come out piecemeal in a series of integration meetings. We take scrupulous notes as the new cor-porate vision for eSuperstars.com is laid out. We're moving to their offices and taking their name. I'll run the collectibles business; Sarah will join the business development team (they already have a CFO); and Fred will join Vince and Jordan as a co-CEO. The rest of our original company will be-come the "charity arm" of the combined entity. But right away it starts shaping up as a land grab—us against them—and Fred, tapping away on his Blackberry, remains worryingly quiet.

"I DON'T LIKE THAT GUY Vince," Sarah says, shuddering. We're stuck in a subway tunnel under Times Square on our way back to our old of-fices. "He's so . . . *creepy*." For the last three hours we've been arguing the merits of our unfinished site versus their unfinished site. In the end, it was decided we'd use theirs, which means all the work we did on ours, all those passionate discussions of names and colors and ad campaigns . . . all of that was for nothing, the last three months wasted. "Those eSuperstars people don't care about us," Sarah says, shaking her head. "They just want access to Dell and Valentine and Spielberg."

"They'll be upset about Spielberg," I say, but Sarah doesn't hear me. She's reading the ads above the subway windows, the tacky messages from language schools, personal-injury law firms, and cosmetic doctors. She likes the doctors best: a dermatologist named Zizmor, a plastic surgeon called Senderoff. She thinks the names are fake.

"I don't understand why Fred is doing this," she says, finally. "The financials just don't make sense. It's like no one ever sat down and thought through the business before they raised money. I mean, how are we going to mass-market *dream experiences*? We might convince Tiger Woods to play one round with a winning bidder if the proceeds are going to his foundation, but he'd have to play hundreds of rounds before we started making any money. Besides, why should charities team up with us if they can hold their own benefit auctions without paying us? And for that matter, how will we get bidders to our site in the first place if they can already find everything on eBay? Because *some* of the proceeds will go to charity? Come on. They can give to charity without our help. It's one of the few things people can still do on their own."

"Maybe that's why we're merging: to get more visibility. We'll be a much bigger company. We'll have a charity side and a for-profit side, we'll offer collectibles and experiences. . . . We'll corner the market on fantasy."

"Our business plan already takes care of that," Sarah says.

MONEY, EVEN SOME, changes everything. When I had none, I learned to live in two-week installments, steering carefully through those last long days to Friday. But now there's padding in those paychecks, hundreds of lingering dollars to spend on photographs, paintings, and shelves for the books I can finally afford (I stride into the Strand one weekend morning and buy back as many of my old books as I can remember, including a copy of *Brightness Falls* that actually *is* mine, complete with illegible notes in margins and favorite passages underlined for easy plagiarism). After a lifetime of cheap wall coverings and compromised closets, I see my new apartment as a measure of progress. Never mind that what I mistook for peace and quiet has turned out to be dark and eerie silence. I just throw money at the problem, stock up on lamps and plants and anything else that might add light and color.

At work we pack up our desks and reassemble them on Park Avenue. The original eSuperstars people have taken all the window offices, leaving us to herd like sheep into a bullpen of makeshift cubicles. Fred keeps saying merging is for the best: it will speed up our timetable, give us more leverage, et cetera, et cetera; but it feels like we've been hijacked by thugs masquerading as entrepreneurs. In the interest of the company, Sarah and I decide to sit apart. In recent days the heavy flirting has become light petting, "Page Six" canoodling. It was inevitable: a cheap fling for shallow times. It won't go anywhere; it can't. She's a pro-life investment banker who admires John Sununu and has no sense of irony.

SOON THE ATMOSPHERE in the eSuperstars office becomes tense. The merger agreement stipulated that no one would get laid off, and no one has. But now, as the meetings drag on, there's nothing for anyone to do. Entire days are spent arguing over the organizational chart on the chalkboard, a dysfunctional corporate family tree that measures the status and importance of every employee. It's heavily skewed in their favor. Fred implores us to stop thinking in terms of *us* versus *them*, but we've been surrounded, usurped, diluted. I want to move forward with the collectibles business despite the lack of a Web site, but Vince announces he'd like to focus exclusively on Dream Experiences in the beginning. "For press purposes," he says. I give him a Halper catalog, tell him the press loves collectibles. He just smiles.

In early April Fred leaves for a long weekend in Vegas, and the environment turns hostile. The eSuperstars people stop talking to us, so Sarah and I tell *our* employees to take the rest of the day off. I start writing a long note to Jack Norton, Michael Dell's man, explaining how awful things have become, how our "CEO triumvirate" is just throwing money—Dell's money—away. I get up to print it out and am walking past Vince's corner office when I hear him laughing with two of his boys: "Too bad she's so uptight, because with those tits she'd be great in bed." They all laugh. I know they're talking about Sarah. Vince hates her because she keeps showing him up in meetings. I can't help myself.

"Like she'd ever fuck you," I say, from just outside the door.

Vince looks up, slightly shocked. "What'd you say?"

"I said, 'Like she'd ever fuck you.' I mean, let's be realistic." Then I walk away.

I pick up the Norton letter and go back toward my desk, running through the possible repercussions. Vince can't fire me for that, because then what he said will come out. But he'll get me somehow, when no one's looking. Or when everyone is. I walk past Sarah, who's diligently e-mailing potential business partners, and kiss the back of her neck.

"Stop," she whispers. "We can't do that stuff here."

I want to tell her what just happened, but that won't help anything. She's going through enough already. America thunders forward while we sit on our hands and wonder what's gone wrong.

I WALK IN ON Monday morning and Fred is already at his desk. His face is drawn, his eyes dark and glazed. He looks like shit. "Went straight through," he says. "It's the only way to do it. Didn't sleep till the flight back. Have you ever been on a red-eye back from Vegas? Somber as a morgue. Everyone's burnt out and busted, but not Uncle Freddie." He looks around the still-deserted office, then unzips a duffle bag at his feet. I crouch down and peer inside, and dozens of neatly bound stacks of bills stare back at me. They're all hundreds.

"How much is in there?"

"Seventy Gs. All-night blackjack run. But I've got a little problem. I can't deposit it anywhere because First Union has no goddamn branches in New York."

"My brother, Douglas, works at First Union," I tell him, "on the investment banking side. His office is just around the corner. Maybe he can—"

"Let's get him over here," Fred says. "I can't carry this bag around all week."

Douglas has been in New York for two years, working as an entry-level analyst at one of New York's top mergers-and-acquisitions firms. He joined First Union over the winter, and from all accounts he's doing well. He's not exactly passionate about finance; he's just good with people and willing to put in the hours. I've told him about this circus a few times, about Fred and

Sarah, Bobby V. and Nancy, and he's been meaning to come over and see a real dot-com in action—or inaction.

When my brother shows up, just after one o'clock, Bobby Valentine is here with Tommy Lasorda, entertaining a group of girls with stories of spring training; Nancy Spielberg is yelling at someone on the phone; and Sarah's in one of her snug shirts. But I'm saving the best for last. When Fred hands him the duffle bag my brother's eyes open up like large moons. Fred asks about the banking business. Doug tries to sputter out an answer, but all this is too much for a Monday.

"I need to get this into my account," Fred says. "Maybe someone in your office could do something. I mean, there must be a way, right?"

"I don't think . . ." Doug's eyes are still on the money, no doubt wondering what exactly people would say if he appeared back at his office after lunch carrying $70,000 in cash for deposit. "I don't think we can deal with . . . I mean . . . we're just the investing arm. Maybe I can get you a phone number or something. . . ."

I shepherd him back out to the elevators. He looks stricken.

SARAH AND I WERE hoping Fred would come back and everything would change, but it just gets worse. We start getting shut out of meetings. Our people ask us what's going on, why they're even coming to work. We ask them to be patient. We sound like Fred. But the original eSuperstars employees aren't doing anything, either. Their salesmen are supposed to be selling Dream Experiences to corporations—our all-important B-to-B side—but the only experiences we have available are meet-and-greets with Bobby Valentine. I have several months' worth of collectibles ready to auction as soon as the site is ready, but no one seems to care.

Still, the checks keep coming, so I keep showing up for work. Sarah and I start taking long lunches upstairs in the private Colgate cafeteria. Occasionally someone asks what department we're in and we say R & D— we're researching new whiter-than-white toothpastes, edible shaving creams, soaps that smell like summer. . . . We sit surrounded by corporate middle managers, eating hanger steaks and roasted chicken. Sometimes we go out for sushi with Fred. He pays as long as we promise not to complain about work, and we can usually hold out until the walk back, and then the floodgates open and Fred bobs and weaves around our questions. Back in the office, Sarah gives me a primer course on buying stocks—P/E ratios, earnings per share, selling short—and soon we're screwing around with our E-Trade accounts and then with each other, having sex in stairwells, in bathrooms, in dressing rooms at Saks. We have afternoon martinis, go to sample sales, buy lingerie at La Perla. It's like I'm having an affair, even though there's no one else. I suppose I'm cheating on my job, but I barely have one. Fred watches us come back in, flushed and slightly askew, and he just shakes his head. What else can he do?

Twenty-nine

ON A FRIDAY IN the middle of April, the NASDAQ starts a stomach-churning freefall. My office, normally humming with the sounds of inactivity, turns stone serious. Three desks away, Fred makes frantic phone calls as his Bloomberg screen tallies the carnage. By noon CEO-watching has become a spectator sport; we watch as Fred and Vince and even Jordan bark sell orders and type out frantic text messages to faceless brokers. Between calls Fred puts his head in his hands and rubs his eyes, like he doesn't believe what he's seeing. On the small TV in the corner, CNBC reporters talk quickly, desperately, as they collide with traders on market floors. But the ticker on the bottom of the screen is all anyone is watching. It tells the story in a sea of bloodred numbers.

I walk up behind Sarah, who is camped out in front of the screen. "Kind of cool, watching the economy fall apart in real time."

"Don't start. This is only a small correction. They've been predicting it." She says this stoically, her belief in systems, in the order of numbers, intact. But two hours later, when the markets close, no rally has ensued. The Dow has fallen 617 points; the NASDAQ 355—almost ten percent of its value. I shudder to think of what's happened to little Inkine or, worse, monolithic Oracle. This may be a correction, but it feels like a funeral. By 6:00 P.M., everyone is gone but Fred, who is at his desk, staring at after-hours numbers. I walk over and ask how bad it is.

"I don't know. What worries me is that all these Internet companies are valued based on future earnings: If the economy sustains its current growth, then they'll see profitability three, four, even five years down the road. But if the economy falters, if the bottom drops out of the *present*, then we'll never get to that future, and anyone who doesn't have enough cash will evaporate."

"Like us."

Fred shifts in his chair. "I've been meaning to talk to you about that," he says. "I think I've found a solution, if you can keep it quiet for a few more days."

"What."

"Another merger—with UltimateBid, our West Coast competitors. They're a great company with strong backing, and they're ahead of us. They actually have a site."

"Imagine that."

"They're aligned with IMG, one of the top celebrity management agencies, so it'll be easy to fulfill those dream experiences. You know how we keep talking about a round of golf with Tiger Woods? Well, they've already done it. I'm telling you, this is a good opportunity."

"What about collectibles?"

"They think it's a great idea."

"You're sure?"

"Absolutely. We've discussed it specifically."

THE (SECOND) OFFICIAL MERGER announcement comes early the following week. Vince gathers the office together and gives us the details. We'll be adopting the UltimateBid name (our fourth in as many months), along with their headquarters in Silicon Valley. Our office will be the East Coast branch. IMG and SFX (the original investors in eSuperstars) will be majority owners, and the current UltimateBid CEO will retain that position. Vince and Jordan will run the New York office, and Fred will stay on in an unofficial capacity. There is no mention of a collectibles business. He ends by cheerily declaring, again, that no one will be laid off. "I personally made sure of that," he says, his gelled hair glistening under the fluorescent yellow office lighting.

Sarah and I make a beeline for the cafeteria. "This is fucking awful," she says, as soon as the elevator doors close. "I don't want to be some mid-level employee in a satellite office. Right now, I'd take a pink slip and a severance package in a second. Why the hell did I ever leave Wall Street?"

"Do they actually give you a *pink slip* when you're fired?"

Sarah cocks her head and looks at me. "What's wrong with you?"

We take our normal window table. Sarah walks off to steal a Colgate croissant while I open the *Post*. Bobby Valentine is on the back cover. According to the article, he made disparaging comments about some of his players during a speech at Wharton a few days ago. Bobby denied saying anything negative, but now a tape of the speech has been produced and the whole affair has blown up. They're calling it "Whartongate."

"I think I might quit if Fred leaves," Sarah says, sitting down next to me. "There won't be anyone left to look out for us."

"He hasn't exactly been doing that while he's been here. I mean, don't you blame him for some of this? I remember when I first met him at Petaluma—God, it seems like two years ago, but I guess it's only been five months—he was so *smart*, so *optimistic*. I know this sounds weird but I was really . . . *taken* by him. He could have been starting a construction company and I would have signed on."

"And instead we got deconstruction. Even in a runaway economy, our model wouldn't have worked. He figured that out too late and now he's doing the best he can, considering he's got twenty people to look out for. Merging always gives a company life—at least until the dust clears. Anyway, you'll be fine: the collectibles business is the only revenue stream that remotely makes sense. The stupid *dream experiences* . . . they're more like nightmares."

We take a fire stairwell back to our floor, stopping halfway down for a quick exchange Sarah likes fooling around in semipublic, an unlocked door away from getting caught. And it *is* kind of thrilling. Our entire relationship is based on dangerous sex in stolen moments. It's as hollow as the age.

When we finally make it back downstairs, Bobby Valentine is sitting at my desk, checking his e-mail. "I'm hiding," he says, when I ask what's going on. "This fucking thing won't go away."

"It's just the press," I say.

Bobby leans back in my chair. "No, this whole thing is my fault. I don't care that I said that crap. Believe me, it's not hard when you've got someone like Rey Ordonez on your team. The problem is . . . I *lied* about it afterward."

It sounds like a confession, and one he should be making to someone other than a halfway-starstruck semiemployee. I lean against the cubicle wall, searching for something clever to say, a witty cliché about living life in a fishbowl or baseball being a long season, but all I can think of is how his honest admission—even if it was about lying—sounds so different from everything else I've been hearing.

"I think that's the first time someone's told the truth around here in months."

The manager of the Mets looks up and grins.

IN MID-MAY our new California-based CEO flies in to address us. We gather around and listen hard for some semblance of a realistic future. I'd like to think there was a time, back when people still memorized phone numbers, when CEOs were formidable, like redwoods. But this man wears soft Italian loafers and relaxed-fit khakis, and when he speaks it's not with the booming voice of authority but with the subdued tones of insider status. He stresses the importance of teamwork, then tells us how lucky we are to have Vince and Jordan leading the way. He says he works in a cubicle just like we do and pauses after this revelation, like it's an applause line. In a final limp-wristed rallying cry, he announces we'll beat eBay at its own game, and as I try to count the number of times I've heard that, he slinks away without meeting any of us. I look across the room and try to catch Fred's eye, but he's staring at the floor.

At the end of the day, walking out of the office with Sarah, we run into our fearless new leader waiting on the curb with Vince. We walk up and introduce ourselves and he shakes our hands with the phony affability of a politician who's stuck listening to a constituent's complaint. I ask if I can spend a few minutes with him discussing the collectibles department. He tells me to come out to California and talk to him next week. Then a limo pulls up and the back door opens. Two girls in miniskirts are waiting inside. I can see their legs, hear them laughing. UltimateBid's upper management climbs in, and the car pulls away.

I FLY OUT TO San Francisco on a Thursday and drive down to our offices the next morning. I'm planning to present our CEO with a full business plan for the collectibles division. Fred says it's a formality; they just need a better understanding of what it all entails. But it's been months since I've appraised a signature or studied the markings on a bat, and most of the collectors who sent me consignments early on have taken them back. How can I convince them to sell their valuable sports memorabilia on a site that specializes in meet-and-greets with Gloria Estefan?

If San Francisco was a hotbed of Internet activity a few years ago, it is now defined by it. I drive south down 101—the real information highway—and turn off just north of Menlo Park. Ultimatebid.com is housed in a low-rise office complex so completely nondescript that it's hard to imagine anything creative occurring within.

I walk inside and present myself to the Barbie-like receptionist, who smiles and speaks at the same time. Behind her lies a maze of colorless cubicles inhabited by dozens of determined twenty-somethings, walking and talking and typing with brisk purpose. The only hint of decoration in the entire place is a banner featuring Heidi Klum in a bikini, framed by the words *UltimateBid.com—Stop Dreaming, Start Bidding.* Barbie asks me to follow her, and so I do, past work stations filled with UltimateBid coffee mugs and baseball caps and employees who probably don't even know there is a New York office. We stop outside the last cubicle, where the CEO is sitting in his chair, doing absolutely nothing. There are no papers on his desk. His phone rests snugly in its cradle. His monitor is on screensaver. The man looks impossibly bored. He has no idea who I am, of course, so I reintroduce myself, recite my recent history—all the way back to Sotheby's—then present him with my plan, which he quickly skims.

"To tell you the truth, I haven't really considered collectibles," he says. "We're in the business of *experiences.*"

"Are you serious? No one's even mentioned any of this?"

"No," he says, unwrapping a stick of gum. "But I think it's important that every employee be heard, and I'm always open to suggestions."

Suggestions? I can feel blood rushing to my head. I just flew across the country to give this guy a plan for the only viable revenue stream he's got, and . . . and . . . "Look, I came all the way out here to give you this. Are you even going to read it? Six months ago I was America's leading authority on sports memorabilia, and now you're paying me and at least twenty other intelligent people a lot of money to sit in New York and do nothing. Excuse me for asking, but what the hell are you guys doing out here?"

I'm asking him to fire me. I'm begging him. *Please*. But he can't even do that.

"I understand your frustration, but everything will sort itself out soon enough. I'll read this and get back to you. Two mergers in two months," he says, with a false chuckle. "We're hardly sitting on our hands." He gets up and walks me back to the door, where he presents me with an UltimateBid pullover. "I'll be in New York soon," he says. "I want to explore a new idea I've come up with, a nonprofit angle. I want to go after charities and foundations. There's untapped potential there. What do you think?"

FLYING HOME, I FINALLY consider the question I've been ignoring for weeks. If I do get fired, what will I do next? I always go back to that AOL party at the Four Seasons. That was the beginning, the hatching of my generation. We led parallel lives for a while after that, the Internet and I, but we joined up eventually. Everyone did. Now, though, I feel like I've been fed through a time machine, and here I am, in my late twenties, with no grad school, no viable trade or expertise, just a short history of mismatched phases. I—*we*—bought into the Internet completely. Ken is still writing Concorde copy for Agency.com; someone told me Gus is doing PR for a Latino Web site; and Casey, my clairvoyant college friend, who claimed to see the future of technology from atop the Golden Gate Bridge, has left HBO to start an Internet production company called NetShoot.com. But if everything collapses, most of the people I know will still have their former careers to return to. I can't go back to Sotheby's, even if I wanted to. They're not hiring. The price-fixing scandal has exploded, Amazon is severing its ties, and last I heard, sothebys.com was in disarray. I have $50,000 in the bank now. I could take a year and really, truly give writing another shot. But I feel so *invested* in all this, literally and figuratively. And I can't stand the thought of failing again.

ONE DAY, JUST BEFORE NOON, I'm scanning fuckedcompany.com to see if we're listed when my phone rings.

"Where are you?" says Ken Hamm. He sounds frantic, out of breath.

"I'm where you just called me."

"Well, we need to meet. How about P. J. Clarke's?"

"Right now?"

"Yes! The fucking Concorde just crashed."

"The Concorde doesn't crash."

"It does now. Taking off from Paris, this morning. Oh, this isn't good. They were having problems selling seats anyway and . . . just get over to Clarke's."

I haven't been to my old haunt in years, and as I walk in it seems more depressing than ever. It's like the place is stuck in time, a slow afternoon in the fifties, and the world is moving farther and farther away. A bartender I don't recognize says Frankie left two years ago. I order a Bloody Mary but it doesn't taste right. Then Ken walks in and slumps onto a stool beside me. He puts his Manhattan Portage bag on the floor.

"Keep an eye on that," I tell him.

"What?"

"Nothing."

He orders a beer and exhales deeply. "Can you believe it? The market crashing is one thing, but the Concorde crashing, too? That was *my* project, *my* plane. I was revamping their entire site, giving it a futuristic feel, and that's hard. Have you ever seen the Concorde? It looks like the setting for a late-seventies cult classic—Skylab meets *A Clockwork Orange*. And now my only source of income is strewn across a field outside Paris."

"I'm sure they won't stop flying completely."

"Oh, just you watch. They've already grounded the whole fleet. It'll be some major international incident. I mean, the *French* are involved."

"So what's the big deal? Now you have time to work on *your* cult classic. What about it? How's your screenplay?"

"How's your book?" Ken retorts.

"I'm not writing one."

"But you should be."

"About what?"

"I don't know. The search for authenticity in an artificial age."

"Who the hell would read that?"

"Either everyone or no one."

"And what makes me an authority?"

"You've been trying on costumes for years."

"Well, one of them was writing. And it didn't fit."

"You hedged your bets, then gave up."

"Oh, *I* gave up. What was the Concorde?"

"A lucrative little sideline that served the dual purpose of paying my bills and keeping me attached, however tenuously, to a small sliver of society. When you've been living inside your head for so long, with only an hour and a half of mediocre film to show for it, you need to reacclimate or risk disappearing into yourself completely. Now, I've been working on this football screenplay for three years, and it's still not ready. You're the only person who even asks about it anymore."

"You know what Don DeLillo said?"

"Oh, God. What?" Ken says, putting his beer down.

"That 'the withheld work of art is the only eloquence left.'"

"When?"

"When what?"

"When did he say that?"

"I don't know. It was in *Mao II*. Whenever that came out . . . like a decade ago."

"Exactly," Ken says. "The era before ours. We've changed so much since then. Now the only eloquence left is having the conviction to create art in the first place. There. That's your book."

Thirty

By MID-AUGUST MOST company-related work in the New York office has ceased, but we're still getting paid, still showing up. Just after ten on a Monday morning, I stroll in to find a phone message from Casey. I know what it's about. NetShoot, his Internet production company, has gotten off to a fast start, and now he wants me to use my Dell connections to help him find investors. I call him back and listen for an hour as he attempts to explain his business. From what little I can glean, NetShoot has something to do with interactive education, but I don't really get it. He's talking about video compression when my screen lights up with an e-mail from Emily, a missive from her latest war zone. I tell Casey to send me his business plan, then hang up quickly.

Emily, she follows the sound of guns. Now she's in the West Bank:

> Hello my sweet . . . What shakes? All is well here, though I'll never be-
> lieve anything I see on American news again. Not to wax political but
> I didn't know hatred until I came here. This is a conflict only America
> can resolve, but we must stop taking sides. The Israelis are every bit as
> brutal as the Palestinians. Theirs is just a different kind of terrorism,
> a subtle land grab backed by a powerful army. I certainly don't con-
> done Palestinian methods, which are mostly unspeakable, but they are
> a repressed and impoverished people subjected to daily humiliations
> at the hands of ghoulish troops. I'm not sure what other choice they
> have. We really need to step in. Clinton tried, I guess, with Arafat, but
> from what I see of Bush and Gore on CNN . . . God help us. Anyway,
> enough. Last weekend I went to Jordan and saw Petra. Remember at
> the end of the *Last Crusade* when Indy and his dad (played by Mr. Sexy
> himself, Sean Connery) rode horses through the crack in the cliff and

came out next to that amazing building carved into the red rock? That's Petra. It's incredible—there's a whole hidden city back there. I fell asleep on the shores of the Red Sea, watching the stars and listening to Bedouins wandering around on the great red sand dunes, their camels clanking away. I leave next Saturday for New York though. The Fordham transfer came through, so you're stuck with me for my last year of law school. Keep your eyes peeled for an apartment. Anywhere is fine—I'm not a downtown snob like you. I'm ready to come home. There are only so many times I can be groped in the back of a minibus or hissed at on the road. And you? How's work? That Fred guy sounds like a con man. And the new apartment? It's liberating living alone. In my old place I danced around naked to the Jackson 5 every morning. Do you still see Ken? Sometimes, when the world is moving too fast, I picture him crouched at his desk, slaving over his twelfth draft. And your Republican girlfriend? I must say . . . when you sell out you go all the way. You need perspective, my boy—mountains, oceans, sandstorms . . . See upheaval, experience revolt. Your soul has been tainted by cheap money. You need my help. xoxo. E.

SIX MONTHS AGO Casey convinced an HBO colleague named Ben Loeb, a senior producer with two Emmys to his credit, that there was a market for their production skills on the Internet, and within weeks they had quit their jobs and cofounded NetShoot. Their idea is simple enough: create a next-generation Internet video production company. But their business plan is hardly ready for prime time. It's rife with unfinished thoughts, unsubstantiated research, unsound numbers. It reads like it was written at 3:00 A.M. Still, what's there is compelling.

With high-speed connections fast replacing dial-up service, the demand for online video is—according to the unattributed study cited on page twelve—expected to grow exponentially over the next five years. NetShoot will become the leading producer of these videos, handling everything from conception to shooting to editing to delivering the final product. Apparently they're on the right track, because they've already landed a $500,000 contract with the Global Education Network, and have several other clients in the pipeline.

I call my friend back, tell him I have some thoughts, and a few hours later Casey, Ben, and I are huddled around a table at Passerby, a hidden hipster lounge tucked among the warehouses of West Chelsea.

"We're creating the next stop on the road to convergence," Casey says, "TV and computer as one, a black box with all the answers. And we have a brief window of opportunity before the land grab starts, so we're going out for a million dollars."

"What's your valuation?"

"What?"

"How much is your company worth? You need to come up with a number so potential investors know how much of the company they're getting for their money."

"We were hoping you might help us with that," Ben says.

"Why not get a small business loan? If you've already got six-figure revenues, it shouldn't be a problem." But the two of them look at me like I've just suggested they walk a block west and jump into the Hudson. Internet entrepreneurs don't get bank loans; they get investors. Capital over debt: it's a model based on promises.

"Because this is a highly scalable business with a quick ROI," Casey says. He's been reading books, as well. "We're thinking IPO in a year and a half. By then we'll have over eight million in sales."

I try to imagine the process that went into calculating that figure.

"Look," Ben says, reading my mind. "We're not finance guys. We're TV producers who see an opportunity, and we're hoping you'll help us raise money, perhaps on a consultancy basis. You're probably swamped at your own company, but we'd like to work with you if you're up for it . . . and we'd definitely make it worth your while."

It's still early but the music is already loud and Passerby's disco floor is throbbing with lights. These guys want to pay me to kick-start another dream. I've become a new-economy pro, an expert on what hasn't happened. Who cares about truth? Who cares that every company I've worked for since Kroll has either been investigated by the FBI or the Justice Department or has faded away in a string of meaningless mergers? Who cares that my mentor is Fred Sterling, a man with two personalities, a man whose very name rings of insincerity? I've spent the last eight months on the wrong side of a closing door, and yet here I am, speaking of something new. I grin as I remember I'm still the proud owner of trytohelp.com. The Internet, like all New Age religions, is full of omens.

THE HAMMER FINALLY, mercifully, comes down in September. The entire New York office is being let go, with the exception of Vince, Jordan, and a few of their hand-picked favorites. In a nod to the changing times, UltimateBid.com will be relaunching as Ultimate, Inc., and will act solely as an eBay ticket and experience provider. I get a month's severance and a cash payout from a rather complex stock buyback scheme that Sarah cooked up. I'm getting the hang of this take-the-money-and-run routine.

Fred stops by a few hours after the announcement. I figure he's going to apologize for the way things have worked out, but instead he whispers the words "Cell Genesys" in my ear. "They're curing cancer, and the stock's got upside." I sold the rest of my Oracle position a few weeks ago, and I've been peppering the windfall into various Internet stocks. Fred says the market should stabilize, and I believe him. For all his secrecy, I still think he's a market genius. Maybe Cell Genesys will cure cancer or, better yet, develop an expensive daily multipill cocktail that brings in billions.

"I've got something for you, too," I say, flippantly, like I'm just returning the favor. And I start telling him about NetShoot. I make it sound as can't-miss as possible, the way Fred always does.

"I like the idea. What are they looking for?"

"One million."

"Let me look at the numbers when they get the plan together. If they add up, I may take the whole round myself."

"I'm thinking of doing some work with them, now that—"

"Which reminds me," Fred says. "The reason I came by. I heard through the grapevine that eBay is looking for a new head of their sports collectibles division, so I gave them your name. It turns out they knew you from Sotheby's. They want to fly you out there for some interviews. Think of all those California girls."

"Fuck both of you," Sarah says, walking by with a boxful of office supplies. She's been cleaning out her desk.

• • •

I FLY OUT TO San Jose with reservations and fly back home the next day, relieved. eBay didn't offer me the job—not that I gave them much choice. I looked around at the overly friendly employees, the colorful playschool motifs of the eBay "campus," and I knew I couldn't work there. It may be an Internet company, but it's already a bustling bureaucracy, a cubicle city housing people with titles like "Senior Director of Business Category Development and Marketing." Everything revolved around the eBay "community," which is funny, considering stock options are what had everyone running around like rabbits on speed. It's a drink-the-Koolaid place, and I wasn't thirsty. In the interviews—six of them in a row—I answered all their questions, suggested ways to get more high-end pieces listed on their site, then announced I couldn't possibly consider the job for anything less than $200,000 a year. On the way back to the airport, I stared out at the brown business parks rolling endlessly into one another. I looked, I really did, but I didn't see one person walking down the spotless streets. Some kind of community. There was an e-mail waiting when I got back to New York, telling me I hadn't gotten the job. On my last day at Ultimate, Inc., I found out Vince had finally gotten me back; he'd told someone at eBay that I had a poor work ethic. No wonder $200,000 seemed a bit rich.

Still, I use the eBay interviews as leverage. Casey needs me, so I tell him I'm seriously considering San Jose. And it works. A few days later he comes back with a full-time offer: VP of Business Development. Ben will be VP of Production, and Casey will be CEO. We'll all make the same amount $75,000 to start—but the two of them will own the company. I tell him I'll think about it.

SARAH SEGUES SMOOTHLY into a job at a hedge fund. I go visit her at her new offices in the Grace Building on Forty-second Street to get her thoughts on NetShoot. She says it won't be easy raising money in this deteriorating climate, no matter how good the idea. The angel investors have all floated away. I tell her what Fred said, how he might put up the entire million by himself, and Sarah laughs. For the next two hours she gives me another crash course in venture capitalism—warrants, founder's shares, convertible preferred stock, antidilution formulas . . . I find Sarah irresistible when she's lecturing me, and soon the door is locked and we're fooling around against the window, which overlooks Bryant Park. It's passionate and absurd and *final*. We both know it. Our relationship was based on convenience, on proximity, and with that gone Sarah and I are done. We dance around town a little longer, but it's shadow dancing, empty and formless. It's an argument at Café Loup that triggers the final scene. She tells me she wants a man with a life plan; a man who doesn't roll his eyes at the mention of faith; a man who knows when to quit.

"The Internet's over," she says. "People figured out they don't *need* it for much more than e-mail and dating. It's just another device, something to play around with when you're bored."

"Kind of like us," I say. She gives me a pitying look, then gets up, smiles at Ethan and Uma, who are sitting a table away, and walks out into the night. All three of us watch her go; her pants are like a second skin.

CASEY AND BEN agree to my terms—10 percent of the company plus the title of cofounder—and I move seamlessly from Park Avenue to the NetShoot offices, in a loft near the Flatiron Building. I spend a month perfecting the business plan, while the production studios hum nearby. At any one time, a dozen people are coming and going, a steady stream of editors, encoders, cameramen, and NYU film-school interns. I try to learn about production by watching Ben, who moves between our three busy edit stations like a skilled conductor keeping his orchestra together.

Casey sets up meetings with anyone he can find. A few are potential clients, of course, but most are tech companies or interactive agencies or even competitors. When I warn Casey that his time might be better spent elsewhere, he assures me his get-togethers are all crucial, that we need to get our name out there. NetShoot's conference room is separated from the rest of the office by a futuristic glass garage door that rumbles up and down at the touch of a button. It's the type of superfluous dot-com gimmick (Ping-Pong tables, massages, yoga, wine and cheese Fridays) that went down well a few months ago but now is just an easy metaphor for all that's gone wrong. But Casey hasn't spent a year banging his head against a cubicle desk, so people keep showing up, and the garage door keeps opening and closing. In the first weeks I give our CEO the benefit of the doubt. Sometimes, hoping there might actually be business to develop, I join him in the back, but it's always the same story:

A friend of a friend of Casey's runs a young tech company based in Cambridge or Reston or Palo Alto. In comes their BD guy, wearing the blue-and-khaki uniform, trailed by three identically dressed comrades who pass out business cards with nebulous titles or, worse, just a name and a logo, leaving me wondering if he's the CEO or just a minion in his first week with the company. Then the garage door comes down and the parade of self-important introductions begins. Everyone is an Internet guru, a market mover, a tech wizard. When it's finally time to turn to work, to technology of one form or another, we usually can't understand what the hell our guests are talking about and have to call Ben in to translate. Ben, always frantic, sits and listens for a few minutes, then scrawls "waste of time" on a pad, passes it over to me, and excuses himself. Still, we need more business, so Casey finds some: online modeling agencies, soft-core porn sites, streaming video nightclubs. . . . They always want the first project free. They bring girls along—strippers, dancers, models—and the garage door goes up and down and up and down and our CEO emerges with a new client: Cake.com or Dark Angel Pictures, Inc.

"It's a loss leader," Casey says, trying to sound upbeat. Ben just shakes his head.

I work by the window, busying myself with market opportunities, revenue models, and roll-out strategies. It strikes me, in the small hours, that I've once again become everything I once despised. I'm a producer; I have the words *Business Development* in my title; I own three plain-blue button-down shirts; and I attend Silicon Alley networking parties, where companies like ours—people like me—trawl for clients that just aren't there. The only people interested in NetShoot are name-tagged, job-hunting Internet migrants, victims of other, earlier dot-com explosions.

I'm writing fiction again, but this time it's a business plan. I've figured out that a service business like ours isn't the type that attracts venture capitalists and scurries down the path toward an IPO, so I've tried to mask this plain truth with pages of theoretical products and untested services: live Webcasts, interactive applications, clickable video, synchronized media, digital management. . . . Ben says he can cover if people ask about any of this. If only we could get someone that interested.

IN MID-OCTOBER, armed with the completed business plan, I fly out to Las Vegas for a Fred Sterling–sponsored weekend. We're staying at the Mirage, in a VIP villa with a hot tub, a pool, and a putting green—all comped by the casino, thanks to Fred's gambling exploits. I've never been to Vegas before, but I've heard Fred's stories, seen Fred's winnings. Of the dozen friends on the trip, several others are Internet millionaires as well, and my goal is to get some NetShoot commitments. I want to pin Fred down, too. I think he kind of owes me.

The flight out is an airborne frat house. The passengers are all drinking, playing gin, telling tall tales of their last Vegas weekend, and as the beverage cart begins another pass, I start worrying about the old lady sitting quietly beside me. Sure enough, it's not long before she reaches up with a shaky bingo wing and presses her call button. The exasperated flight attendant hurries over, but the woman doesn't ask for earplugs or a seat change; she asks for a double vodka on the rocks. Then she reaches over and pulls a book out of her bag: *Slot Smarts: Winning Strategies at the Slot Machine.*

"I need to brush up," she says. "It'll be a long night."

THE MIRAGE IS EXACTLY that, or would be, if it weren't sur-rounded by newer, larger optical wonders. When I asked Fred how I'd find him in the casino he told me to just listen, so I walk in through the front doors, leave my bags with a bellhop, and just stand there. It's the sound of the slots that gets me first, and then the air, unnatural and cool, and only then the people, thousands of voices—gasping and crying and laughing—emanating from every endless direction. Still I can hear Fred's shouting ris-ing above the cacophony. I follow the noise, past rows of slots, past poker tables and roulette wheels, until I see the green blackjack tables, dozens of them, crowded lilypads on a polluted lake. I spot a table surrounded by on-lookers, and as I edge my way past them, Fred erupts from his seat. "AL-WAYS FUCKING DOUBLE DOWN!" he shouts, and the crowd cheers as the dealer slides chips across the table at him. Fred adds them to a large stack, and then, turning to acknowledge the people, he sees me on the out-skirts. He waves me through, and now I can see . . . he's at the table with Jerry from Atlanta and a few others I recognize. I give him a rough hug as the next hands are dealt. Fred bets two white chips.

"How much are the white ones worth?" I ask a round-headed man wearing flip-up shades and a Las Vegas is Radioactive T-shirt.

"Five G's," he says, wistfully.

Five grand? He must have a stack of twenty-five in front of him, along with a healthy sprinkling of thousand-dollar yellows. That's upwards of $150,000. No wonder he attracts a crowd. I watch Fred win four hands in a row, and then the dealer wipes his hands clean and is replaced by a stoic Asian woman. Jerry and the others immediately call it quits. Fred plays one more hand but gets smoked. He looks at his towering stacks, at the unsmiling dealer, then announces he's had enough, as well.

"Just warming up," he tells the assembled throng.

Half an hour later we're sitting down to a catered affair in the backyard of our villa, being attended to by two waiters and a half dozen near-naked women, the latter sent over by the hotel, like champagne or extra toothpaste. Everyone is chattering at once, replaying what they witnessed at the card table, Fred Sterling on one of his signature runs. The story is already growing, the numbers spiraling upward, $200,000, $250,000, and maybe it's true. The girls slide their way around the tables in transparent dresses, sniffing out the heavy hitters. But the money men are hard to spot these days—they could be anyone—and the girls must think so, too, because a few of them give up and slink over to the pool, where they strip down to bikinis or nothing and slip into the water. Their bodies are like sculptures, enduring testaments to form. A few minutes and then I can't watch anymore. I go inside, start wandering around. In a small secondary suite I walk in on some guy pouring blue diamond-shape pills into a small bowl. And there are other bowls, other offerings: ecstasy, weed, and coke, a mountain of it, lying, literally, on a silver platter. I walk back outside, feeling like I've already done something wrong. Who are these people? And how did I become one of them?

There's a performance after dinner, a sex show, and soon the girls start slipping into bedrooms with paying customers. Fred, who's been out in the pool, strolls into the living room naked. He's ready to hit the tables again. As the party enters its steamy midlife, he slips his bathrobe back on and leads a core group of us back to the casino floor.

It's a grand entrance: We surround our terry-cloth hero like corner men around a prizefighter and march out to do battle. All that's missing is the music. It's 2:00 A.M. but the Mirage is still mobbed. Fred chooses his table and offers me the seat next to him. Within minutes the crowd is three deep behind us. Fred is gambling with $5,000 chips. I'm gambling $25 chips. But at the tables it's just a different color, that's all. A win is still a win; a loss is still a loss. I'm way below the $100 table minimum, but they're making an exception to keep Fred happy. Vegas was built on such backhanded hospitality. I told myself I wouldn't gamble more than $500 this weekend, but I'm burning through it fast, one hand after another—$25, $50, $25—so I sit a few out, and Fred, who is having his shoulders rubbed by a girl with a "Sexual Deviant" tattoo etched below her navel, starts playing my position, as well. And he wins two, three, four hands in a row. He starts betting ten grand a hand on each spot, his and mine, and with every victory the drunken crowd behind us roars in approval. When the cards have all been dealt and the dealer pauses to shuffle, Fred picks up a white chip and flicks it at me with his thumb. I catch it with two hands. "Thanks, your spot was on fire," he says. He's just given me $5,000 like it's meter money. *Five thousand dollars!* I pocket it quickly and edge away from the table before he can change his mind and take it back.

So this is freedom's endgame: previously played football games being watched on giant TVs by men with money on the outcomes; sleepy Asian gamblers nodding their way through Baccarat; fleshy teenagers searching for Siegfried and Roy's white tigers; frat boys chatting up hookers at the video poker machines; and hundreds of blue-haired grandmothers sitting on stools, feeding coins into slots, mechanically, like toll takers handing out thruway tickets.

I take a seat at the only $25 table I can find and immediately hit another cold streak. I double my bets and soon the $5,000 has become $3,000. There's no way to tell time. And I don't know how drunk I am. In Vegas the drinks are free if you're playing cards, and I think I've had at least ten of them. Maybe they water them down, or maybe I'm in that weird time-deficient zone that casinos strive for, where you can let your vices take over completely, without interruption. The world falls away and I sit there for what seems like hours, hitting, sticking, hitting, sticking, hitting, hitting. . . . At some point I hear a rumor that the sun is coming up.

WE PLAY GOLF the next day at Shadow Creek, the Mirage's ultra-private course. Back at the suite, I try to piece together our round. I know we played eighteen holes, though all I remember is looking up at the colorless desert mountains from some lush green fairway and thinking how synthetic everything was. Now I'm in a bedroom, the one with all the trays, trying to catch a few minutes' sleep, but it's already cocktail hour again. A new shift of girls has arrived, and more guys, too, dozens of them, word having spread about our secret slice of heaven. I look outside; there's action in the pool, on the putting green, and now someone's knocking on the door. This is no time for rest.

At some point Fred hits the tables again. He could, of course, be in a roped-off V.I.P. area, playing his $10,000 hands in plush privacy, but he likes it out here, among the people and the noise, the girls and the drinks, and the cards that keep coming up aces. I head off down the strip for a few hours, manage to lose another $1,000, then wander back to the Mirage. It must be 3:00 A.M. I listen for Fred but don't hear him. The casino is dead; everyone's wiped out. I walk over to the tables and spot Jerry, playing by himself, gambling $25 chips, like me.

"Where's the crowd?" I ask.

"The cards turned," Jerry says, matter-of-factly, without looking up. He points to a table twenty yards away, and there's Fred, wedged between a fat man in a fedora and a kid in a UCLA cap. His shoulders are slumped, his elbows on the table. "Last time I checked, he'd blown through about two hundred thousand. That was about an hour ago. He's lost everything he won . . . and then some."

I wish Jerry luck, then make my way to Fred's table. His chip bag is empty. He's betting yellows now, *mellow yellows*, and when I sit down he tries to sound upbeat.

"Temporary setback," he says. "A few bad hands. It happens when you're playing for the big money." For a moment he rallies around his words, tells the dealer he's going to take back all his white chips—all forty of them, sitting quietly across the table in their submerged trenches—but the dealer doesn't even crack a smile. I watch Fred go bust twice more, and that's enough. I leave him to his demons and head back to the suite, stopping along the way to put $100 on black and watch it come up dead red.

In the rooms, bodies are strewn everywhere—on couches, carpets, chairs. Everyone's asleep except for a couple having synchronized sex in the pool. I pick up my duffel bag—it's weighed down by the untouched NetShoot business plans—and check for available beds. But they're all taken and the best I can do is a bathtub. I find a few pillows, lock the door, and lie down. I'm so tired I could fall asleep on a kitchen counter.

WHEN I OPEN my eyes—minutes later? hours?—Jerry's yelling my name. I pull myself out of my porcelain coffin and unlock the door.

"*There* you are," he says. "We've been looking everywhere for you. We've got to get out of here. Fred busted through his credit line and they won't let him gamble anymore, which means we have to leave. Security's on their way." Behind him, people are scurrying about, zipping up bags, packing up pills.

"How much was his credit line?" I ask.

"I don't know, maybe two hundred thousand."

"But I thought Fred was like their favorite customer."

"He *was*," Jerry says, "but things change quickly out here. They *escorted* him out of the casino, and now he's down the strip, at the Paris. They extended him a new line and sent a limo over to pick him up. He just can't stop playing."

Jerry heads out to supervise the cleanup. I brush my teeth with my finger. It must be late morning. Sunday. There's a group leaving for the airport, but my flight doesn't leave until 6:00 P.M., so I grab my bag and head out into the desert sunlight. The Strip is packed with families and shoppers and old couples coming back from breakfast buffets. I walk past one sprawling gambling mecca after another, then turn left at the Eiffel Tower. Fred is in an elevated glass V.I.P. area in the center of the floor. It's just him, the dealer, and some kind of facilitator—a casino host, they call them—a nebulous Mickey Rourke type who promises the world and delivers it, all of it, until the money runs out. Such are the terms of a Las Vegas friendship. I sidle up and take a seat beside him.

He doesn't say much. He doesn't say anything. I'm not sure he completely registers my presence. He's in whatever dark place comes after forty or fifty hours without sleep, with only cards, one hand after another, slowly running you to ruin. He's gambling with $5,000 chips again, and when I ask how it's going, he says he's down slightly, and that he doesn't like the vibe here. He says the drinks taste funny. When I ask what slightly means, he says eighty or ninety grand. By my count, that means he's lost close to $300,000 in less than forty-eight hours. I don't know how much Fred Sterling is worth (it's an endlessly debated question), but even if it's millions, a $300,000 hit has to hurt. A lot. The dealers switch and Fred's cards stay cold. His stack starts dwindling. I watch him hit on seventeen by accident and go bust when he would have won. I play a few hands—the last of the $5,000—but his bad luck is contagious. I suggest we stop for a while, have some lunch, regroup. . . . And he *wants* to leave the table, I can see him trying, but leaving means he's lost, and so he stays seated, orders more chips, tells the dealer to get ready for a run. And now here we go again, $5,000 at a time. It was less than a year ago that I told anyone who would listen that I had found my mentor. Now look at him. Sometime after three I leave him alone, mumbling about margin calls. He doesn't even notice me go.

The flight back is grim, an airborne boulevard of broken dreams. Seems everyone lost this weekend. But no one lost like Fred. The bubble just burst for good.

Thirty-one

IN THREE MONTHS the NASDAQ has fallen from over 4,200 to less than 2,600, my E-Trade account has been decimated, and the Internet has become a punch line, a subject brought up by smug parents, by value investors who claim they never bought the hype. But we have a *new* concept, we keep telling each other, a good idea. And we're only looking for one million dollars—nothing, in the scheme of things.

On a windy late-fall afternoon, I take the subway to see Sarah. I want to get her thoughts before the investor meetings start. In chilly Bryant Park, she skims the new NetShoot business plan, making margin notes in pencil.

"What do you think?" I ask, finally.

"Honestly? I think there are some fundamental problems here."

"No there aren't," I say, reflexively. "Like what?"

"Well, you have this whole introduction about how Internet video is so crucial because everyone is switching from dial-up connections to high-speed DSL. But then, in the *competitive advantage* section, you say that Net-Shoot's 'proprietary encoding and editing *techniques*' allow you to make your fifty-six K videos stream better than anyone else's."

"Exactly. My partners are, like, leading authorities on this stuff. They can make video files small enough to fit through phone wires. They've won Emmys."

"But don't you see the inherent contradiction? How can you be banking on a world of high-speed Internet access when your only real talent is for making video look good at *low* speeds? It has to be one or the other."

"That's kind of a nitpicky thing."

"No it's not. It's the basis of your whole business. Look, this is what I do all day. I look at business plans, most of which I don't understand. But Net-

Shoot is pretty simple. You're not some complex tech play; you're a service business, and a good one for all I know, but the sector you're servicing is as popular as the plague right now."

"I really just wanted you to look at the numbers."

HELP COMES JUST in time—help, that is, in a diversionary sense. Emily has arrived in New York and is sharing a flower-district apartment with a torch singer. It's the first time the two of us have lived in the same place since St. George's, and we happily spend the fall together—as friends. She missed the dot-com boom years and doesn't understand what I'm doing at NetShoot. I try to explain but it doesn't work.

Within a month she's restless. Most of her Fordham classmates are applying for jobs at law firms, but Emily wants to get back out there, save the world from itself. In the interim she's taken a part-time job as a bike-delivery person for kozmo.com, the much-hyped, much-troubled Internet retail service, because she read that it was one of the most dangerous jobs in America. So now she rides around, a shock of blurry blond hair, dodging cab doors, delivering movies and food and minor electronics.

We don't talk about work or school. No, we talk about lives we *could* be leading, will be leading, once we get back on track. She urges me to start keeping a journal, so I give it a shot. And to my surprise it feels good to be writing again, however tenuously.

11/14/00 2:49 a.m.

So here we are . . . What the hell do people write about in journals? What does Emily write about? Is this a shrink or a soapbox? A blackboard or a friend? Back from drinks at Cedar Tavern with Shelton, who is working for a dot-com fashion site that's running out of money. Hadn't seen her in ages, and we talked cautiously of how life has been. I told her about NetShoot. I tried to sound excited but she saw through it. We played gin at a back booth and drank for hours. Speed Levitch, that manic tour guide from *The Cruise*, was sitting across from us. He was talking to a friend in rapid-fire bursts of slanted insight. Then Winona Ryder sat down with one of her hundred exes (some guy from Soul Asylum, whom Shelton recognized but I didn't) in the booth

behind me. Her hair was dyed blond, and no one else recognized her.
She kept playing eighties songs on the jukebox, and complaining to her
rocker boy that men were afraid to ask her out. It was a night like that.
We drank until we couldn't focus on the cards. At some point Speed
Levitch got up, put his coat on, and said, sadly, "This is no world for
a clown." And he's right. We followed him out a few minutes later.
Shelton was going to another party, so we hugged good night and I
walked home like I always do in New York.

SOME DAYS I THINK NetShoot might really work. We had our first
funding meetings this week. The potential investors wanted to see our office
in action, but we don't have much business right now, so we called all the actresses we knew and had them come in and pretend to work for us. By the
time the money men strolled in, the place looked like a phone-sex agency.

Our presentation was separated into three sections: Casey did the
overview, Ben explained the business of production, and I handled the financials. The practice sessions had gone well, but in front of real people,
Casey started going off on tangents. The investors couldn't understand him,
and their eyes began wandering to the glass garage door and the salacious
figures in the office. But Ben got us back on track, and when we got to the
numbers, I did my best Fred Sterling imitation and it worked. They looked
at our illogical figures ($48 million in Y5 revenues) and didn't flinch. They
asked questions, but nothing tough or penetrating, nothing that Sarah
would have asked. Instead they brought up Michael Dell and HBO, all the
connections we had in common, as if we were one big friendly circle. They
invited us to play golf. They did everything but write us a check. NetShoot
sounded like a home run, they said, the best idea they'd heard in ages. But
they'd have to get back to us. They walked out ogling our office workers,
winking at us conspiratorially. They made me shiver.

1/8/01 8:00 a.m.
    Sitting in Florent on a snowy Monday morning, completely jet-
lagged. Got back from Australia last night to find my E-Trade account
had been ravished by the falling market, but I have no one to blame but
myself.

Perth was extraordinary. Giles and Jennie had their second (real) wedding on a white beach with surfers and Aussie girls providing the breathtaking background. Everyone was so laid-back. The Aussies like people right away. And they let the world come to them. Jennie's friends taught me to DJ, and we all did ecstasy on New Year's in Margaret River, the glorious end of the continent, of the world. It was the most fun you can have without a lover, which was the problem, but probably healthy for a change.

Big day today. Lunchtime pitch with Jack Norton from MSD Capital, followed by a "How can we work together?" meeting with my brother's company, payforview.com (should be interesting: two brothers with no idea what they're doing end up in the same stupid industry. Why didn't Douglas stay in banking? I guess everyone needs their Internet fix, just to see what they're missing, what they've missed); then the Whitney exhibition with Claire. Just what I need. . . . Why does she still haunt me like this? Why does she call me so innocently just as she's finally slipping from view? And now she lives a few short blocks away, above Tea and Sympathy on Greenwich Ave. Sometimes I think I still love her, that we could make it work now that we're older, have had more time, more experience . . . and then I think I'm just grabbing at memories.

Read Adam Gopnik's *Paris to the Moon* while I was Down Under. Oh, to write like him. I swear, I sat there—in airports, on beaches—and conjured this Paris he knew, this world he'd constructed, and I rediscovered what writing can do. The everyday incidents made magic through words. There was this scene—I've practically memorized it—when Gopnik and his five-year-old son Luke run into Cressida, Luke's first crush, swimming in the pool at the Ritz:

> She was floating as elegantly as an angel, just above the mermaids, a little on her side, her long blond braids trailing in the water behind her. I think my heart stopped a little at that moment too. Luke's certainly had stopped and then restarted. He leaped right in, before I could stop him, and head up—like a puppy, like a millionaire's wife—he swam out to his love in the water. . . .

The essay was rife with issues of class and foreignness and all that, but the love story in miniature was an allegory, too, for Gopnik's own life—the loss of spontaneity and craving, the certain settling down of love that comes with marriage, with time, with familiarity. Great writers start with great themes. I miss trying to make words work.

MORE THAN A DOZEN meetings and no solid commitments. Talk about bad timing. . . . The economy has fallen apart, Bush is in office, the NASDAQ is still in freefall, and half of young New York is unemployed. NetShoot has downsized, as well—it's back to three of us until we can get funded. I tell Ben and Casey we need to switch gears. Going after venture capital isn't working. We'll get the money in increments. My partners start nodding. We write target lists of wealthy friends, high net worth individuals, then start working the phones.

Our pitch isn't bad. Through trial and lots of error we've landed on Corporate E-Learning—employee training, CEO announcements, sales seminars, earnings reports. . . . Fortune 500 companies can save millions using Web video to disseminate this kind of information. It sounds good, reads even better. But there's a problem. Ben and I decide to do the next series of pitches—our last chance, really—without Casey. He's too much of a loose cannon. Gently we tell him we don't need three people in the meetings. He doesn't take it well, but he gets the picture. Marketing kits are printed up; the Web site is redesigned; the business plan is adjusted; and then, like a gift from above, Ben lands a small deal with Pepsi. *Now*, we're ready.

My failure to corner the Vegas boys was a blessing in disguise, as we approach them now with our amended mission and listen, mildly shocked, as Jerry and several others pledge $25,000 apiece. Ben and I take our luck to Wall Street, pitch friends at Goldman Sachs and Citigroup. We pitch my father. And we pitch Fred Sterling, officially. I'm hoping Fred might still go in for a big number, two hundred grand, maybe two fifty, but he tells us he's hurting right now. He offers $25,000, like the others. He says it's the best he can do.

By March, we've raised over $300,000, all but $45,000 of which is coming from my investors—*my* friends and family. We decide to close the round and raise the rest later. But I'm starting to feel nervous. It all seemed fine when we were out there hustling, but now, with the money all but in the bank, I realize *I'm* suddenly assuming all the risk in a company I only have a 10 percent stake in. If NetShoot folds, I'll be left holding the bag. Casey and Ben will slip back into that grand mosaic of television, and I'll have failed not only myself (I'm accustomed to that) but everyone around me. My partners know plenty of wealthy people. Is there some reason they couldn't find any takers? Then again, funding was my job, my only job, and I've barely succeeded. This isn't my company; I forced my way in through the side door. I should have faith enough not to worry about what might go wrong, but I don't. Not after last year.

I take Ben aside to express my concerns. We've become close, and when I tell him I'm not comfortable with the current arrangement, he says he knew I wouldn't be. I tell him I want an even third of the founders' stock, but Ben has something else in mind.

"Look," he says, "we can't afford three seventy-five-thousand-dollar salaries with only three hundred grand in the bank."

"Then we'll cut back, pay ourselves fifty thousand until we get it off the ground."

"Or we can cut someone out," Ben says. He motions toward Casey's desk, toward our CEO. "Think about it. I'm doing all the work, you're raising all the money, and he's . . . he's . . ."

"My friend," I say. And he is. Casey and I went to school together, traveled cross-country together. He's been talking about the Internet for years. We can't fire him—NetShoot was *his* idea. But Ben's right: we can't go on like this, either. Casey can't make decisions, he gets nervous in meetings, and he spends a great deal of time courting Internet porn companies. We need to hire a sales force, a tech team, a receptionist; we need to buy new equipment and build a studio. And there just isn't room for incompetence. I sound like my father.

I tell Ben the only way I'll agree to the purge is if we give Casey the option of shutting the whole company down. He started it; he can pull the plug. Or he can agree with our plan, and we'll go on, with the money, without him. There can be no middle ground. On a Monday at the end of March, Casey unsuspectingly lowers the garage door. And then we lower the boom. It's awful. He calls us every name in the book, and I'm not sure he's wrong. But we don't waver. Casey storms out dramatically, but he's back fifteen minutes later, and for a long time he sits at his desk looking at the wall. I try not to watch him. It's too depressing. Then he comes back to the conference room, where Ben and I are studying numbers, pretending it's business as usual.

"You two assholes can do whatever you want. The way this is going, you're probably doing me a favor anyway." And then he's gone.

Ben nods, I nod, and the fratricide is complete.

5/9 10:30 a.m.

Woke up early this morning—Saturday—and the apartment was smoky. My throat was sore, I was coughing, and I couldn't see across the room. Have woken up like this before, hazy, unable to process, but always after blazing nights on the town, nights that spun and dragged till dawn. This is real smoke. It smells like cinders. I wasn't out that late last night. Emily and I rented *Ride with the Devil*, the new Ang Lee film starring the one and only Jewel, and of course it was awful, completely unwatchable. At least she hasn't gone hip-hop yet.

Later we walked to Pastis for a burger. We sat at the bar and watched downtown New York shuffle in and out. I started telling her about Casey. I keep thinking about what we did—what *I* did—to him, and the reasons have receded while the act has loomed large. I'm not sure what NetShoot is worth, but I don't think it's worth a friendship. What's happening to me, to us, all of us who are chasing the remnants of someone else's gold rush? We've all lost ourselves. And there was Emily, going on about art films, about the World Bank, about this incredible Phil Gourevitch book on the genocide in Rwanda. At some point she dropped me off at home, and I fell asleep thinking of our friendship—how intriguingly cerebral, how sprinkled with affection, and still, how squarely platonic it is. Deep down I know it should be. She's my best friend, and I'll do anything to keep it that way. Maybe that's true love.

I think I'm oxygen deprived. There was a note about the boiler posted by the mailboxes, but I never read it. I've opened the windows, turned on the fan, but the smoke won't dissipate. I'm living in a dream state, a vague gray, filled with characters and concern. I keep coming up with book ideas, novel thoughts, but nothing sticks, nothing comes through to the other side. I need to get past wanting to write and find a *reason* to write. A purpose beyond the act itself. Like Bingham. Like Gopnik. Like every writer who is sincere. NetShoot is all-consuming, but strangely unconsuming. I'm there all day and half the night, but barely. It's just a place to go, a child I'm responsible for. It's this other stuff that keeps me up. These visions in the smog.

I TRY TO WRITE when I can't sleep. The smoke has cleared but all the life has been sucked out with it, and now it's just me, alone, staring at an empty desk. I'll grab a pillow and sit on my wide window frame, listening to New York in its darkest hours—the noise, the heat, the life that leads to so much distraction. I plot out stories in my journal. I would like to write them. I would like to stop all this and start over. Reinvent myself—again. It's the most American of ideas, and I've become an expert. But there's always some problem—money or confidence, time or temperament. Excuses swirl around the city like trash on a windy day.

BEN AND I MOVE NetShoot to a modern office space on Thirty-fourth Street. It's specifically designed to house start-ups like ours, but there are no more start-ups like ours, so the building is almost deserted. "Act as if . . . ," Ben keeps telling me, and I think I know what he means. He's saying the Internet has become a charade. It's all about the illusion of legitimacy, and the thing is, there are spots out there   even now—for the chosen few, and if we can give the right answers, fake it well enough, we might just make it.

After work most days I'll walk down Tenth Avenue to meet Emily at the Half King. She likes the place because it's co-owned by Sebastian Junger. He bought his share with money he made from *The Perfect Storm*. Emily has a crush on him, he being the brawny, adventurous type she favors. One evening we walk in and there he is, sitting a few stools away. Emily eyes him nervously. We order drinks and she tells me she's applied for a full-time position at the UN. New York is wearing on her, she says, and there's something about America that's starting to make her nervous. I get up to go to the bathroom, and when I come back, Sebastian Junger is sitting in my seat.

I can't hear what they're talking about, but Emily is sitting upright and looking into his eyes. I'm sure it's some far-off adventure I could only dream about. Junger's a foreign-affairs journalist for *Vanity Fair* now, and I let the two world travelers talk alone, unfettered, while I stare at liquor labels, pretending I'm not jealous. Twenty minutes later I'm about to leave when Emily comes over to get me. "Let's go," she says. "He's really intriguing, but he's already made it. I like hanging out with lost causes."

Walking east, back into the grid of our lives, we pass a homeless man propped up against the side of Parke & Ronen on Ninth Avenue. I have my head down, barely looking, when I catch a glimpse of the cap on his head. It says RxCentric.com. I was at the party, a year ago, when they gave those away. Fred Sterling had just closed on another round of financing, and I remember how he stood up and threw those caps into the crowd, and how people fought for them like they were foul balls. It was a year of bold pronouncements and endless toasts, and it seems so easy, looking back now, to see that there was something very wrong. It was Emily, in one of her e-mails from Kosovo, who first said the rising tide would go back out. But I couldn't then imagine the erosion it would leave in its place. The homeless man is muttering to himself. A lot of people are muttering to themselves again. I fish a dollar out of my pocket and hand it to him. Then I walk Emily home. The flower stores are all closed.

Thirty-two

EMILY CONVINCES ME to go running with her in the mornings. She says I
need the exercise. Apparently she buzzed my door yesterday at 8:00 A.M.,
but I didn't hear her. I'm ready this morning, though, and when the buzzer
goes off I walk out in my running shoes, and together we make our way toward the Hudson River. It's a dazzling day; the air carries the hint of the
coming fall, and the high, cloudless sky is a deep, atmospheric blue. It's time
to reset, restart. Emily just got offered a job with the UN, a two-year contract with the High Commissioner for Refugees in Bosnia. She'd been interviewing all summer, searching for a ticket to the darker corners of the globe
the way others search for lovers. But now, as we walk west through the
meat-packing district, she seems strangely indecisive, as if she may have finally fallen for New York. We walk around purveyor trucks backed up onto
sidewalks, past men in white coats loading the last meats of the day, car-
casses bound for butchers, markets, and restaurants across the city. Sidewalks are being hosed down, and I look away as pieces of blood-stained
bone ride the current of water toward the sewers.

We cross the West Side Highway and the foul odor of slaughter gives way
to the gentle salt breeze of open water. The docks have been renovated, and
now a smooth path runs along the river from Thirty-fourth Street to Bat-
tery Park at the southern tip of the island. We start jogging south but stop
near Charles Street because I'm tight and need to stretch. That's the kind of
shape I'm in. We start talking about *The Corrections*. Emily says something
about the importance of big books. I'm looking out over the water toward
Jersey City, and when I turn back to her to agree, I see a plane, just above
her head, flying low, north to south, over the center of the city. It's a large
plane, a cargo or passenger plane, and I think, briefly, that it must be part
of a commercial, a publicity fly-by for a new airline. That's how low it is. It's

flying crisply, unwavering, in perfect control. Then it banks slightly left, and at some point, as it passes over SoHo, I realize what will happen next. Emily asks if I've heard what she just said. I point at the sky with my mouth half open. And she turns around just in time to see the plane explode as it disappears into the south tower of the World Trade Center. It looks like it's been swallowed. A second goes by, the speed of sound, before the noise catches up: a dull boom, flat and far away. There are flames and smoke almost immediately, but what is most striking, as the wind ripples in off the water, is what is left on the side of the building—the symmetrical silhouette, body and two wings, tilted slightly to the left, in the dead center.

Things like this happen slowly. Emily gasps and puts her hand on my shoulder. There is a girl wearing headphones Rollerblading toward us. She's our age. Her back is to the towers and she hasn't seen the crash yet. Watching her skate, in the last moments of her innocence, is like watching the past. I want her to keep going and never turn around. But she stops when she sees my face, Emily's face. She looks behind her and starts shaking. Then she takes her headphones off. The outline of the plane is on fire; black smoke is pouring out from the inside.

Emily says, "*Oh, my God.*"

The girl on Rollerblades looks at us, her pretty face draining of color. Her brow furrows and her lips purse and there is a question, a hundred questions, swelling in her mind. But then she puts her headphones back on and skates away, like what she just saw isn't real. Emily starts moving toward the towers, as if magnetically attracted to catastrophe.

Everything is open by the river. My eyes move north across the neighborhoods leading uptown. I want some kind of confirmation, but the city isn't speaking. Not yet. I look back at the Trade Center and feel like I'm in some kind of lacuna, a big gaping gap in time, between past and future, the world that was and the one that will be.

"... the type of plane?" Emily is saying.

"What?"

"Did you see the type of plane?"

"It looked big. A commercial plane, maybe."

"How was it flying?"

"Like it was in control. Look where it hit: they must have been aiming for it."

From where we're standing, the World Trade Center still looks strong. The plane struck near the top. Perhaps the damage is localized.

"Let's go down there," Emily says. "Maybe we can help."

We begin running again, passing people staring at the sky. Still, it's calm. It's all just too unbelievable. Somewhere far away, a police siren starts to wail, and I'm struck with the odd thought that this scene is no longer ours, that it has passed on now to the larger public and left us with just the unbelievable image, the searing memory. I wonder if that girl with the headphones has turned around again.

We run faster. The West Side Highway starts falling into chaos, cars weaving their way uptown, others stopping, a few even turning around. We pass people on cell phones, an entire city trying to speak at once. A food vendor at the foot of one of the piers has stopped unfurling his umbrella and is tuning a transistor radio. Mostly, though, we're looking up as we run. We can't take our eyes off the building.

"All that smoke," Emily says, catching her breath. "It must be bad up there."

"I think . . . I think it was a *terrorist* attack."

"You can't just assume that. Maybe some pilot passed out on approach."

"On approach to where?"

But I know what Emily's thinking. A few months ago, when I asked about her summer in the West Bank, she was almost contrite, her previously Western views having shifted with what she experienced. She said it was a struggle without answers, two cultures that could never compromise. She saw Palestinian children throw pebbles at tanks; she saw Israeli soldiers humiliating old Muslim men at checkpoints; she saw two sides, with ancient prides and hatreds, fighting over land—arid, rotting, ruined holy land—that belonged to everyone and no one. When she came back to the States, where sides were long ago taken, she turned against our government, called them cowards, said we'd pay for our policies. Now, staring up at the burning building, I'm sure she's hoping she was wrong, that one has nothing to do with the other. This must be some smaller hatred, some awful mistake.

We're south of Canal Street now, and sirens are everywhere, ringing out a great symphony of anguish. The Trade Center is no longer a far-off spectacle. It's close. The air is gray with what looks like ash. And debris is raining down, debris and paper, an endless stream glittering like tickertape, a parade of devastation. People are moving past us, going the other way. They are screaming, shaking, hysterically crying. The first fire truck barrels by; the cab is full and firemen are hanging from the sides. Every one of them is staring at the hole a half mile up. And no one is speaking. We slow to a walk. I'm thinking of something awful.

"Imagine sitting at your desk way up there, then hearing a noise outside and turning around to see a plane coming straight—"

"Look!" Emily shouts, pointing toward the Statue of Liberty. There's another plane there. It looks like the first one, even bigger. Or maybe we're just closer. It's coming in from the west, from Jersey, and now it's over the water, moving fast and turning hard. I can almost make out the colors. It banks sharply to the left, and from my angle it looks like it might miss the south tower on the right side. There is time for one more thought before impact, and again it's oddly logistical. I wonder what the fuck air traffic control at Newark is doing.

The plane does hit the building. It completes its sweeping turn and slices through the exposed side of the second tower. The explosion is larger, louder, more violent than the first. The ground moves under my feet. All around us people are running for their lives, as if some tidal wave is chasing them. And it *is*, a tidal wave of destruction, of remains—a tidal wave of what's left. Emily is still moving toward the towers, wading against tormented humanity.

"No" is what she keeps saying.

"Do you think they're terrorists now?" I shout against the noise.

"Those people in there . . ."

I grab her hand, suddenly thinking for the first time of our own safety. "Come on, we need to get out of here," I yell. "Someone's attacking us."

She stops moving. I tug her arm. "Okay . . ."

We take one more look at the unfolding devastation before us. A few months ago I'd been in Tower Two for a meeting. It was a morning just like this, and Ben and I were way up on one of the top floors, pitching NetShoot to a roomful of bankers. They sat and listened politely, sipping their coffee, checking their Blackberrys. They weren't the least bit interested in our presentation. But Jesus, they're up there now, up above where the second plane just hit. I remember we had to change elevators once, maybe twice, as we made our way up. I can only imagine—

A body is falling from the top of Tower One. I spot it halfway down, twisting but still, unmoving, resigned. It's such a long way down. I look at Emily. I don't think she saw it; she was turning away. We start running up the same path we came down. The West Side Highway is inundated with emergency vehicles, racing down from every part of the city, and I keep looking across the river to make sure the whole world isn't collapsing. We stop to catch our breath near Spring Street.

"Maybe we should stay here a minute," I say, surveying the skyline. "If there's another one, it'll probably hit the Empire State or somewhere in Midtown, so . . ." I hear myself saying this but can't believe the words. Here we are, dodging flying bombs on a sunny American morning.

A group has gathered around the food cart we passed earlier, searching for information, trying to stifle their sobs. The vendor has his radio working now, and we can hear the announcers asking people to call in. They're saying something about a small commuter plane with propellers. They have no idea. I look out across the Hudson and see another plane, flying low, on approach to Newark. I half expect it to veer off course and come crashing down like the others. I feel so helpless. I start looking for boats, just in case. Something has gone so terribly wrong.

Emily grabs my hand, squeezes it tight. We move farther north, walking now, not quite sure what to do, where to go. We keep turning around, sneaking peeks at the smoking buildings, like kids cheating on some horrid exam.

"How long since the first plane crashed?" I ask.

"I don't know. Maybe half an hour."

"Don't you think we should have fighter jets up there by now? I read that they can scramble those things in, like, fifteen minutes."

But Emily is looking back downtown again. From here, half a mile away, lower Manhattan looks like one giant digital effect. From here we can't see the debris, can't hear the turmoil. Just the sound of sirens, a city of sirens, wailing in unison.

"Hey, Em, did . . . did you see the falling—"

"Yes."

I want to tell Emily she is beautiful. I want to tell her how much she means to me, right now, as the city falls apart.

"We need to find a TV," she says, "so we can see what's going on."

At another time, to a different person, I might note the intrinsic absurdity of that comment. We just *saw* what's going on. We saw more than I ever want to see again. But George Trow's future is now our present, his context, our context. News coverage has become more important than the event itself. It makes perfect sense, kind of.

We decide to go back to my apartment. The noise is becoming overwhelming, and in something close to shock, we start jogging again, past more fire trucks loaded down with men, until we get back up to the meatpacking district. On West Fourteenth Street, two fashionable women in their early fifties have their hands cupped around their eyes and are staring through the glass doors of Jeffrey, the upscale clothing store. They're looking for signs of movement inside. As we pass, one of them turns to the other and adjusts her handbag.

"Does this mean they'll cancel Fashion Week?" she asks.

Thirty-three

We spend a lot of time together these days, Emily and I, volunteering at Ground Zero, holding signs up on the West Side Highway, and watching the news, hour after hour, day after day. We search for ways to help, but there are too many of us roaming downtown New York, all wanting to do something positive, constructive, meaningful. It's not a bad thing.

A few weeks have passed and everyone has gotten back in touch. "Just checking in," we say to each other, but really we need to be close again to people who've known us well. Sarah Connelly is getting engaged to a banker, and Fred Sterling is in Gamblers Anonymous. Casey's gone back to HBO, Giles has gone back to England, and the great Gustavo Chavez has talked his way into a job in the Bush Administration. I saw Shelton being interviewed on the Metro channel's fashion report, looking fabulous in some outfit I couldn't even begin to describe. Even Claire has found herself: she and Devon have moved in together, and recently she sold her first six-figure book. I'm happy for her.

I went out with Ken Hamm last night and listened to him wonder out loud if art had become frivolous, selfish, without merit, and there I was, in a lovely role-reversal, telling my bleeding-heart friend that individual creativity, in this age of broken economies, crooked cultures, and falling empires, is more important than ever. He sighed, he rubbed his eyes, and then he smiled.

Emily calls me early on a sunny Saturday in October.

"Get out of bed, we're going on an adventure," she says. "Meet me at Chelsea Market in twenty minutes." She hangs up before I can protest.

I slip on some clothes and walk the few blocks west, wondering what she's got in store. When I get there she's waiting outside with a sly grin on her face. She hands me a cup of coffee and starts leading me up Tenth Avenue, past gas stations and train yards and windowless buildings. It's not until we turn left on desolate Thirty-third Street that I look above me and realize where we're going.

The High Line is an abandoned elevated train line that winds up the West Side of Manhattan, from the meat-packing district to the Javits Center. It's a curious structure, suspended in time amid the cavernous dance clubs and art galleries of industrial west Chelsea. Emily snuck up there a few days after the towers came down, looking for a respite from the misery, from the loss, from where the world was heading. I asked her what it was like. She said I'd have to see for myself.

Emily leads me to a sleepy truck depot. A man in a guard shack is listening to baseball on the radio. (Yes, they're playing baseball again. America grieved for days, and when it was time to move forward, we turned on the games or went out to the ballpark, and for a small time—nine innings here and there—we could be whole again.) She grabs my hand and darts behind a truck. We squeeze past fenders and through fences and soon we're at the back of the lot, kneeling near a clump of bushes, the trucks keeping us hidden from view.

"The tracks start there," she says, pointing at a ramp rising out of the earth on the other side of the brush. "A private railroad company still owns the High Line, so I don't think they can arrest us once we're up there."

"You mean this is illegal?"

"Oh, come on, just follow me, and stay low." I hurry along the tracks after her, climbing above the city as the gravel slowly gives way to tall grass, hyacinths, adolescent trees. Soon we're in our own secret park, and the acrid stench of decay relinquishes its hold. Below us, in the Penn Station train yard, a dispatcher barks out numbers.

"How have I lived here so long and never noticed this?" I say, catching my breath.

"Because that's New York. You miss things the first or second or tenth time around. Almost no one knows about it. Giuliani keeps threatening to tear it down, but . . . well, it looks like he's found a greater calling now." She pauses as we come upon a graffiti-covered barricade spanning the entire width of the structure. For a moment I think we're stuck, but Emily gets down on her stomach and starts wriggling through a small hole underneath the metal blockade. I follow her, sliding along the old railroad stones, until I'm clear through to the other side. Then I dust myself off and look around.

It's beautiful up here, two stories above the city. There are wild flowers everywhere. We keep walking down the tracks, above gallery rooftops, until we reach a small clearing where we can see in every direction: the lonely, stoic Empire State; the moatlike Hudson, filled at the moment with warships; and, straight ahead, the end of the island, still smoldering in the awful aftermath.

We sit down on a rail, and for a long time we don't speak. Below us, around us, the city is forging ahead through these days of anxious confusion, eerie patriotism, anointed heroes. I know what Emily is going to say before she opens her mouth. She's going to say good-bye. Emily runs toward things; she ran toward the burning buildings when the rest of New York was running away. Now it's time to run toward another challenge, some other place where she's needed more than here. When she says it— that she's going back to the Balkans—she does so almost apologetically, as if she knows she's leaving me behind.

Everything comes and goes in New York. Except dreams. They cling to you like reputations, until you either shake them or live up to them. And try as I might, I can't shake mine. And so I tell Emily *my* news: that I just sold my half of NetShoot to my partner, Ben. It's his company anyway. He's going to turn it into a TV production shop, which is what it should have been all along. If it doesn't catch on quickly, he promises he'll turn off the spigot and return what's left of the cash to the investors. And so I have a little money. Not a lot, but enough to live on for a year, maybe a year and a half. It's time enough to write a book. Or try. I've come full circle. I have no job, I have no girlfriend, and my coffinlike apartment spews forth fumes in the night. But I do have experience—six years in a city that eats its young or makes them strong—and nothing can compare with that. We stare a lot these days, at buildings there and gone, and now, next to Emily, I listen to the silence and look at the midtown skyline. It's the same view I once had in Montclair, when I was still a child, new here and hopeful. Only now the buildings are closer, the city more genuine. And I know it so well.

All that time I spent looking the wrong way, messing up moments, living one life and craving another. I remember what my mother once said, about never realizing you're living through memorable times because it's just your life, an endless present, one day after the next. The history gets attached later, she said, and usually it does, but the last few weeks have changed all that, attached a legacy before its time, and allowed us to glimpse our lives from a distance, from above, from a rusting train line forgotten in all this sprawl. And I see now, all those years, jobs, women, apartments . . . all that *time*, gathering speed through the century's end and beyond, all of that was worthwhile, indeed necessary, to get to here, this point, this beginning.

I've always wanted words to mean something, and now they can. They have a context. I don't think I'm ready to write a novel, a fictional story from scratch—not yet—but there are things I can speak to, things I have learned. I've learned about longing. And I've learned the real meaning of authenticity.

The cheerless end of dreams: that's how Ken summed up the last few years. But I disagree. In an age like this we find out who we are. Spend enough time on the surface of things, live enough years in a city of façades, and when you do dive you'll dive deep. There are two parts to being a writer: desire and purpose. Desire I've had for a long time, but purpose is trickier. Purpose is what carries us through. I want to write about a genuine life, about journeys and dreams and all the stuff we learn as kids. Because it's the same when we're older. We make decisions. We gain experience. And at some point, we all have a story to tell. I spent years dreaming of writing, and now, finally, *finally*, I'll write about those years of dreaming.

And that's what I tell Emily. I talk forever, six years piled up, and when I'm done, when I've told her I don't care what happens, that I'll write the book, start it tomorrow and see it through to the end, she stands and dusts off her jeans. "I knew what you were going to say, too," she says. "And it's about time." Then we laugh and hug, for a long while, ushering in our real lives, suspended above the wounded city I call home.

Acknowledgments

IN SOME WAYS, this book was written before I ever started typing, but it took a few years and the help of more than a few people to get the words just right.

I'd like to thank everyone who appears in these pages for putting up with all this. It's not easy being written about, and though I've done my best to portray events as they occurred, I'm very much aware that this is only one person's point of view. In particular, I'd like to mention my parents, Marcia Harrison and Gene Goodwillie, who have been incredibly supportive despite the perilous nature of the subject matter; my brother, Douglas Goodwillie, who isn't so bad for a banker; and my dear friends Emily Edson and Ken Hamm, who seem, more and more, to represent the heart and soul of this book.

Thanks, too, to all those whose names I've changed to protect whatever needed protecting.

The end of this story was just the beginning of another, and I wouldn't have gotten through these past years without the wisdom and encouragement of Arabella Phillimore, Zoë Rosenfeld, Kieran and Jenny Brew, Trey Goodwillie, Meredith Kovach, KaDee Strickland, Kevin Raidy, Leonard Ellis, Mallory May, Katherine Fowler, Ginger Knowlton, Dr. Scott Sherman, Bradfield Hughes, Jason Herrick, Phil Musser, Maeve Gallagher, Patrick Nicholson, Rick Festa, Kate Hayes, Lizzie West, Duncan Halden, Leelila Strogov, Jennifer Angerer, Karen Kolodny, Sally Amon, Steve Goodwillie, and the Woodstock crowd.

Thanks to those who read and commented on early versions of the manuscript, including Brian DeFiore, Elisabeth Weed, Kirsten Manges, Sebastian Junger, Carol Todd, Michael Balser, Janie Swann, Meghan Daum, Stuart Evers, Amanda Cordano, and John Manley.

At Algonquin, many thanks to Elisabeth Scharlatt, Brunson Hoole, and Judit Bodnar.

Alice Spence, Alexandra Rowley, and Theresa Sellitti were generous with their time and spirit.

Dan Hollins, Susan Shapiro, Jack Finefrock, and P. F. Kluge preached the importance of the written word, and I stupidly believed them.

The Chelsea Hotel, the New York Society Library, and various buildings at NYU provided calm, shelter, and just enough quiet.

And thanks to Jack MacRae and the staff at 192 Books. How lucky I am to have New York's best bookstore just down the street.

Two people are responsible for this book.

Kathy Pories, the most talented of editors, read my take on things and kind of liked it. Thanks for your instincts, your dedication, your time, and your trust.

And finally . . . Kate Garrick, an incredible agent and even better friend, took this book on when it was still an unwieldy pile of papers blowing around downtown Manhattan. She shaved them down and shaped them up and soon thereafter gave me the best news I'd ever heard. Thanks for everything.